Course   Foundations of
Information Systems

Course Number   **INFO 530**

Drexel University

College of Information Science and Technology

create

http://create.mcgraw-hill.com

ISBN-10: 0390759813   ISBN-13: 9780390759818

Contents

Credits

The Context of Systems Analysis and Design Methods

Chapter Preview and Objectives

This is a book about systems analysis and design as applied to information systems and computer applications. No matter what your chosen occupation or position in any business, you will likely participate in systems analysis and design. Some of you will become *systems analysts*, the key players in systems analysis and design activities. The rest of you will work *with* systems analysts as projects come and go in your organizations. This chapter introduces you to information systems from four different perspectives. You will understand the context for systems analysis and design methods when you can:

▌ Define *information system* and name seven types of information system applications.

▌ Identify different types of *stakeholders* who use or develop information systems, and give examples of each.

▌ Define the unique role of *systems analysts* in the development of information systems.

▌ Identify those *skills* needed to successfully function as an information systems analyst.

▌ Describe current *business drivers* that influence information systems development.

▌ Describe current *technology drivers* that influence information systems development.

▌ Briefly describe a simple *process* for developing information systems.

Introduction

It is Bob Martinez's first week at work as an analyst/programmer. Fresh out of college with a degree in computer information systems technology, Bob is eager to work with information systems in the real world. His employer is SoundStage Entertainment Club, one of the fastest-growing music and video clubs in America. SoundStage is just beginning systems analysis and design work on a reengineering of their member services information system. Bob has been appointed to the project team.

This morning was the kickoff meeting for the project, a meeting that included the vice president of member services, director of the audio club, director of the game club, director of marketing, director of customer services, and director of warehouse operations. With that lineup Bob was glad to mainly keep silent at the meeting and rely on his boss, Sandra Shepherd, a senior systems analyst. He was amazed at how well Sandra was able to speak the language of each of the participants and to explain the plans for the new information system in terms they could understand and with benefits they could appreciate. Bob had thought that being just out of college he would know more about cutting-edge technology than most of his co-workers. But Sandra seemed to understand everything about e-commerce and using mobile technologies plus many things of which Bob was only vaguely aware. He made a note to read up on ERP systems as that had come up in the discussion. By the end of the meeting Bob had a new appreciation for the job of systems analyst and of all the things he had yet to learn.

system a group of interrelated components that function together to achieve a desired result.

A Framework for Systems Analysis and Design

information system (IS) an arrangement of people, data, processes, and **information technology** that interact to collect, process, store, and provide as output the information needed to support an organization.

information technology (IT) a contemporary term that describes the combination of computer technology (hardware and software) with telecommunications technology (data, image, and voice networks).

transaction processing system (TPS) an information system that captures and processes data about business transactions.

management information system (MIS) an information system that provides for management-oriented reporting based on transaction processing and operations of the organization.

As its title suggests, this is a book about *systems analysis and design methods*. In this chapter, we will introduce the subject using a simple but comprehensive visual framework. Each chapter in this book begins with a *home page* (see page 4) that quickly and visually shows which aspects of the total framework we will be discussing in the chapter. We'll build this visual framework slowly over the first four chapters to avoid overwhelming you with too much detail too early. Thereafter, each chapter will highlight those aspects of the full framework that are being taught in greater detail in that chapter.

Ultimately, this is a book about "analyzing" business requirements for information systems and "designing" *information systems* that fulfill those business requirements. In other words, the *product* of systems analysis and design is an information system. That product is visually represented in the visual framework as the large rectangle in the center of the picture.

A **system** is a group of interrelated components that function together to achieve a desired result. For instance, you may own a home theater system made up of a DVD player, receiver, speakers, and display monitor.

Information systems (IS) in organizations capture and manage data to produce useful information that supports an organization and its employees, customers, suppliers, and partners. Many organizations consider information systems to be essential to their ability to compete or gain competitive advantage. Most organizations have come to realize that *all* workers need to participate in the development of information systems. Therefore, information systems development is a relevant subject to you regardless of whether or not you are studying to become an information systems professional.

Information systems come in all shapes and sizes. They are so interwoven into the fabric of the business systems they support that it is often difficult to distinguish between business systems and their support information systems. Suffice it to say that information systems can be classified according to the functions they serve. **Transaction processing systems (TPSs)** process business transactions such as orders, time cards, payments, and reservations. **Management information systems (MISs)** use the transaction data to produce information needed by managers to run the business.

Decision support systems (DSSs) help various decision makers identify and choose between options or decisions. **Executive information systems (EISs)** are tailored to the unique information needs of executives who plan for the business and assess performance against those plans. **Expert systems** capture and reproduce the knowledge of an expert problem solver or decision maker and then simulate the "thinking" of that expert. **Communication and collaboration systems** enhance communication and collaboration between people, both internal and external to the organization. Finally, **office automation systems** help employees create and share documents that support day-to-day office activities.

> **decision support system (DSS)** an information system that either helps to identify decision-making opportunities or provides information to help make decisions.

As illustrated in the chapter home page, information systems can be viewed from various perspectives, including:

- The players in the information system (the "team").
- The business drivers influencing the information system.
- The technology drivers used by the information system.
- The process used to develop the information system.

Let's examine each of these perspectives in the remaining sections of the chapter.

> **executive information system (EIS)** an information system that supports the planning and assessment needs of executive managers.

The Players—System Stakeholders

Let's assume you are in a position to help build an information system. Who are the **stakeholders** in this system? Stakeholders for information systems can be broadly classified into the five groups shown on the left-hand side of Figure 1-1. Notice that each stakeholder group has a different perspective of the same information system. The *systems analyst* is a unique stakeholder in Figure 1-1. The systems analyst serves as a facilitator or coach, bridging the communications gap that can naturally develop between the nontechnical system owners and users and the technical system designers and builders.

> **expert system** an information system that captures the expertise of workers and then simulates that expertise to the benefit of nonexperts.

All the above stakeholders have one thing in common—they are what the U.S. Department of Labor calls **information workers.** The livelihoods of information workers depend on decisions made based on information. Today, more than 60 percent of the U.S. labor force is involved in producing, distributing, and using information. Let's examine the five groups of information workers in greater detail.

Let's briefly examine the perspectives of each group. But before we do so, we should point out that these groups actually define "roles" played in systems development. In practice, any individual person may play more than one of these roles. For example, a system owner might also be a system user. Similarly, a systems analyst may also be a system designer, and a system designer might also be a system builder. Any combination may work.

> **communications and collaboration system** an information system that enables more effective communications between workers, partners, customers, and suppliers to enhance their ability to collaborate.

> Systems Owners

For any information system, large or small, there will be one or more **system owners.** System owners usually come from the ranks of management. For medium to large information systems, system owners are usually middle or executive managers. For smaller systems, system owners may be middle managers or supervisors. System owners tend to be interested in the bottom line—how much will the system cost? How much value or what benefits will the system return to the business? Value and benefits can be measured in different ways, as noted in the margin checklist.

> **office automation system** an information system that supports the wide range of business office activities that provide for improved work flow between workers.

> **stakeholder** any person who has an interest in an existing or proposed information system. Stakeholders may include both technical and nontechnical workers. They may also include both internal and external workers.

> Systems Users

System users make up the vast majority of the information workers in any information system. Unlike system owners, system users tend to be less concerned with costs and benefits of the system. Instead, as illustrated in Figure 1-1, they are concerned with the functionality the system provides to their jobs and the system's ease of learning and ease of use. Although users have become more technology-literate over the years,

> **information worker** any person whose job involves creating, collecting, processing, distributing, and using information.

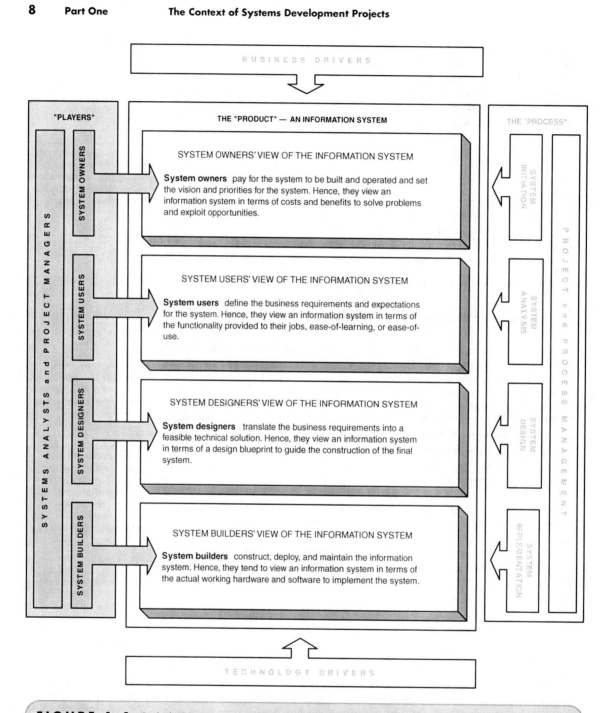

FIGURE 1-1 Stakeholders' Perspective of an Information System

their primary concern is to get the job done. Consequently, discussions with most users need to be kept at the business requirements level as opposed to the technical requirements level. Much of this book is dedicated to teaching you how to effectively identify and communicate business requirements for an information system.

There are many classes of system users. Each class should be directly involved in any information system development project that affects them. Let's briefly examine these classes.

Internal System Users   Internal system users are employees of the businesses for which most information systems are built. Internal users make up the largest percentage of information system users in most businesses. Examples include:

- *Clerical and service workers*—perform most of the day-to-day transaction processing in the average business. They process orders, invoices, payments, and the like. They type and file correspondence. They fill orders in the warehouse. And they manufacture goods on the shop floor. Most of the fundamental data in any business is captured or created by these workers, many of whom perform manual labor in addition to processing data. Information systems that target these workers tend to focus on transaction processing speed and accuracy.
- *Technical and professional staff*—consists largely of business and industrial specialists who perform highly skilled and specialized work. Examples include lawyers, accountants, engineers, scientists, market analysts, advertising designers, and statisticians. Because their work is based on well-defined bodies of knowledge, they are sometimes called **knowledge workers.** Information systems that target technical and professional staff focus on data analysis as well as generating timely information for problem solving.
- *Supervisors, middle managers, and executive managers*—are the decision makers. Supervisors tend to focus on day-to-day problem solving and decision making. Middle managers are more concerned with tactical (short-term) operational problems and decision making. Executive managers are concerned with strategic (long-term) planning and decision making. Information systems for managers tend to focus entirely on information access. Managers need the right information at the right time to identify and solve problems and make good decisions.

External System Users   The Internet has allowed traditional information system boundaries to be extended to include other businesses or direct consumers as system users. These external system users make up an increasingly large percentage of system users for modern information systems. Examples include:

- *Customers*—any organizations or individuals that purchase our products and services. Today, our customers can become direct users of our information systems when they can directly execute orders and sales transactions that used to require intervention by an internal user. For example, if you purchased a company's product via the Internet, you became an external user of that business's sales information system. (There was no need for a separate internal user of the business to input your order.)
- *Suppliers*—any organizations from which our company may purchase supplies and raw materials. Today, these suppliers can interact directly with our company's information systems to determine our supply needs and automatically create orders to fill those needs. There is no longer always a need for an internal user to initiate those orders to a supplier.
- *Partners*—any organizations from which our company purchases services or with which it partners. Most modern businesses contract or outsource a number of basic services such as grounds maintenance, network management, and many others. And businesses have learned to partner with other businesses to more quickly leverage strengths to build better products more rapidly.
- *Employees*—those employees who work on the road or who work from home. For example, sales representatives usually spend much of their time on the road. Also, many businesses permit workers to telecommute (meaning "work from home") to reduce costs and improve productivity. As mobile or remote users, these employees require access to the same information systems as those needed by internal users.

POSSIBLE VALUES AND BENEFITS OF INFORMATION SYSTEMS

Increased Business Profit
Reduced Business Costs
Costs and Benefits of the System
Increased Market Share
Improved Customer Relations
Increased Efficiency
Improved Decision Making
Better Compliance with Regulations
Fewer Mistakes
Improved Security
Greater Capacity

system user a "customer" who will use or is affected by an information system on a regular basis—capturing, validating, entering, responding to, storing, and exchanging data and information.

knowledge worker any worker whose responsibilities are based on a specialized body of knowledge.

> **remote user** a user who is not physically located on the premises but who still requires access to information systems.

External system users are increasingly referred to as **remote users** and **mobile users.** They connect to our information systems through laptop computers, handheld computers, and smart phones—either wired or wireless. Designing information systems for these devices presents some of the most contemporary of challenges that we will address in this book.

> Systems Designers

> **mobile user** a user whose location is constantly changing but who requires access to information systems from any location.

> **system designer** a technical specialist who translates system users' business requirements and constraints into technical solutions. She or he designs the computer databases, inputs, outputs, screens, networks, and software that will meet the system users' requirements.

System designers are technology specialists for information systems. As Figure 1-1 shows, system designers are interested in information technology choices and in the design of systems that use chosen technologies. Today's system designers tend to focus on technical specialties. Some of you may be educating yourselves to specialize in one of these technical specialties, such as:

- *Database administrators*—specialists in database technologies who design and coordinate changes to corporate databases.
- *Network architects*—specialists in networking and telecommunications technologies who design, install, configure, optimize, and support local and wide area networks, including connections to the Internet and other external networks.
- *Web architects*—specialists who design complex Web sites for organizations, including public Web sites for the Internet, internal Web sites for organizations (called *intranets*), and private business-to-business Web sites (called *extranets*).
- *Graphic artists*—relatively new in today's IT worker mix, specialists in graphics technology and methods used to design and construct compelling and easy-to-use interfaces to systems, including interfaces for PCs, the Web, handhelds, and smart phones.
- *Security experts*—specialists in the technology and methods used to ensure data and network security (and privacy).
- *Technology specialists*—experts in the application of specific technologies that will be used in a system (e.g., a specific commercial software package or a specific type of hardware).

> Systems Builders

> **system builder** a technical specialist who constructs information systems and components based on the design specifications generated by the system designers.

System builders (again, see Figure 1-1) are another category of technology specialists for information systems. Their role is to construct the system according to the system designers' specifications. In small organizations or with small information systems, systems designers and systems builders are often the same people. But in large organizations and information systems they are often separate jobs. Some of you may be educating yourselves to specialize in one of their technical specialties, such as:

- *Applications programmers*—specialists who convert business requirements and statements of problems and procedures into computer languages. They develop and test computer programs to capture and store data and to locate and retrieve data for computer applications.
- *Systems programmers*—specialists who develop, test, and implement operating systems-level software, utilities, and services. Increasingly, they also develop reusable software "components" for use by applications programmers (above).
- *Database programmers*—specialists in database languages and technology who build, modify, and test database structures and the programs that use and maintain them.
- *Network administrators*—specialists who design, install, troubleshoot, and optimize computer networks.
- *Security administrators*—specialists who design, implement, troubleshoot, and manage security and privacy controls in a network.

- *Webmasters*—specialists who code and maintain Web servers.
- *Software integrators*—specialists who integrate software packages with hardware, networks, and other software packages.

Although this book is not directly intended to educate the system builder, it is intended to teach system designers how to better communicate design specifications to system builders.

> Systems Analysts

As you have seen, system owners, users, designers, and builders often have very different perspectives on any information system to be built and used. Some are interested in generalities, while others focus on details. Some are nontechnical, while others are very technical. This presents a communications gap that has always existed between those who need computer-based business solutions and those who understand information technology. The **systems analyst** bridges that gap. You can (and probably will) play a role as either a systems analyst or someone who works with systems analysts.

As illustrated in Figure 1-1, their role intentionally overlaps the roles of all the other stakeholders. For the system owners and users, systems analysts identify and validate business problems and needs. For the system designers and builders, systems analysts ensure that the technical solution fulfills the business needs and integrate the technical solution into the business. In other words, systems analysts *facilitate* the development of information systems through interaction with the other stakeholders.

There are several legitimate, but often confusing, variations on the job title we are calling "systems analyst." A *programmer/analyst* (or *analyst/programmer*) includes the responsibilities of both the computer programmer and the systems analyst. A *business analyst* focuses on only the nontechnical aspects of systems analysis and design. Other synonyms for "systems analyst" are systems consultant, business analyst, systems architect, systems engineer, information engineer, information analyst, and systems integrator.

Some of you will become systems analysts. The rest of you will routinely work with systems analysts who will help you solve your business and industrial problems by creating and improving your access to the data and information needed to do your job. Let's take a closer look at systems analysts as the key facilitators of information systems development.

The Role of the Systems Analyst   Systems analysts understand both business and computing. They study business problems and opportunities and then transform business and information requirements into specifications for information systems that will be implemented by various technical specialists including computer programmers. Computers and information systems are of value to a business only if they help solve problems or effect improvements.

Systems analysts initiate *change* within an organization. Every new system changes the business. Increasingly, the very best systems analysts literally change their organizations—providing information that can be used for competitive advantage, finding new markets and services, and even dramatically changing and improving the way the organization does business.

The systems analyst is basically a *problem solver.* Throughout this book, the term *problem* will be used to describe many situations, including:

- Problems, either real or anticipated, that require corrective action.
- Opportunities to improve a situation despite the absence of complaints.
- Directives to change a situation regardless of whether anyone has complained about the current situation.

The systems analyst's job presents a fascinating and exciting challenge to many individuals. It offers high management visibility and opportunities for important

systems analyst a specialist who studies the problems and needs of an organization to determine how people, data, processes, and information technology can best accomplish improvements for the business.

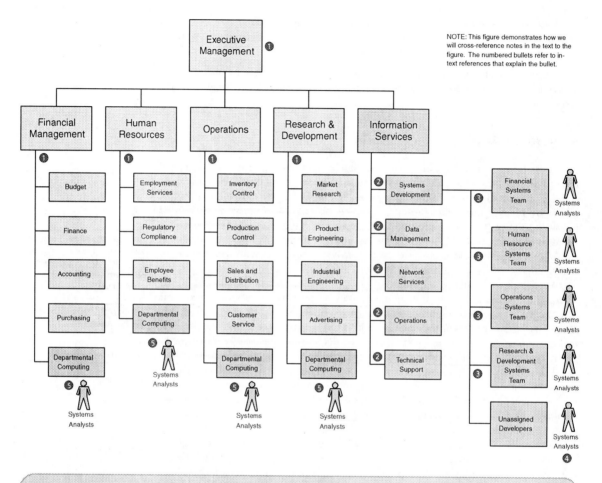

NOTE: This figure demonstrates how we will cross-reference notes in the text to the figure. The numbered bullets refer to in-text references that explain the bullet.

FIGURE 1-2   Systems Analysts in a Typical Organization

decision making and creativity that may affect an entire organization. Furthermore, this job can offer these benefits relatively early in your career (compared to other entry-level jobs and careers).

Where Do Systems Analysts Work?   Every business organizes itself uniquely. But certain patterns of organization seem to reoccur. Figure 1-2 is a representative organization chart. The following numbered bullets cross-reference and emphasize key points in the figure:

❶ System owners and system users are located in the functional units and subunits of the business, as well as in the executive management.

❷ System designers and builders are usually located in the information systems unit of the business. Most systems analysts work also for the information services unit of an organization.

❸ As shown in the figure, systems analysts (along with systems designers and builders) may be permanently assigned to a team that supports a specific business function (e.g., financial systems).

Numbers 2 and 3 above represent a traditional approach to organizing systems analysts and other developers. Numbers 4 and 5 below represent strategies intended to emphasize either efficiency or business expertise. All of the strategies can be combined in a single organization.

The Next Generation:
Career Prospects for Systems Analysts

Many of you are considering or preparing for a career as a systems analyst. The life of a systems analyst is both challenging and rewarding. But what are the prospects for the future? Do organizations need systems analysts? Will they need them in the foreseeable future? Is the job changing for the future, and if so, how? These questions are addressed in this box.

According to the U.S. Department of Labor, computer-related jobs account for 5 out of the 20 fastest-growing occupations in the economy. What's more, these fastest-growing computer-related occupations pay better than many other jobs.

In 2002, 468,000 workers were classified as systems analysts. By 2012, that number will grow to 653,000, an increase of 39%. This means that at least 185,000 new systems analysts must be educated and hired (not including those needed to replace the ones who retire or move into managerial positions or other occupations). The need is increasing because industry needs systems analysts to meet the seemingly endless demand for more information systems and software applications. As some programming jobs are being out-sourced to independent contractors and other countries, the need grows even greater for skilled systems analysts, who can create solid design specifications for remote development teams. Opportunities for success will be the greatest for the most educated, qualified, skilled, and experienced analysts.

What happens to the successful systems analyst? Does a position as a systems analyst lead to any other careers? Indeed, there are many career paths. Some analysts leave the information systems field and join the user community. Their experience with developing business applications, combined with their total systems perspective, can make experienced analysts unique business specialists. Alternatively, analysts can become project managers, information systems managers, or technical specialists (for databases, telecommunications, microcomputers, and so forth). Finally, skilled systems analysts are often recruited by the consulting and outsourcing industries. The career path opportunities are virtually limitless.

As with any profession, systems analysts can expect change. While it is always dangerous to predict changes, we'll take a shot at it. We believe that organizations will become increasingly dependent on external sources for their systems analysts—consultants and outsourcers. This will be driven by such factors as the complexity and rapid change of technology, the desire to accelerate systems development, and the continued difficulty in recruiting, retaining, and retraining skilled systems analysts (and other information technology professionals). In many cases, internally employed systems analysts will manage projects through consulting or outsourcing agreements.

We believe that an increasing percentage of tomorrow's systems analysts will not work in the information systems department. Instead, they will work directly for a business unit within an organization. This will enable them to better serve their users. It will also give users more power over what systems are built and supported.

Finally, we also believe that a greater percentage of systems analysts will come from noncomputing backgrounds. At one time most analysts were computer specialists. Today's computer graduates are becoming more business-literate. Similarly, today's business and noncomputing graduates are becoming more computer-literate. Their full-time help and insight will be needed to meet demand and to provide the business background necessary for tomorrow's more complex applications.

Next Generation

❹ Systems analysts (along with system designers and builders) may also be pooled and temporarily assigned to specific projects for any business function as needed. (Some organizations believe this approach yields greater efficiency because analysts and other developers are always assigned to the highest-priority projects regardless of business area expertise.)

❺ Some systems analysts may work for smaller, departmental computing organizations that support and report to their own specific business functions. (Some organizations believe this structure results in systems analysts that develop greater expertise in their assigned business area to complement their technical expertise.)

All of the above strategies can, of course, be reflected within a single organization.

Regardless of where systems analysts are assigned within the organization, it is important to realize that they come together in *project teams*. Project teams are usually created and disbanded as projects come and go. Project teams must also include appropriate representation from the other stakeholders that we previously discussed (system owners, system users, system designers, and system builders). Accordingly, we will emphasize team building and teamwork throughout this book.

Skills Needed by the Systems Analyst   For those of you with aspirations of becoming a systems analyst, this section describes the skills you will need to develop. This book introduces many systems analysis and design concepts, tools, and techniques. But you will also need skills and experiences that neither this book nor your systems analysis and design course can fully provide.

When all else fails, the systems analyst who remembers the basic concepts and principles of "systems thinking" will still succeed. No tool, technique, process, or methodology is perfect in all situations! But concepts and principles of systems thinking will always help you adapt to new and different situations. This book emphasizes systems thinking.

Not too long ago, it was thought that the systems analyst's only real tools were paper, pencil, and a flowchart template. Over the years, several tools and techniques have been developed to help the systems analyst. Unfortunately, many books emphasize a specific class of tools that is associated with one methodology or approach to systems analysis and design. In this book, we propose a "toolbox" approach to systems analysis and design. As you read this book, your toolbox will grow to include many tools from different methodologies and approaches to systems analysis and design. Subsequently, you should pick and use tools based on the many different situations you will encounter as an analyst—the right tool for the right job!

In addition to having formal systems analysis and design skills, a systems analyst must develop or possess other skills, knowledge, and traits to complete the job. These include:

- *Working knowledge of information technologies*—The analyst must be aware of both existing and emerging information technologies. Such knowledge can be acquired in college courses, professional development seminars and courses, and in-house corporate training programs. Practicing analysts also stay current through disciplined reading and participation in appropriate professional societies. (To get started, see the Suggested Readings at the end of this and subsequent chapters.)
- *Computer programming experience and expertise*—It is difficult to imagine how systems analysts could adequately prepare business and technical specifications for a programmer if they didn't have some programming experience. Most systems analysts need to be proficient in one or more high-level programming languages.
- *General knowledge of business processes and terminology*—Systems analysts must be able to communicate with business experts to gain an understanding of their problems and needs. For the analyst, at least some of this knowledge comes only by way of experience. At the same time, aspiring analysts should avail themselves of every opportunity to complete basic business literacy courses available in colleges of business. Relevant courses may include financial accounting, management or cost accounting, finance, marketing, manufacturing or operations management, quality management, economics, and business law.
- *General problem-solving skills*—The systems analyst must be able to take a large business problem, break down that problem into its parts, determine problem causes and effects, and then recommend a solution. Analysts must avoid the tendency to suggest the solution before analyzing the problem. For aspiring analysts, many colleges offer philosophy courses that teach

The Context of Systems Analysis and Design Methods   **Chapter One**   **15**

FIGURE 1-3

The Systems
Analyst as a
Facilitator

problem-solving skills, critical thinking, and reasoning. These "soft skills" will
serve an analyst well.

- *Good interpersonal communication skills*—An analyst must be able to communicate effectively, both orally and in writing. Almost without exception,
your communications skills, not your technical skills, will prove to be the
single biggest factor in your career success or failure. These skills are learn-
able, but most of us must force ourselves to seek help and work hard to
improve them. Most schools offer courses such as business and technical
writing, business and technical speaking, interviewing, and listening—all useful skills for the systems analyst. These skills are taught in Chapter 6.

- *Good interpersonal relations skills*—As illustrated in Figure 1-3, systems
analysts interact with all stakeholders in a systems development project.
These interactions require effective interpersonal skills that enable the analyst to deal with group dynamics, business politics, conflict, and change.
Many schools offer valuable interpersonal-skills development courses on
subjects such as teamwork, principles of persuasion, managing change and
conflict, and leadership.

- *Flexibility and adaptability*—No two projects are alike. Accordingly, there is
no single, magical approach or standard that is equally applicable to all projects. Successful systems analysts learn to be flexible and to adapt to unique
challenges and situations. Our aforementioned toolbox approach is intended
to encourage flexibility in the use of systems analysis and design tools and
methods. But you must develop an attitude of adaptability to properly use
any box of tools.

- *Character and ethics*—The nature of the systems analyst's job requires a
strong character and a sense of right and wrong. Analysts often gain access
to sensitive or confidential facts and information that are not meant for
public disclosure. Also, the products of systems analysis and design are usually considered the intellectual property of the employer. There are several
standards for computer ethics. One such standard, from the Computer
Ethics Institute, is called "The Ten Commandments of Computer Ethics" and
is shown in Figure 1-4.

> **FIGURE 1-4** Ethics for Systems Analysts

The Ten Commandments of Computer Ethics

1. Thou shalt not use a computer to harm other people.
2. Thou shalt not interfere with other people's computer work.
3. Thou shalt not snoop around in other people's computer files.
4. Thou shalt not use a computer to steal.
5. Thou shalt not use a computer to bear false witness.
6. Thou shalt not copy or use proprietary software for which you have not paid.
7. Thou shalt not use other people's computer resources without authorization or proper compensation.
8. Thou shalt not appropriate other people's intellectual output.
9. Thou shalt think about the social consequences of the program you are writing or the system you are designing.
10. Thou shalt always use a computer in ways that insure consideration and respect for your fellow humans.

Source: Computer Ethics Institute.

> External Service Providers

external service provider (ESP) a systems analyst, system designer, or system builder who sells his or her expertise and experience to other businesses to help those businesses purchase, develop, or integrate their information systems solutions; may be affiliated with a consulting or services organization.

Those of you with some computing experience may be wondering where consultants fit in our taxonomy of stakeholders. They are not immediately apparent in our visual framework. But they are there! Any of our stakeholder roles may be filled by internal or external workers. Consultants are one example of an **external service provider (ESP)**. Most ESPs are systems analysts, designers, or builders who are contracted to bring special expertise or experience to a specific project. Examples include technology engineers, sales engineers, systems consultants, contract programmers, and systems integrators.

> The Project Manager

project manager an experienced professional who accepts responsibility for planning, monitoring, and controlling projects with respect to schedule, budget, deliverables, customer satisfaction, technical standards, and system quality.

We've introduced most of the key players in modern information systems development—systems owners, users, designers, builders, and analysts. We should conclude by emphasizing the reality that these individuals must work together as a team to successfully build information systems and applications that will benefit the business. Teams require leadership. For this reason, usually one or more of these stakeholders takes on the role of **project manager** to ensure that systems are developed on time, within budget, and with acceptable quality. As Figure 1-1 indicates, most project managers are experienced systems analysts. But in some organizations, project managers are selected from the ranks of what we have called "system owners." Regardless, most organizations have learned that project management is a specialized role that requires distinctive skills and experience.

Business Drivers for Today's Information Systems

Another way to look at our information system product is from the perspective of business drivers. Using Figure 1-5, let's now briefly examine the most important business trends that are impacting information systems. Many trends quickly become fads, but here are some business trends we believe will influence systems development in the

FIGURE 1-5 Business Drivers for an Information System

coming years. Many of these trends are related and integrated such that they form a new business philosophy that will impact the way everyone works in the coming years.

> Globalization of the Economy

Since the 1990s, there has been a significant trend of economic globalization. Competition is global, with emerging industrial nations offering lower-cost or higher-quality alternatives to many products. American businesses find themselves with new international competitors. On the other hand, many American businesses have discovered new and expanded international markets for their own goods and services. The bottom line is that most businesses were forced to reorganize to operate in this global economy.

How does economic globalization affect the players in the systems game? First, information systems and computer applications must be internationalized. They must support multiple languages, currency exchange rates, international trade regulations, and different business cultures and practices. Second, most information systems ultimately require information consolidation for performance analysis and decision making. The aforementioned language barriers, currency exchange rates, transborder information regulations, and the like, complicate such consolidation. Finally, there exists a demand for players who can communicate, orally and in writing, with management and users that speak different languages, dialects, and slang. Opportunities for international employment of systems analysts should continue to expand.

> Electronic Commerce and Business

In part due to the globalization of the economy, and in part because of the pervasiveness of the Internet, businesses are changing or expanding their business model to implement **electronic commerce (e-commerce)** and **electronic business (e-business)**. The Internet is fundamentally changing the rules by which business is conducted. We live in a world where consumers and businesses will increasingly expect to conduct commerce (business transactions) using the Internet. But the impact is even more substantive. Because people who work in the business world have become so comfortable with "surfing the Web," organizations are increasingly embracing the Web interface as a suitable architecture for conducting day-to-day business *within* the organization.

There are three basic types of e-commerce- and e-business-enabled information systems applications:

- Marketing of corporate image, products, and services is the simplest form of electronic commerce application. The Web is used merely to "inform" customers about products, services, and policies. Most businesses have achieved this level of electronic commerce.
- *Business-to-consumer (B2C)* electronic commerce attempts to offer new, Web-based channels of distribution for traditional products and services. You, as a typical consumer, can research, order, and pay for products directly via the Internet. Examples include Amazon.com (for books and music) and E-trade.com (for stocks and bonds). Both companies are businesses that were created on the Web. Their competition, however, includes traditional businesses that have added Web-based electronic commerce front ends as an alternative consumer option (such as Barnes and Noble and Merrill Lynch). Figure 1-6 illustrates a typical B2C Web storefront.
- *Business-to-business (B2B)* electronic commerce is the real future. This is the most complex form of electronic commerce and could ultimately evolve into electronic business—the complete, paperless, and digital processing of virtually all business transactions that occur within and between businesses.

One example of B2B electronic commerce is electronic procurement. All businesses purchase raw materials, equipment, and supplies—frequently tens or hundreds of millions of dollars worth per year. B2B procurement allows employees to browse electronic storefronts and catalogs, initiate purchase requisitions and work orders, route requisitions and work orders electronically for expenditure approvals, order the goods and services, and pay for the delivered goods and completed services—all

electronic commerce (e-commerce) the buying and selling of goods and services by using the Internet.

electronic business (e-business) the use of the Internet to conduct and support day-to-day business activities.

FIGURE 1-6 An Electronic Commerce Storefront

without the traditional time-consuming and costly paper flow and bureaucracy. Figure 1-7 illustrates a sample Web-based procurement storefront.

Largely due to the trend toward these e-business and e-commerce applications, most new information systems applications are being designed for an Internet architecture. Not that long ago, we were redesigning most applications to operate within a *Windows* user interface. Today, we increasingly see applications designed to run within an Internet browser such as *Internet Explorer* or *Netscape*. The choice of a desktop operating system, such as *Windows, Macintosh,* or *Linux,* is becoming less important than the availability of the browser itself.

> Security and Privacy

As the digital economy continues to evolve, citizens and organizations alike have developed a heightened awareness of the security and privacy issues involved in today's economy. Security issues tend to revolve around business continuity; that is, "How will the business continue in the event of a breach or disaster—any event that causes a disruption of business activity?" Additionally, businesses must ask themselves, "How can the business protect its digital assets from outside threats?" It is true that these questions ultimately come down to technology; however, the concerns have become fundamental business concerns.

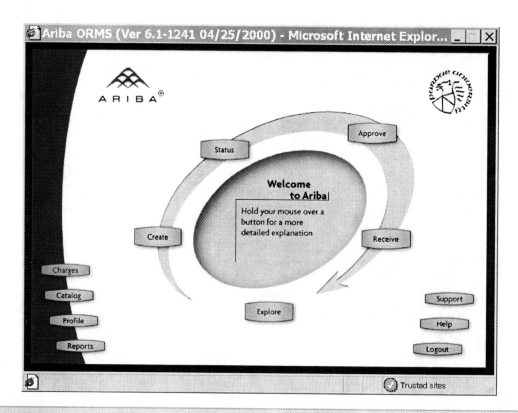

FIGURE 1-7   An Electronic Commerce Procurement Storefront

Related to security is the issue of privacy. Consumers are increasingly demanding privacy in the digital economy. Governments are regulating privacy issues, and the regulations will likely become more stringent as the digital economy continues to evolve. Go to your favorite commercial Web sites. Almost every business now has a privacy policy. Consumer groups are beginning to analyze and monitor such privacy policies, holding companies accountable and lobbying governments for stricter regulations and enforcement.

As information systems are developed and changed, you will increasingly be expected to incorporate more stringent security and privacy controls. In the global economy, you will need to become sensitive to a wide array of regulations that vary considerably from one country to another. Certainly, security and privacy mechanisms will be subject to the same internal audits that have become routine in systems that support or interact with financial systems.

> Collaboration and Partnership

Collaboration and partnership are significant business trends that are influencing information systems applications. Within organizations, management is emphasizing the need to break down the walls that separate organization departments and functions. Management speaks of "cross-functional" teams that collaborate to address common business goals from interdisciplinary perspectives. For example, new product design used to be the exclusive domain of engineers. Today, new product design typically involves a cross-functional team of representatives from many organizational units, such as engineering, marketing, sales, manufacturing, inventory control, distribution, and, yes, information systems.

Similarly, the trend toward collaboration extends beyond the organization to include other organizations—sometimes even competitors. Organizations choose to directly collaborate as partners in business ventures that make good business sense. Microsoft and Oracle sell competitive database management systems. But Microsoft and Oracle also partner to ensure that Oracle applications will operate on a Microsoft database. Both companies benefit financially from such cooperation.

In a similar vein, businesses have learned that it can be beneficial for their information systems to interoperate with one another. For example, while Wal-Mart could generate its own restocking orders for merchandise and send them to its suppliers, it makes more sense to integrate their respective inventory control systems. Suppliers can monitor Wal-Mart's inventory levels directly and can automatically initiate business-to-business transactions to keep the shelves stocked with their merchandise. Both companies benefit. (Of course, this also raises the aforementioned issue of requirements for good security.)

> Knowledge Asset Management

What is knowledge? *Knowledge* is the result of a continuum of how we process raw data into useful information. Information systems collect raw **data** by capturing business facts (about products, employees, customers, and the like) and processing business transactions. Data gets combined, filtered, organized, and analyzed to produce **information** to help managers plan and operate the business. Ultimately, information is refined by people to create **knowledge** and expertise. Increasingly, organizations are asking themselves, "How can the company manage and share knowledge for competitive advantage? And as workers come and go, how can the workers' knowledge and expertise be preserved within the organization?"

Thirty years of data processing and information systems have resulted in an enormous volume of data, information, and knowledge. All three are considered critical *business* resources, equal in importance to the classic economic resources of land, labor, and capital.

The need for knowledge asset management impacts information systems on a variety of fronts. Although we have captured (and continue to capture) a great amount of data and information in information systems, they are loosely integrated in most organizations—indeed, redundant and contradictory data and information are common in information systems. As new information systems are built, we will increasingly be expected to focus on integration of the data and information that can create and preserve knowledge in the organizations for which we work. This will greatly complicate systems analysis and design. In this book, we plan to introduce you to many tools and techniques that can help you integrate systems for improved knowledge management.

> Continuous Improvement and Total Quality Management

Information systems automate and support **business processes.** In an effort to continuously improve a business process, **continuous process improvement (CPI)** examines a business process to implement a series of small changes for improvement. These changes can result in cost reductions, improved efficiencies, or increased value and profit. Systems analysts are both affected by continuous process improvements and expected to initiate or suggest such improvements while designing and implementing information systems.

Another ongoing business driver is **total quality management (TQM).** Businesses have learned that quality has become a critical success factor in competition. They have also learned that quality management does not begin and end with the products and services sold by the business. Instead, it begins with a culture that recognizes that

data raw facts about people, places, events, and things that are of importance in an organization. Each fact is, by itself, relatively meaningless.

information data that has been processed or reorganized into a more meaningful form for someone. Information is formed from combinations of data that hopefully have meaning to the recipient.

knowledge data and information that are further refined based on the facts, truths, beliefs, judgments, experiences, and expertise of the recipient. Ideally information leads to *wisdom*.

business processes tasks that respond to business events (e.g., an order). Business processes are the work, procedures, and rules required to complete the business tasks, independent of any information technology used to automate or support them.

continuous process improvement (CPI) the continuous monitoring of business processes to effect small but measurable improvements in cost reduction and value added.

total quality management (TQM) a comprehensive approach to facilitating quality improvements and management within a business.

everyone in the business is responsible for quality. TQM commitments require that every business function, including information services, identify quality indicators, measure quality, and make appropriate changes to improve quality.

Information systems, and hence systems analysts, are part of the TQM requirement. Our discussions with college graduate recruiters suggest that an "obsessive" attitude toward quality management will become an essential characteristic of successful systems analysts (and all information technology professionals). Throughout this book, continuous process improvement and total quality management will be an underlying theme.

> Business Process Redesign

As stated earlier, many information systems support or automate business processes. Many businesses are learning that those business processes have not changed substantially in decades and that those business processes are grossly inefficient and/or costly. Many business processes are overly bureaucratic, and all their steps do not truly contribute value to the business. Unfortunately, information systems have merely automated many of these inefficiencies. Enter business process redesign!

business process redesign (BPR) the study, analysis, and redesign of fundamental business processes to reduce costs and/or improve value added to the business.

Business process redesign (BPR) involves making substantive changes to business processes across a larger system. In effect, BPR seeks to implement more substantial changes and improvements than does CPI. In a BPR, business processes are carefully documented and analyzed for timeliness, bottlenecks, costs, and whether or not each step or task truly adds value to the organization (or, conversely, adds only bureaucracy). Business processes are then redesigned for maximum efficiency and lowest possible costs.

So how does BPR affect information systems? There are two basic ways to implement any information system—build it or buy it. In other words, you can write the software yourself, or you can purchase and implement a commercial software package. In both cases, BPR figures prominently. In writing your own software, it is useful to redesign business processes before writing the software to automate them. This way, you avoid automating underlying inefficiencies. Alternatively, in purchasing software packages, most businesses have discovered it is easier to redesign the business processes to work with the software package than to attempt to force (and even cripple) the software package to work with existing business processes.

Technology Drivers for Today's Information Systems

Advances in information technology can also be drivers for information systems (as suggested in Figure 1-8). In some cases, outdated technologies can present significant problems that drive information system development projects. In other cases, newer technologies present business opportunities. Let's examine several technologies that are influencing today's information systems.

> Networks and the Internet

Scott McNealy, Sun Computer's charismatic CEO, is often cited as stating, "The network has become the computer." Few would argue that today's information systems are installed on a network architecture consisting of local and wide area networks. These networks include mainframe computers, network servers, and a variety of desktop, laptop, and handheld client computers. But today, the most pervasive networking technologies are based on the Internet. Some of the more relevant Internet technologies that you need to become aware of, if not develop some basic skill with, are described in the following list. (For now, don't be intimidated by these terms—we

FIGURE 1-8   Technology Drivers for an Information System

will be teaching you more about these technologies and how to design systems that use them throughout this textbook.)

- *xHTML* and *XML* are the fundamental languages of Web page authoring and Internet application development. Extensible Hypertext Markup Language (xHTML) is the emerging second-generation version of HTML, the language used to construct Web pages. Extensible Markup Language (XML) is the language used to effectively transport data content along with its proper interpretation over the Internet. Introductory xHTML and XML courses have become core requirements in most information systems and information technology college curricula.

- *Scripting* languages are simple programming languages designed specifically for Internet applications. Examples include *Perl, VBScript,* and *JavaScript.* These languages are increasingly taught in college Web development and programming courses.
- Web-specific programming languages such as *Java* and *Cold Fusion* have emerged to specifically address construction of complex, Web-based applications that involve multiple servers and Web browsers. These languages are also becoming prevalent in college programming curricula.
- *Intranets* are essentially private Internets designed for use by employees of an organization. They offer the look and feel of the Internet; however, security and firewalls restrict their use to employees.
- *Extranets,* like intranets, are private Internets. But extranets are for use between specific organizations. Only the employees of those identified businesses can access and use the extranet. For example, an automotive manufacturer such as Chevrolet might set up an extranet for the sole use of its dealers. Through this extranet, the manufacturer can communicate information about parts, problems, sales incentives, and the like.
- *Portals* (in corporations) are "home pages" that can be customized to the specific needs of different individuals who use them. For example, portal technology can define Web pages that provide appropriate information and applications for different roles in the same company. Each individual's role determines which information and applications that person can use from her or his Web page. Examples of roles include "customer," "supplier," and different types of "employee." Portals can also effectively integrate public Internet, private intranet, and extranet content into each individual user's home page.
- *Web services* are the latest rage. Web services are reusable, Web-based programs that can be called from any other Internet program. For example, let's say you need to write a program to accept credit card payments over the Web. Sure, you could write, debug, and test the credit card validation program yourself. But an alternative approach would be to purchase the right to use a credit card validation program over the Web. By doing so, you need not maintain responsibility for the credit card validation code. You need only "call" the Web service from your program, much as you would call an internal subroutine. Of course, you will pay for the privilege of using Web services since somebody had to write the original Web service program.

These are but a few of the network and Internet technologies that you should seek out during your education. But you must recognize the volatility of the Internet and accept that these and other technologies will emerge and disappear frequently in the near future.

> Mobile and Wireless Technologies

Wireless Handheld

Mobile and wireless technologies are poised to significantly change the next generation of information systems. Handheld computers, or *personal data assistants* (*PDAs,* such as the HP *iPaq,* Palm, and RIM *BlackBerry*®), have become common in the ranks of information workers. These devices are increasingly including wireless capabilities (see margin photo) that provide Web access and e-mail. *Cell phones* are also increasingly featuring Internet and e-mail capabilities. And now, integrated devices such as *smart phones* are emerging that integrate the capabilities of PDAs and cell phones into a single device (see margin photo). For those who prefer separate devices, technologies like *Bluetooth* are emerging to allow the separate devices to interoperate as one logical device while preserving each one's form factors and advantages.

Additionally, laptop computers are increasingly equipped with wireless and mobile capabilities to allow information workers to more easily move between locations while preserving connectivity to information systems. All of these technical trends will significantly impact the analysis and design of new information systems. Increasingly, wireless access must be assumed. And the limitations of mobile devices and screen sizes must be accommodated in an information system's design. This textbook will teach and demonstrate tools and techniques to deal with the design of emerging mobile applications.

Smart Phone

> Object Technologies

Today, most contemporary information systems are built using **object technologies.** Today's pervasive programming languages are object-oriented. They include *C++*, *Java*, *Smalltalk*, and *Visual Basic .NET.* Object technologies allow programmers to build software from software parts called *objects.* (We will get into more specifics about objects later in this book.) Object-oriented software offers two fundamental advantages over nonobject software. First, objects are reusable. Once they are designed and built, objects can be reused in multiple information systems and applications. This reduces the time required to develop future software applications. Second, objects are extensible. They can be changed or expanded easily without adversely impacting any previous applications that used them. This reduces the lifetime costs of maintaining and improving software.

The impact of object technology is significant in the world of systems analysis and design. Prior to object technologies, most programming languages were based on so-called *structured methods.* Examples include *COBOL* (the dominant language), *C*, *FORTRAN, Pascal,* and *PL/1.* It is not important at this time for you to be able to differentiate between structured and object technologies and methods. Suffice to say, structured methods are inadequate to the task of analyzing and designing systems that will be built using object technologies. Accordingly, **object-oriented analysis and design** methods have emerged as the preferred approach for building *most* contemporary information systems. For this reason, we will integrate object-oriented analysis and design tools and techniques throughout this book to give you a competitive advantage in tomorrow's job market.

At the same time, structured tools and techniques are still important. Databases, for example, are still commonly designed using structured tools. And structured tools are still preferred by many systems analysts for analyzing and designing work flows and business processes. Thus, we will also teach you several popular structured tools and techniques for systems analysis and design.

It is easy to become a devout disciple of one analysis and design strategy, such as structured analysis and design or object-oriented analysis and design. You should avoid doing so! We will advocate both and teach you when and how to combine structured and object-oriented tools and techniques for systems analysis and design. As we write this chapter, this approach—called **agile development**—is gaining favor among experienced analysts who have become weary of overly prescriptive methods that usually insist that you use only *one* methodology's tools and processes. At the risk of oversimplifying agile methods, think of it as assembling a toolbox of different tools and techniques—structured, object-oriented, and others—and then selecting the best tool or technique for whatever problems or need you encounter as a systems analyst.

> Collaborative Technologies

Another significant technology trend is the use of collaborative technologies. Collaborative technologies are those that enhance interpersonal communications and teamwork. Four important classes of collaborative technologies are e-mail, instant messaging, groupware, and work flow.

Everybody knows what e-mail is. But e-mail's importance in information systems development is changing. Increasingly, modern information systems are *e-mail-enabled;*

object technology a software technology that defines a system in terms of objects that consolidate data and behavior (into objects). Objects become reusable and extensible components for the software developers.

object-oriented analysis and design a collection of tools and techniques for systems development that will utilize object technologies to construct a system and its software.

agile development a systems development strategy wherein the system developers are given the flexibility to select from a variety of appropriate tools and techniques to best accomplish the tasks at hand. Agile development is believed to strike an optimal balance between productivity and quality for systems development.

that is, e-mail capabilities are built right into the application software. There is no need to switch to a dedicated e-mail program such as *Outlook.* The application merely invokes the user's or organization's default e-mail program to enable relevant messages to be sent or received.

Related to e-mail technology is instant messaging (e.g., AOL's *Instant Messenger* and Microsoft's *MSN Messenger Service*). Instant messaging was popularized in public and private "chat rooms" on the Internet. But instant messaging is slowly being incorporated into enterprise information systems applications as well. For example, instant messaging can implement immediate response capabilities into a help system for a business application. Imagine being able to instantly send and receive messages with the corporate help desk when using a business application. The productivity and service-level implications are significant.

Finally, groupware technology allows teams of individuals to collaborate on projects and tasks regardless of their physical location. Examples of groupware technologies include Lotus's *SameTime* and Microsoft's *NetMeeting.* Using such groupware allows multiple individuals to participate in meetings and share software tools across a network. As with e-mail and instant messaging, groupware capabilities can be built into appropriate business applications.

Clearly, systems analysts and system designers must build these innovative collaborative technologies into their applications.

> Enterprise Applications

Virtually all organizations, large and small, require a core set of enterprise applications to conduct business. As shown in Figure 1-9, for most businesses the core applications include financial management, human resource management, marketing and sales, and operations management (inventory and/or manufacturing control). At one time, most organizations custom-built most or all of these core enterprise applications. But today, these enterprise applications are frequently purchased, installed, and configured for the business and integrated into the organization's business processes. Why? Because these core enterprise applications in different organizations or industries tend to be more alike than they are different.

Today, these "internal" core applications are being supplemented with other enterprise applications that integrate an organization's business processes with those of its suppliers and customers. These applications, called *customer relationship management* and *supply chain management,* are also illustrated in Figure 1-9.

The trend toward the use of purchased enterprise applications significantly impacts systems analysis and design. Purchased and installed enterprise applications are never sufficient to meet all of the needs for information systems in any organization. Thus, systems analysts and other developers are asked to develop value-added applications to meet additional needs of the business. But the purchased and installed enterprise applications become a technology constraint. Any custom application must properly integrate with and interface to the purchased enterprise applications. This is often called **systems integration,** and this is the business and systems environment into which most of you will graduate. Let's briefly explore some of the more common enterprise applications and describe their implications for systems analysis and design.

Enterprise Resource Planning (ERP)   As previously noted, the core business information system applications in most businesses were developed in-house incrementally over many years. Each system had its own files and databases with loose and awkward integration of all applications. During the 1990s, businesses tried very hard to integrate these legacy information systems, usually with poor results. Organizations would have probably preferred to redevelop these core business applications (see Figure 1-9 again) from scratch as a single *integrated* information system. Unfortunately, few if any businesses had enough resources to attempt this. Recognizing that the basic applications needed by most businesses were more similar than different, the software industry developed a solution—**enterprise resource planning (ERP)**

---

systems integration the process of building a unified information system out of diverse components of purchased software, custom-built software, hardware, and networking.

---

enterprise resource planning (ERP) a software application that fully integrates information systems that span most or all of the basic, core business functions (including transaction processing and management information for those business functions).

REPRESENTATIVE ERP VENDORS

SSA

Oracle/PeopleSoft

SAP AG (the Market Leader)

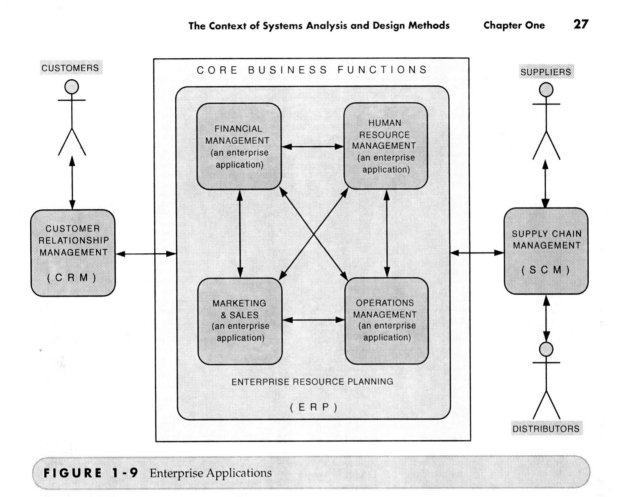

FIGURE 1-9 Enterprise Applications

applications. An ERP solution is built around a common database shared by common business functions. Examples of ERP software vendors are listed in the margin.

An ERP solution provides the core information system functions for the entire business. But usually an organization must redesign its business processes to fully exploit and use an ERP solution. Most organizations must still supplement the ERP solution with custom software applications to fulfill business requirements that are unique to the industry or business. For most organizations, an ERP implementation and integration represents the single largest information system project ever undertaken by the organization. It can cost tens of millions of dollars and require a small army of managers, users, analysts, technical specialists, programmers, and consultants.

ERP applications are significant to systems analysts for several reasons. First, systems analysts may be involved in the decision to select and purchase an ERP solution. Second, and more common, systems analysts are frequently involved in the customization of the ERP solution, as well as the redesign of business processes to use the ERP solution. Third, if custom-built applications are to be developed within an organization that uses an ERP core solution, the ERP system's architecture significantly impacts the analysis and design of the custom application that must coexist and interoperate with the ERP system.

Supply Chain Management   Today, many organizations are expending effort on enterprise applications that extend support beyond their core business functions. Companies are extending their core business applications to interoperate with their suppliers and distributors to more efficiently manage the flow of raw materials and products between their respective organizations. These **supply chain management (SCM)** applications utilize the Internet as a means for integration and communications.

REPRESENTATIVE SCM VENDORS

i2 Technologies
Manugistics
SAP
SCT

supply chain management (SCM) a software application that optimizes business processes for raw material procurement through finished product distribution by directly integrating the logistical information systems of organizations with those of their suppliers and distributors.

The Farms

Food Processing Plants   Freight Companies   Distribution Centers   Freight Companies

The Restaurants

FIGURE 1-10 Supply Chain

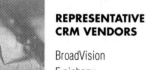

**REPRESENTATIVE
CRM VENDORS**

BroadVision
E.piphany
Kana
Amdocs
Oracle/PeopleSoft
Siebel (the Market Leader)
SAP

**customer relationship
management (CRM)** a
software application that provides customers with access
to a business's processes
from initial inquiry through
postsale service and support.

For example, Figure 1-10 demonstrates a logical supply chain ending at restaurants belonging to a franchise (e.g., Outback, Red Lobster, Wendy's). Notice that this supply chain includes many businesses and carriers to achieve its final result—ensuring that the restaurants have adequate food supplies to do business. Any delays or problems in any single link of this supply chain will adversely affect one and all. For that reason, several of these businesses will implement supply chain management using SCM software technology to plan, implement, and manage the chain. Examples of supply chain management vendors are listed in the margin. (It should be noted that several ERP application vendors are extending ERP software applications to include SCM capabilities. The SCM market is due for a shakeout because there are too many vendors for all to succeed.)

SCM applications are significant to systems analysts for the same reasons as stated for ERP applications. As an analyst, you may be involved in the evaluation and selection of an SCM package. Or you may be expected to implement and perhaps customize such packages to meet the organization's needs. And again, you may expect to participate in redesigning existing business processes to work appropriately with the SCM solution.

Customer Relationship Management   Many companies have discovered that highly focused customer relationship management can create loyalty that results in increased sales. Thus, many businesses are implementing **customer relationship management (CRM)** solutions that enable customer self-service via the Internet.

The theme of all CRM solutions is a focus on the "customer." CRM is concerned with not only providing effective customer inquiry responses and assistance but also helping the business better profile its customer base for the purpose of improving customer relations and marketing. Examples of CRM vendors are listed in the margin. As was the case with SCM technologies, many ERP vendors are developing or acquiring CRM capabilities to complement and extend their ERP solutions. And as with SCM, the larger number of players will likely be reduced through acquisition and attrition.

CRM technology impacts systems analysts in precisely the same ways as those we described for ERP and SCM technology. In many businesses, new applications must interface with a core, CRM enterprise application.

Enterprise Application Integration   Many companies face the significant challenge of integrating their existing legacy systems with new applications such as ERP, SCM, and CRM solutions. Any company that wants to do business across the Internet will also have to meet the challenge of integrating its systems with those of other organizations and their different systems and technologies. To meet this challenge, many organizations are looking at enterprise application integration software. **Enterprise application integration (EAI)** involves linking applications, whether purchased or developed in-house, so that they can transparently interoperate with one another. This is illustrated conceptually in Figure 1-11. Some vendors offering EAI tools are listed in the margin.

REPRESENTATIVE EAI VENDORS

BEA Systems
IBM (MQSeries)
Mercator Software
TIBCO Software

enterprise application integration (EAI) the process and technologies used to link applications to support the flow of data and information between those applications. EAI solutions are usually based on **middleware**.

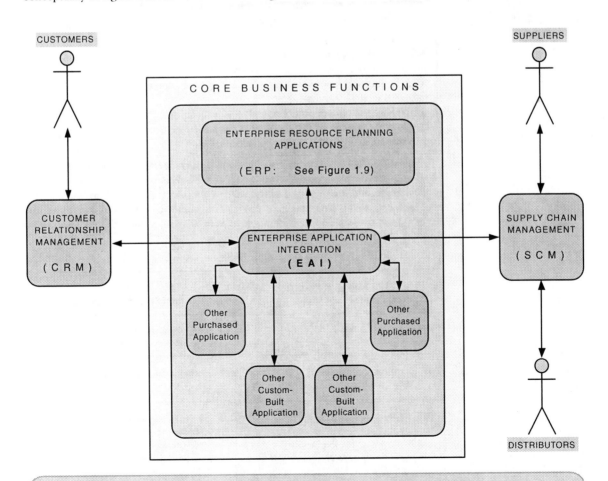

FIGURE 1-11 Enterprise Application Integration

30   **Part One**   **The Context of Systems Development Projects**

---
middleware software (usually purchased) used to translate and route data between different applications.

Again, this market is rapidly expanding and contracting. The tools are used to define and construct communication pipelines between differing applications and technologies.

Today, as any new information system is developed, it must be integrated with all the information systems that preceded it. These "legacy" information systems may have been purchased or built in-house. Regardless, systems analysts and other developers must consider application integration for any new information system to be developed. And EAI technologies are at the core of the integration requirements.

A Simple System Development Process

Thus far you have learned about different types of information systems, the players involved in developing those systems, and several business and technology drivers that influence the development of information systems. In this section you will learn about another information system perspective, the "process" for developing an information system.

---
system development process a set of activities, methods, best practices, deliverables, and automated tools that stakeholders use to develop and maintain information systems and software.

Most organizations have a formal **system development process** consisting of a standard set of processes or steps they expect will be followed on any system development project. While these processes may vary greatly for different organizations, a common characteristic can be found: Most organizations' system development process follows a problem-solving approach. That approach typically incorporates the following general problem-solving steps:

1. Identify the problem.
2. Analyze and understand the problem.
3. Identify solution requirements and expectations.
4. Identify alternative solutions and choose the best course of action.
5. Design the chosen solution.
6. Implement the chosen solution.
7. Evaluate the results. (If the problem is not solved, return to step 1 or 2 as appropriate.)

Figure 1-12 adds a system development process perspective that we will use (with appropriate refinements) throughout this book as we study the development process, tools, and techniques. For the sake of simplicity our initial problem-solving approach establishes four stages or phases that must be completed for any system development project—system initiation, system analysis, system design, and system

Our Simplified System Development Process	General Problem-Solving Steps
System initiation	1. Identify the problem. (Also plan for the solution of the problem.)
System analysis	2. Analyze and understand the problem. 3. Identify solution requirements and expectations.
System design	4. Identify alternative solutions and choose the best course of action. 5. Design the chosen solution.
System implementation	6. Implement the chosen solution. 7. Evaluate the results. (If the problem is not solved, return to step 1 or 2 as appropriate.)

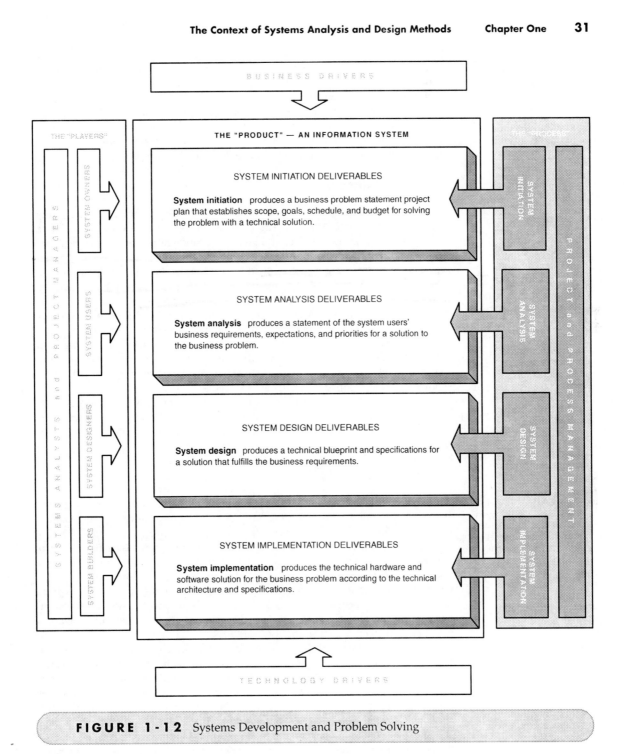

FIGURE 1-12 Systems Development and Problem Solving

implementation. The table on the previous page shows the correlation between the above general problem-solving steps and our process.

It is important to note that any system development process must be managed on a project-by-project basis. You learned earlier that at least one stakeholder accepts responsibility as the project manager for ensuring that the system is developed on time, within budget, and with acceptable quality. The activity of managing a project is referred to as **project management.** Accordingly, in Figure 1-12 we have added a process for project management. Also, to ensure that all projects are

project management the activity of defining, planning, directing, monitoring, and controlling a project to develop an acceptable system within the allotted time and budget.

process management
the ongoing activity that
defines, improves, and
coordinates the use of an
organization's chosen
methodology (the "process")
and standards for all system
development projects.

managed according to the same development process, we have included **process management** as an ongoing activity. Notice that project and process management overlap all of the process phases.

Let's *briefly* examine our system development process in Figure 1-12 to expand your understanding of each phase and activity in the process. Given a problem to be solved or a need to be fulfilled, what will we do during system initiation, analysis, design, and implementation? Also, who will be involved in each phase?

> System Initiation

system initiation the initial
planning for a project to define
initial business scope, goals,
schedule, and budget.

Information system projects are usually complicated. They require a significant time, effort, and economic investment. The problems to be solved are frequently stated vaguely, which means that the initial envisioned solution may be premature. For these reasons, system projects should be carefully planned. System initiation establishes project scope and the problem-solving plan. Thus, as shown in Figure 1-12, we see that **system initiation** establishes the project scope, goals, schedule, and budget required to solve the problem or opportunity represented by the project. Project scope defines the area of the business to be addressed by the project and the goals to be achieved. Scope and goals ultimately impact the resource commitments, namely, schedule and budget, that must be made to successfully complete the project. By establishing a project schedule and budget against the *initial* scope and goals, you also establish a *baseline* against which all stakeholders can accept the reality that any future changes in scope or goals *will* impact the schedule and budget.

Figure 1-12 also shows that project managers, system analysts, and system owners are the primary stakeholders in a system analysis. This book will teach you many tools and techniques for initiating a system project and establishing a suitable project plan.

> System Analysis

system analysis the study
of a business problem domain
to recommend improvements
and specify the business
requirements and priorities
for the solution.

The next step in our system development process is **system analysis.** System analysis is intended to provide the project team with a more thorough understanding of the problems and needs that triggered the project. As such, the business area (scope of the project—as defined during system initiation) may be studied and analyzed to gain a more detailed understanding of what works, what doesn't, and what's needed. As depicted in Figure 1-12, the system analysis requires working with system users to clearly define business requirements and expectations for any new system that is to be purchased or developed. Also, business priorities may need to be established in the event that schedule and budget are insufficient to accomplish all that is desired.

Recall the business drivers discussed earlier in the chapter. These (and future) business drivers most closely affect system analysis, which often defines business requirements in response to the business drivers. For example, we discussed a current trend toward e-business and e-commerce. This business driver may influence the business requirement for any information system, leading us to establish project goals to conduct all business transactions on the Web.

The completion of a system analysis often results in the need to update many of the deliverables produced earlier, during system initiation. The analysis may reveal the need to revise the business scope or project goals—perhaps we now feel the scope of the project is too large or too small. Accordingly, the schedule and budget for the project may need to be revised. Finally, the feasibility of the project itself becomes questionable. The project could be canceled or could proceed to the next phase.

As shown in Figure 1-12, project managers, system analysts, and system users are the primary stakeholders in a system analysis. Typically, results must be summarized and defended to the system owners, who will pay to design and implement an information system to fulfill the business requirements. This book will teach you many tools and techniques for performing a system analysis and documenting user requirements.

> System Design

Given an understanding of the business requirements for an information system, we can now proceed to **system design.** During system design we will initially need to explore alternative technical solutions. Rarely is there only one solution to any problem. For example, today most companies need to choose between purchasing a solution that is good enough and building a custom solution in-house. (We'll explore options such as this throughout this book.)

system design the specification or construction of a technical, computer-based solution for the business requirements identified in a system analysis. (Note: Increasingly, the design takes the form of a working prototype.)

Once a technical alternative is chosen and approved, the system design phase develops the technical blueprints and specifications required to implement the final solution. These blueprints and specifications will be used to implement required databases, programs, user interfaces, and networks for the information system. In the case where we choose to purchase software instead of build it, the blueprints specify how the purchased software will be integrated into the business and with other information systems.

Recall the technology drivers discussed in the last section of the chapter. These (and future) technology drivers most closely impact the system design process and decisions. Many organizations define a common information technology architecture based on these technology drivers. Accordingly, all system designs for new information systems must conform to the standard IT architecture.

As depicted in Figure 1-12, project managers, system analysts, and system designers are the primary stakeholders in a system design. This book will teach you many tools and techniques for performing a system design.

> System Implementation

The final step in our simple system development process is **system implementation.** As shown in Figure 1-12, system implementation constructs the new information system and puts it into operation. It is during system implementation that any new hardware and system software are installed and tested. Any purchased application software and databases are installed and configured. And any custom software and databases are constructed using the technical blueprints and specifications developed during system design.

system implementation the construction, installation, testing, and delivery of a system into production (meaning day-to-day operation).

As system components are constructed or installed, they must be individually tested. And the complete system must also be tested to ensure that it works properly and meets user requirements and expectations. Once the system has been fully tested, it must be placed into operation. Data from the previous system may have to be converted or entered into start-up databases, and system users must be trained to properly use the system. Finally, some sort of transition plan from older business processes and information systems may have to be implemented.

And once again, as depicted in Figure 1-12, project managers, system analysts, and system builders are the primary stakeholders in a system implementation. While this book will teach you some of the tools and techniques for performing a system implementation, most of these methods are taught in programming, database, and networking courses. This book emphasizes system initiation, analysis, and design skills, but it will also teach you the unique system implementation tools and techniques that are most commonly performed by systems analysts and, therefore, are not typically covered in these other information technology courses.

> System Support and Continuous Improvement

We would be remiss not to briefly acknowledge that implemented information systems face a lifetime of support and continuous improvement. But where is that shown in Figure 1-12? It is there! But it is subtle.

Implemented information systems are rarely perfect. Your users will find errors (bugs) and you will discover, on occasion, design and implementation flaws that require attention and fixes. Also, business and user requirements constantly change. Thus, there will be a need to continuously improve any information system until the time it becomes obsolete. So where does system support and change fit into our development process?

A change made for system support or improvement is merely another project, sometimes called a *maintenance* or *enhancement* project. Such a project should follow the exact same problem-solving approach defined for any other project. The only difference is the effort and budget required to complete the project. Many of the phases will be completed much more quickly, especially if the original stakeholders properly documented the system as initially developed. Of course, if they did not, a system improvement project can quickly consume much greater time, effort, and money. Much of what we will teach you in this book is intended to help you appropriately document information systems to significantly reduce lifetime costs of supporting and improving your information systems.

Learning Roadmap

Each chapter will provide guidance for self-paced instruction under the heading "Learning Roadmap." Recognizing that different students and readers have different backgrounds and interests, we will propose appropriate learning paths—most within this book, but some beyond the scope of this book.

Most readers should proceed directly to Chapter 2 because the first four chapters provide much of the context for the remainder of the book. Several recurring themes, frameworks, and terms are introduced in those chapters to allow you to define your own learning path from that point forward. This chapter focused on information systems from four different perspectives:

- The *players*—both developers and users of information systems.
- The *business drivers* that currently influence information systems.
- The *technology drivers* that currently influence information systems.
- The *process* of developing information systems.

Chapter 2 will take a closer look at the *product* itself—information systems— from an architectural perspective appropriate for systems development. We will define how different players and development stages view an information system.

Looking further ahead, Chapter 3 more closely examines the *process* of systems development. Chapter 4 completes the introduction to systems analysis and design methods by examining the *management* of systems development.

Summary

1. Information systems in organizations capture and manage data to produce useful information that supports an organization and its employees, customers, suppliers, and partners.
2. Information systems can be classified according to the functions they serve, including:

a. Transaction processing systems that process business transactions such as orders, time cards, payments, and reservations.
b. Management information systems that use transaction data to produce information needed by managers to run the business.

c. Decision support systems that help various decision makers identify and choose between options or decisions.

d. Executive information systems that are systems tailored to the unique information needs of executives who plan for the business and assess performance against the plans.

e. Expert systems that are systems that capture and reproduce the knowledge of an expert problem solver or decision maker and then simulate the "thinking" of that expert.

f. Communication and collaboration systems that enhance communication and collaboration between people, both internal and external to the organization.

g. Office automation systems that help employees create and share documents that support day-to-day office activities.

3. Information systems can be viewed from various perspectives, including from the perspective of the "players," the "business drivers" influencing the information system, the "technology drivers" used by the information system, and the "process" used to develop the information system.

4. Information workers are the stakeholders in information systems. Information workers include those people whose jobs involve the creation, collection, processing, distribution, and use of information. They include:

a. System owners, the sponsors and chief advocates of information systems.

b. System users, the people who use or are impacted by the information system on a regular basis. Geographically, system users may be internal or external.

c. System designers, technology specialists who translate system users' business requirements and constraints into technical solutions.

d. System builders, technology specialists who construct the information system based on the design specifications.

e. Systems analysts, who facilitate the development of information systems and computer applications. They coordinate the efforts of the owners, users, designers, and builders. Frequently, they may play one of those roles as well. Systems analysts perform systems analysis and design.

5. In addition to having formal systems analysis and design skills, a systems analyst must develop or

possess the following skills, knowledge, and traits:

a. Working knowledge of information technologies.

b. Computer programming experience and expertise.

c. General knowledge of business processes and terminology.

d. General problem-solving skills.

e. Good interpersonal communication skills.

f. Good interpersonal relations skills.

g. Flexibility and adaptability.

h. Character and ethics.

6. Any stakeholder role may be filled by an internal or external worker referred to as an external service provider (ESP). Most ESPs are systems analysts, designers, or builders who are contracted to bring special expertise or experience to a specific project.

7. Most information systems projects involve working as a team. Usually one or more of the stakeholders (team members) takes on the role of project manager to ensure that the system is developed on time, within budget, and with acceptable quality. Most project managers are experienced systems analysts.

8. Business drivers influence information systems. Current business drivers that will continue to influence the development of information systems include:

a. Globalization of the economy.

b. Electronic commerce and business.

c. Security and privacy.

d. Collaboration and partnership.

e. Knowledge asset management.

f. Continuous improvement and total quality management.

g. Business process redesign.

9. Information technology can be a driver of information systems. Outdated technologies can present problems that drive the need to develop new systems. Newer technologies such as the following are influencing today's information systems:

a. Networks and the Internet:

i) *xHTML* and *XML* are the fundamental languages of Web page authoring and Internet application development. Extensible Hypertext Markup Language (xHTML) is the emerging second-generation version of HTML, the language used to construct Web pages. Extensible Markup Language (XML) is the language used to effectively transport data content along with its proper interpretation over the Internet.

ii) *Scripting* languages are simple programming languages designed specifically for Internet applications.

iii) Web-specific programming languages such as *Java* and *Cold Fusion* have emerged to specifically address construction of complex, Web-based applications that involve multiple servers and Web browsers.

iv) *Intranets* are essentially private Internets designed for use by employees of an organization. They offer the look and feel of the Internet; however, security and firewalls restrict their use to employees.

v) *Extranets,* like intranets, are private Internets. But extranets are for use between specific organizations. Only the employees of those identified businesses can access and use the extranet.

vi) *Portals* (in corporations) are "home pages" that can be customized to the specific needs of different individuals who use them. For example, portal technology can define Web pages that provide appropriate information and applications for different roles in the same company. Each individual's role determines which information and applications that person can use from her or his Web page.

vii) Web services are reusable, Web-based programs that can be called from any other Internet program.

b. Mobile and wireless technologies—Increasingly, wireless access must be assumed. And the limitations of mobile devices and screen sizes must be accommodated in an information system's design. All of the following technical trends will significantly impact the analysis and design of new information systems:

i) Handheld computers, or *personal data assistants* (such as the HP *iPaq*, Palm, and RIM *BlackBerry*) have become common in the ranks of information workers. These devices are increasingly including wireless capabilities that provide Web access and e-mail

ii) *Cell phones* are also increasingly featuring Internet and e-mail capabilities.

iii) Integrated devices such as *smart phones* are emerging that integrate the capabilities

of PDAs and cell phones into a single device.

iv) Technologies like *Bluetooth* are emerging to allow separate devices to interoperate as one logical device while preserving each one's form factors and advantages.

c. Object technologies—Most contemporary information systems are built using object technologies. Object technologies allow programmers to build software from software parts called objects. Object-oriented software offers the advantage of reusability and extensibility.

d. Collaborative technologies—Collaborative technologies are those that enhance interpersonal communications and teamwork. Four important classes of collaborative technologies are e-mail, instant messaging, groupware, and work flow.

e. Enterprise applications—Virtually all organizations, large and small, require a core set of enterprise applications to conduct business. For most businesses the core applications include financial management, human resource management, marketing and sales, and operations management (inventory and/or manufacturing control). At one time, most organizations custom-built most or all of these core enterprise applications. But today, these enterprise applications are frequently purchased, installed, and configured for the business and integrated into the organization's business processes. These "internal" core applications are being supplemented with other enterprise applications that integrate an organization's business processes with those of its suppliers and customers. These applications are called customer relationship management (CRM) and supply chain management (SCM). Enterprise application integration (EAI) involves linking applications, whether purchased or developed in-house, so that they can transparently interoperate with one another.

10. Many organizations have a formal systems development process consisting of a standard set of processes or steps they expect will be followed on any systems development project. Systems development processes tend to mirror general problem-solving approaches. This chapter presented a simplified system development process that is composed of the following phases:

a. System initiation—the initial planning for a project to define initial business scope, goals, schedule, and budget.

b. System analysis—the study of a business process domain to recommend improvements and specify the business requirements and priorities for the solution.

c. System design—the specification or construction of a technical, computer-based solution for the business requirements identified in system analysis.

d. System implementation—the construction, installation, testing, and delivery of a system into operation.

11. Information systems face a lifetime of support and continuous improvement. A change made for system support or improvement is merely another project, sometimes called a maintenance or enhancement project. These projects follow the exact same problem-solving approach defined for any other project, but they require less effort and budget.

12. Sequential development requires that each development process (phase) be completed—one after the other. This approach is referred to as the waterfall approach. An alternative development approach is iterative (or incremental) development. This approach requires completing enough analysis, design, and implementation as is necessary to fully develop a part of the new system. Once that version of the system is implemented, the strategy is to then perform some additional analysis, design, and implementation in order to release the next version of the system. These iterations continue until all parts of the entire information system have been developed.

Review Questions

1. Why are information systems (IS) essential in organizations?

2. Why do systems analysts need to know who the stakeholders are in the organization?

3. Who are the typical stakeholders in an information system? What are their roles?

4. Please explain what the consequences are if an information system lacks a system owner.

5. What are the differences between internal users and external users? Give examples.

6. What are the differences between the role of system analysts and the role of the rest of the stakeholders?

7. What kind of knowledge and skills should a system analyst possess?

8. In addition to the business and computing knowledge that system analysts should possess, what are the other essential skills that they need to effectively complete their jobs?

9. Why are good interpersonal communication skills essential for system analysts?

10. What are some of the business drivers for today's information systems?

11. What are the differences between electronic commerce (e-commerce) and electronic business (e-business)?

12. What are the differences between information and knowledge?

13. What are the most important technology drivers for today's information systems?

14. What are the four steps in a system development process? What happens in each step?

15. Why is system initiation essential in the system development process?

Problems and Exercises

1. Assume you are a systems analyst who will be conducting a requirements analysis for an individually owned brick-and-mortar retail store with a point-of-sale system. Identify who the typical internal and external users might include.

2. Assume you are a systems analyst for a consulting company and have been asked to assist the chief executive officer (CEO) of a regional bank. The bank recently implemented a plan to reduce the number of staff, including loan officers, as a strategy to maintain profitability. Subsequently, the bank has experienced chronic problems with backlogged loan requests because of the limited number of loan officers who are able to review and approve or disapprove loans. The CEO of the bank is interested in solutions that would allow the approval process to move faster without increasing the number of loan officers, and has

engaged your company to come up with suggestions. What is one type of system that you might recommend to the bank?

3. How do communication and collaboration systems improve efficiency and effectiveness? What are some of the communication and collaboration systems that are being used by an increasing number of organizations?

4. Identify the type of information system that clerical workers in an organization would typically use and why.

5. As information systems increase in complexity and comprehensiveness, ethical issues regarding accessing and using data from these systems are also increasing. What are some of these ethical issues?

6. What are business to consumer (B2C) and business to business (B2B) Web applications, and what are some examples of each type?

7. While system development processes and methodologies can vary greatly, identify and briefly explain the "generic" phases of the system development process that are described in the textbook and which must be completed for any project. You are a contractor with a systems integration company.

8. Your company has a contract with a local firm to link all of their systems so they can transparently work together. Their applications include a number of existing legacy systems, which were built at different times by different developers using a variety of languages and platforms, as well as several newer contemporary applications. What is the term for this type of linking? What type of tool would you most likely use, and what are some examples of these tools?

9. Your company has asked you to develop a new Web-based system to replace its existing legacy system. There will be very little change in business requirements and functionality from the existing legacy system. Suggest which system development process you might use and why.

10. You recently joined a retail sales company which has recently bought out and assimilated a commercial industrial supply house. You have been asked to lead a project to develop a consolidated inventory-tracking system. Suggest which system development process you might use and why.

11. Your company president sits down beside you just before a meeting is to begin and tells you that people keep saying the customer needs to install a CRM, but doesn't really know what it is. The company president then asks you to explain it in nontechnical terms in the next 30 seconds.

12. Industry studies indicate that mobile and wireless technology has become one of the major technology drivers for designing new information systems. Why is this the case and what is the impact?

13. Briefly explain the impact of Web services on Web development. Give some examples of Web services.

14. Identify in which phase of the development process the following activities belong:

   a. Development of the technical blueprint or design document.
   b. Project scheduling.
   c. Integration testing.
   d. Interviewing system users to define business requirements.

15. What are the two most important advantages of object-oriented software technologies over structured software technologies?

Projects and Research

1. Research the average and/or median salaries for IT professionals. You can use a variety of methods to find this information, such as searching the Web for online sites that publish the results of salary surveys for IT professionals. You can also look at classified ads in newspapers, trade magazines, and/or online.

   a. Is there a significant difference between typical salaries for system analysts, designers and developers?

   b. Roughly, what is the difference in the typical salaries for these different groups?
   c. What do you think are the reasons for the difference?
   d. Is there a gender gap in the salaries of IT professionals? Discuss any trends that you found, and the implications.

2. Contact the chief information officers (CIOs) or top IT managers of several local or regional organizations. Ask them about the process or

methodology they use for system development in their organizations, and why they utilize that particular approach.

   a. Describe and compare the different approaches that you have found.

   b. Which approach do you believe to be the most effective approach?

   c. Why?

3. Career choices and personal skills:

   a. At this point in your education, if you had to choose between becoming a systems analyst, systems designer, or systems builder, which one would you choose?

   b. Why?

   c. Now divide a piece of paper into two columns. On one side, list the personal skills and traits you think are most important for each of these three groups of systems analysts, designers, and builders. In the second column, list at least five skills and traits that you feel to be your strongest ones, then map them to the skills and traits you listed for each of the three groups. With which group do you have the most skills and traits in common?

   d. Is this group the same one as the one you would choose in Question 3a? Why do you think this is (or is not) the case?

4. Your school library should have journals and periodicals dating back at least several decades, or may subscribe to online research services which do. Look at several recent articles in information technology journals regarding systems analysis, as well as several articles from at least 25 years ago.

   a. Compare the recent articles to the older ones. Do there appear to be significant differences in the typical knowledge, skills, abilities, and/or experience that systems analysts needed 25 years ago compared to now?

   b. If you found some differences, what are the ones that you consider most important?

   c. What do you think are some of the reasons for these changes?

   d. Now get out your crystal ball and look into the future 25 years from now. What differences do you predict between the systems analysts of today and those in 25 years?

5. Search the Web for several articles and information on ethical issues related to information technology professionals.

   a. What articles did you find?

   b. Based on your research, which ethical issues do you think systems analysts might face during their careers?

   c. Pick a particular ethical issue and explain the steps you would take if you were confronted with this issue.

   d. What would you do if you found your best friend and co-worker had committed a serious ethical violation? Facts to consider: The violation may never be discovered, but it will cost your company many thousands of dollars in higher costs over the next several years. Your company has a stringent policy of firing employees who commit serious ethical violations. Make sure to explain your reasons for the action(s) you would take, if any.

6. Search the Web or business periodicals in your library such as Forbes Magazine for information on three or four chief information officers of large companies or organizations.

   a. Which industry sector, companies, and CIOs did you find?

   b. For each CIO that you researched, what was their predominant experience prior to becoming a CIO; that is, did they have an information technology background, a business background, or both?

   c. For each CIO, what is their level of education?

   d. How many years has each been a CIO, and for approximately how many different companies has each one worked?

   e. Based upon your research, what knowledge and skills does a CIO need in order to be successful? Why?

Minicases

1. What do you think will be possible technologically 10 years from now? How about 20 or 30 years from now? Research a new and interesting technology that is in the research and development stage. Prepare a presentation using a movie clip and PowerPoint on this technology and present it

to the class. Submit a short paper on the impacts this new technology might have on society and/or businesses.

2. Consider outsourcing: It is many times the case that at least part of the development process is outsourced. In fact, project leaders today must be

capable of handling geographically diverse teams as well as timeline and resource constraints. Outsourcing brings to the table increased efficiency and economic gains to the societies that are interacting. However, these gains are not quickly realized, and the negative impacts on a society that is outsourcing can be significant from a jobs perspective. Dr. Mankiw, as an economic advisor to President Bush, publicly touted the benefits of outsourcing and was deeply criticized for his stance. Do you think that it is good or bad for a business to outsource work? Do you think there are ethical dilemmas for companies who outsource? Find at least two articles on the impacts of outsourcing, and bring them to share with the class.

3. You are a network administrator, and as part of your job, you monitor employee e-mails. You discover that your boss is cutting corners on a system that your company is developing in order to finish the project more quickly and to stay under budget. There is a flaw in the system as a result, and this flaw will cause a network crash if more than 20 people are on the network at a time. The client expects approximately 12 people on the network at any given time. You are sure, as apparently your boss is, that the customer will not find out until well after the project is accepted (if ever). What do you do?

4. A systems analyst must be both technically proficient and capable of successful customer communication. Developing a good system requires a complete understanding of user requirements. Many times, users don't know what is available (technologically) or even what they would like from a system. What are characteristics of good communication?

Team and Individual Exercises

1. Get together into small groups of two. The first person will decide on a task that he/she wishes to be completed—for instance, sharpen a pencil or write down the name of the professor. It should be simple and straightforward. That person is to communicate on paper using only diagrams and no words (verbal or written) what he/she wishes to be done, and give it to person number two. Person number two should then complete the requested task.

2. What did you discover from this exercise? How long did it take until the second person understood what the first person was asking for? Was

there miscommunication? Write down your thoughts and observations, and share them with the class.

3. Individual exercise: Imagine a really cool technology. The sky is the limit, and anything is possible. How does this technology impact your life? Does it impact business?

4. Individual exercise: Think back on the last time someone told you something *couldn't* be done. What was it? Did you listen to them? Why or why not?

Suggested Readings

Ambler, Scott. *Agile Modeling: Effective Practices for eXtreme Programming and the Unified Process.* New York: John Wiley & Sons, 2002. This book has significantly shaped our thinking about the software development process. Those of you who are critical of the "extreme-programming" movement need not fear that our enthusiasm for this suggested reading indicates an endorsement of extreme programming. We simply like the sanity that Scott brings to the process of systems and software development through the use of flexible methods within the context of an iterative process. We will reference this book in several chapters.

Ernest, Kallman; John Grillo; and James Linderman. *Ethical Decision Making and Information Technology: An Introduction with Cases,* 2nd ed. Burr Ridge, IL: McGraw-Hill/Irwin, 1995. This is an excellent textbook for teaching ethics in an MIS curriculum. It is a collection of case studies that can complement a systems analysis and design course.

Gartner Group IT Symposium and Expo (annual). Our university's management information unit has long subscribed to the Gartner Group's service that reports on industry trends, the probabilities for success of trends and technologies, and suggested strategies for information technology transfer. Gartner research has played a significant, ongoing role in helping us to chart business and technology drivers as described in this chapter. We have also been fortunate to be able to attend Gartner's annual IT symposium. Gartner Group reports and symposiums have influenced each edition of the book. For more information about the Gartner Group, see www.gartner.com.

Gause, Donald, and Gerald Weinberg. *Are Your Lights On? How to Figure Out What the Problem REALLY Is.* New York: Dorset House Publishing, 1990. Yes, this is not a recent book, but neither are the fundamentals of problem solving. Here's a short and easy-to-read book about general problem solving. You can probably read the entire book in one night, and it could profoundly improve your problem-solving potential as a systems analyst (or, for that matter, any other profession).

Levine, Martin. *Effective Problem Solving,* 2nd ed. Englewood Cliffs, NJ: Prentice Hall, 1994. This is another older book, but as we stated before, problem-solving methods are timeless. At only 146 pages, this title can serve as an excellent professional reference.

Weinberg, Gerald. *Rethinking Systems Analysis and Design.* New York: Dorset House Publishing, 1988. Don't let the date fool you. This is one of the best and most important books on this subject ever written. This book may not teach any of the popular systems analysis and design methods of our day, but it challenges the reader to leap beyond those methods to consider something far more important—the people side of systems work. Dr. Weinberg's theories and concepts are presented in the context of dozens of delightful fables and short experiential stories. We are grateful to him for our favorite systems analysis fable of all time, "The Three Ostriches."

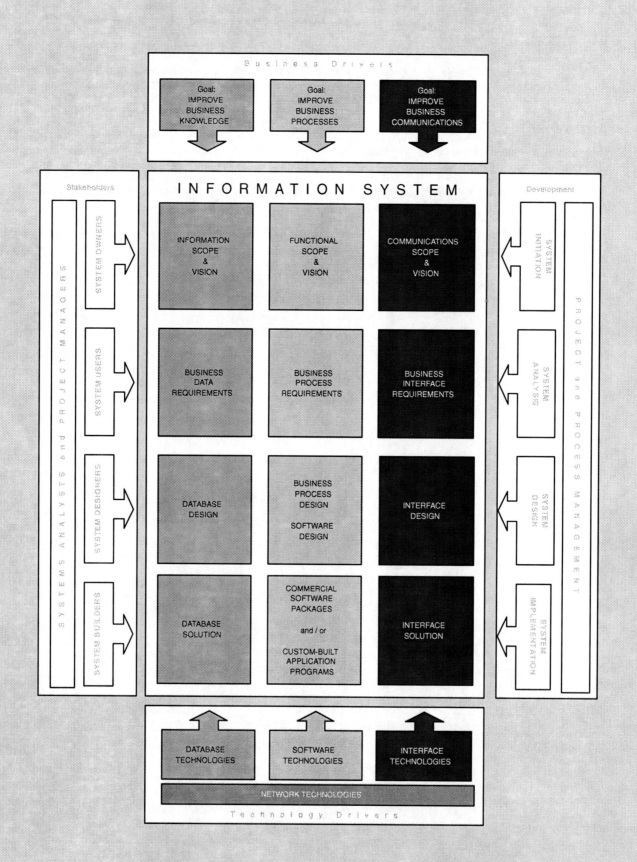

Information System Building Blocks

Chapter Preview and Objectives

Systems analysis and design methods are used to develop information systems for organizations. Before learning the *process* of building systems, you need a clear understanding of the *product* you are trying to build. This chapter takes an architectural look at information systems and applications. We will build a framework for information systems architecture that will subsequently be used to organize and relate all of the chapters in this book. The chapter will address the following areas:

▮ Differentiate between *front-* and *back-office* information systems.

▮ Describe the different classes of information system applications (*transaction processing, management information, decision support, expert, communication and collaboration,* and *office automation systems*) and how they interoperate to supplement one another.

▮ Describe the role of information systems architecture in systems development.

▮ Identify three high-level goals that provide system owners and system users with a perspective of an information system.

▮ Name three goal-oriented perspectives for any information systems.

▮ Identify three technologies that provide system designers and builders with a perspective of an information system.

▮ Describe four building blocks of the KNOWLEDGE goal for an information system.

▮ Describe four building blocks of the PROCESS goal for an information system.

▮ Describe four building blocks of the COMMUNICATIONS goal for an information system.

▮ Describe the role of network technologies as it relates to KNOWLEDGE, PROCESSES, and COMMUNICATIONS building blocks.

Introduction

The SoundStage member services system project is getting underway. Bob Martinez has been assigned the task of conducting initial meetings with groups of system users to gain their perspective on the system and what it must accomplish. He quickly discovered that everyone had a different perspective and expressed that perspective in a different language. In college, majoring in computer information systems technology, Bob tended to think about information systems in terms of programming languages, networking technologies, and databases. He found that the others didn't think in those terms. The system users talked about manual forms and how they were routed. They talked about policies and procedures and reports they needed. As he met with managers he heard them talk about strategic plans and how the system could give the organization a competitive edge.

It reminded Bob of the old story he had heard about three blind men who came upon an elephant. One felt the trunk and concluded that an elephant was like a snake. Another felt a leg and concluded that an elephant was like a tree. The third felt an ear and concluded that an elephant was like a fan. It didn't take Bob long to realize that the owners' and users' perspectives were just as valid as his. An information system is more than technology. It is mainly a tool that serves the goals of the organization.

The Product—Information Systems

front-office information system an information system that supports business functions that extend out to the organization's customers.

In Chapter 1 you were introduced to information systems from four different perspectives, including stakeholders, business drivers, technology drivers, and the process of systems development. As suggested by the *home page* (see p. 42), this chapter will more closely examine the information system "product."

Organizations are served not by a single information system but, instead, by a federation of information systems that support various business functions. This idea is illustrated in Figure 2-1. Notice that most businesses have both **front-office**

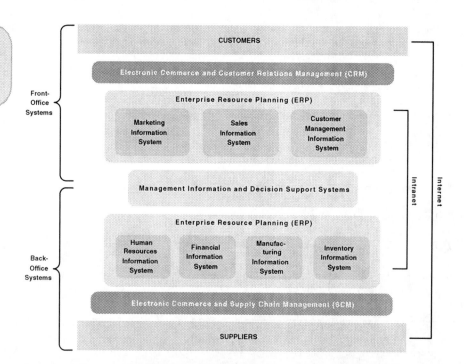

FIGURE 2-1

A Federation of Information Systems

information systems that support business functions that reach out to customers (or constituents) and **back-office information systems** that support internal business operations as well as interact with suppliers. These front- and back-office information systems feed data to management information systems and decision support systems that support management needs of the business. Contemporary information systems are interfacing with customers and suppliers using electronic commerce technology, customer relations management (CRM), and supply chain management (SCM) applications (see descriptions in Chapter 1) over the Internet. Finally, most companies have some sort of intranet (internal to the business) to support communications between employees and the information systems.

In Chapter 1 you learned that there are several classes of information system applications (see opposite page). Each class serves the needs of different types of users. In practice, these classes overlap such that it isn't always easy to differentiate one from another. The various applications should ideally interoperate to complement and supplement one another. Take a few moments to study Figure 2-2, which illustrates typical roles of information systems in an organization. The rounded rectangles represent various information systems. Notice that an organization can and will have multiple transaction-processing systems, office automation systems, and the like. The "drum" shapes represent stored data. Notice that an organization has multiple

back-office information system an information system that supports internal business operations of an organization, as well as reaches out to suppliers.

FIGURE 2-2 Information Systems Applications

46   **Part One**   **The Context of Systems Development Projects**

sets of stored data, and only some of them work together. We call your attention to the following number annotations on the diagram:

❶ The first transaction processing system responds to an input transaction's data (e.g., an order). It produces transaction information to verify the correct processing of the input transaction.

❷ The second transaction processing system merely produces an output transaction (e.g., an invoice). Such a system may respond to something as simple as the passage of time (e.g., it is the end of the month; therefore, generate all invoices).

❸ The first management information system simply produces reports or information (e.g., sales analysis reports) using data stored in transactional databases (maintained by the aforementioned transaction processing systems).

❹ The second management information system uses business models (e.g., MRP) to produce operational management information (e.g., a production schedule).

❺ Notice that an MIS may use data from more than one transactional database.

❻ Notice that snapshots of data from the transactional databases populate a data warehouse. The snapshots may be taken at various time intervals, and different subsets of data may be included in various snapshots. The data in the warehouse will be organized to ensure easy access and inquiry by managers.

❼ Decision support and executive information systems applications will typically provide read-only access to the data warehouses to produce decision support and executive management information.

❽ An expert system requires a special database that stores the expertise in the form of rules and heuristics.

❾ An expert system either accepts problems as inputs (e.g., Should we grant credit to a specific customer?), or senses problems in the environment (e.g., Is the lathe producing parts within acceptable specifications?), and then responds to a problem with an appropriate solution based on the system's expertise.

❿ Personal office automation systems tend to revolve around the data and business processing needs of an individual. Such systems are typically developed by the users themselves (and run on personal computers).

⓫ Work group office automation systems are frequently message-based (e.g., e-mail-based) and are smaller-scale solutions to departmental needs. As shown in the figure, they can access or import data from larger, transaction processing systems.

In the average business, there will be many instances of each of these different applications.

A Framework for Information Systems Architecture

information systems architecture a unifying framework into which various stakeholders with different perspectives can organize and view the fundamental building blocks of information systems.

It has become fashionable to deal with the complexity of modern information systems by using the term *architecture*. Information technology professionals speak of data architectures, application architectures, network architectures, software architectures, and so forth. An **information systems architecture** serves as a higher-level framework for understanding different views of the fundamental building blocks of an information system. Essentially, information systems architecture provides a foundation for organizing the various components of any information system you care to develop.

Different stakeholders have different perspectives on or views of an information system. System owners and system users tend to focus on three common business goals of any information system. These goals are typically established in response to one or more of the business drivers you read about in Chapter 1. These goal-oriented perspectives of an information system include:

- The goal to improve *business knowledge.* Knowledge is a product of information and data.
- The goal to improve *business processes* and services.
- The goal to improve *business communications* and people collaboration.

The role of the system designers and builders is more technical. As such, their focus tends to be placed more on the technologies that may be used by the information system in order to achieve the business goal. The system designers' and builders' perspectives of an information system tend to focus more on:

- The *database technologies* that support business accumulation and use of business knowledge.
- The *software technologies* that automate and support business processes and services.
- The *interface technologies* that support business communications and collaboration.

As shown in Figure 2-3, the intersection of these perspectives (rows and columns) defines *building blocks* for an information system. In the next section, we will describe all these information system building blocks.

NOTE: Throughout this book, we use a consistent color scheme for both the framework and the various tools that relate to, or document, the building blocks. The color scheme is based on the building blocks as follows:

- represents something to do with KNOWLEDGE
- represents something to do with PROCESSES
- represents something to do with COMMUNICATIONS

The information system building blocks do not exist in isolation. They must be carefully synchronized to avoid inconsistencies and incompatibilities within the system. For example, a database designer (a *system designer*) and a programmer (a *system builder*) have their own architectural views of the system; however, these views must be compatible and consistent if the system is going to work properly. Synchronization occurs both horizontally (across any given row) and vertically (down any given column).

In the remainder of this chapter, we'll briefly examine each focus and perspective—the building blocks of information systems.

> KNOWLEDGE Building Blocks

Improving business knowledge is a fundamental goal of an information system. As you learned in Chapter 1, business knowledge is derived from data and information. Through processing, data is refined to produce information that results in knowledge. Knowledge is what enables a company to achieve its mission and vision.

The KNOWLEDGE column of your framework is illustrated in Figure 2-4. Notice at the bottom of the KNOWLEDGE column that our goal is to capture and store business data using DATABASE TECHNOLOGIES. Database technology (such as *Access, SQL Server, DB2,* or *Oracle*) will be used to organize and store data for all information systems. Also, as you look down the KNOWLEDGE column, each of our different stakeholders has different perspectives of the information system. Let's examine those views and discuss their relevance to the KNOWLEDGE column.

System Owners' View of KNOWLEDGE   The average system owner is not interested in raw data. The system owner is interested in information that adds new business knowledge. Business knowledge and information help managers make

48   Part One   The Context of Systems Development Projects

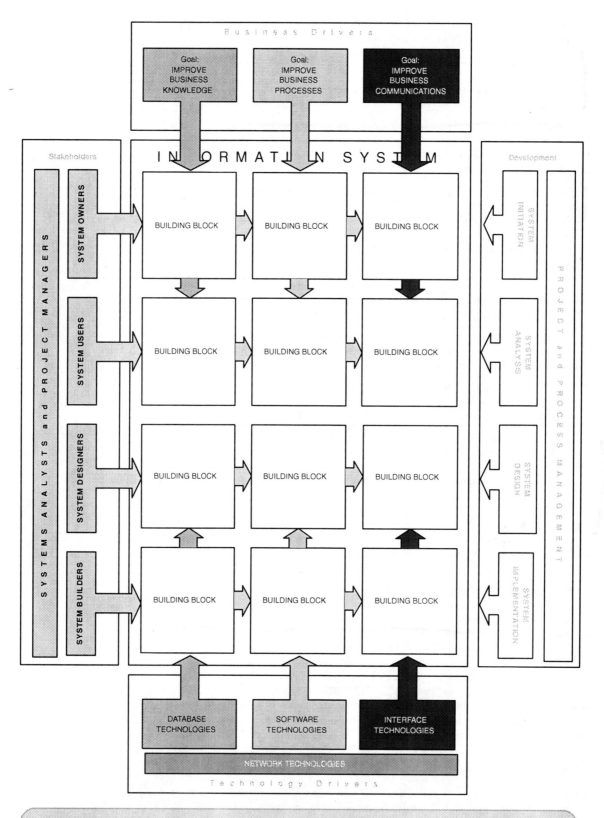

FIGURE 2-3   Information System Perspectives and Focuses

FIGURE 2-4   A BUSINESS KNOWLEDGE Perspective of Information Systems

intelligent decisions that support the organization's mission, goals, objectives, and competitive edge.

Business knowledge may initially take the form of a simple list of business entities and business rules. Examples of business entities might include CUSTOMERS, PRODUCTS, EQUIPMENT, BUILDINGS, ORDERS, and PAYMENTS. What do business entities have to do with knowledge? Information is produced from raw data that describe these business entities. Therefore, it makes sense that we should quickly identify relevant business entities about which we need to capture and store data.

It is also useful to understand simple business associations or rules that describe how the business entities interact. Examples of useful business rules for a sales system might include the following:

- A CUSTOMER <u>can place</u> ORDERS—an ORDER <u>must be placed by</u> a CUSTOMER.
- An ORDER <u>sells</u> PRODUCTS—a PRODUCT <u>may be sold on</u> an ORDER.

Intuitively, a system's database needs to track these business entities and rules in order to produce useful information (for example, "Has CUSTOMER 2846 placed any unfilled ORDERS?").

System owners are concerned with the big picture. They are generally not interested in details (such as what fields describe a CUSTOMER or an ORDER). The primary role of system owners in a systems development project should be to define the scope and vision for the project. For KNOWLEDGE, scope can be defined in simple terms such as the aforementioned business entities and rules. System owners define project vision and expectations in terms of their insight into problems, opportunities, and constraints as they relate to the business entities and rules.

System Users' View of KNOWLEDGE   Information system users are knowledgeable about the data that describe the business. As information workers, they capture, store, process, edit, and use that data every day. They frequently see the data only in terms of how data are currently stored or how they think data should be stored. To them, the data are recorded on forms, stored in file cabinets, recorded in books and binders, organized into spreadsheets, or stored in computer files and databases. The challenge in systems development is to correctly identify and verify users' business data requirements. **Data requirements** are an extension of the business entities and rules that were initially identified by the system owners. System users may identify additional entities and rules because of their greater familiarity with the data. More importantly, system users must specify the exact data attributes to be stored and the precise business rules for maintaining that data. Consider the following example:

> A system owner may identify the need to store data about a business entity called CUSTOMER. System users might tell us that we need to differentiate between PROSPECTIVE CUSTOMERS, ACTIVE CUSTOMERS, and INACTIVE CUSTOMERS because they know that slightly different types of data describe each type of customer. System users can also tell us precisely what data must be stored about each type of customer. For example, an ACTIVE CUSTOMER might require such data attributes as CUSTOMER NUMBER, NAME, BILLING ADDRESS, CREDIT RATING, and CURRENT BALANCE. Finally, system users are also knowledgeable about the precise rules that govern entities and relationships. For example, they might tell us that the credit rating for an ACTIVE CUSTOMER must be PREFERRED, NORMAL, or PROBATIONARY and that the default for a new customer is NORMAL. They might also specify that only an ACTIVE CUSTOMER can place an ORDER, but an ACTIVE CUSTOMER might not necessarily have any current ORDERS at any given time.

Notice from the above example that the system user's data requirements can be identified independently of the DATABASE TECHNOLOGY that can or will be used to store the data. System users tend to focus on the "business" issues as they pertain to

data requirement a representation of users' data in terms of entities, attributes, relationships, and rules.

the data. It is important that the system users provide data requirements that are consistent with and complementary to the information scope and vision provided by the system owners.

System Designers' View of KNOWLEDGE   The system designer's KNOWLEDGE perspective differs significantly from the perspectives of system owners and system users. The system designer is more concerned with the DATABASE TECHNOLOGY that will be used by the information system to support business knowledge. System designers translate the system users' business data requirements into database designs that will subsequently be used by system builders to develop computer databases that will be made available via the information system. The system designers' view of data is constrained by the limitations of whatever database management system (DBMS) is chosen. Often, the choice has already been made and the developers must use that technology. For example, many businesses have standardized on an enterprise DBMS (such as *Oracle, DB2,* or *SQL Server*) and a work group DBMS (such as *Access*).

In any case, the system designer's view of KNOWLEDGE consists of data structures, database schemas, fields, indexes, and other technology-dependent components. Most of these technical specifications are too complex to be reasonably understood by system users. The systems analyst and/or database specialists design and document these technical views of the data. This book will teach tools and techniques for transforming business data requirements into database schemas.

System Builders' View of KNOWLEDGE   The final view of KNOWLEDGE is relevant to the system builders. In the KNOWLEDGE column of Figure 2-4, system builders are closest to the actual database management system technology. They must represent data in very precise and unforgiving languages. The most commonly encountered database language is *SQL (Structured Query Language)*. Alternatively, many database management systems, such as *Access* and *Visual FoxPro* include proprietary languages or facilities for constructing a new database.

Not all information systems use database technology to store their business data. Many older legacy systems were built with *flat-file* technologies such as VSAM. These flat-file data structures were constructed directly within the programming language used to write the programs that use those files. For example, in a *COBOL* program the flat-file data structures are expressed as PICTURE clauses in a DATA DIVISION. It is not the intent of this book to teach either database or flat-file construction languages, but only to place them in the context of the KNOWLEDGE building block of information systems.

> PROCESS Building Blocks

Improving business and services processes is another fundamental goal of an information system. Processes deliver the desired functionality of an information system. Processes represent the *work* in a system. People may perform some processes, while computers and machines perform others.

The PROCESS building blocks of information systems are illustrated in Figure 2-5. Notice at the bottom of the PROCESS column that SOFTWARE TECHNOLOGIES will be used to automate selected processes. As you look down the PROCESS column, each of our different stakeholders has different perspectives of the information system. Let's examine those views and discuss their relevance to the PROCESS column.

System Owners' View of PROCESSES   As usual, system owners are generally interested in the big picture. They tend to focus not so much on work flow and procedures as on high-level **business functions,** such as those listed in the margin of page 53. Organizations are often organized around these business fuctions with a vice president

business function a group of related processes that support the business. Functions can be decomposed into other subfunctions and eventually into processes that do specific tasks.

52   Part One   The Context of Systems Development Projects

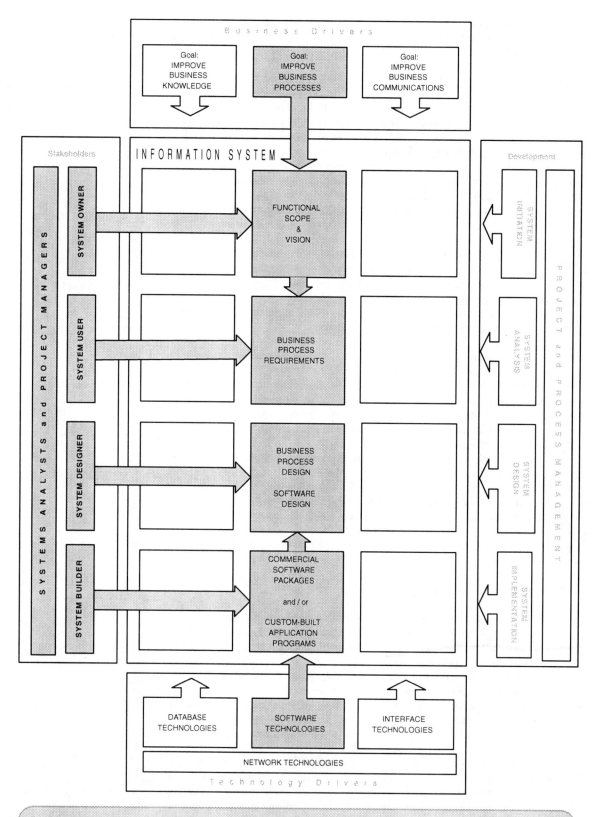

FIGURE 2-5 A BUSINESS PROCESS Perspective of Information Systems

overseeing each function. Unlike business events (such as CUSTOMER SUBMITS ORDER) that have a definite beginning and end, a business function has no starting time or stopping time.

Historically, most information systems were (or are) *function-centered.* That means the system supported one business function. An example would be a SALES INFORMATION SYSTEM that supports only the initial processing of customer orders. Today, many of these single-function information systems are being redesigned as cross-functional information systems that support several business functions. As a contemporary alternative to the traditional SALES INFORMATION SYSTEM, a cross-functional ORDER FULFILLMENT INFORMATION SYSTEM would also support all relevant processes subsequent to the processing of the customer order. This would include filling the order in the warehouse, shipping the products to the customer, billing the customer, and providing any necessary follow-up service to the customer—in other words, all business processes required to ensure a complete and satisfactory response to the customer order, regardless of which departments are involved.

As shown in Figure 2-5, the system owners view a system's business PROCESSES with respect to the functional scope being supported by the systems and to a vision or expectation for improvements. The system's business functions are frequently documented by systems analysts in terms of simple lists of business events and responses to those events. Some examples of business events and responses are as follows:

- Event: CUSTOMER SUBMITS ORDER
  Response: CUSTOMER RECEIVES ORDERED PRODUCTS

- Event: EMPLOYEE SUBMITS PURCHASE REQUISITION FOR SUPPLIES
  Response: EMPLOYEE RECEIVES REQUESTED SUPPLIES

- Event: END OF MONTH
  Response: INVOICE CUSTOMERS AGAINST ACCOUNTS

With respect to each event and response identified, system owners would identify perceived problems, opportunities, goals, objectives, and constraints. The costs and benefits of developing information systems to support business functions would also be discussed. As was the case with KNOWLEDGE, system owners are not concerned with PROCESS details. That level of detail is identified and documented as part of the system users' view of processes.

System owners also frequently identify services and levels of service that they seek to provide to customers, suppliers, and employees. A popular example is customer, supplier, or employee *self*-service. Human resource systems, for example, increasingly provide employees with the ability to enter their own transactions such as change of address, medical claims, and training requests. System owners also identify needs for information systems to improve service by reducing errors and improving service.

This book will teach you how to identify and document project scope in terms of relevant business functions, business events, and responses.

System Users' View of PROCESSES   Returning again to Figure 2-5, we are ready to examine the system users' view of processes. Users are concerned with the business processes, or "work," that must be performed in order to provide the appropriate responses to business events. System users specify the business process in terms of **process requirements** for a new system. Process requirements are often documented in terms of activities, data flows, or work flow.

These process requirements must be precisely specified, especially if they are to be automated or supported by software technology. Business process requirements are frequently defined in terms of **policies** and **procedures.** Policies are explicit rules that must be adhered to when completing a business process. Procedures are the precise steps to be followed in completing the business process. Consider the following example:

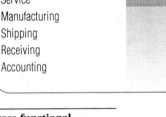

TYPICAL BUSINESS FUNCTIONS

Sales
Service
Manufacturing
Shipping
Receiving
Accounting

cross-functional information system a system that supports relevant business processes from several business functions without regard to traditional organizational boundaries such as divisions, departments, centers, and offices.

process requirements a user's expectation of the processing requirements for a business process and its information systems.

policy a set of rules that govern a business process.

procedure step-by-step set of instructions and logic for accomplishing a business process.

CREDIT APPROVAL is a policy. It establishes a set of rules for determining whether or not to extend credit to a customer. That credit approval policy is usually applied within the context of a specific CREDIT CHECK procedure that established the correct steps for checking credit against the credit policy.

work flow the flow of transactions through business processes to ensure appropriate checks and approvals are implemented.

Process requirements are also frequently specified in terms of **work flow.** Most businesses are very dependent on checks and balances to implement work flow. For example, a purchase requisition may be initiated by any employee. But that requisition follows a specific work flow of approvals and checks before it becomes a purchase order transaction that is entered into an information processing system. Of course, these checks and balances can become cumbersome and bureaucratic. Systems analysts and users seek an approproriate balance between checks and balances and service and performance.

Once again, the challenge in systems development is to identify, express, and analyze business process requirements exclusively in business terms that can be understood by system users. Tools and techniques for process modeling and documentation of policies and procedures are taught extensively in this book.

System Designers' View of PROCESSES   As was the case with the KNOWLEDGE building block, the system designer's view of business processes is constrained by the limitations of specific application development technologies such as *Java, Visual Basic.NET, C++*, and *C#*. Sometimes the analyst is able to choose the software technology; however, often the choices are limited by software architecture standards that specify which software and hardware technologies must be used. In either case, the designer's view of processes is technical.

Given the business processes from the system users' view, the designer must first determine which processes to automate and how to best automate those processes. Models are drawn to document and communicate how selected business processes are, or will be, implemented using the software and hardware.

Today, many businesses purchase commercial off-the-shelf (COTS) software instead of building that software in-house. In fact, many businesses prescribe that software that can be purchased should never be built—or that only software that provides true competitive advantage should be built. In the case of purchasing software, business processes must usually be changed or adapted to work with the software. Hence, in this scenario the business process design specifications must document how the software package will be integrated into the enterprise.

software specifications the technical design of business processes to be automated or supported by computer programs to be written by system builders.

Alternatively, in the case of building software in-house, business processes are usually designed first. And the business process specifications must then be supplemented with **software specifications** that document the technical design of computer programs to be written. You may have encountered some of these software specifications in a programming course. As was the case with KNOWLEDGE, some of these technical views of PROCESSES can be understood by users but most cannot. The designers' intent is to prepare software specifications that (1) fulfill the business process requirements of system users and (2) provide sufficient detail and consistency for communicating the software design to system builders. The systems design chapters in this book teach tools and techniques for transforming business process requirements into both business process design and software design specifications.

System Builders' View of PROCESSES   System builders represent PROCESSES using precise computer programming languages or application development environments (ADEs) that describe inputs, outputs, logic, and control. Examples include *C++, Visual Basic .NET, C#* (part of the Microsoft *Visual Studio .NET* ADE), and *Java* (available in ADEs such as IBM *WebSphere* and BEA *WebLogic*). Additionally, some applications and database management systems provide their own internal languages for programming. Examples include *Visual Basic for Applications* (in *Access*) and

PL-SQL (in *Oracle*). All these languages are used to write custom-built **application programs** that automate business processes.

This book does not teach application programming. We will, however, demonstrate how some of these languages provide an excellent environment for rapidly developing a system using prototyping software. **Prototyping** has become the design technique of choice for many system designers and builders. Prototypes typically evolve into the final version of the system or application.

As mentioned earlier, sometimes decisions may involve purchasing a commercial software package as a system solution. In this scenario, the system builder may need to focus on customization that must be done to the software package. The system builder may also be expected to develop application programs that must be integrated with the commercial package to extend the package's functional capabilities. Finally, the system builder must also focus on program utilities that must be written to help with the conversion and integration of the commercial program and existing systems.

application program a language-based, machine-readable representation of what a software process is supposed to do or how a software process is supposed to accomplish its task.

prototyping a technique for quickly building a functioning but incomplete model of the information system using rapid application development tools.

> COMMUNICATIONS Building Blocks

Let's examine our final building block—COMMUNICATIONS. A common goal of most organizations is to improve business communications and collaboration between employees and other constituents. Communication improvements in information systems are typically directed toward two critical interface goals for an information system:

- Information systems must provide effective and efficient communication interfaces to the system's users. These interfaces should promote teamwork and coordination of activities.
- Information systems must interface effectively and efficiently with *other* information systems—both with those within the business and increasingly with other businesses' information systems.

The COMMUNICATIONS building blocks of information systems are illustrated in our framework in Figure 2-6. Notice at the bottom of the COMMUNICATION column that it utilizes INTERFACE TECHNOLOGIES to implement the communication interfaces. And once again, as you look down the COMMUNICATION column, each of our different stakeholders has different views of the system. Let's examine those views and discuss their relevance to systems development.

System Owners' View of COMMUNICATION The system owners' view of COMMUNICATION is relatively simple. Early in a systems development project, system owners need to specify:

- With which business units, employees, customers, and external businesses must the new system interface?
- Where are these business units, employees, customers, and external businesses located?
- Will the system have to interface with any other information, computer, or automated systems?

Answers to these questions help to define the communications scope of an information systems development project. Minimally, a suitable system owners' view of information system communication scope and vision might be expressed as a simple list of business locations or systems with which the information system must interface. Again, relevant problems, opportunities, or constraints may be identified and analyzed.

System Users' View of COMMUNICATION System users' view of COMMUNICATION is more in terms of the information system's inputs and outputs. Those inputs and outputs can take many forms; however, the business interface requirements are more

Foundations of Information Systems

52

56   **Part One**   **The Context of Systems Development Projects**

FIGURE 2-6 A BUSINESS COMMUNICATIONS Perspective of Information Systems

important than the technical format. The inputs and outputs represent how the proposed system would interact with users, employees, business units, customers, and other businesses.

The details of those inputs and outputs are important. System users might specify the details in the form of a list of fields (and their values) that make up the inputs or outputs. Alternatively, and because system users have become comfortable with the graphical user interface (e.g., *Windows* or Web browsers) for the system, the details might be specified in the form of prototypes. System users are increasingly demanding that their custom-built information system applications have the same "look and feel" as their favorite PC tools such as word processors and spreadsheets. This common graphical user interface makes each new application easier to learn and use.

Both list and prototype approaches to documenting the system users' view of COMMUNICATION will be addressed in various chapters of this book.

System Designers' View of COMMUNICATION   System designers must be concerned with the technical design of both the user and the system-to-system communication interfaces. We call these **interface specifications.** Let's begin with the user interface.

Users and designers can be involved in interface design. But whereas system users are interested in requirements and format, system designers have other interests such as consistency, compatibility, completeness, and user dialogues. The **user dialogue** (sometimes called *interface navigation*) specifies how the user will navigate through an application to perform useful work.

The trend toward graphical user interfaces (GUIs) such as *Windows* and Web browsers has simplified life for system users but complicated the design process for system designers. In a typical *Windows* application, there are many different things users can do at any given time—type something, click the left mouse button on a menu item or toolbar icon, press the F1 key for help, maximize the current window, minimize the current window, switch to a different program, and many others. Accordingly, the system designer views the interface in terms of various system states, events that change the system from one state to another, and responses to those events. Today, there are many more design decisions and considerations the system designer must address to document the dialogue of a graphical user interface solution. Tools used to document user dialogues will be discussed in the design unit of this book.

Web interfaces have further complicated the designer's activities. Society has come to expect more glitz in Web interfaces. For that reason, it is not at all uncommon for the design team to include graphical design specialists and human–computer interface specialists to ensure that the interface for a Web server is both compelling and easy to use.

Although not depicted in Figure 2-6, modern system designers may also design *keyless interfaces* such as bar coding, optical character recognition, pen, and voice or handwriting recognition. These alternatives reduce errors by eliminating the keyboard as a source of human error. However, these interfaces, like graphical user interfaces, must be carefully designed to both exploit the underlying technology and maximize the return on what can be a sizable investment.

Finally, and as suggested earlier, system designers are also concerned with system-to-system interfaces. Increasingly, system interfaces are the most difficult to design and implement. For instance, consider a procurement information system that is used to initiate and purchase everything from supplies to equipment. A procurement system must interface with other information systems such as human resources (to determine authority to purchase and approve orders), accounting (to determine if funds are available against an account), receiving (to determine if ordered goods were received, and accounts payable (to initiate payment). These interfacing systems may use very different software and databases. This can greatly complicate system interface design. System interfaces become even more complex when the interface is between information systems in different businesses. For example, in the aforementioned system, we might want to enable our procurement system to directly interface with a supplier's order fulfillment system.

interface specifications technical designs that document how system users are to interact with a system and how a system interacts with other systems.

user dialogue a specification of how the user moves from window to window or page to page, interacting with the application programs to perform useful work.

Legacy information systems in most businesses were each built with the technologies and techniques that represented the best practices at the time when they were developed. Some systems were built in-house. Others were purchased from software vendors or developed with consultants. As a result, the integration of these heterogeneous systems can be difficult. Consequently, the need for different systems to interoperate is pervasive. Accordingly, the time system designers spend on system-to-system integration is frequently as much as or more than the time they spend on system development. The system designer's mission is to find or build interfaces between these systems that (1) do not create maintenance projects for the legacy systems, (2) do not compromise the superior technologies and design of the new systems, and (3) are ideally transparent to the system users.

System Builders' View of COMMUNICATION   System builders construct, install, test, and implement both user and system-to-system interface solutions using INTERFACE TECHNOLOGY (see Figure 2-6). For user interfaces, the interface technology is frequently embedded into the *application development environment (ADE)* used to construct software for the system. For example, ADEs such as those for *Visual Studio .NET,* and *Powerbuilder* include all the interface technology required to construct a *Windows* graphical user interface (GUI). ADEs such as those for *Java* and *Cold Fusion* provide similar functionality for Web interfaces. Alternatively, the user interface could be constructed with a stand-alone interface technology that supports *xHTML* (e.g., Macromedia's *Dreamweaver*).

System-to-system interfaces are considerably more complex than user interfaces to construct or implement. One system-to-system interfacing technology that is currently popular is middleware. **Middleware** is a layer of utility software that sits in between application software and systems software to transparently integrate differing technologies so that they can interoperate.

middleware utility software that allows application software and systems software that utilize differing technologies to interoperate.

One common example of middleware is the open database connectivity (ODBC) tools that allow application programs to work with different database management systems without having to be rewritten to take into consideration the nuances and differences of those database management systems. Programs written with ODBC commands can, for the most part, work with any ODBC-compliant database (which includes dozens of different database management systems). Similar middleware products exist for each of the columns in our information system framework. System designers help to select and apply these products to integrate systems.

At the time of this writing, *XML (eXtensible Markup Language)* has emerged as an evolving standard for system-to-system communication. *XML* is unique in its ability to share data between systems through data streams that not only include the data but also include the meaning and structural definitions for that data. *XML* capabilities are the new frontier for software that implements electronic data exchange over the Web.

Once again, this book is not about system construction; however, we present the system builder's view because the other COMMUNICATION views lead to the construction of the actual communication interfaces.

Network Technologies and the IS Building Blocks

In this chapter, we unveiled a framework for information systems architecture that was initially inspired by the work of John Zachman.[1] The Zachman "Framework for Information Systems Architecture" achieved international recognition and use. The Zachman framework is a matrix (similar to the chapter map at the beginning of this chapter). The rows correspond to what Zachman calls *perspectives* of different

---

[1]John A. Zachman, "A Framework for Information Systems Architecture," *IBM Systems Journal* 26, no. 3 (1987), pp. 276–292.

FIGURE 2-7

The Role of the Network in Information Systems

people involved in systems development and use. The columns correspond to *focuses* on different aspects of the information system. Zachman's architecture includes a separate column that closely equates to what our framework recognizes as NETWORK TECHNOLOGIES. (We have chosen to omit that column because network frameworks are more typically covered in data communications and networking textbooks—and those textbooks tend to focus on the Open Systems Interconnect (OSI) framework as opposed to Zachman's.)

But unquestionably, today's information systems are built on networks. Figure 2-7 shows a modern high-level information systems framework that demonstrates the contemporary layering of an information system's KNOWLEDGE, PROCESSES, and COMMUNICATIONS building blocks on NETWORK TECHNOLOGIES. Today's best-designed information systems tend to separate these layers and force them to communicate across the network. This *clean-layering* approach allows any one building block to be replaced with another while having little or no impact on the other building blocks. For example, the DATABASE TECHNOLOGY, SOFTWARE TECHNOLOGY, or INTERFACE TECHNOLOGY could be changed without impacting the other building blocks.

It is not the intent of this book to teach network technology. Most information systems and technology programs offer courses that can expand your understanding of network technology.

So where are we now? If you have already read Chapter 1, you learned about information systems development projects with a focus on the stakeholders, the process, and the business and technical drivers that influence the need for new systems. If you haven't already done so, you should at least skim Chapter 1 to learn about the *context of systems analysis and design methods.*

In Chapter 2, you learned about the product itself—information systems—in terms of basic building blocks. This architectural perspective focused on the different information system views of the various stakeholders. You learned that system owners and users view information systems from the standpoint of achieving goals—improving business knowledge, processes, and communications—whereas system designers and builders view information systems in terms of technology that supports the achievement of goals.

Most readers should proceed directly to Chapter 3, which introduces you to the process of information system development. You'll learn about information systems problem solving, methodologies, and development technology as you expand your education in the fundamentals for systems analysis and design methods.

Learning Roadmap

Summary

1. Organizations are served by a federation of information systems that support various business functions. Businesses have front-office information systems that support business functions that extend out to their customers and back-office information systems that support internal business operations and interact with suppliers.

2. The many classes of information system applications overlap and interoperate to complement and supplement one another.

3. Information systems architecture provides a unifying framework into which various stakeholders with different perspectives can organize and view the fundamental building blocks of information systems:

   a. System owners and system users tend to focus on three common business goals of any information system—improvements in business knowledge, business processes, and business communications.

   b. System designers and builders tend to focus on technologies used by the information system in order to achieve the business goals. They focus on the database technologies that support business knowledge, software technologies that support business processes, and interface technologies that support business communications.

4. The three views represented in the model are:

   a. KNOWLEDGE—the business knowledge that helps managers make intelligent decisions.

   b. PROCESSES—the activities (including management) that carry out the mission of the business.

   c. COMMUNICATIONS—how the system interfaces with its users and other information systems.

5. Improving business knowledge is a fundamental goal of an information system:

   a. The system owner is interested in information that adds new business knowledge.

   b. Information system users are knowledgeable about the data that describes the business. This data is used to create information and subsequent business knowledge.

   c. System designers are concerned with the database technology that will be used by the information system to support business knowledge.

   d. System builders focus on the actual database management system technology used to store the business data that will support business knowledge.

6. Improving business processes is a fundamental goal of an information system:

   a. System owners are interested in the business functions the groups of related processes, that support a business.

   b. System users specify the business process in terms of process requirements for a new system. Business process requirements are frequently defined in terms of policies and procedures. Policies are explicit rules that must be adhered to when completing business processes. Procedures are the precise steps to be followed in completing business processes.

   c. System designers view business processes in terms of the application development environment and the software technology used to develop the system. Many businesses purchase commercial off-the-shelf software solutions instead of building the software in-house.

   d. System builders focus on custom-built applications programs that automate business processes.

7. A common goal of most organizations is to improve business communications:

   a. System owners define the communications scope of an information system development project.

   b. System users view communications in terms of the information system's inputs and outputs.

   c. System designers are concerned with the technical design of both user and system-to-system communication interfaces.

   d. System builders are concerned with the interface technology they use to implement user and system-to-system communication interfaces.

8. Today's information systems are built on networks. Network technology allows properly designed information systems to separate the KNOWLEDGE, PROCESS, and COMMUNICATION building blocks and force them to communicate across the network.

Information System Building Blocks   **Chapter Two   61**

 ## Review Questions

1. What is the difference between front-office information systems and back-office information systems?
2. How do transaction processing systems (TPSs), management information systems (MISs), and decision support systems (DSSs) interact with each other?
3. Why do we need to identify the information system architecture?
4. What are the three business goal–oriented perspectives or views of an information system that systems owners and system users tend to focus on? What are the three technological perspectives that system designers and builders tend to focus on?
5. How are the business perspectives and the technology perspectives of an information system related?
6. In any given building blocks of an information system, the views of four groups of stakeholders need to be taken into account during the development of the system. What are these four stakeholder groups?

7. Briefly describe how system designers and system builders tend to view KNOWLEDGE in a system.
8. Understanding business functions is essential in the process building block of an information system. What are six high-level business functions typical of many companies?
9. If you were the system owner of an online CD store, list two business functions of your online store in terms of business events and responses to those events.
10. Give an example of a policy and the procedures needed to implement the policy.
11. What is prototyping? Why do we need such a technique?
12. What are the two most critical goals in the communication building blocks?
13. What is user dialogue?
14. Why has the increasing use of graphical user interfaces (GUI) complicated the design process for system designers?
15. What role does network technology play in developing an information system?

 ## Problems and Exercises

1. Companies generally need to use more than one information system to support all their different business functions. These functions are frequently referred to as either front-office information systems or back-office systems. Define each of these two types of systems and identify some of the typical business functions supported by them.
2. As a systems analyst, designer, or builder, you will frequently be involved with your organization's information systems architecture. What is an information systems architecture, and what is its purpose?
3. Although system owners and system users generally have different perspectives of their organization's information system, both groups tend to focus on three business goals that are common to any information system. What are these goal-oriented perspectives, and what is their importance?
4. In an information system, the process building blocks represent the work that occurs in a sys-

tem, which may be performed by people or by computers and machinery. Stakeholders tend to have different views or perspectives of these building blocks. What are these different stakeholder perspectives regarding processes, and how they differ from each other?
5. Assume you are a systems designer and your organization is building a new inventory management system. In reviewing the requirements documentation, it appears that an error was made and some additional data elements were left out that are needed to meet the business or technical objectives of the inventory management system. What should you **not** do at this point?
6. Assume you are designing a retail point-of-sale (POS) system for your company. What are the typical system interfaces of a point-of-sale system that need to be taken into account in designing the POS system?
7. As business technology becomes more powerful and sophisticated, many businesses are redesigning

Foundations of Information Systems

their single-function information systems, such as sales, into cross-functional information systems that provide integrated support for separate, but related, business functions. Assume that you are designing an order management system that will integrate all business functions triggered by the submission of a sales order. What typical business functions would be included in a cross-functional information system?

8. Middleware is frequently used in systems integration projects when different information systems are tied together to exchange data via system-to-system interfaces. Briefly define middleware, explain its benefits, and provide an example.

9. In identifying and documenting business requirements, systems analysts need to be able to distinguish between laws, policies, and procedures. Why is this important?

10. It is common for system owners and system users to have very different views of the same business processes used in an information system. Why do you think this is? Consider an airline that is developing a customer self-check-in system at airports. What do you think the perspective of the system owners is? What about the system users? Give examples of how the business processes for an airline check-in system will be viewed by the system owners and system users.

11. System designers and system builders also tend to have very different views of system building blocks. Explain the different ways that designers and builders might view the communication building blocks using the customer self check-in system scenario described in the last question.

12. System designers frequently have a number of technical design options to choose from when designing interfaces between different systems and applications. What should designers always keep in mind when designing these interfaces?

13. The framework for information systems architecture used in this textbook is derived from the pioneering framework developed by John Zachman. What is one of the advantages of designing systems based upon this or similar frameworks?

14. At times, an organization may choose to purchase a commercial off-the-shelf (COTS) software package. What do you think are the pros and cons of using off-the-shelf applications compared to custom-built applications?

15. If an organization chose a COTS package as their solution, would the view of the system builder be the same as for a custom-built application? If not, how would it be different?

Projects and Research

1. Select a medium to large organization. The organization can be in the public or private sector, and it can be one with which you are personally familiar or one for which information is readily available.

   a. Describe the organization you have selected (type of organization, mission, products or services, size, annual sales or revenues, etc.).
   b. Select one of the major information systems the organization uses and/or is developing, and describe it.
   c. In the organization you selected, who would typically be the owner of this system?
   d. Describe, from the viewpoint of the owner, the information produced by this system.
   e. If the organization initiated a project to replace or modify this system, how might the system owner define the scope and vision of the project within the context of the organization you selected
   f. Who are the typical users of this system?

   g. Describe, from the perspective of the users, the information produced by this system.
   h. What is an essential difference in how system owners and users view the information produced by the system?

2. Contact and interview two or three systems analysts, in different organizations if possible, regarding this chapter's subtopic on communication building blocks.

   a. Describe the nature of each analyst's company or organization, its mission, and current business issues or needs.
   b. How important does each of the system analysts consider communications with system users versus system builders; that is, which is more important and why?
   c. Do they find it more difficult to communicate with the system users or with the system builders? Why?

d. If they were CIOs for a day, what would each of them change about the way their designers communicate with system users and builders?

e. Which viewpoints do you agree with, or do you have a totally different one than the people you interviewed? Justify your answer.

3. Select an information system used by a medium to large organization. It can be one with which you are personally familiar or one whose organizational structure and information system you have researched.

   a. What is the nature of the organization you have selected, its mission, and the high-level purpose of their information system?

   b. Who is the owner of the system?

   c. If you were the owner of the system, describe how you would see the system processes from that viewpoint.

   d. Who are the users of the system?

   e. If you were one of the system users, describe how you would see the system processes from that viewpoint.

   f. If you were the system designer, describe the system processes from that viewpoint.

   g. What are the essential differences in viewpoints?

4. Imagine that you are the owner of a small business and are searching on the Web for a company that can supply the products or services needed by your business. Find several business-to-business (B2B) Web sites that offer the products or services for which your business is looking. Familiarize yourself with their Web sites from the viewpoint of a typical business customer who is visiting these sites for the first time.

   a. What is the nature of your organization, and for what type of goods or services are you looking?

   b. Which B2B sites did you find on the Web?

   c. Compare the different sites. If all other things were equal (price, availability, brands offered, etc.), would you be more likely to purchase goods or services from one than the other(s), solely because of differences in their Web sites? Why or why not?

   d. From the viewpoint of a business customer, do you think design or usability is more important for a Web site? Explain your answer.

   e. From the viewpoint of a consumer, would your answer be the same as in the preceding question? Explain.

5. Research several articles published in the last few years in your library and/or on the Web that discuss ethical issues related to systems design.

   a. What articles were you able to find?

   b. Describe some of the situations and ethical issues that might arise from time to time in systems design.

   c. Pick one of the situations described in (b) and describe what you believe to be the system designer's ethical obligation, if any.

   d. (Extra credit) Do you think that requiring IT professionals, that is, systems analysts, designers, and builders, to be licensed or certified would increase professionalism and/or reduce unethical behavior? Why or why not?

6. The textbook uses a framework for describing information systems architecture that is based upon John Zachman's "Framework for Information Systems Architecture" model. Using the Web or your school library, research other frameworks for describing IS architectures, and select one, such as Open Systems Interconnect (OSI).

   a. Which frameworks did you find, and which did you select?

   b. Describe its approach to communicating systems architecture. Include a diagram if applicable.

   c. What are its similarities to the framework used in the textbook?

   d. What are its differences?

   e. If you were a systems owner, which one would you find easier to understand?

   f. If you were a systems analyst, which one would you find easier to understand?

Minicases

1. An IT manager requests an amount of funds to upgrade the e-mail server. Without the necessary upgrade, the server will be burdened by the sheer amount of e-mail and will run the risk of crashing. The business manager denies the request, citing the past reliability of the server, and expresses concern at the recent large IT expenditures. The business manager leaves the conversation wondering what IT investments are really necessary, and if the IT manager is just creating "job security."

The IT manager, likewise, leaves the meeting frustrated at not having the tools he/she needs to do the job properly. The IT manager knows that when the server crashes, it will be his/her responsibility to fix.

   a. Do you think this happens often in business?
   b. What perspectives do you think each are taking on the problem?
   c. How could each have communicated those perspectives and business needs better?

2. Interview at least one person in marketing, customer service, and accounting/payroll in the same company. What types of information do they handle? Do they share information across departments? Do you notice overlap in information or in data entry?
3. Government service departments are deeply burdened by the amount of data that they hold and process. Interview someone from a service department and draft a short essay. Service departments that must sift through vast amounts of data are those that deal with, for example, missing persons, child protective services, DMV, and tracking of persons on probation following a

crime. You should include, but are not limited to, topics such as:

- What is the department's (or person's) job?
- What kind of data do they collect and analyze?
- What kind of analyses do they do on the data?
- How much information do they collect, from whom, and what programs do they use?

4. Your neighborhood grocery store, Wow Grocery, always seems to be running out of your favorite ice cream. In frustration, you ask the store manager why they always seem to be out. The store manager, Bob, tells you that the small store cannot afford an inventory management system, so inventory is updated manually. This means that oftentimes the store must either stock extra quantities of well-liked items or risk running out. Unfortunately, Wow Grocery does not have a large enough freezer to store additional stocks of ice cream. As a result, the store runs out of the ice cream quite frequently.
5. What can Wow Grocery do to automate or manage its inventory system without spending much money? Draft your solution into a short paper.

Team and Individual Exercises

1. How do you solve a seemingly insolvable problem? As a team, develop a methodology for solving the following question: How many homes are there in the United States that are painted yellow?
2. Try something you have not done before (legal, not dangerous, and rated G). Share with the class

what you did, and why you did it. Why is it important to try and experience new things?
3. Share (with your team) an unethical incident that you have observed. How did that incident affect you directly? What indirect impact did it have on others?

Suggested Readings

Galitz, Wilbert O. *The Essential Guide to User Interface Design: An Introduction to GUI Design Principles and Techniques,* 2nd ed. New York: John Wiley & Sons, 2002.

Goldman, James E.; Phillip T. Rawles; and Julie R. Mariga. *Client/Server Information Systems: A Business-Oriented Approach.* New York: John Wiley & Sons, 1999. For students who are looking for a student-oriented introduction to information technology architecture and data communications, we recommend our colleagues' book because it was written for business and information systems majors to provide a comprehensive survey of the technology that supports today's information systems.

Inmon, W. H. *Building the Data Warehouse,* 3rd ed. New York: John Wiley & Sons, 2002.

Sethi, Vikram, and William R. King. *Organizational Transformation through Business Process Reengineering.* Upper Saddle River, NJ: Prentice Hall, 1998.

Taylor, David, and Alyse D. Terhune. *Doing E-Business: Strategies for Thriving in an Electronic Marketplace.* New York: John Wiley & Sons, 2000.

Zachman, John A. "A Framework for Information System Architecture." *IBM Systems Journal* 26, no. 3 (1987). We adapted the matrix model for information system building blocks from Mr. Zachman's conceptual framework. We first encountered John Zachman on the lecture circuit, where he delivers a remarkably informative and entertaining talk on the same subject as this article. Mr. Zachman's framework has drawn professional acclaim and inspired at least one conference on his model. His framework is based on the concept that architecture means different things to different people. His framework suggests that information systems consist of three distinct "product-oriented" views—data, processes, and technology (which we renamed *communications*)—to which we added a fourth view, "interface." The Zachman framework offers six different audience-specific views—for each of those product views—the ballpark and owner's views (which we renamed as *owner's* and *user's views*, respectively), the designer's and builder's views (which we combined into our *designer's view*), and an out-of-context view (which we called the *builder's view*).

Information Systems Development

Chapter Preview and Objectives

This chapter more closely examines the systems development process that was first introduced in Chapter 1. Successful systems development is governed by some fundamental, underlying principles that we introduce in this chapter. We also introduce a basic, representative systems development methodology as a disciplined approach to developing information systems. Although such an approach will not guarantee success, it will greatly improve the chances of success. You will know that you understand information systems development when you can:

▌ Describe the motivation for a standard systems development process in terms of the Capability Maturity Model (CMM) for quality management.

▌ Differentiate between the system life cycle and a system development methodology.

▌ Describe 10 basic principles of systems development.

▌ Define problems, opportunities, and directives—the triggers for systems development projects.

▌ Describe the PIECES framework for categorizing problems, opportunities, and directives.

▌ Describe the essential phases of systems development. For each phase, describe its purpose, inputs, and outputs.

▌ Describe cross life-cycle activities that overlap multiple system development phases.

▌ Describe typical, alternative "routes" through the essential phases of systems development. Describe how routes may be combined or customized for different types of projects.

▌ Describe various automated tools for systems development.

Introduction

Work is getting underway at SoundStage Entertainment Club for the systems analysis and design of their member services information system. But the more Bob Martinez learns about the system, the more confused he gets. Bob can recall some of his programming assignments in college. Most of them were just a page or two of bulleted points listing required features. It was pretty easy to get your head around that. But the new SoundStage system will involve tracking member contacts and purchase requirements, promotions, sales, shipments, inventory, multiple warehouses, Web sites, and more. Bob wonders how they will even list all the requirements, let alone keep them straight. How will they know what data they need to track? How will they know what every piece of programming needs to do? He mentioned that to his boss, Sandra. She said it was all about following "the methodology." He remembered something about methodology from a systems analysis class. At the time it seemed like a lot of unnecessary work. But he is starting to see now that on a large project, following an established method may be the only path that is safe to travel.

The Process of Systems Development

systems development process a set of activities, methods, best practices, deliverables, and automated tools that stakeholders (from Chapter 1) use to develop and continuously improve information systems and software (from Chapters 1 and 2).

This chapter introduces a focus on information systems development. We will examine a **systems development process.** Notice we did not say "the" process—there are as many variations on the process as there are experts and authors. We will present one representative process and use it consistently throughout this book. The chapter home page shows an expanded number of phases compared to the home page of Chapter 1. This is because we have factored the high-level phases such as system analysis and system design from Chapter 1 into multiple phases and activities. We have also refined the size and place of the stakeholder roles to reflect "involvement" as opposed to emphasis or priority. And we have edited and enhanced the building blocks to indicate deliverables and artifacts of system development. All of these modifications will be explained in due time.

Why do organizations embrace standardized processes to develop information systems? Information systems are a complex product. Recall from Chapter 2 that an information system includes data, process, and communications building blocks and technologies that must serve the needs of a variety of stakeholders. Perhaps this explains why as many as 70 percent or more of information system development projects have failed to meet expectations, cost more than budgeted, and are delivered much later than promised. The Gartner Group suggests that "consistent adherence to moderately rigorous methodology guidelines can provide 70 percent of [systems development] organizations with a productivity improvement of at least 30 percent within two years."[1]

Increasingly, organizations have no choice but to adopt and follow a standardized systems development process. First, using a consistent process for systems development creates efficiencies that allow management to shift resources between projects. Second, a consistent methodology produces consistent documentation that reduces lifetime costs to maintain the systems. Finally, the U.S. government has mandated that any organization seeking to develop software for the government must adhere to certain quality management requirements. A consistent process promotes quality. And many other organizations have aggressively committed to total quality management goals in order to increase their competitive advantage. In order to realize quality and productivity improvements, many organizations have turned to project and process management frameworks such as the Capability Maturity Model, discussed in the next section.

---

[1]Richard Hunter, "AD Project Portfolio Management," *Proceedings of the Gartner Group IT98 Symposium/Expo* (CD-ROM). The Gartner Group is an industry watchdog and research group that tracks and projects industry trends for IT managers.

> The Capability Maturity Model

It has been shown that as an organization's information system development process matures, project timelines and cost decrease while productivity and quality increase. The Software Engineering Institute at Carnegie Mellon University has observed and measured this phenomenon and developed the **Capability Maturity Model (CMM)** to assist all organizations to achieve these benefits. The CMM has developed a wide following, both in industry and government. Software evaluation based on CMM is being used to qualify information technology contractors for most U.S. federal government projects.

The CMM framework for systems and software is intended to help organizations improve the maturity of their systems development processes. The CMM is organized into five maturity levels (see Figure 3-1):

- *Level 1—Initial:* This is sometimes called anarchy or chaos. At this level, system development projects follow no consistent process. Each development team uses its own tools and methods. Success or failure is usually a function of the skill and experience of the team. The process is unpredictable and not repeatable. A project typically encounters many crises and is frequently over budget and behind schedule. Documentation is sporadic or not consistent from one project to the next, thus creating problems for those who must maintain a system over its lifetime. Almost all organizations start at Level 1.

- *Level 2—Repeatable:* At this level, project management processes and practices are established to track project costs, schedules, and functionality. The focus is on project management. A system development process is always followed, but it may vary from project to project. Success or failure is still a function of the skill and experience of the project team; however, a concerted effort is made to repeat earlier project successes. Effective project management practices lay the foundation for standardized processes in the next level.

Capability Maturity Model (CMM) a standardized framework for assessing the maturity level of an organization's information systems development and management processes and products. It consists of five levels of maturity.

FIGURE 3-1

The Capability Maturity Model (CMM)

TABLE 3-1 Impact of System Development "Process" on Quality

CMM Project Statistics for a Project Resulting in 200,000 Lines of Code

Organization's CMM Level	Project Duration (months)	Project Person-Months	Number of Defects Shipped	Median Cost ($ millions)	Lowest Cost ($ millions)	Highest Cost ($ millions)
1	30	600	61	5.5	1.8	100+
2	18.5	143	12	1.3	.96	1.7
3	15	80	7	.728	.518	.933

Source: Master Systems, Inc.

system development methodology a formalized approach to the systems development process; a standardized process that includes the activities, methods, best practices, deliverables, and automated tools to be used for information systems development.

- *Level 3—Defined:* In this level, a standard **system development** process (sometimes called a *methodology*) is purchased or developed. All projects use a tailored version of this process to develop and maintain information systems and software. As a result of using the standardized process for all projects, each project results in consistent and high-quality documentation and deliverables. The process is stable, predictable, and repeatable.
- *Level 4—Managed:* In this level, measurable goals for quality and productivity are established. Detailed measures of the standard system development process and product quality are routinely collected and stored in a database. There is an effort to improve individual project management based on this collected data. Thus, management seeks to become more proactive than reactive to systems development problems (such as cost overruns, scope creep, schedule delays, etc.). Even when a project encounters unexpected problems or issues, the process can be adjusted based on predictable and measurable impacts.
- *Level 5—Optimizing:* In this level, the standardized system development process is continuously monitored and improved based on measures and data analysis established in Level 4. This can include changing the technology and best practices used to perform activities required in the standard system development process, as well as adjusting the process itself. Lessons learned are shared across the organization, with a special emphasis on eliminating inefficiencies in the system development process while sustaining quality. In summary, the organization has institutionalized continuous systems development process improvement.

It is very important to recognize that each level is a prerequisite for the next level.

Currently, many organizations are working hard to achieve at least CMM Level 3 (sometimes driven by a government or organizational mandate). A central theme to achieving Level 3 (Defined) is the use of a standard process or methodology to build or integrate systems. As shown in Table 3-1, an organization can realize significant improvements in schedule and cost by institutionalizing CMM Level 3 process improvements.[2]

> Life Cycle versus Methodology

system life cycle the factoring of the lifetime of an information system into two stages, (1) systems development and (2) systems operation and maintenance—first you build it; then you use and maintain it. Eventually, you cycle back to redevelopment of a new system.

The terms *system life cycle* and *system development methodology* are frequently and incorrectly interchanged. Most system development processes are derived from a natural **system life cycle.** The system life cycle just happens. Figure 3-2 illustrates two

[2]White Paper, "Rapidly Improving Process Maturity: Moving Up the Capability Maturity Model through Outsourcing" (Boston: Keane, 1997, 1998, p.11).

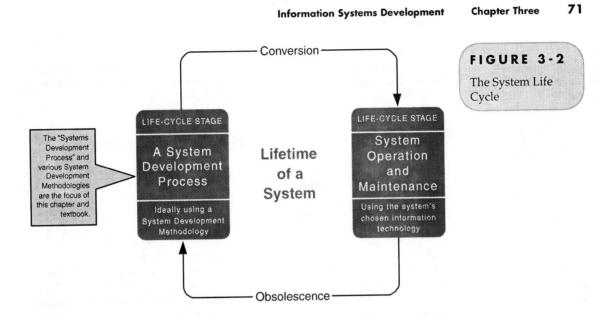

FIGURE 3-2

The System Life Cycle

The "Systems Development Process" and various System Development Methodologies are the focus of this chapter and textbook.

LIFE-CYCLE STAGE

A System Development Process

Ideally using a System Development Methodology

Conversion

Lifetime of a System

LIFE-CYCLE STAGE

System Operation and Maintenance

Using the system's chosen information technology

Obsolescence

life-cycle stages. Notice that there are two key events that trigger a change from one stage to the other:

- When a system cycles from development to operation and maintenance, a *conversion* must take place.
- At some point in time, *obsolescence* occurs (or is imminent) and a system cycles from operation and maintenance to redevelopment.

Actually, a system may be in more than one stage at the same time. For example, one version may be in *operation and support* while the next version is in *development.*

So how does this contrast with a systems development methodology? A systems development methodology "executes" the systems development stage of the system life cycle. Each individual information system has its own system life cycle. The methodology is the standard process to build and maintain that system and all other information systems through their life cycles. Consistent with the goals of the CMM, methodologies ensure that:

- A consistent, reproducible approach is applied to all projects.
- There is reduced risk associated with shortcuts and mistakes.
- Complete and consistent documentation is produced from one project to the next.
- Systems analysts, designers, and builders can be quickly reassigned between projects because all use the same process.
- As development teams and staff constantly change, the results of prior work can be easily retrieved and understood by those who follow.

Methodologies can be purchased or homegrown. Why purchase a methodology? Many information system organizations can't afford to dedicate staff to the development and continuous improvement of a homegrown methodology. Methodology vendors have a vested interest in keeping their methodologies current with the latest business and technology trends. Homegrown methodologies are usually based on generic methodologies and techniques that are well documented in books and on Web sites. Examples of system development methodologies are listed in the margin on the following page. You should be able to research most of them on the Web. Many of their underlying methods will be taught in this textbook.

Throughout this book, we will use a methodology called *FAST,* which stands for *Framework for the Application of Systems Thinking. FAST* is not a real-world commercial methodology. We developed it as a composite of the best practices we've

FAST a hypothetical methodology used throughout this book to demonstrate a representative systems development process. The acronym's letters stand for *Framework for the Application of Systems Thinking.*

REPRESENTATIVE SYSTEM DEVELOPMENT METHODOLOGIES

Architected Rapid Application Development (Architected RAD)

Dynamic Systems Development Methodology (DSDM)

Joint Application Development (JAD)

Information Engineering (IE)

Rapid Application Development (RAD)

Rational Unified Process (RUP)

Structured Analysis and Design (old, but still occasionally encountered)

eXtreme Programming (XP)

Note: There are many commercial methodologies and software tools (sometimes called *methodware*) based on the above general methodologies.

encountered in many commercial and reference methodologies. Unlike many commercial methodologies, *FAST* is not prescriptive. That is to say, *FAST* is an agile framework that is flexible enough to provide for different types of projects and strategies. Most important, *FAST* shares much in common with both the book-based and the commercial methodologies that you will encounter in practice.

> Underlying Principles for Systems Development

Before we examine the *FAST* methodology, let's introduce some general principles that should underlie all systems development methodologies.

Principle 1: Get the System Users Involved   Analysts, programmers, and other information technology specialists frequently refer to "my system." This attitude has, in part, created an "us versus them" conflict between technical staff and their users and management. Although analysts and programmers work hard to create technologically impressive solutions, those solutions often backfire because they don't address the real organization problems. Sometimes they even introduce new organization problems. For this reason, system user involvement is an absolute necessity for successful systems development. Think of systems development as a partnership between system users, analysts, designers, and builders. The analysts, designers, and builders are responsible for systems development, but they must engage their owners and users, insist on their participation, and seek agreement from all stakeholders concerning decisions that may affect them.

Miscommunication and misunderstandings continue to be a significant problem in many systems development projects. However, owner and user involvement and education minimize such problems and help to win acceptance of new ideas and technological change. Because people tend to resist change, information technology is often viewed as a threat. The best way to counter that threat is through constant and thorough communication with owners and users.

Principle 2: Use a Problem-Solving Approach   A system development methodology is, first and foremost, a problem-solving approach to building systems. The term *problem* is broadly used throughout this book to include (1) real problems, (2) opportunities for improvement, and (3) directives from management. The classical problem-solving approach is as follows:

1. Study and understand the problem, its context, and its impact.
2. Define the requirements that must be met by *any* solution.
3. Identify candidate solutions that fulfill the requirements, and select the best solution.
4. Design and/or implement the chosen solution.
5. Observe and evaluate the solution's impact, and refine the solution accordingly.

Systems analysts should approach all projects using some variation of this problem-solving approach.

Inexperienced or unsuccessful problem solvers tend to eliminate or abbreviate one or more of the above steps. For example, they fail to completely understand the problem, or they prematurely commit to the first solution they think of. The result can range from (1) solving the wrong problem, to (2) incorrectly solving the problem, (3) picking the wrong solution, or (4) picking a less-than-optimal solution. A methodology's problem-solving process, when correctly applied, can reduce or eliminate these risks.

Principle 3: Establish Phases and Activities   All methodologies prescribe phases and activities. The number and scope of phases and activities vary from author to author, expert to expert, methodology to methodology, and business to business. The chapter home page at the beginning of this chapter illustrates the eight phases of our *FAST* methodology in the context of your information systems framework. The phases

FIGURE 3-3   Overlap of System Development Phases and Activities

are listed on the far right-hand side of the illustration. In each phase, the focus is on those building blocks and on stakeholders that are aligned to the left of that phase.

The phases are: scope definition, problem analysis, requirements analysis, logical design, decision analysis, physical design and integration, construction and testing, and installation and delivery. Each of these phases will be discussed later in this chapter. These phases are not absolutely sequential. The phases tend to overlap one another, as illustrated in Figure 3-3. Also, the phases may be customized to the special needs of a given project (e.g., deadlines, complexity, strategy, resources). In this chapter, we will describe each customization as alternative routes through the methodology and problem-solving process.

Principle 4: Document throughout Development   When do you document the programs you write? Be honest. We must confess that, like most students, we did our documentation after we wrote the programs. We knew better, but we postdocumented anyway. That just does not work in the business world. In medium to large organizations, system owners, users, analysts, designers, and builders come and go. Some will be promoted; some will have extended medical leaves; some will quit the organization; and still others will be reassigned. To promote good communication between constantly changing stakeholders, documentation should be a working byproduct of the entire systems development effort.

Documentation enhances communications and acceptance. Documentation reveals strengths and weaknesses of the system to multiple stakeholders. It stimulates user involvement and reassures management about progress. At the same time, some methodologies have been criticized for expecting too much documentation that adds little value to the process or resulting system. Our *FAST* methodology advocates a balance between the value of documentation and the effort to produce it. Experts call this *agile modeling*.

Principle 5: Establish Standards   In a perfect world, all information systems would be integrated such that they behave as a single system. Unfortunately, this never happens because information systems are developed and replaced over a very long period of time. Even organizations that purchase and install an enterprise resource planning (ERP) product usually discover that there are applications and needs that fall outside the ERP system. Systems integration has become critical to the success of any organization's information systems.

To achieve or improve systems integration, organizations turn to standards. In many organizations, these standards take the form of enterprise information technology architecture. An IT architecture sets standards that serve to direct technology solutions and information systems to a common technology vision or configuration.

An information technology architecture typically standardizes on the following (note: it is not important that you know what all these sample technologies are):

- *Database technology*—What database engine(s) will be used (e.g., *Oracle*, IBM *DB2*, Microsoft *SQL Server*)? On what platforms will they be operated (e.g., *UNIX, Linux, Windows XP, MVS*)? What technologies will be used to load data into online transaction processing (OLTP) databases, operational data stores, and data warehouses (i.e., Extract Transform and Load [ETL])?
- *Software technology*—What application development environment(s)/language(s) will be used to write software (e.g., IBM's *Websphere* with *Java*, Microsoft's *Visual Studio .NET* with *Visual Basic .NET, Visual C++,* and/or *Visual C#*; Syebase's *Powerbuilder,* Oracle's *Oracle Forms*)?
- *Interface technology*—How will user interfaces be developed—with *MS Windows* components or Web languages and components (e.g., an *xHTML* editor such as Macromedia's *Dreamweaver,* a portal engine such as IBM's *Websphere*)? How will data be exchanged between different information systems (e.g., a data broker such as IBM's *MQ Messaging,* an XML-based data exchange, or a custom programmed interface)?

Notice how these architectural questions closely correspond to the technology drivers in your information system model.

In the absence of an IT architecture, each information system and application may be built using radically different technologies. Not only does this make it difficult to integrate applications, but it creates resource management problems—IT organizations cannot as easily move developers between projects as priorities change or emergencies occur because different teams are staffed with technical competencies based on the various technologies used and being used to develop information systems. Creating an enterprise IT architecture and driving projects and teams to that architecture make more sense.

As new technologies emerge, an IT architecture must change. But that change can be managed. The chief technology officer (CTO) in an organization is frequently charged with technology exploration and IT architecture management. Given that architecture, all information systems projects are constrained to implement new systems that conform to the architecture (unless otherwise approved by the CTO).

Principle 6: Manage the Process and Projects   Most organizations have a system development process or methodology, but they do not always use it consistently on projects. Both the process and the projects that use it must be managed. **Process management** ensures that an organization's chosen process or management is used consistently on and across all projects. Process management also defines and improves the chosen process or methodology over time. **Project management** ensures that an information system is developed at minimum cost, within a specified time frame, and with acceptable quality (using the standard system development process or methodology). Effective project management is essential to achieving CMM Level 2 success. Use of a repeatable process gets us to CMM Level 3. CMM Levels 4 and 5 require effective process management. Project management can occur without a standard process, but in mature organizations all projects are based on a standardized and managed process.

Process management and project management are influenced by the need for quality management. Quality standards are built into a process to ensure that the activities and deliverables of each phase will contribute to the development of a high-quality information system. They reduce the likelihood of missed problems and requirements, as well as flawed designs and program errors (bugs). Standards also make the IT organization more agile. As personnel changes occur, staff can be relocated between projects with the assurance that every project is following an understood and accepted process.

process management an ongoing activity that documents, teaches, oversees the use of, and improves an organization's chosen methodology (the "process") for systems development. Process management is concerned with phases, activities, deliverables, and quality standards that should be consistently applied to all projects.

project management the process of scoping, planning, staffing, organizing, directing, and controlling a project to develop an information system at minimum cost, within a specified time frame, and with acceptable quality.

Principle 7: Justify Information Systems as Capital Investments Information systems are capital investments, just like a fleet of trucks or a new building. System owners commit to this investment. Notice that the initial commitment occurs early in a project, when system owners agree to sponsor and fund the project. Later (during the phase called *decision analysis*), system owners recommit to the more costly technical decisions. In considering a capital investment, two issues must be addressed:

1. For any problem, there are likely to be several possible solutions. The systems analyst and other stakeholders should not blindly accept the first solution suggested. The analyst who fails to look at alternatives may be doing the business a disservice.
2. After identifying alternative solutions, the systems analyst should evaluate each possible solution for feasibility, especially for **cost-effectiveness.** Cost-effectiveness is measured using a technique called *cost-benefit analysis.*

Like project and process management, cost-benefit analysis is performed throughout the system development process.

A significant advantage of the phased approach to systems development is that it provides several opportunities to reevaluate cost-effectiveness, risk, and feasibility. There is often a temptation to continue with a project only because of the investment already made. In the long run, canceled projects are usually much less costly than implemented disasters. This is extremely important for young analysts to remember.

Most system owners want more from their systems than they can afford or are willing to pay for. Furthermore, the scope of most information system projects increases as the analyst learns more about the business problems and requirements as the project progresses. Unfortunately, most analysts fail to adjust estimated costs and schedules as the scope increases. As a result, the analyst frequently and needlessly accepts responsibility for cost and schedule overruns.

Because information systems are recognized as capital investments, system development projects are often driven by enterprise planning. Many contemporary information technology business units create and maintain a **strategic information systems plan.** Such a plan identifies and prioritizes information system development projects. Ideally, a strategic information systems plan is driven by a **strategic enterprise plan** that charts a course for the entire business.

Principle 8: Don't Be Afraid to Cancel or Revise Scope There is an old saying: "Don't throw good money after bad." In other words, don't be afraid to cancel a project or revise scope, regardless of how much money has been spent so far—cut your losses. To this end, we advocate a **creeping commitment** approach to systems development.[3] With the creeping commitment approach, multiple feasibility checkpoints are built into any systems development methodology. At each checkpoint feasibility is reassessed. All previously expended costs are considered sunk (meaning not recoverable). They are, therefore, irrelevant to the decision. Thus, the project should be reevaluated at each checkpoint to determine if it remains feasible to continue investing time, effort, and resources into the project. At each checkpoint, the analyst should consider the following options:

- Cancel the project if it is no longer feasible.
- Reevaluate and adjust the costs and schedule if project scope is to be increased.
- Reduce the scope if the project budget and schedule are frozen and not sufficient to cover all project objectives.

The concept of sunk costs is more or less familiar to most financial analysts, but it is frequently forgotten or not used by the majority of systems analysts, most system users, and even many system owners.

cost-effectiveness the result obtained by striking a balance between the lifetime costs of developing, maintaining, and operating an information system and the benefits derived from that system. Cost-effectiveness is measured by cost-benefit analysis.

strategic information systems plan a formal strategic plan (3 to 5 years) for building and improving an information technology infrastructure and the information system applications that use that infrastructure.

strategic enterprise plan a formal strategic plan (3 to 5 years) for an entire business that defines its mission, vision, goals, strategies, benchmarks, and measures of progress and achievement. Usually, the strategic enterprise plan is complemented by strategic business unit plans that define how each business unit will contribute to the enterprise plan. The information systems plan (above) is one of those unit-level plans.

creeping commitment a strategy in which feasibility and risks are continuously reevaluated throughout a project. Project budgets and deadlines are adjusted accordingly.

[3]Thomas Gildersleeve, *Successful Data Processing Systems Analysis,* 2nd ed. (Englewood Cliffs, NJ: Prentice Hall, 1985), pp. 5–7.

risk management the process of identifying, evaluating, and controlling what might go wrong in a project before it becomes a threat to the successful completion of the project or implementation of the information system. Risk management is driven by risk analysis or assessment.

PRINCIPLES OF SYSTEMS DEVELOPMENT

Get the System Users Involved.

Use a Problem-Solving Approach.

Establish Phases and Activities.

Document throughout Development.

Establish Standards.

Manage the Process and Projects.

Justify Information Systems as Capital Investments.

Don't Be Afraid to Cancel or Revise Scope.

Divide and Conquer.

Design Systems for Growth and Change.

In addition to managing feasibility throughout the project, we must manage risk. **Risk management** seeks to balance risk and reward. Different organizations are more or less averse to risk, meaning that some are willing to take greater risks than others in order to achieve greater rewards.

Principle 9: Divide and Conquer   Whether you realize it or not, you learned the divide-and-conquer approach throughout your education. Since high school, you've been taught to outline a paper before you write it. Outlining is a divide-and-conquer approach to writing. A similar approach is used in systems development. We divide a system into subsystems and components in order to more easily conquer the problem and build the larger system. In systems analysis, we often call this *factoring*. By repeatedly dividing a larger problem (system) into more easily managed pieces (subsystems), the analyst can simplify the problem-solving process. This divide-and-conquer approach also complements communication and project management by allowing different pieces of the system to be communicated to different and the most appropriate stakeholders.

The building blocks of your information system framework provide one basis for dividing and conquering an information system's development. We will use this framework throughout the book.

Principle 10: Design Systems for Growth and Change   Businesses change over time. Their needs change. Their priorities change. Accordingly, information systems that support a business must change over time. For this reason, good methodologies should embrace the reality of change. Systems should be designed to accommodate both growth and changing requirements. In other words, well-designed information systems can both scale up and adapt to the business. But regardless of how well we design systems for growth and change, there will always come a time when they simply cannot support the business.

System scientists describe the natural and inevitable decay of all systems over time as *entropy*. As described earlier in this section, after a system is implemented it enters the *operations and maintenance* stage of the life cycle. During this stage the analyst encounters the need for changes that range from correcting simple mistakes, to redesigning the system to accommodate changing technology, to making modifications to support changing user requirements. Such changes direct the analyst and programmers to rework formerly completed phases of the life cycle. Eventually, the cost of maintaining the current system exceeds the costs of developing a replacement system—the current system has reached entropy and becomes obsolete.

But system entropy can be managed. Today's tools and techniques make it possible to design systems that can grow and change as requirements grow and change. This book will teach you many of those tools and techniques. For now, it's more important to simply recognize that flexibility and adaptability do not happen by accident—they must be built into a system.

We have presented 10 principles that should underlie any methodology. These principles are summarized in the margin and can be used to evaluate any methodology, including our *FAST* methodology.

A Systems Development Process

In this section we'll examine a logical process for systems development. (Reminder: *FAST* is a hypothetical methodology created for learning purposes.) We'll begin by studying types of system projects and how they get started. Then we'll introduce the eight *FAST* phases. Finally, we'll examine alternative variations, or "routes" through the phases, for different types of projects and development strategies.

> Where Do Systems Development Projects Come From?

System owners and system users initiate most projects. The impetus for most projects is some combination of **problems, opportunities,** and **directives.** To simplify this discussion, we will frequently use the term *problem* to collectively refer to problems, opportunities, and directives. Accordingly, *problem solving* refers to solving problems, exploiting opportunities, and fulfilling directives.

There are far too many potential system problems to list them all in this book. However, James Wetherbe developed a useful framework for classifying problems.[4] He calls it *PIECES* because the letters of each of the six categories, when put together, spell the word "pieces." The categories are:

P   the need to correct or improve *performance.*
I   the need to correct or improve *information* (and data).
E   the need to correct or improve *economies,* control costs, or increase profits.
C   the need to correct or improve *control* or security.
E   the need to correct or improve *efficiency* of people and processes.
S   the need to correct or improve *service* to customers, suppliers, partners, employees, and so on.

Figure 3-4 expands on each of the PIECES categories.

The categories of the PIECES framework are neither exhaustive nor mutually exclusive—they overlap. Any given project is usually characterized by one or more categories, and any given problem or opportunity may have implications with respect to more than one category. But PIECES is a practical framework (used in *FAST*), not just an academic exercise. We'll revisit PIECES several times in this book.

Projects can be either planned or unplanned. A *planned project* is the result of one of the following:

- An *information systems strategy plan* has examined the business as a whole to identify those system development projects that will return the greatest strategic (long-term) value to the business.
- A *business process redesign* has thoroughly analyzed a series of business processes to eliminate redundancy and bureaucracy and to improve efficiency and value added. Now it is time to redesign the supporting information system for those redesigned business processes.

The opposite of planned projects are *unplanned projects*—those that are triggered by a specific problem, opportunity, or directive that occurs in the course of doing business. Most organizations have no shortage of unplanned projects. Anyone can submit a proposed project based on something that is happening in the business. The number of unplanned-project proposals can easily overwhelm the largest information systems organization; therefore, they are frequently screened and prioritized by a **steering committee** of system owners and IT managers to determine which requests get approved. Those requests that are not approved are **backlogged** until resources become available (which sometimes never happens).

Both planned and unplanned projects go through the same essential system development process. Let's now examine the project phases in somewhat greater detail.

> The *FAST* Phases

FAST, like most methodologies, consists of phases. The number of phases will vary from one methodology to another. In Chapter 1 you were introduced to the four classic phases of the system development life cycle. The *FAST* methodology employs

problem an undesirable situation that prevents the organization from fully achieving its mission, vision, goals, and/or objectives.

opportunity a chance to improve the organization even in the absence of an identified problem.

directive a new requirement that's imposed by management, government, or some external influence.

steering committee an administrative body of system owners and information technology executives that prioritizes and approves candidate system development projects.

backlog a repository of project proposals that cannot be funded or staffed because they are a lower priority than those that have been approved for system development. Note that priorities change over time; therefore, a backlogged project might be approved at some future date.

[4]James Wetherbe and Nicholas P. Vitalari, *Systems Analysis and Design: Traditional, Best Practices,* 4th ed. (St. Paul, MN: West Publishing, 1994), pp. 196–199. James Wetherbe is a respected information systems educator, researcher, and consultant.

The PIECES Problem-Solving Framework and Checklist

The following checklist for problem, opportunity, and directive identification uses Wetherbe's PIECES framework. Note that the categories of PIECES are not mutually exclusive; some possible problems show up in multiple lists. Also, the list of possible problems is not exhaustive. The PIECES framework is equally suited to analyzing both manual and computerized systems and applications.

PERFORMANCE

A. Throughput – the amount of work performed over some period of time.
B. Response times – the average delay between a transaction or request, and a response to that transaction or request.

INFORMATION (and Data)

A. Outputs
  1. Lack of any information
  2. Lack of necessary information
  3. Lack of relevant information
  4. Too much information – "information overload"
  5. Information that is not in a useful format
  6. Information that is not accurate
  7. Information that is difficult to produce
  8. Information is not timely to its subsequent use
B. Inputs
  1. Data is not captured
  2. Data is not captured in time to be useful
  3. Data is not accurately captured – contains errors
  4. Data is difficult to capture
  5. Data is captured redundantly – same data captured more than once
  6. Too much data is captured
  7. Illegal data is captured
C. Stored data
  1. Data is stored redundantly in multiple files and/or databases
  2. Same data items have different values in different files (poor data integration)
  3. Stored data is not accurate
  4. Data is not secure to accident or vandalism
  5. Data is not well organized
  6. Data is not flexible – not easy to meet new information needs from stored data
  7. Data is not accessible

ECONOMICS

A. Costs
  1. Costs are unknown
  2. Costs are untraceable to source
  3. Costs are too high
B. Profits

1. New markets can be explored
2. Current marketing can be improved
3. Orders can be increased

CONTROL (and Security)

A. Too little security or control
  1. Input data is not adequately edited
  2. Crimes (e.g., fraud, embezzlement) are (or can be) committed against data
  3. Ethics are breached on data or information – refers to data or information getting to unauthorized people
  4. Redundantly stored data is inconsistent in different files or databases
  5. Data privacy regulations or guidelines are being (or can be) violated
  6. Processing errors are occurring (either by people, machines, or software)
  7. Decision-making errors are occurring
B. Too much control or security
  1. Bureaucratic red tape slows the system
  2. Controls inconvenience customers or employees
  3. Excessive controls cause processing delays

EFFICIENCY

A. People, machines, or computers waste time
  1. Data is redundantly input or copied
  2. Data is redundantly processed
  3. Information is redundantly generated
B. People, machines, or computers waste materials and supplies
C. Effort required for tasks is excessive
D. Material required for tasks is excessive

SERVICE

A. The system produces inaccurate results
B. The system produces inconsistent results
C. The system produces unreliable results
D. The system is not easy to learn
E. The system is not easy to use
F. The system is awkward to use
G. The system is inflexible to new or exceptional situations
H. The system is inflexible to change
I. The system is incompatible with other systems

FIGURE 3-4 The PIECES Framework for Problem Identification eight phases to better define periodic milestones and the deliverables. The grid below compares the *FAST* phases to the classic phases. As you can see, both sets of phases cover the same ground, but *FAST* is more detailed.

FAST Phases	Classic Phases			
	Project Initiation	System Analysis	System Design	System Implementation
Scope definition	X			
Problem analysis	X	X		
Requirements analysis		X		
Logical design		X		
Decision analysis	(a system analysis transition phase)			
Physical design and integration			X	
Construction and testing			X	X
Installation and delivery				X

Figure 3-5 illustrates the phases of the *FAST* methodology. Each phase produces deliverables that are passed to the next phase. And documentation accumulates as you complete each phase. Notice that we have included an iconic representation of the building blocks to symbolize this accumulation of knowledge and work-in-process artifacts during system development. Notice also that a project starts with some combination of PROBLEMS, OPPORTUNITIES, and DIRECTIVES from the user community (the green arrow) and finishes with a WORKING BUSINESS SOLUTION (the red arrow) for the user community.

Figure 3-6 shows the *FAST* methodology from the perspective of your information system building blocks that you learned in Chapters 1 and 2. The phases are on the right-hand side. The deliverables are built around the building blocks for knowledge, processes, and communications. The stakeholders are on the left-hand side. Notice how we have expanded and duplicated some stakeholders to reflect their involvement opposite the phases in which they primarily participate.

NOTE: The remainder of this section briefly describes each of the eight basic phases. Throughout this discussion, we will be referring to the process flowchart in Figure 3-5, as well as the building blocks view of the process in Figure 3-6. Also throughout the discussion, all terms printed in SMALL CAPS refer to phases, prerequisites (inputs), and deliverables (outputs) shown in Figures 3-5 and 3-6.

Scope Definition   The first phase of a typical project is SCOPE DEFINITION. The purpose of the scope definition phase is twofold. First, it answers the question, "Is this problem worth looking at?" Second, and assuming the problem *is* worth looking at, it establishes the size and boundaries of the project, the project vision, any constraints or limitations, the required project participants, and, finally, the budget and schedule.

In Figure 3-6, we see that the participants in the scope definition phase primarily include SYSTEM OWNERS, PROJECT MANAGERS, and SYSTEM ANALYSTS. System users are generally excluded because it is too early to get into the level of detail they will eventually bring to the project.

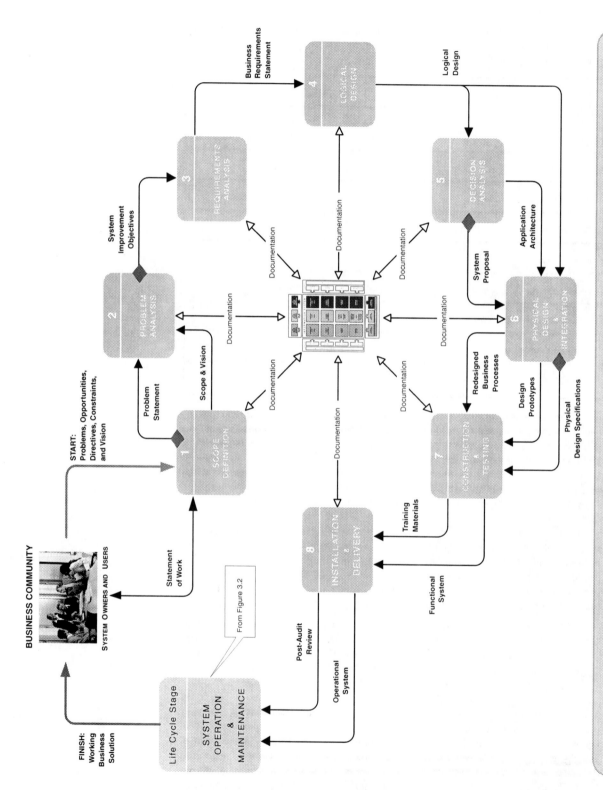

FIGURE 3-5 Process View of System Development

FIGURE 3-6 Building Blocks View of System Development

problem statement a statement and categorization of problems, opportunities, and directives; may also include constraints and an initial vision for the solution. Synonyms include *preliminary study* and *feasibility assessment.*

constraint any factor, limitation, or restraint that may limit a solution or the problem-solving process.

scope creep a common phenomenon wherein the requirements and expectations of a project increase, often without regard to the impact on budget and schedule.

statement of work a contract with management and the user community to develop or enhance an information system; defines vision, scope, constraints, high-level user requirements, schedule, and budget. Synonyms include *project charter, project plan,* and *service-level agreement.*

In Figure 3-5, we see that the scope definition phase is triggered by some combination of PROBLEMS, OPPORTUNITIES, and DIRECTIVES (to which we will add CONSTRAINTS and VISION). There are several deliverables or outcomes of a scope definition. One important outcome is a PROBLEM STATEMENT, a succinct overview of the problems, opportunities, and/or directives that triggered the project. The PIECES framework provides an excellent outline for a **problem statement.** The goal here is not to solve the problems, opportunities, and directives but only to catalog and categorize them. We should also identify any **constraints** that may impact the proposed project. Examples of constraints include budget limits, deadlines, human resources available or not available, business policies or government regulations, and technology standards. Finally, the system owners should be asked for at least a high-level vision for the system improvements they are seeking.

Given a basic understanding of problems, opportunities, directives, constraints, and vision, we need to establish initial scope. Thus, an initial SCOPE STATEMENT is another important outcome of this phase. Scope defines how big we think the project is. Your information system building blocks provide a useful framework for defining scope. Figure 3-6 illustrates that scope and vision can be defined in terms of INFORMATION, FUNCTIONS, and INTERFACES. Scope can, and frequently does, change during a project. But by documenting initial scope, you establish a baseline for controlling **scope creep** on both the budget and the schedule.

Given the initial problem and scope statements for the project, the analyst can staff the project team, estimate the budget for system development, and prepare a schedule for the remaining phases. Ultimately, this phase concludes with a "go or no-go" decision from system owners. Either the system owners agree with the proposed scope, budget, and schedule for the project, or they must reduce scope (to reduce costs and time) or cancel the project. This feasibility checkpoint is illustrated in Figure 3-5 as a diamond.

The final and most important deliverable is a STATEMENT OF WORK. **A statement of work** is a contract or agreement to develop the information system. It consolidates the problem statement, scope statement, and schedule and budget for all parties who will be involved in the project.

Problem Analysis   There is always an existing system, regardless of whether it currently uses information technology. The PROBLEM ANALYSIS phase studies the existing system and analyzes the findings to provide the project team with a more thorough understanding of the problems that triggered the project. The analyst frequently uncovers new problems and answers the most important question, "Will the benefits of solving these problems exceed the costs of building the system to solve these problems?"

Once again, Figure 3-6 provides a graphical overview of the problem analysis phase in terms of your information system building blocks. Notice that the participants still include the SYSTEM OWNERS but that this phase begins to actively involve the SYSTEM USERS as well. The system users are the business subject matter experts in any project. (Notice the intentional expansion of the system users' perspective to overlap many phases—remember principle 1: "Get the system users involved.") Of course, PROJECT MANAGERS and SYSTEM ANALYSTS are always involved in all phases of a project.

As shown in Figure 3-5, the prerequisites for the problem analysis phase are the SCOPE and PROBLEM STATEMENTS as defined and approved in the scope definition phase. The deliverable of the problem analysis phase is a set of SYSTEM IMPROVEMENT OBJECTIVES derived from a thorough understanding of the business problems. These objectives do not define inputs, outputs, or processes. Instead, they define the business criteria on which any new system will be evaluated. For instance, we might define a system improvement objective as any of the following:

Reduce the time between order processing and shipping by three days.
Reduce bad credit losses by 45 percent.
Comply with new financial aid federal qualification requirements by January 1.

Think of system improvement objectives as the *grading criteria* for evaluating any new system that you might eventually design and implement. System improvement objectives may be presented to system owners and users as a written recommendation or an oral presentation.

Depending on the complexity of the problem and the project schedule, the team may or may not choose to formally document the existing system. Such documentation frequently occurs when the business processes are considered dated or overly bureaucratic. Documentation of the existing system is sometimes called an "AS IS" BUSINESS MODEL. The as-is model may be accompanied by analysis demonstrating inefficiencies, bottlenecks, or other problems related to the business processes.

Every existing system has its own terminology, history, culture, and nuances. Learning those aspects of the system is an important by-product of this phase. From all of the information gathered, the project team gains a better understanding of the existing system's problems and opportunities. After reviewing the findings, the system owners will either agree or disagree with the recommended system improvement objectives. And consistent with the creeping commitment principle, we include another go or no-go feasibility checkpoint (the red diamond) at the end of the phase. The project can be either:

- Canceled if the problems are deemed no longer worth solving.
- Approved to continue to the next phase.
- Reduced or expanded in scope (with budget and schedule modifications) and then approved to continue to the next phase.

Requirements Analysis Given system owner approval to continue from the problem analysis phase, now you can design a new system, right? No, not yet! What capabilities should the new system provide for its users? What data must be captured and stored? What performance level is expected? Careful! This requires decisions about *what* the system must do, *not how* it should do those things. The REQUIREMENTS ANALYSIS phase defines and prioritizes the *business* requirements. Simply stated, the analyst approaches the users to find out what they need or want out of the new system, carefully avoiding any discussion of technology or technical implementation. This is perhaps the most important phase of systems development. Errors and omissions in requirements analysis result in user dissatisfaction with the final system and costly modifications.

Returning again to Figure 3-6, notice that the participants primarily include both SYSTEM USERS (which may include owners who will actually *use* the system) and SYSTEMS ANALYSTS. PROJECT MANAGERS are also involved. SYSTEM DESIGNERS are omitted from this phase in order to prevent premature attention to technology solutions. The building blocks can themselves provide the framework for defining many business requirements, including BUSINESS DATA REQUIREMENTS, BUSINESS PROCESS REQUIREMENTS, and BUSINESS AND SYSTEM INTERFACE REQUIREMENTS. Because the business requirements are intended to solve problems, the PIECES framework can also provide a useful outline, this time for a requirements statement.

In Figure 3-5, we see that the SYSTEM IMPROVEMENT OBJECTIVES from the problem analysis phase are the prerequisite to the requirements analysis phase. The deliverable is a BUSINESS REQUIREMENTS STATEMENT. Again, this requirements statement does not specify any technical possibilities or solutions. The requirements statement may be a document as small as a few pages, or it may be extensive with a page or more of documentation per requirement.

To produce a business requirements statement, the systems analyst works closely with system users to identify needs and priorities. This information is collected by way of interviews, questionnaires, and facilitated meetings. The challenge to the team is to validate those requirements. The system improvement objectives provide the "grading key" for business requirements: *Does each requirement contribute to meeting one or more system improvement objectives?* Chapters 6 and 7 will introduce systems analysis tools and techniques for identifying and documenting user requirements.

Typically, requirements must also be prioritized. Priorities serve two purposes. First, if project timelines become stressed, requirements priorities can be used to rescope the project. Second, priorities can frequently be used to define iterations of design and construction to create staged releases or versions of the final product.

The requirements analysis phase should never be skipped or shortchanged. One of the most common complaints about new systems and applications is that they don't really satisfy the users' needs. This usually happens when system designers and builders become preoccupied with a technical solution before fully understanding the business needs. System designers and builders are dependent on competent systems analysts to work with users to define and document complete and accurate business requirements before applying any technology.

Logical Design   Business requirements (above) are usually expressed in words. Systems analysts have found it useful to translate those words into pictures called **system models** to validate the requirements for completeness and consistency. (Figure 3-5 is an example of a common system model called a *data flow diagram*.) System modeling implements a timeless concept: "A picture is worth a thousand words."

The LOGICAL DESIGN PHASE translates business requirements into system models. The term **logical design** should be interpreted as "technology independent," meaning the pictures illustrate the system independent of any possible technical solution—hence, they model business requirements that must be fulfilled by any technical solution we might want to consider.

Different methodologies require or recommend different amounts and degrees of system modeling or logical design. Prescriptive methodologies like *structured analysis and design, information engineering,* and the *Rational Unified Process (RUP)* usually require that many types and/or instances of system models be drawn in various levels of detail. Fortunately, computer-automated tools are available to assist the systems analyst in these drawing tasks. Alternatively, agile methodologies like *architected rapid application development* and *extreme programming* recommend "just enough modeling." This so-called *agile modeling* seeks to prevent the project from degenerating into a condition called **analysis paralysis.** This textbook leans toward agile methods but recognizes that complex problems may best be solved using more prescriptive approaches.

In Figure 3-6, we see that the participants include SYSTEM ANALYSTS (who draw the models) and SYSTEM USERS (who validate the models). PROJECT MANAGERS are always included to ensure that modeling meets standards and does not deter overall project progress. We can draw (1) LOGICAL DATA MODELS that depict data and information requirements, (2) LOGICAL PROCESS MODELS that depict business processes requirements, and (3) LOGICAL INTERFACE MODELS that depict business and system interface requirements.[5]

In Figure 3-5, we see that the prerequisite to logical design is the BUSINESS REQUIREMENTS STATEMENT from the previous phase. In practice, the requirements analysis and logical design phases almost always have considerable overlap. In other words, as business requirements are identified and documented, they can be modeled. The deliverables of logical design are the LOGICAL SYSTEM MODELS AND SPECIFICATIONS themselves. Depending on the methodology used, the level of detail in the specifications will vary. For example, we may define a business rule that specifies the legitimate values for a data attribute such as *Credit Rating* or a rule that specifies the business policy for a *Credit Check.*

---

system model a picture of a system that represents reality or a desired reality. System models facilitate improved communication between system users, system analysts, system designers, and system builders.

---

logical design the translation of business user requirements into a system model that depicts only the business requirements and not any possible technical design or implementation of those requirements. Common synonyms include *conceptual design* and *essential design,* the latter of which refers to modeling the "essence" of a system, or the "essential requirements" independent of any technology. The antonym of logical design is *physical design* (defined later in this chapter).

---

analysis paralysis a satirical term coined to describe a common project condition in which excessive system modeling dramatically slows progress toward implementation of the intended system solution.

---

[5]Those of you already familiar with *object-oriented* modeling should note that object models tend to blur the boundaries of our framework somewhat, but the framework can still be applied since the problem to be solved is still driven by the three fundamental business goals illustrated in our framework. This will be demonstrated in the object-oriented analysis and design chapters of this book.

Before we move on to the next phase, we should note that the SCOPE DEFINITION, PROBLEM ANALYSIS, REQUIREMENTS ANALYSIS, and LOGICAL DESIGN PHASES are collectively recognized by most experts as *system analysis*. Some experts would also include our next phase, DECISION ANALYSIS. But we consider it to be a system analysis to system design transition phase because it makes the transition from the business concerns of system owners and users to the technology concerns of system designers and builders. And of course, systems analysts are the common thread that ensures continuity as we make this transition. Let's examine the transition.

Decision Analysis   Given business requirements and the logical system models, there are usually numerous alternative ways to design a new information system to fulfill those requirements. Some of the pertinent questions include the following:

- How much of the system should be automated with information technology?
- Should we purchase software or build it ourselves (called the *make-versus-buy decision*)?
- Should we design the system for an internal network, or should we design a Web-based solution?
- What information technologies (possibly emerging) might be useful for this application?

These questions are answered in the DECISION ANALYSIS phase of the methodology. The purpose of this phase is to (1) identify candidate technical solutions, (2) analyze those candidate solutions for feasibility, and (3) recommend a candidate system as the target solution to be designed.

In Figure 3-6, we see that the decision analysis phase is positioned halfway through the development process. Half the building blocks are positioned higher, and half are positioned lower. This is consistent with the decision analysis phase's role as a transition from analysis to design—and from business concerns of SYSTEM USERS to those of SYSTEM DESIGNERS (and, ultimately, system builders). Designers (the technical experts in specific technologies) begin to play a role here along with system users and SYSTEM ANALYSTS. Analysts help to define and analyze the alternatives. Decisions are made regarding the technologies to be used as part of the application's architecture. Ultimately, SYSTEM OWNERS will have to approve or disapprove the approved decisions since they are paying for the project.

Figure 3-5 shows that a decision analysis is triggered by validated business requirements plus any logical system models and specifications that expand on those requirements. The project team solicits ideas and opinions for technical design and implementation from a diverse audience, possibly including IT software vendors. Candidate solutions are identified and characterized according to various criteria. It should be noted that many modern organizations have information technology and architecture standards that constrain the number of candidate solutions that might be considered and analyzed. (The existence of such standards is illustrated at the bottom of your information system building blocks model in Figure 3-6.) After the candidate solutions have been identified, each one is evaluated by the following criteria:

- *Technical feasibility*—Is the solution technically practical? Does our staff have the technical expertise to design and build this solution?
- *Operational feasibility*—Will the solution fulfill the user's requirements? To what degree? How will the solution change the user's work environment? How do users feel about such a solution?
- *Economic feasibility*—Is the solution cost-effective (as defined earlier in the chapter)?
- *Schedule feasibility*—Can the solution be designed and implemented within an acceptable time period?
- *Risk feasibility*—What's the probability of a successful implementation using the technology and approach?

The project team is usually looking for the *most* feasible solution—the solution that offers the best combination of technical, operational, economic, schedule, and risk feasibility. Different candidate solutions may be most feasible on a single criterion; however, one solution will usually prove *most* feasible based on all of the criteria.

The key deliverable of the decision analysis phase is a SYSTEM PROPOSAL. This proposal may be written and/or presented verbally. Several outcomes are possible. The creeping commitment feasibility checkpoint (again, the red diamond) may result in any one of the following options:

- Approve and fund the system proposal for design and construction (possibly including an increased budget and timetable if scope has significantly expanded).
- Approve or fund one of the alternative candidate solutions.
- Reject all the candidate solutions and either cancel the project or send it back for new recommendations.
- Approve a reduced-scope version of the proposed solution.

Optionally, the decision analysis phase may also produce an APPLICATION ARCHITECTURE for the approved solution. Such a model serves as a high-level blueprint (like a simple house floor plan) for the recommended or approved proposal.

Before we move on, you may have noticed in Figure 3-6 a variation on the SYSTEM PROPOSAL deliverable called a REQUEST FOR SYSTEM PROPOSALS (or RFP). This variation is for a recommendation to purchase the hardware and/or software solution as opposed to building it in-house. We'll defer any further discussion of this option until later in the chapter when we discuss the commercial package integration variation of our basic process.

Physical Design and Integration   Given approval of the SYSTEM PROPOSAL from the decision analysis phase, you can finally design the new system. The purpose of the PHYSICAL DESIGN AND INTEGRATION phase is to transform the business requirements (represented in part by the LOGICAL SYSTEM MODELS) into PHYSICAL DESIGN SPECIFICATIONS that will guide system construction. In other words, physical design addresses greater detail about *how* technology will be used in the new system. The design will be constrained by the approved ARCHITECTURAL MODEL from the previous phase. Also, design requires adherence to any internal technical design standards that ensure completeness, usability, reliability, performance, and quality.

Physical design is the opposite of logical design. Whereas logical design dealt exclusively with business requirements independent of any technical solution, physical design represents a specific technical solution. Figure 3-6 demonstrates the physical design phase from the perspective of your building blocks. Notice that the design phase is concerned with technology-based views of the system: (1) PHYSICAL DATABASE DESIGN SPECIFICATIONS, (2) PHYSICAL BUSINESS PROCESS and SOFTWARE DESIGN SPECIFICATIONS, and (3) PHYSICAL USER AND SYSTEM INTERFACE SPECIFICATIONS. The SYSTEM DESIGNER and SYSTEM ANALYST (possibly overlapping roles for some of the same individuals) are the key participants; however, certain aspects of the design usually have to be shared with the SYSTEM USERS (e.g., screen designs and work flow). You may have already had some exposure to physical design specifications in either programming or database courses.

There are two extreme philosophies of physical design.

- *Design by specification*—Physical system models and detailed specifications are produced as a series of written (or computer-generated) blueprints for construction.
- *Design by prototyping*—Incomplete but functioning applications or subsystems (called *prototypes*) are constructed and refined based on feedback from users and other designers.

In practice, some combination of these extremes is usually performed.

No new information system exists in isolation from other existing information systems in an organization. Consequently, a design must also reflect system integration concerns. The new system must be integrated both with other information systems

physical design the translation of business user requirements into a system model that depicts a technical implementation of the users' business requirements. Common synonyms include *technical design* or, in describing the output, *implementation model*. The antonym of physical design is *logical design* (defined earlier in this chapter).

and with the business's processes themselves. Integration is usually reflected in physical system models and design specifications.

In summary, Figure 3-5 shows that the deliverables of the physical design and integration phase include some combination of PHYSICAL DESIGN MODELS AND SPECIFICATIONS, DESIGN PROTOTYPES, and REDESIGNED BUSINESS PROCESSES. Notice that we have included one final go or no-go feasibility checkpoint for the project (the red diamond). A project is rarely canceled after the design phase unless it is hopelessly over budget or behind schedule. On the other hand, scope could be decreased to produce a minimum acceptable product in a specified time frame. Or the schedule could be extended to build a more complete solution in multiple versions. The project plan (schedule and budget) would need to be adjusted to reflect these decisions.

It should be noted that in modern methodologies, there is a trend toward merging the design phase with our next phase, construction. In other words, the design and construction phases usually overlap.

Construction and Testing   Given some level of PHYSICAL DESIGN MODELS AND SPECIFICA-TIONS (and/or DESIGN PROTOTYPES), we can begin to construct and test system components for that design. Figure 3-5 shows that the primary deliverable of the CONSTRUCTION AND TESTING phase is a FUNCTIONAL SYSTEM that is ready for implementation. The purpose of the construction and testing phase is twofold: (1) to build and test a system that fulfills business requirements and physical design specifications, and (2) to implement the interfaces between the new system and existing systems. Additionally, FINAL DOCUMEN-TATION (e.g., help systems, training manuals, help desk support, production control instructions) will be developed in preparation for training and system operation. The construction phase may also involve installation of purchased software.

Your information system framework (Figure 3-6) identifies the relevant building blocks and activities for the construction phase. The focus is on the last row of building blocks. The project team must construct or install:

- DATABASES—Databases may include *online transaction processing (OLTP)* databases to support day-to-day business transactions, *operational data stores (ODS)* to support day-to-day reporting and queries, and *data warehouses* to support data analysis and decision support needs.
- COMMERCIAL SOFTWARE PACKAGES and/or CUSTOM-BUILT SOFTWARE—Packages are installed and customized as necessary. Application programs are constructed according to the physical design and/or prototypes from the previous phase. Both packages and custom software must be thoroughly tested.
- USER AND SYSTEM INTERFACES—User interfaces (e.g., Windows and Web interfaces) must be constructed and tested for usability and stability. System-to-system interfaces must be either constructed or implemented using application integration technologies. Notice that MIDDLEWARE (a type of system software) is often used to integrate disparate database, software, and interface technologies. We'll talk more about middleware in the design unit of this book.

Figure 3-6 also identifies the participants in this phase as SYSTEM BUILDERS, SYSTEM ANALYSTS, SYSTEM USERS, and PROJECT MANAGERS. SYSTEM DESIGNERS may also be involved to clarify design specifications.

You probably already have some experience with part of this activity—application programming. Programs can be written in many different languages, but the current trend is toward the use of visual and object-oriented programming languages such as *Java*, *C++*, or *Visual Basic*. As components are constructed, they are typically demonstrated to users in order to solicit feedback.

One of the most important aspects of construction is conducting tests of both individual system components and the overall system. Once tested, a system (or version of a system) is ready for INSTALLATION AND DELIVERY.

Installation and Delivery   What's left to do? New systems usually represent a departure from the way business is currently done; therefore, the analyst must provide for a smooth transition from the old system to the new system and help users cope with normal start-up problems. Thus, the INSTALLATION AND DELIVERY phase serves to deliver the system into operation (sometimes called *production*).

In Figure 3-5, the FUNCTIONAL SYSTEM from the construction and testing phase is the key input to the INSTALLATION AND DELIVERY phase. The deliverable is an OPERATIONAL SYSTEM. SYSTEM BUILDERS install the system from its development environment into the production environment. SYSTEM ANALYSTS must train SYSTEM USERS, write various user and production control manuals, convert existing files and databases to the new databases, and perform final system testing. Any problems may initiate rework in previous phases thought to be complete. System users provide continuous feedback as new problems and issues arise. Essentially, the installation and delivery phase considers the same building blocks as the construction phase.

To provide a smooth transition to the new system, a conversion plan should be prepared. This plan may call for an abrupt cutover, where the old system is terminated and replaced by the new system on a specific date. Alternatively, the plan may run the old and new systems in parallel until the new system has been deemed acceptable to replace the old system.

The installation and delivery phase also involves training individuals who will use the final system and developing documentation to aid the system users. The implementation phase usually includes some form of POST-AUDIT REVIEW to gauge the success of the completed systems project. This activity promotes continuous improvement of the process and future project management.

System Operation and Maintenance   Once the system is placed into operation, it will require ongoing **system support** for the remainder of its useful, productive lifetime. System support consists of the following ongoing activities:

- *Assisting users*—Regardless of how well the users have been trained and how thorough and clear the end-user documentation is, users will eventually require additional assistance as unanticipated problems arise, new users are added, and so forth.
- *Fixing software defects (bugs)*—Software defects are errors that slipped through the testing of software. These are inevitable, but they can usually be resolved, in most cases, by knowledgeable support.
- *Recovering the system*—From time to time, a system failure may result in a program "crash" and/or loss of data. Human error or a hardware or software failure may cause this. The systems analyst or technical support specialists may then be called on to recover the system—that is, to restore a system's files and databases and to restart the system.
- *Adapting the system to new requirements*—New requirements may include new business problems, new business requirements, new technical problems, or new technology requirements.

Eventually, we expect that the user feedback and problems, or changing business needs, will indicate that it is time to start over and reinvent the system. In other words, the system has reached entropy, and a new project to create an entirely new system development process should be initiated.

> Cross Life-Cycle Activities

System development also involves a number of **cross life-cycle activities.** These activities, listed in the margin definition, are not explicitly depicted in Figure 3-5, but they are vital to the success of any project. Let's briefly examine each of these activities.

Fact-Finding   There are many occasions for **fact-finding** during a project. Fact-finding is most crucial to the early phases of a project. It is during these phases that

system support the ongoing technical support for users of a system, as well as the maintenance required to deal with any errors, omissions, or new requirements that may arise.

cross life-cycle activity any activity that overlaps multiple phases of the system development process. Examples include *fact-finding*, *documentation*, *presentation*, *estimation*, *feasibility analysis*, *project and process management*, *change management*, and *quality management*.

fact-finding the formal process of using research, interviews, meetings, questionnaires, sampling, and other techniques to collect information about system problems, requirements, and preferences. It is also called *information gathering* or *data collection*.

the project team learns about a business's vocabulary, problems, opportunities, constraints, requirements, and priorities. But fact-finding is also used during the decision analysis, physical design, construction and testing, and installation and delivery phases—only to a lesser extent. It is during these latter phases that the project team researches technical alternatives and solicits feedback on technical designs, standards, and working components.

Documentation and Presentation   Communication skills are essential to the successful completion of any project. In fact, poor communication is frequently cited as the cause of project delays and rework. Two forms of communication that are common to systems development projects are **documentation** and **presentation.**

Clearly, documentation and presentation opportunities span all the phases. In Figure 3-7, the black arrows represent various instances of documentation of a phase. The red arrows represent instances where presentations are frequently required. Finally, the green arrows represent the storage of documentation and other artifacts of systems development in a **repository.** A repository saves documentation for reuse and rework as necessary.

Feasibility Analysis   Consistent with our creeping commitment approach to systems development, **feasibility analysis** is a cross life-cycle activity. Different measures of **feasibility** are applicable in different phases of the methodology. These measures include technical, operational, economic, schedule, and risk feasibility, as described when we introduced the decision analysis phase. Feasibility analysis requires good **estimation** techniques.

Process and Project Management   Recall that the CMM considers systems development to be a *process* that must be managed on a project-by-project basis. For this reason and others, process management and project management are ongoing, cross life-cycle activities. Both types of management were introduced earlier, but their definitions are repeated in the margin on page ••• for your convenience. **Process management** defines the methodology to be used on every project—think of it as the *recipe* for building a system. **Project management** is concerned with administering a single instance of the process as applied to a single project.

Failures and limited successes of systems development projects often outnumber successful projects. Why is that? One reason is that many systems analysts are unfamiliar with, or undisciplined in how to properly apply, tools and techniques of systems development. But most failures are attributed to poor leadership and management. This mismanagement results in unfulfilled or unidentified requirements, cost overruns, and late delivery.

> Sequential versus Iterative Development

The above discussion of phases might lead you to assume that systems development is a naturally sequential process, moving in a one-way direction from phase to phase. Such sequential development is, in fact, one alternative. This approach is depicted in part (a) of Figure 3-8. In the figure we have used the four classic phases rather than the eight *FAST* phases in the interest of simplicity. This strategy requires that each phase be "completed" one after the other until the information system is finished. In reality, the phases may somewhat overlap one another in time. For example, some system design can be started prior to the completion of system analysis. Given its waterfall-like visual appearance, this approach is often called the **waterfall development approach.**

The waterfall approach has lost favor with most modern system developers. A more popular strategy, shown in part (b) of Figure 3-8, is commonly referred to as the **iterative development approach,** or incremental development process. This

documentation the ongoing activity of recording facts and specifications for a system for current and future reference.

presentation the ongoing activity of communicating findings, recommendations, and documentation for review by interested users and managers. Presentations may be either written or verbal.

repository a database and/or file directory where system developers store all documentation, knowledge, and artifacts for one or more information systems or projects. A repository is usually automated for easy information storage, retrieval, and sharing.

feasibility analysis the activity by which feasibility is measured and assessed.

feasibility a measure of how beneficial the development of an information system would be to an organization.

estimation the calculated prediction of the costs and effort required for system development. A somewhat facetious synonym is *guesstimation*, usually meaning that the estimation is based on experience or empirical evidence but is lacking in rigor—in other words, a *guess*.

process management an ongoing activity that documents, teaches, oversees the use of, and improves an organization's chosen methodology (the "process") for systems development. Process management is concerned with phases, activities, deliverables, and quality standards that should be consistently applied to all projects.

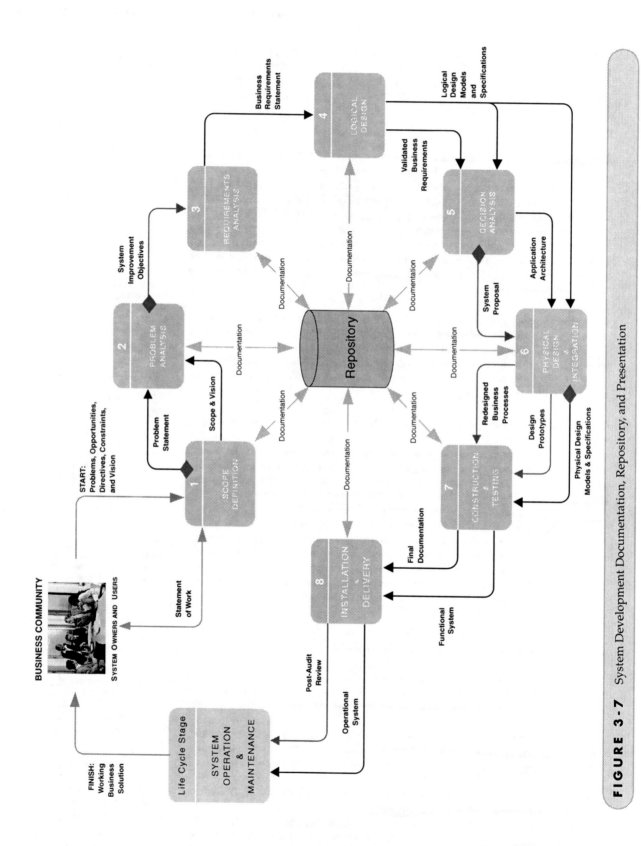

FIGURE 3-7   System Development Documentation, Repository, and Presentation

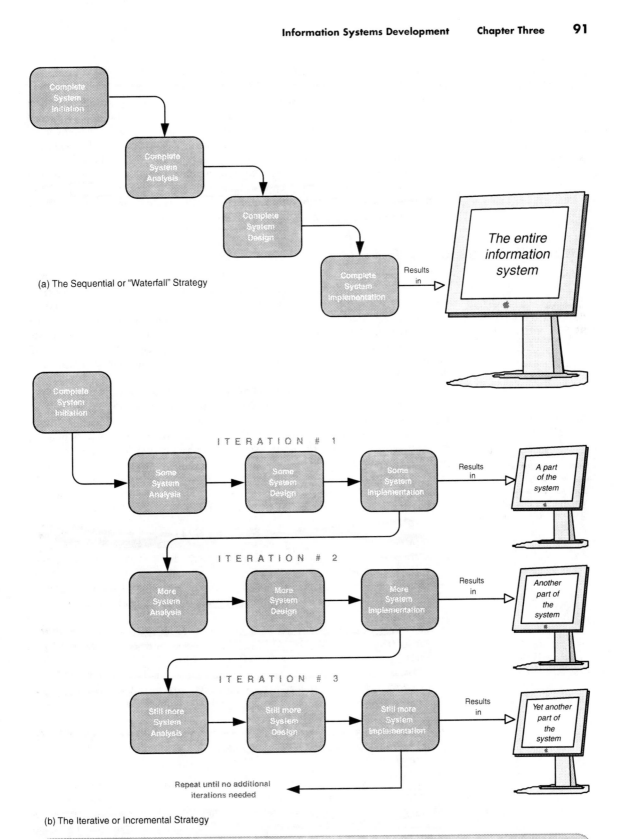

(a) The Sequential or "Waterfall" Strategy

(b) The Iterative or Incremental Strategy

FIGURE 3-8   Sequential versus Iterative Systems Development Approach

project management the process of scoping, planning, staffing, organizing, directing, and controlling a project to develop an information system at minimum cost, within a specified time frame, and with acceptable quality.

approach requires completing enough analysis, design, and implementation to be able to fully develop a *part* of the new system and place it into operation as quickly as possible. Once that version of the system is implemented, the strategy is to then perform some additional analysis, design, and implementation to release the next version of the system. These iterations continue until all parts of the entire information system have been implemented. The popularity of this iterative and incremental process can be explained simply: System owners and users have long complained about the excessive time required to develop and implement information systems using the waterfall approach. The iterative approach allows versions of useable information to be delivered in regular and shorter time frames. This results in improved customer (system owner and user) satisfaction.

Alternative Routes and Strategies

waterfall development approach an approach to systems analysis and design that completes each phase one after another and only once.

iterative development approach an approach to systems analysis and design that completes that entire information system in successive iterations. Each iteration does some analysis, some design, and some construction. Synonyms include incremental and spiral.

Given any destination, there are many routes to that destination and many modes of transport. You could take the superhighway, highways, or back roads, or you could fly. Deciding which route is best depends on your goals and priorities. Do you want to get there fast, or do you want to see the sights? How much are you willing to spend? Are you comfortable with the mode of travel? Just as you would pick your route and means to a travel destination, you can and should pick a route and means for a systems development destination.

So far, we've described a basic set of phases that comprise our *FAST* methodology. At one time, a "one size fits all" methodology was common for most projects; however, today a variety of types of projects, technologies, and development strategies exist—one size no longer fits all projects! Like many contemporary methodologies, *FAST* provides alternative routes and strategies to accommodate different types of projects, technology goals, developer skills, and development paradigms.

In this section, we will describe several *FAST* routes and strategies. Before we do so, examine Figure 3-9 on the following page. The figure illustrates a taxonomy or classification scheme for methodological strategies. Notice the following:

- Methodologies and routes can support the option of either *building software solutions* in-house or *buying a commercial software solution* from a software vendor. Generally, many of the same methods and techniques are applicable to both options.
- Methodologies may be either very *prescriptive* ("Touch all the bases; follow all the rules") or relatively *adaptive* ("Change as needed within certain guidelines").
- Methodologies can also be characterized as *model-driven* ("Draw pictures of the system") or *product-driven* ("Build the product and see how the users react").
- Model-driven methodologies are rapidly moving to a focus on the *object-oriented* technologies being used to construct most of today's systems (more about this later). Earlier model-driven approaches emphasized either process modeling *or* data modeling.
- Finally, product-driven approaches tend to emphasize either rapid *prototyping* or writing program *code* as soon as possible (perhaps you've heard the term *extreme programming*).

So many strategies! Which should you choose? A movement is forming known as *agile methods*. In a nutshell, advocates of agile methods suggest that system analysts and programmers should have a tool box of methods that include tools and techniques from all of the above methodologies. They should choose their tools and techniques based on the problem and situation. *FAST* is an agile methodology. It advocates the integrated use of tools and techniques from many methodologies, applied in the context of repeatable processes (as in CMM Level 3). That said, let's examine some of the route variations and strategies for the *FAST* process. As we

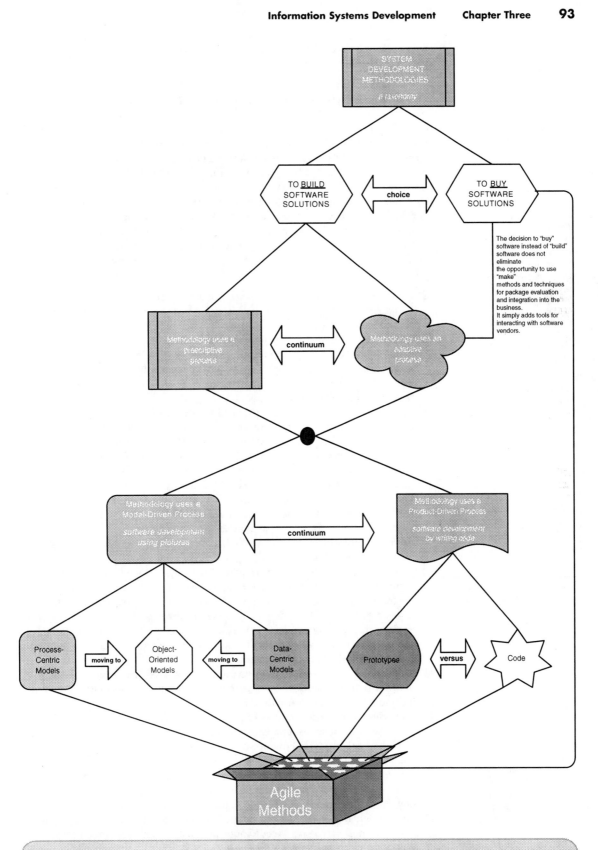

F I G U R E 3 - 9 A Taxonomy for System Development Methodologies and Strategies navigate through each route, we will use red typefaces and arrows to highlight those aspects of the route that differ from the basic route you've already learned.

> The Model-Driven Development Strategy

One of the oldest and most commonly used approaches to analyzing and designing information systems is based on system modeling. As a reminder, a system model is a picture of a system that represents reality or a desired reality. System models facilitate improved communication between system users, system analysts, system designers, and system builders. In the *FAST* methodology, system models are used to illustrate and communicate the KNOWLEDGE, PROCESS, or INTERFACE building blocks of information systems. This approach is called **model-driven development.**

> **model-driven development** a system development strategy that emphasizes the drawing of system models to help visualize and analyze problems, define business requirements, and design information systems.

The model-driven development route for *FAST* is illustrated in Figure 3-10. The model-driven approach does not vary much from the basic phases we described earlier. We call your attention to the following notes that correspond to the numbered bullets:

❶ System models may exist from the project that created the current system. Be careful! These models are notorious for being out of date. But they can still be useful as a point of departure.

❷ Earlier you learned that it is important to define scope for a project. One of the simplest ways to communicate scope is by drawing MODELS THAT SHOW SCOPE DEFINITION. Scope models show which aspects of a problem are within scope and which aspects are outside scope. This is sometimes called a *context diagram* or context model.

❸ Some system modeling techniques call for extensive MODELS OF THE EXISTING SYSTEM to identify problems and opportunities for system improvement. This is sometimes called the *as-is system model.* Modeling of the current system has waned in popularity today. Many project managers and analysts view it as counterproductive or of little value added. The exception is modeling of as-is business processes for the purpose of business process redesign.

❹ The requirements statement is one of the most important deliverables of system development. It sometimes includes MODELS THAT DEPICT HIGH-LEVEL BUSINESS REQUIREMENTS. One of the most popular modeling techniques today is called *use case* (introduced in Chapter 7). Use cases identify requirements and track their fulfillment through the life cycle.

> **logical model** a pictorial representation that depicts *what* a system is or does. Synonyms include essential model, conceptual model, and business model.

❺ Most model-driven techniques require that analysts document business requirements with **logical models** (defined earlier). Business requirements are frequently expressed in LOGICAL MODELS THAT DEPICT MORE DETAILED USER REQUIREMENTS. They show only *what* a system must be or must do. They are implementation *in*dependent; that is, they depict the system independent of any possible technical implementation. Hence, they are useful for depicting and validating business requirements.

❻ As a result of the decision analysis phase, the analyst may produce system MODELS THAT DEPICT APPLICATION ARCHITECTURE. Such models illustrate the planned technical implementation of a system.

❼ Many model-driven techniques require that analysts develop MODELS THAT DEPICT PHYSICAL DESIGN SPECIFICATIONS (defined earlier in this chapter). Recall that **physical models** show not only what a system is or does but also *how* the system is implemented with technology. They are implementation *de*pendent because they reflect technology choices and the limitations of those technology choices. Examples include database schemas, structure charts, and flowcharts. They serve as a blueprint for construction of the new system.

> **physical model** a technical pictorial representation that depicts what a system is or does and *how* the system is implemented. Synonyms include implementation model and technical model.

❽ New information systems must be interwoven into the fabric of an organization's business processes. Accordingly, the analyst and users may develop MODELS OF REDESIGNED BUSINESS PROCESSES.

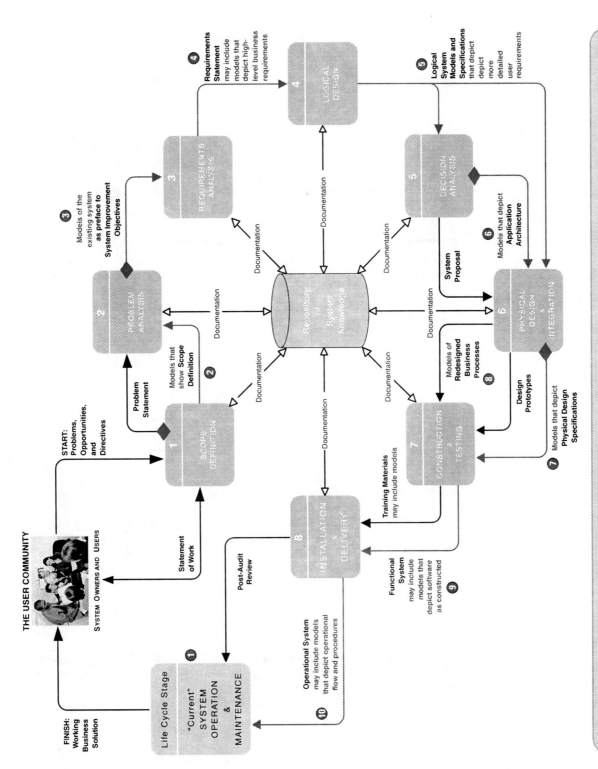

FIGURE 3-10 The Model-Driven System Development Strategy

⑨ Construction translates the physical system models into software. In some cases, automated tools exist to automatically translate software into PHYSICAL MODELS THAT DEPICT SOFTWARE CONSTRUCTED. This is called *reverse engineering*.

⑩ Finally, the operational system may include MODELS THAT DEPICT FLOW AND PROCEDURE. For example, system models may document backup and recovery procedures.

In summary, system models can be produced as a portion of the deliverables for most phases. Model-driven approaches emphasize system modeling. Once implemented, the system models serve as documentation for any changes that might be needed during the operation and support stage of the life cycle.

The model-driven approach is believed to offer several advantages and disadvantages, as listed below:

Advantages

- Requirements specification tends to be more thorough and better documented.
- Business requirements and system designs are easier to validate with pictures than words.
- It is easier to identify, conceptualize, and analyze alternative technical solutions.
- Design specifications tend to be more sound, stable, adaptable, and flexible because they are model based and more thoroughly analyzed *before* they are built.
- Systems can be constructed more correctly the first time when built from thorough and clear model based specifications. Some argue that code-generating software can automatically generate skeleton or near-complete code from good system models.

Disadvantages

- It is time-consuming. It takes time to collect the facts, draw the models, and validate those models. This is especially true if users are uncertain or imprecise about their system requirements.
- The models can only be as good as the users' understanding of those requirements.
- Pictures are not software—some argue that this reduces the users' role in a project to passive participation. Most users don't get excited about pictures. Instead, they want to see working software, and they gauge project progress by the existence of software (or its absence).
- The model-driven approach is considered by some to be inflexible—users must fully specify requirements before design, design must fully document technical specifications before construction, and so forth. Some view such rigidity as impractical.

process modeling a process-centered technique popularized by the *structured analysis and design* methodology that used models of business process requirements to derive effective software designs for a system. Structured analysis introduced a modeling tool called the *data flow diagram* to illustrate the flow of data through a series of business processes. Structured design converted data flow diagrams into a process model called *structure charts* to illustrate a top-down software structure that fulfills the business requirements.

Model-driven development is most effective for systems for which requirements are well understood and which are so complex that they require large project teams to complete. The approach also works well when fulfillment of user expectations and quality is more important than cost and schedule.

There are several different model-driven techniques. They differ primarily in terms of the types of models that they require the systems analyst to draw and validate. Let's briefly examine three of the most popular model-driven development techniques that will be taught in this book. Please note that we are introducing only the techniques here, not the models. We'll teach the models themselves later, in the "how to" chapters.

Process Modeling **Process modeling** was founded in the structured analysis and design methodologies in 1978. While structured analysis and design has lost favor as a methodology, process modeling remains a viable and important technique. Recall that your information system building blocks include several possible focuses: KNOWLEDGE, PROCESSES, and INTERFACES. Process modeling focuses on the PROCESS column of building blocks. *Flowcharts* are one type of process model (used primarily by SYSTEM BUILDERS) that you may have encountered in a programming course. Process modeling has enjoyed something of a renaissance with the emergence of business process redesign (introduced in Chapter 1).

Data flow diagrams and structure charts have contributed significantly to reducing the communications gap that often exists between nontechnical system owners and users and technical system designers and builders. Process modeling is taught in this book.

Data Modeling   Recall that KNOWLEDGE improvement is a fundamental goal and set of building blocks in your framework. Knowledge is the product of *information,* which in turn is the product of *data.* **Data modeling** methods emphasize the knowledge building blocks, especially data. In the data modeling approach, emphasis is placed on diagrams that capture business data requirements and translate them into database designs. Arguably, data modeling is the most widely practiced system modeling technique. Hence, it will be taught in this book.

> **data modeling** a data-centered technique used to model business data requirements and design database systems that fulfill those requirements. The most frequently encountered data models are *entity relationship diagrams.*

Object Modeling   Object modeling is the result of technical advancement. Today, most programming languages and methods are based on the emergence of object technology. While the concepts of object technology are covered extensively throughout this book, a brief but oversimplified introduction is appropriate here.

For the past 30 years, techniques like process and data modeling deliberately separated the concerns of PROCESSES from those of DATA. In other words, process and data models were separate and distinct. Because virtually all systems included processes *and* data, the techniques were frequently used in parallel and the models had to be carefully synchronized. Object techniques are an attempt to eliminate the separation of concerns, and hence the need for synchronization of data and process concerns. This has given rise to **object modeling** methods.

Business objects correspond to real things of importance in the business such as *customers* and the *orders* they place for *products.* Each object consists of *both* the data that describes the object and the processes that can create, read, update, and delete that object. With respect to your information system building blocks, object-oriented analysis and design (OOAD) significantly changes the paradigm. The DATA and PROCESS columns (and, arguably, the INTERFACE column as well) are essentially merged into a single OBJECT column. The models then focus on identifying objects, building objects, and assembling appropriate objects, as with *Legos,* into useful information systems.

> **object modeling** a technique that attempts to merge the data and process concerns into singular constructs called *objects.* Object models are diagrams that document a system in terms of its objects and their interactions. Object modeling is the basis for *object-oriented analysis and design* methodologies.

The current popularity of object technology is driving the interest in object models and OOAD. For example, most of today's popular operating systems like Microsoft *Windows* and Apple *Mac/OS* have object-oriented user interfaces ("point and click," using objects such as windows, frames, drop-down menus, radio buttons, checkboxes, scroll bars, and the like). Web user interfaces like Microsoft *Internet Explorer* and Netscape *Navigator* are also based on object technology. Object programming languages such as *Java, C++, C#, Smalltalk,* and *Visual Basic .NET* are used to construct and assemble such object-oriented operating systems and applications. And those same languages have become the tools of choice for building next-generation information system applications. Not surprisingly, object modeling techniques have been created to express business and software requirements and designs in terms of objects. This edition of this book extensively integrates the most popular object modeling techniques to prepare you for systems analysis and design that ultimately produces today's object-based information systems and applications.

> The Rapid Application Development Strategy

rapid application development (RAD) a system development strategy that emphasizes speed of development through extensive user involvement in the rapid, iterative, and incremental construction of a series of functioning **prototypes** of a system that eventually evolves into the final system (or a version).

In response to the faster pace of the economy in general, **rapid application development (RAD)** has become a popular route for accelerating systems development. The basic ideas of RAD are:

- To more actively involve system users in the analysis, design, and construction activities.
- To organize systems development into a series of focused, intense workshops jointly involving SYSTEM OWNERS, USERS, ANALYSTS, DESIGNERS, and BUILDERS.
- To accelerate the requirements analysis and design phases through an iterative construction approach.
- To reduce the amount of time that passes before the users begin to see a working system.

prototype a small-scale, representative, or working model of the users' requirements or a proposed design for an information system. Any given prototype may omit certain functions or features until such time as the prototype has sufficiently evolved into an acceptable implementation of requirements.

The basic principle behind prototyping is that users know what they want when they see it working. In RAD, a **prototype** eventually evolves into the final information system. The RAD route for *FAST* is illustrated in Figure 3-11. Again, the red text and flows indicate the deviations from the basic *FAST* process. We call your attention to the following notes that correspond to the numbered bullets:

❶ The emphasis is on reducing time in developing applications and systems; therefore, the initial problem analysis, requirements analysis, and decision analysis phases are consolidated and accelerated. The deliverables are typically abbreviated, again in the interest of time. The deliverables are said to be INITIAL, meaning "expected to change" as the project progresses.

　　After the above initial analysis, the RAD uses an iterative approach, as discussed earlier in the chapter. Each iteration emphasizes only enough new functionality to be accomplished within a few weeks.

❷ LOGICAL AND PHYSICAL DESIGN SPECIFICATIONS are usually significantly abbreviated and accelerated. In each iteration of the cycle, only some design specifications will be considered. While some system models may be drawn, they are selectively chosen and the emphasis continues to be on rapid development. The assumption is that errors can be caught and fixed in the next iteration.

❸ In some, but rarely all, iterations, some business processes may need to be redesigned to reflect the likely integration of the evolving software application.

❹ In each iteration of the cycle, SOME DESIGN PROTOTYPES or SOME PARTIAL FUNCTIONAL SYSTEM elements are constructed and tested. Eventually, the completed application will result from the final iteration through the cycle.

❺ After each prototype or partial functional subsystem is constructed and tested, system users are given the opportunity to experience working with that prototype. The expectation is that users will clarify requirements, identify new requirements, and provide BUSINESS FEEDBACK on design (e.g., ease of learning, ease of use) for the next iteration through the RAD cycle.

❻ After each prototype or functioning subsystem is constructed and tested, system analysts and designers will review the application architecture and design to provide TECHNICAL FEEDBACK and direction for the next iteration through the RAD cycle.

❼ Based on the feedback, systems analysts will identify REFINED SYSTEM IMPROVEMENT OBJECTIVES and/or BUSINESS REQUIREMENTS. This analysis tends to focus on revising or expanding objectives and requirements and identifying user concerns with the design.

❽ Based on the feedback, systems analysts and system designers will identify a REFINED APPLICATION ARCHITECTURE and/or DESIGN CHANGES.

❾ Eventually, the system (or a version of the system) will be deemed worthy of implementation. This CANDIDATE RELEASE VERSION OF THE FUNCTIONAL SYSTEM is system tested and placed into operation. The next version of the system may continue iterating through the RAD cycle.

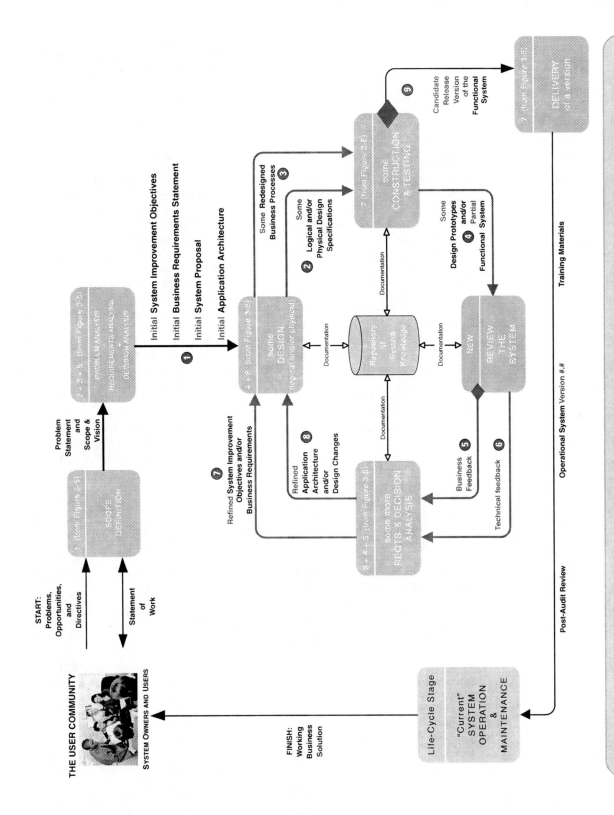

FIGURE 3-11 The Rapid Application Development (RAD) Strategy

100   Part One   The Context of Systems Development Projects

timeboxing the imposition of a nonextendable period of time, usually 60 to 90 days, by which the first (or next) version of a system must be delivered into operation.

Although not a rigid requirement for RAD, the duration of the prototyping loop can be limited using a technique called **timeboxing.** Timeboxing seeks to deliver an operational system to users and management on a regular, recurring basis. Advocates of timeboxing argue that management and user enthusiasm for a project can be enhanced and sustained because a working version of the system is implemented on a regular basis.

The RAD approach offers several advantages and disadvantages:

Advantages

- It is useful for projects in which the user requirements are uncertain or imprecise.
- It encourages active user and management participation (as opposed to a passive reaction to nonworking system models). This increases end-user enthusiasm for the project.
- Projects have higher visibility and support because of the extensive user involvement throughout the process.
- Users and management see working, software-based solutions more rapidly than they do in model-driven development.
- Errors and omissions tend to be detected earlier in prototypes than in system models.
- Testing and training are natural by-products of the underlying proto-typing approach.
- The iterative approach is a more natural process because change is an expected factor during development.

Disadvantages

- Some argue that RAD encourages a "code, implement, and repair" mentality that increases lifetime costs required to operate, support, and maintain the system.
- RAD prototypes can easily solve the wrong problems since problem analysis is abbreviated or ignored.
- A RAD-based prototype may discourage analysts from considering other, more worthy technical alternatives.
- Sometimes it is best to throw a prototype away, but stakeholders are often reluctant to do so because they see this as a loss of time and effort in the current product.
- The emphasis on speed can adversely impact quality because of ill-advised shortcuts through the methodology.

RAD is most popular for small- to medium-size projects. We will demonstrate prototyping and RAD techniques in appropriate chapters of this book.

> The Commercial Application Package Implementation Strategy

Sometimes it makes more sense to buy an information system solution than to build one in-house. In fact, many organizations increasingly expect to build software in-house only when there is a competitive advantage to be gained. And for many core applications such as human resources, financials, procurement, manufacturing, and distribution, there is little competitive value in building your own system—hence a **commercial application package** is purchased. Accordingly, our *FAST* methodology includes a commercial software package route.

commercial application package a software application that can be purchased and customized (within limits) to meet the business requirements of a large number of organizations or a specific industry. A synonym is *commercial off-the-shelf (COTS) system.*

The ultimate commercial solution is enterprise resource planning, or ERP (defined in Chapter 1). ERP solutions provide *all* of the core information system applications for an entire business. For most organizations, an ERP implementation represents the single largest information system project ever undertaken by the organization. It can cost tens or hundreds of millions of dollars and require a small army of managers, users, analysts, technical specialists, programmers, consultants, and contractors.

The *FAST* methodology's route for commercial application package integration is not really intended for ERP projects. Indeed, most ERP vendors provide their own implementation methodology (and consulting partners) to help their customers implement such a massive software solution. Instead, our *FAST* methodology provides a route for implementing all other types of information system solutions that may be purchased by a business. For example, an organization might purchase a commercial application package for a single business function such as accounting, human resources, or procurement. The package must be selected, installed, customized, and integrated into the business and its other existing information systems.

The basic ideas behind our commercial application package implementation route are:

- Packaged software solutions must be carefully selected to fulfill business needs—"You get what you ask and pay for."
- Packaged software solutions not only are costly to purchase but can be costly to implement. In fact, the package route can actually be more expensive to implement than an in-house development route.
- Software packages must usually be customized for and integrated into the business. Additionally, software packages usually require the redesign of existing business processes to adapt to the software.
- Software packages rarely fulfill all business requirements to the users' complete satisfaction. Thus, some level of in-house systems development is necessary in order to meet the unfulfilled requirements.

The commercial application package implementation route is illustrated in Figure 3-12. Once again, the red typeface and arrows indicate differences from the basic *FAST* process. We call your attention to the following notes that correspond to the numbered bullets:

❶ It should be noted that the decision to purchase a package is determined in the problem analysis phase. The red diamond represents the "make versus buy" decision. The remainder of this discussion assumes that a decision to buy has been approved.

❷ Problem analysis usually includes some initial TECHNOLOGY MARKET RESEARCH to identify what package solutions exist, what features are in the software, and what criteria should be used to evaluate such application packages. This research may involve software vendors, IT research services (such as the Gartner Group), or consultants.

❸ After defining business requirements, the requirements must be communicated to the software vendors who offer viable application solutions. The business (and technical) requirements are formatted and communicated to candidate software vendors as either a REQUEST FOR PROPOSAL (RFP) or a REQUEST FOR QUOTATION (RFQ). The double-ended arrow implies that there may need to be some clarification of requirements and criteria.

❹ Vendors submit PROPOSALS or QUOTATIONS for their application solutions. These proposals are evaluated against the business and technical requirements specified in the RFP. The double-ended arrow indicates that claimed features and capabilities must be validated and in some instances clarified. This occurs during the decision analysis phase.

❺ A CONTRACT AND ORDER is negotiated with the winning vendor for the software and possibly for services necessary to install and maintain the software.

❻ The vendor provides the BASELINE COMMERCIAL APPLICATION software and documentation. Services for installation and implementation of the software are frequently provided by the vendor or its service providers (certified consultants).

❼ When an application package is purchased, the organization must nearly always change its business processes and practices to work efficiently with the package. The need for REDESIGNED BUSINESS PROCESSES is rarely greeted with enthusiasm,

request for proposal (RFP) a formal document that communicates business, technical, and support requirements for an application software package to vendors that may wish to compete for the sale of that application package and services.

request for quotation (RFQ) a formal document that communicates business, technical, and support requirements for an application software package to a single vendor that has been determined as being able to supply that application package and services.

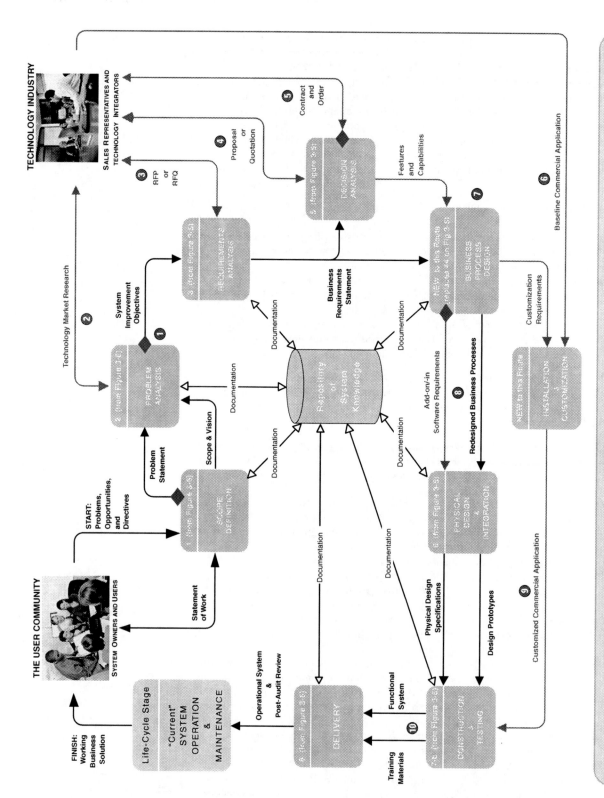

FIGURE 3-12   The Commercial Application Package Implementation Strategy

but they are usually necessary. In many cases, the necessary changes are not wrong—they are just different and unfamiliar. System users tend to be uncomfortable with changing the way they have always done something.

❽ An application package rarely meets all business requirements upon installation. Typically, a **gap analysis** must be performed to determine which business requirements are not fulfilled by the package's capabilities and features. For requirements that will not be fulfilled, the following options exist:

- Request customizations of the package within allowable limits as specified by the software vendor. Most commercial application packages allow the purchaser to set specific options, preferences, and defined values and ranges for certain parameters. Within limits, these customizations allow you to "personalize" the package to the business accounting and business practices. Such necessary CUSTOMIZATION REQUIREMENTS need to be specified.

- Define ADD-ON SOFTWARE REQUIREMENTS. Add-on software requirements specify programs that must be designed and constructed to augment the commercial application package and deliver additional functionality. It should be noted that add-on programs carry some risk that they may have to be modified in the future when a new version of the software becomes available. But this risk is nominal, and most organizations take the risk in order to provide additional functionality.

- Define ADD-IN SOFTWARE REQUIREMENTS. Add-in software requirements are very dangerous! They specify changes to the actual commercial application package to meet business requirements. In other words, users are requesting that changes be made to the purchased software, its database, or its user interfaces. At best, such changes can make version upgrades extremely difficult and prohibitively expensive. At worst, such changes can invalidate technical support from the vendor. (And most vendors encourage keeping versions relatively current by canceling technical support on older versions.) Changing program code and database structures should be discouraged. Insistence by users is often a symptom of unwillingness to adapt business processes to work with the application. Many organizations prohibit changes to application packages and force users to adapt in order to preserve their upgrade path.

❾ The BASELINE COMMERCIAL APPLICATION is installed and tested. Allowable changes based on options, preferences, and parameters are completed and tested. Note: These customizations within the limits specified by the software vendor will typically carry forward to version upgrades. In most instances the vendor has provided for this level of CUSTOMIZED COMMERCIAL APPLICATION.

❿ Any add-on (or add-in) software changes are designed and constructed to meet additional business requirements. The system is subsequently tested and placed into operation using the same activities described in the basic *FAST* process.

The commercial application package strategy offers its own advantages and disadvantages:

| **gap analysis** a comparison of business and technical requirements for a commercial application package against the capabilities and features of a specific commercial application package for the purpose of defining the requirements that cannot be met. |

Advantages

- New systems can usually be implemented more quickly because extensive programming is not required.
- Many businesses cannot afford the staffing and expertise required to develop in-house solutions.
- Application vendors spread their development costs across all customers that purchase their software. Thus, they can invest in continuous

Disadvantages

- A successful COTS implementation is dependent on the long-term success and viability of the application vendor—if the vendor goes out of business, you can lose your technical support and future improvements.
- A purchased system rarely reflects the ideal solution that the business might achieve with an in-house-developed system that could be

improvements in features, capabilities, and usability that individual businesses cannot always afford.

- The application vendor assumes responsibility for significant system improvements and error corrections.
- Many business functions are more similar than dissimilar for all businesses in a given industry. For example, business functions across organizations in the health care industry are more alike than different. It does not make good business sense for each organization to "reinvent the wheel."

customized to the precise expectations of management and the users.

- There is almost always at least some resistance to changing business processes to adapt to the software. Some users will have to give up or assume new responsibilities. And some people may resent changes they perceive to be technology-driven instead of business-driven.

Regardless, the trend toward purchased commercial application packages cannot be ignored. Today, many businesses require that a package alternative be considered prior to engaging in any type of in-house development project. Some experts estimate that by the year 2005 businesses will purchase 75 percent of their new information system applications. For this reason, we will teach systems analysis tools and techniques needed by system analysts to function in this environment.

> Hybrid Strategies

The *FAST* routes are not mutually exclusive. Any given project may elect to or be required to use a combination of, or variation of, more than one route. The route to be used is always selected during the *scope definition* phase and is negotiated as part of the *statement of work*. One strategy that is commonly applied to both model-driven and rapid application development routes is an incremental strategy. Figure 3-13 illustrates one possible implementation of an incremental strategy in combination with rapid application development. The project delivers the information system into operation in four stages. Each stage implements a version of the final system using a RAD route. Other variations on routes are possible.

> System Maintenance

All routes ultimately result in placing a new system into operation. System maintenance is intended to guide projects through the operation and support stage of their life cycle—which could last decades! Figure 3-14 places system maintenance into perspective. System maintenance in *FAST* is not really a unique route. As illustrated in the figure, it is merely a smaller-scale version of the same *FAST* process (or route) that was used to originally develop the system. The figure demonstrates that the starting point for system maintenance depends on the problem to be solved. We call your attention to the following numbered bullets in the figure:

❶ Maintenance and reengineering projects are triggered by some combination of user and technical feedback. Such feedback may identify new problems, opportunities, or directives.

❷ The maintenance project is initiated by a SYSTEM CHANGE REQUEST that indicates the problems, opportunities, or directives.

❸ The simplest fixes are SOFTWARE BUGS (errors). Such a project typically jumps right into a RECONSTRUCTION AND RETESTING phase and is solved relatively quickly.

❹ Sometimes a DESIGN FLAW in the system becomes apparent after implementation. For example, users may frequently make the same mistake due to a confusing screen design. For this type of maintenance project, the PHYSICAL DESIGN AND INTEGRATION phase would need to be revisited, followed of course by the construction and delivery phases.

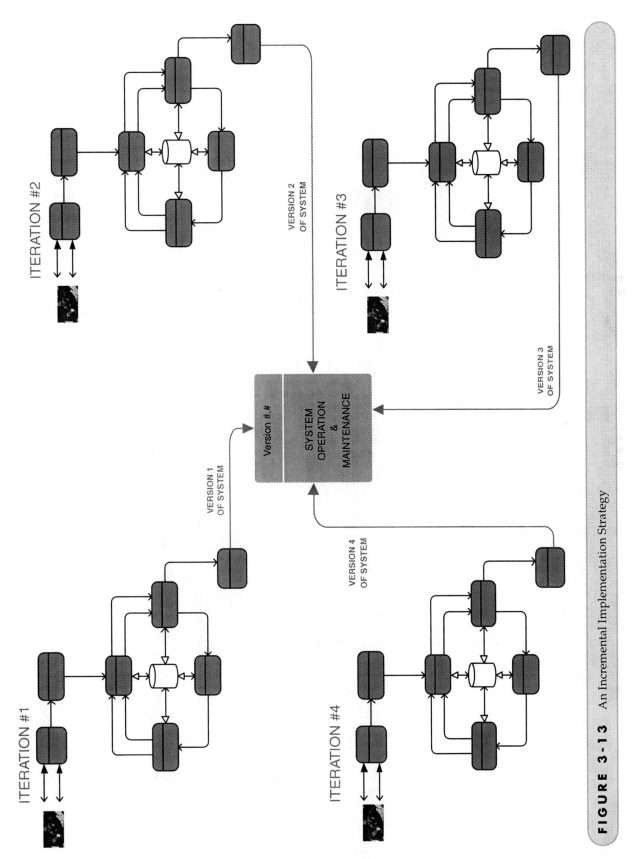

FIGURE 3-13 An Incremental Implementation Strategy

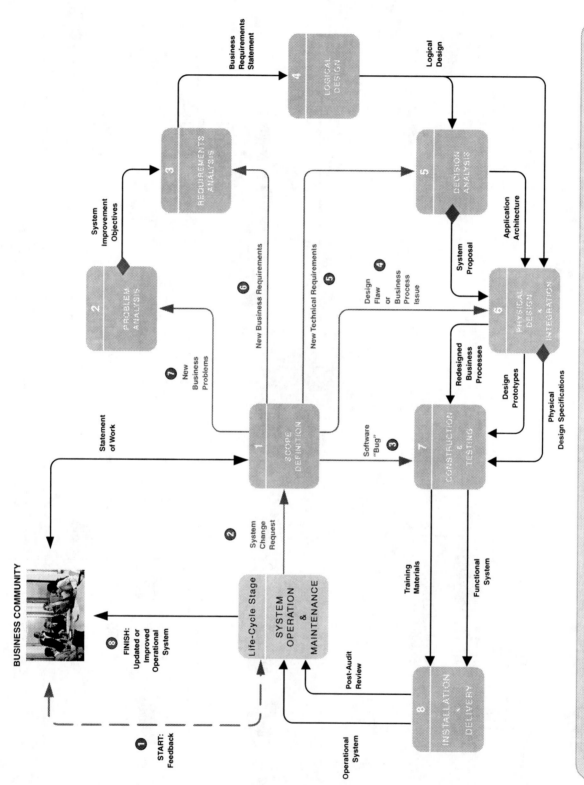

FIGURE 3-14 A System Maintenance Perspective

In some cases a BUSINESS PROCESS ISSUE may become apparent. In this case, only the business process needs to be redesigned.

❺ On occasion, NEW TECHNICAL REQUIREMENTS might dictate a change. For example, an organization may standardize on the newest version of a particular database management system such as *SQL Server* or *Oracle*. For this type of project, the DECISION ANALYSIS phase may need to be revisited to first determine the risk and feasibility of converting the existing, operational database to the new version. As appropriate, such a project would subsequently proceed to the physical design, construction, and delivery phases as necessary.

❻ Businesses constantly change; therefore, business requirements for a system also change. One of the most common triggers for a reengineering project is a NEW (or revised) BUSINESS REQUIREMENT. Given the requirement, the REQUIREMENTS ANALYSIS phase must be revisited with a focus on the impact of the new requirement on the existing system. Based on requirements analysis, the project would then proceed to the logical design, decision analysis, physical design, construction, and delivery phases.

Time out! By now, you've noticed that maintenance and reengineering projects initiate in different phases of the basic methodology. You might be concerned that repeating these phases would require excessive time and effort. Keep in mind, however, that the scope of maintenance and reengineering projects is much, much smaller than the original project that created the operational system. Thus, the work required in each phase is much less than you might have guessed.

❼ Again, as businesses change, significant NEW BUSINESS PROBLEMS, opportunities, and constraints can be encountered. In this type of project, work begins with the PROBLEM ANALYSIS phase and proceeds as necessary to the subsequent phases.

❽ In all cases, the final result of any type of maintenance or reengineering project is an updated operational business system that delivers improved value to the system users and owners. Updates may include revised programs, databases, interfaces, or business processes.

As described earlier in the chapter, we expect all systems to eventually reach entropy. The business and/or technical problems and requirements have become so troublesome as to warrant "starting over."

That completes our introduction to the systems development methodology and routes. Before we end this chapter, we should introduce the role of automated tools that support systems development.

Automated Tools and Technology

You may be familiar with the old fable of the cobbler (shoemaker) whose own children had no shoes. That situation is not unlike the one faced by some systems developers. For years we've been applying information technology to solve our users' business problems; however, we've sometimes been slow to apply that same technology to our own problem—developing information systems. In the not-too-distant past, the principal tools of the systems analyst were paper, pencil, and flowchart template.

Today, entire suites of automated tools have been developed, marketed, and installed to assist systems developers. While system development methodologies do not always require automated tools, most methodologies do benefit from such technology. Some of the most commonly cited benefits include:

• Improved productivity—through automation of tasks.
• Improved quality—because automated tools check for completeness, consistency, and contradictions.
• Better and more consistent documentation—because the tools make it easier to create and assemble consistent, high-quality documentation.

- Reduced lifetime maintenance—because of the aforementioned system quality improvements combined with better documentation.
- Methodologies that really work—through rule enforcement and built-in expertise.

Chances are that your future employer is using or will be using this technology to develop systems. We will demonstrate the use of various automated tools throughout this textbook. There are three classes of automated tools for developers:

- Computer-aided systems modeling.
- Application development environments.
- Project and process managers.

Let's briefly examine each of these classes of automated tools.

> Computer-Assisted Systems Engineering

Systems developers have long aspired to transform information systems and software development into engineering-like disciplines. The terms *systems engineering* and *software engineering* are based on a vision that systems and software development can and should be performed with engineering-like precision and rigor. Such precision and rigor are consistent with the model-driven approach to systems development. To help systems analysts better perform system modeling, the industry developed automated tools called **computer-assisted software engineering (CASE)** tools. Think of CASE technology as software that is used to design and implement other software. This is very similar to the computer-aided design (CAD) technology used by most contemporary engineers to design products such as vehicles, structures, machines, and so forth. Representative modeling products are listed in the margin. Most modeling products run on personal computers, as depicted in Figure 3-15.

CASE Repositories   At the center of any true CASE tool's architecture is a developer's database called a **CASE repository.** The repository concept was introduced earlier (see Figure 3-7).

Around the CASE repository is a collection of tools, or facilities, for creating system models and documentation.

CASE Facilities   To use the repository, the CASE tools provide some combination of the following facilities, illustrated in Figure 3-16:

- *Diagramming tools* are used to draw the system models required or recommended in most system development methodologies. Usually, the shapes on one system model can be linked to other system models and to detailed descriptions (see next item below).
- *Dictionary tools* are used to record, delete, edit, and output detailed documentation and specifications. The descriptions can be associated with shapes appearing on system models that were drawn with the diagramming tools.
- *Design tools* can be used to develop mock-ups of system components such as inputs and outputs. These inputs and outputs can be associated with both the aforementioned system models and the descriptions.
- *Quality management tools* analyze system models, descriptions and specifications, and designs for completeness, consistency, and conformance to accepted rules of the methodologies.
- *Documentation tools* are used to assemble, organize, and report on system models, descriptions and specifications, and prototypes that can be reviewed by system owners, users, designers, and builders.
- *Design and code generator tools* automatically generate database designs and application programs or significant portions of those programs.
- *Testing tools* simulate transactions and data traffic, measure performance, and provide configuration management of test plans and test scripts.

Forward and Reverse Engineering   As previous stated, CASE technology automates system modeling. Today's CASE tools provide two distinct ways to develop system models—**forward engineering** and **reverse engineering.** Think of reverse

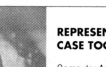

REPRESENTATIVE CASE TOOLS

Computer Associates' *Erwin*
Oracle's *Designer 2000*
Popkin's *System Architect*
Rational *ROSE*
Visible Systems' *Visible Analyst*

---

computer-assisted software engineering (CASE) the use of automated software tools that support the drawing and analysis of system models and associated specifications. Some CASE tools also provide prototyping and code generation capabilities.

CASE repository a system developers' database where developers can store system models, detailed descriptions and specifications, and other products of systems development. Synonyms data include data *dictionary* and *encyclopedia*.

---

forward engineering a CASE tool capability that can generate initial software or database code directly from system models.

---

reverse engineering a CASE tool capability that can automatically generate initial system models from software or database code.

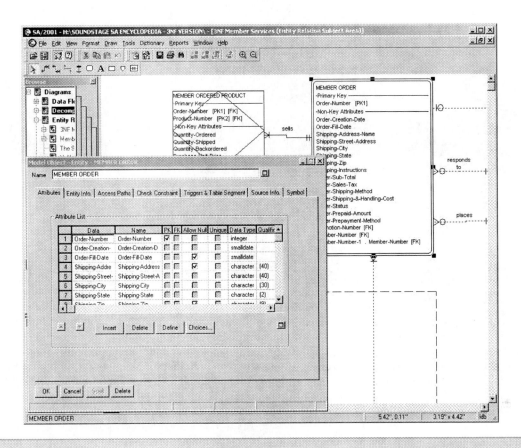

FIGURE 3-15   Screen Capture of *System Architect* CASE Tool

engineering as allowing you to generate a flowchart from an existing program and of forward engineering as allowing you to generate a program directly from a flowchart. CASE tools that allow for bidirectional, forward, and reverse engineering are said to provide for "round-trip engineering." For example, you reverse engineer a poorly designed system into a system model, edit and improve that model, and then forward engineer the new model into an improved system.

> Application Development Environments

The emphasis on speed and quality in software development has resulted in RAD approaches. The potential for RAD has been amplified by the transformation of programming language compilers into complete **application development environments (ADEs).** ADEs make programming simpler and more efficient. Indeed, most programming language compilers are now integrated into an ADE. Examples of ADEs (and the programming languages they support, where applicable) are listed in the margin.

Application development environments provide a number of productivity and quality management facilities. The ADE vendor provides some of these facilities. Third-party vendors provide many other facilities that can integrate into the ADE.

- *Programming languages* or *interpreters* are the heart of an ADE. Powerful debugging features and assistance are usually provided to help programmers quickly identify and solve programming problems.
- *Interface construction tools* help programmers quickly build the user interfaces using a component library.

REPRESENTATIVE ADEs

IBM's *Websphere (Java)*
Borland's *J Builder (Java)*
Macromedia's *Cold Fusion*
Microsoft's *Visual Studio.NET (VB .NET, C#, C++.NET)*
Oracle's *Developer*
Sybase's *Powerbuilder*

application development environment (ADE) an integrated software development tool that provides all the facilities necessary to develop new application software with maximum speed and quality. A common synonym is *integrated development environment (IDE)*.

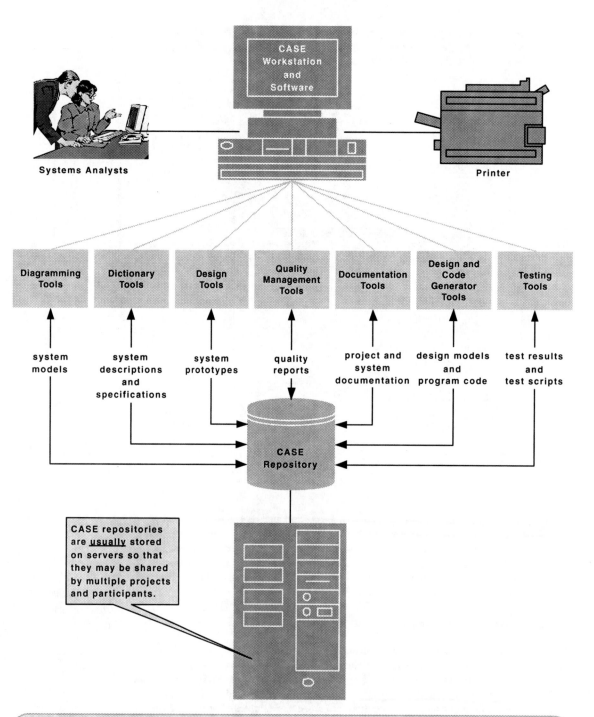

FIGURE 3-16 CASE Tool Architecture

- *Middleware* is software that helps programmers integrate the software being developed with various databases and computer networks.
- *Testing tools* are used to build and execute test scripts that can consistently and thoroughly test software.
- *Version control* tools help multiple programmer teams manage multiple versions of a program, both during development and after implementation.
- *Help authoring tools* are used to write online help systems, user manuals, and online training.
- *Repository links* permit the ADE to integrate with CASE tool products as well as other ADEs and development tools.

> Process and Project Managers

A third class of automated tools helps us manage the system development methodology and projects that use the methodology. While CASE tools and ADEs are intended to support analysis, design, and construction of new information systems and software, **process manager application** and **project manager application** tools are intended to support cross life-cycle activities. Microsoft's *Project* and Niku's *Open Workbench* and *Project Manager* are examples of automated project management tools. Because process and project management is the subject of the next chapter, you'll learn more about these automated tools in that chapter.

process manager application an automated tool that helps to document and manage a methodology and routes, its deliverables, and quality management standards. An emerging synonym is *methodware*.

project manager application an automated tool that helps to plan system development activities (preferably using the approved methodology), estimate and assign resources (including people and costs), schedule activities and resources, monitor progress against schedule and budget, control and modify schedule and resources, and report project progress.

This chapter, along with the first two, completes the minimum context for studying systems analysis and design. We have described that context in terms of the three Ps—the participants (the stakeholders; Chapter 1), the product (the information system; Chapter 2), and the process (the system development; Chapter 3). Armed with this understanding, you are now ready to study systems analysis and/or design methods.

For many of you, Chapter 4, "Project Management," will provide a more complete context for studying systems analysis and design. It builds on Chapter 3 by emphasizing a variety of management issues related to the system development process. These include methodology management, resource management, management of expectations, change management, and others.

For those of you who skip the project and process management chapter, your next assignment will depend on whether your goal is:

- A comprehensive survey of systems development—We recommend you continue your sequential path to Chapter 5, "Systems Analysis." In that chapter you will study in greater depth the scope definition, problem analysis, requirements analysis, and logical design phases that were introduced in Chapter 3.
- The study of systems analysis techniques—Again, we recommend you continue your sequential path to Chapter 5, "Systems Analysis." Chapter 5 will provide a context for subsequently studying the tools and techniques of systems analysis.
- The study of systems design techniques—You might still want to quickly skim or review Chapter 5, "Systems Analysis," for context. Then continue your detailed study in Chapter 12, "System Design." In that chapter, you will learn more about the process and strategies for system design and construction of information systems.

Learning Roadmap

Summary

1. A systems development process is a set of activities, methods, best practices, deliverables, and automated tools that stakeholders use to develop and continuously improve information systems and software.

2. The Capability Maturity Model (CMM) is a framework for assessing the maturity level of an organization's information systems development and management processes and products. It defines the need for a system development process.

3. A system life cycle divides the life of an information system into two stages, *systems development* and *systems operation and maintenance*.

4. A systems development methodology is a process for the system development stage. It defines a set of activities, methods, best practices, deliverables, and automated tools that systems developers and project managers are to use to develop and maintain information systems and software.

5. The following principles should underlie all systems development methodologies:

    a. Get the system users involved.
    b. Use a problem-solving approach.
    c. Establish phases and activities.
    d. Document throughout development.
    e. Establish standards.
    f. Manage the process and projects.
    g. Justify information systems as capital investments.
    h. Don't be afraid to cancel or revise scope.
    i. Divide and conquer.
    j. Design systems for growth and change.

6. System development projects are triggered by problems, opportunities, and directives:

    a. Problems are undesirable situations that prevent the organization from fully achieving its purpose, goals, and/or objectives.
    b. Opportunities are chances to improve the organization even in the absence of specific problems.
    c. Directives are new requirements that are imposed by management, government, or some external influence.

7. Wetherbe's PIECES framework is useful for categorizing problems, opportunities, and directives. The letters of the PIECES acronym correspond to Performance, Information, Economics, Control, Efficiency, and Service.

8. Traditional, basic systems development phases include:

    a. Scope definition
    b. Problem analysis
    c. Requirements analysis
    d. Logical design
    e. Decision analysis
    f. Physical design and integration
    g. Construction and testing
    h. Installation and delivery

9. Cross life-cycle activities are activities that overlap many or all phases of the methodology. They may include:

    a. Fact-finding, the formal process of using research, interviews, meetings, questionnaires, sampling, and other techniques to collect information about systems, requirements, and preferences.
    b. Documentation, the activity of recording facts and specifications for a system for current and future reference. Documentation is frequently stored in a repository, a database where systems developers store all documentation, knowledge, and products for one or more information systems or projects.
    c. Presentation, the activity of communicating findings, recommendations, and documentation for review by interested users and managers. Presentations may be either written or verbal.
    d. Feasibility analysis, the activity by which feasibility, a measure of how beneficial the development of an information system would be to an organization, is measured and assessed.
    e. Process management, the ongoing activity that documents, manages the use of, and improves an organization's chosen methodology (the "process") for systems development.
    f. Project management, the activity of defining, planning, directing, monitoring, and controlling a project to develop an acceptable system within the allotted time and budget.

10. There are different routes through the basic systems development phases. An appropriate route is selected during the scope definition phase. Typical routes include:

    a. Model-driven development strategies, which emphasize the drawing of diagrams to help visualize and analyze problems, define business requirements, and design information systems. Alternative model-driven strategies include:

   i) Process modeling
  ii) Data modeling
 iii) Object modeling

b. Rapid application development (RAD) strategies, which emphasize extensive user involvement in the rapid and evolutionary construction of working prototypes of a system to accelerate the system development process.

c. Commercial application package implementation strategies, which focus on the purchase and integration of a software package or solution to support one or more business functions and information systems.

d. System maintenance, which occurs after a system is implemented and lasts throughout the system's lifetime. Essentially, system maintenance executes a smaller-scale version of the development process with different starting points depending on the type of problem to be solved.

11. Automated tools support all systems development phases:

a. Computer-aided systems engineering (CASE) tools are software programs that automate or support the drawing and analysis of system models and provide for the translation of system models into application programs.

   i) A CASE repository is a system developers' database. It is a place where developers can store system models, detailed descriptions and specifications, and other products of systems development.

  ii) Forward engineering requires that the systems analyst draw system models, either from scratch or from templates. The resulting models are subsequently transformed into program code.

 iii) Reverse engineering allows a CASE tool to read existing program code and transform that code into a representative system model that can be edited and refined by the systems analyst.

b. Application development environments (ADEs) are integrated software development tools that provide all the facilities necessary to develop new application software with maximum speed and quality.

c. Process management tools help us document and manage a methodology and routes, its deliverables, and quality management standards.

d. Project management tools help us plan system development activities (preferably using the approved methodology), estimate and assign resources (including people and costs), schedule activities and resources, monitor progress against schedule and budget, control and modify schedule and resources, and report project progress.

Review Questions

1. Explain why having a standardized system development process is important to an organization.
2. How are system life cycle and system development methodology related?
3. What are the 10 underlying principles for systems development?
4. Why is documentation important throughout the development process?
5. Why are process management and project management necessary?
6. What is risk management? Why is it necessary?
7. Which stakeholders initiate most projects? What is the impetus for most projects?
8. Who are the main participants in the scope definition? What are their goals in the scope definition?
9. What are the three most important deliverables in scope definition?
10. Who are the main participants in the requirements analysis phase? Why are they the main participants?
11. What feasibility analyses are made in the decision analysis?
12. What is model-driven development?
13. Why is model-driven development popular?
14. What is rapid application development (RAD)?
15. What benefits can RAD bring to the system development process?
16. What is computer-assisted software engineering (CASE)? List some examples of CASE.

Problems and Exercises

1. The Capability Maturity Model (CMM) was developed by the Software Engineering Institute at Carnegie Mellon, and is widely used by both the private and public sectors. What is the purpose of the CMM framework and how does it achieve this?

2. List the five maturity levels, and briefly describe each of them.

3. Table 3-1 in the textbook illustrates the difference in a typical project's duration, person-months, quality, and cost, depending upon whether an organization's system development process is at CMM level 1, 2, or 3. Between which two CMM levels does an organization gain the greatest benefit in terms of percentage of improvement? What do you think is the reason for this?

4. *Systems development methodology* and *system life cycle* are two terms that are frequently used and just as frequently misused. What is the difference between the two terms?

5. Describe how using a systems development methodology is in line with CMM goals and can help an organization increase its maturity level.

6. A number of underlying principles are common to all systems development methodologies. Identify these underlying principles and explain them.

7. The PIECES framework was developed by James Wetherbe as a means to classify problems. Identify the categories, then categorize the following problems using the PIECES framework:

    a. Duplicate data is stored throughout the system.
    b. There is a need to port an existing application to PDA devices.
    c. Quarterly sales reports need to be generated automatically.
    d. Employees can gain access to confidential portions of the personnel system.
    e. User interfaces for the inventory system are difficult and confusing, resulting in a high frequency of incorrect orders.

8. Each phase of a project includes specific deliverables that must be produced and delivered to the next phase. Using the textbook's hypothetical *FAST* methodology, what are the deliverables for the requirements analysis, logical design, and physical design/integration phases?

9. Scope definition is the first phase of the *FAST* methodology, and it is either the first phase or part of the first phase of most methodologies. What triggers the scope phase, which stakeholders are involved in this phase, what two essential questions need to be answered, and what three important deliverables come out of this phase?

10. The requirements analysis phase is an essential part of a system development methodology. According to the *FAST* methodology, which stakeholders typically participate in this phase? What is the primary focus of requirements analysis? What is *not* the focus? How should each proposed requirement be evaluated? What critical error must be avoided?

11. In the *FAST* methodology, as well as most system methodologies, system owners and system designers do not participate in the requirements analysis phase. What do you think the reason is for this?

12. What is the essential purpose of the logical design phase? How does it accomplish this? How are technological solutions incorporated in this phase? What are some common synonyms for this phase used by other methodologies? Who are the typical participants in this phase? What is agile modeling and what is its purpose? What are the deliverables coming out of this phase? In terms of the development team, what critical transition takes place by the end of this phase?

13. What is the essential purpose of the physical design phase? Who must be involved in this phase, and who may be involved? What are the two philosophies of physical design on the different ends of the continuum, and how are they different? Is this a likely phase in which a project might be canceled? With what other phase is there likely to be overlap, and what do you think is the reason for this?

14. A customer has engaged your software development company to develop a new order-processing system. However, the time frames are very tight and inflexible for delivery of at least the basic part of the new system. Further, user requirements are sketchy and unclear. What are two system development strategies that might be advantageous to use in this engagement?

15. What is the potential downside to using the strategies described in the preceding question?

Projects and Research

1. The Software Engineering Institute (SEI) at Carnegie Mellon University has developed a series of related Capability Maturity Models (CMMs). You can read about these different CMM products at SEI's Web site (http://www.sei.cmu.edu).

   a. Identify the current CMM products being maintained or developed by SEI.
   b. What are their differences and similarities?
   c. If you were to rate your organization, or an organization with which you are familiar, using the CMM described in the textbook, at which level would it be? Why?
   d. What steps would you recommend that your organization take in order to advance to the next CMM level?
   e. Do you feel that the time, cost, and resources to advance to the next level would be worth the perceived benefits for your organization? Why or why not?

2. You are a new project manager and have been assigned responsibility for an enterprise information systems project that touches every division in your organization. The chief executive officer stated at project initiation that successfully implementing this project was the number 1 priority of your organization. The project is in midst of the requirements analysis phase. While it is on schedule, you notice that attendance of the system users and owners at meetings on requirements has been dropping. A more experienced project manager has told you not to worry, that this is normal. Should you be concerned?

3. There are many different systems development methodologies in use, each with its own terminology, and number and scope of phases. Search the Web for information on two or three of these other systems development methodologies, then do the following:

   a. Note the systems development methodologies that you found. When, by whom, and why were they developed?
   b. What phases and terminology do they employ?
   c. Draw a matrix comparing their phases to the textbook's *FAST* methodology.
   d. What significant differences did you find?
   e. Do you see any advantages or disadvantages in any of the methodologies that you found compared to the *FAST* methodology?

4. The *PIECES* framework, which was developed by James Wetherbe and is described in the textbook,

is intended to be a framework for classifying problems, opportunities, and directives.

   Contact one of the systems analysts for your organization, your school, and/or another organization. Ask them about the information systems used in their organization and to describe what the problems are in general terms. Select three of these systems:

   a. Describe the systems you selected, their problems, and the organizations that use them.
   b. Use the *PIECES* framework in the textbook to categorize each system's problems.
   c. Describe the *PIECES* category or categories you found for each problem. Did each problem generally have one or more categories associated with it?
   d. For the systems used by different organizations, what commonality did you find in the categories of problems? If you found a great deal of commonality of categories, do you think this is significant or just coincidental?
   e. Where in the systems development life cycle do you think the PIECES framework would be of the greatest value?

5. Computer-assisted software engineering (CASE) tools can significantly help developers improve productivity, quality, and documentation. Conduct an informal survey of about a dozen information technology departments regarding whether they use CASE tools, and if so, what type. Also, find out how long they have been using the CASE tools and whether they are used for all or just some projects. Add any other questions you may find meaningful. Try to split your survey between public and private sector agencies, and/or large and small organizations.

   a. What types of organizations did you survey?
   b. What did you ask?
   c. What were the results?
   d. Given the limited and informal nature of this survey, were you able to find any patterns or trends?
   e. Based upon your readings and your survey, what are your feelings regarding the use of CASE tools?

6. Projects at times are canceled or abandoned, sometime by choice, sometimes not. Research the Web for articles on project abandonment strategies, and select two of them.

a. What articles did you select?

b. What are their central themes, findings, and recommendations regarding project abandonment?

c. Compare and contrast their findings and their recommendations. Which strategy would you choose, if any?

d. Do you think that abandoning a project is always avoidable and/or always represents a failure?

Minicases

1. Interview at least two project managers. What are their experiences with *scope creep?*

2. George is the CEO of a major corporation that has been trying to develop a program that captures the keystrokes of employees on their computers. The project is currently $100,000 over budget and behind schedule and will require at least another $50,000 and six months to complete. The CEO wants to continue the project because so much has already been invested in it. What is your recommendation? Why?

3. Beatrice is an excellent manager—she is very capable of managing the bureaucratic process and following the business rules in her corporation.

She is a "by the book" person who can always be counted on to do things "right." Will Beatrice make a good *project manager?* Why or why not?

4. A company is trying to decide between using an off-the-shelf program or developing a custom program for inventory management. The off-the-shelf product is less expensive than the custom solution and still has most of the needed functionality. The CEO believes that the missing capability can be addressed through tweaking the program once it is purchased. As the CIO of the company, what are your concerns and recommendations to the CEO?

Team and Individual Exercises

1. (Team) Hold team meetings using different communications mediums. Examples: phone, e-mail, virtual environment. What did you notice about the impact of the technology on the meeting? Was the productivity of the meetings the same for each medium? How did the team feel about the impact of the technologies on the team relationships?

2. (Individual) The analysis and design of an information system, done well, often eliminates jobs in a company. Economic theory strongly supports the

creation of new jobs when this happens, but generally there is a time lag between the structural loss of jobs and the creation of new jobs. How do you feel about that?

3. (Team or Individual) Visit a neonatal intensive care unit at a highly regarded medical center (such as UC San Francisco). Write a short paper on your thoughts of the involved technology and the impact it has on people's lives. At the professor's discretion, share with the class.

Suggested Readings

Ambler, Scott. *Agile Modeling: Effective Practices for eXtreme Programming and the Unified Process.* New York: John Wiley & Sons, 2002. This is the definitive book on agile methods and modeling.

Application Development Trends (monthly periodical). Framingham, MA: Software Productivity Group, Inc. This is our favorite periodical for keeping up with the latest trends in methodology and automated tools. Each month features several articles on different topics and products.

DeMarco, Tom. *Structured Analysis and System Specification.* Englewood Cliffs, NJ: Prentice Hall, 1978. This is the classic book on structured systems analysis, a process-centered, model-driven methodology.

Gane, Chris. *Rapid Systems Development.* Englewood Cliffs, NJ: Prentice Hall, 1989. This book presents a nice overview of RAD that combines model-driven development and prototyping in the correct balance.

Gildersleeve, Thomas. *Successful Data Processing Systems Analysis,* 2nd ed. Englewood Cliffs, NJ: Prentice Hall,

1985. We are indebted to Gildersleeve for the creeping commitment approach. The classics never become obsolete.

Jacobson, Ivar; Grady Booch; and James Rumbaugh. *The Unified Software Development Process.* Reading, MA: Addison-Wesley, 1999. The Rational Unified Process is a currently popular example of a model-driven, object-oriented methodology.

McConnell, Steve. *Rapid Development.* Redmond, WA: Microsoft Press, 1996. Chapter 7 of this excellent reference book provides what may be the definitive summary of system development life cycle and methodology variations that we call "routes" in our book.

Orr, Ken. *The One Minute Methodology.* New York: Dorsett House, 1990. Must reading for those interested in exploring the need for methodology. This very short book can be read in one sitting. It follows the satirical story of an analyst's quest for the development silver bullet, "the one minute methodology."

Paulk, Mark C.; Charles V. Weber; Bill Curtis; and Mary Beth Chrissis. *The Capability Maturity Model: Guidelines for Improving the Software Process.* Reading, MA: Addison-Wesley, 1995. This book fully describes version 1.1 of the Capability Maturity Model. Note that version 2.0 was under development at the time we were writing this chapter.

Wetherbe, James. *Systems Analysis and Design: Best Practices,* 4th ed. St. Paul, MN: West, 1994. We are indebted to Wetherbe for the PIECES framework.

5

Systems Analysis

Chapter Preview and Objectives

In this chapter you will learn more about the systems analysis phases in a systems development project—namely, the scope definition, problem analysis, requirements analysis, and decision analysis phases. The first three phases are collectively referred to as *systems analysis*. The latter phase provides transition between systems analysis and systems design. You will know that you understand the process of systems analysis when you can:

▌ Define systems analysis and relate the term to the scope definition, problem analysis, requirements analysis, logical design, and decision analysis phases of this book's systems development methodology.

▌ Describe a number of systems analysis approaches for solving business system problems.

▌ Describe the scope definition, problem analysis, requirements analysis, logical design, and decision analysis phases in terms of your information system building blocks.

▌ Describe the scope definition, problem analysis, requirements analysis, logical design, and decision analysis phases in terms of purpose, participants, inputs, outputs, techniques, and steps.

▌ Identify the chapters in this textbook that can help you learn specific systems analysis tools and techniques.

NOTE: Although some of the tools and techniques of systems analysis are previewed in this chapter, it is *not* the intent of this chapter to teach those tools and techniques. This chapter teaches only the *process* of systems analysis. The tools and techniques will be taught in the subsequent six chapters.

Introduction

Bob Martinez remembers learning in college that systems analysis defines what an information system needs to do while system design defines how it needs to do it. At the time, it sounded like a simple two-step process. Now, as he begins working on the SoundStage Member Services system project, he sees that there are multiple phases and several steps within systems analysis and system design.

The SoundStage project is at the beginning of systems analysis, in what Sandra, his boss, calls the scope definition phase. After that they'll do problem analysis, requirements analysis, and decision analysis. It sounds like a lot of work just to understand *what* the system needs to do. But this is a complicated system. As Sandra says, would you build a house without a good set of plans?

What Is Systems Analysis?

systems analysis a problem-solving technique that decomposes a system into its component pieces for the purpose of studying how well those component parts work and interact to accomplish their purpose.

systems design a complementary problem-solving technique (to systems analysis) that reassembles a system's component pieces back into a complete system—hopefully, an improved system. This may involve adding, deleting, and changing pieces relative to the original system.

information systems analysis those development phases in an information systems development project that primarily focus on the business problem and requirements, independent of any technology that can or will be used to implement a solution to that problem.

repository a location (or set of locations) where systems analysts, systems designers, and system builders keep all of the documentation associated with one or more systems or projects.

In Chapter 3 you learned about the systems development process. In that chapter we purposefully limited our discussion to only briefly examining each phase. In this chapter, we take a much closer look at those phases that are collectively referred to as **systems analysis.** Formally defined in the margin, systems analysis is the study of a system and its components. It is a prerequisite to **systems design,** the specification of a new and improved system. This chapter will focus on systems analysis. Chapter 12 will do the same for systems design.

Moving from this classic definition of systems analysis to something a bit more contemporary, we see that *systems analysis* is a term that collectively describes the early phases of systems development. Figure 5-1 uses color to identify the systems analysis phases in the context of the full classic route for our *FAST* methodology (from Chapter 3). There has never been a universally accepted definition of systems analysis. In fact, there has never been universal agreement on when information systems analysis ends and when information systems design begins. For the purpose of this book, **information systems analysis** emphasizes *business* issues, *not* technical or implementation concerns.

Systems analysis is driven by the business concerns of SYSTEM OWNERS and SYSTEM USERS. Hence, it addresses the KNOWLEDGE, PROCESS, and COMMUNICATIONS building blocks from SYSTEM OWNERS' and SYSTEM USERS' perspectives. The SYSTEMS ANALYSTS serve as facilitators of systems analysis. This context is illustrated in the chapter home page that preceded the objectives for this chapter.

The documentation and deliverables produced by systems analysis tasks are typically stored in a repository. A repository may be created for a single project or shared by all projects and systems. A repository is normally implemented as some combination of the following:

- A network directory of word processing, spreadsheet, and other computer-generated files that contain project correspondence, reports, and data.
- One or more CASE tool dictionaries or encyclopedias (as discussed in Chapter 3).
- Printed documentation (such as that stored in binders and system libraries).
- An *intranet* Web site interface to the above components (useful for communication).

Hereafter, we will refer to these components collectively as the **repository.**

This chapter examines each of our five systems analysis phases in greater detail. But first, let's examine some overall strategies for systems analysis.

FIGURE 5-1 The Context of Systems Analysis

Systems Analysis Approaches

Fundamentally, systems analysis is about *problem solving.* There are many approaches to problem solving; therefore, it shouldn't surprise you that there are many approaches to systems analysis. These approaches are often viewed as *competing* alternatives. In reality, certain combinations can and should actually complement one another. This was characterized in Chapter 3 as *agile methods.* Let's briefly examine the varied approaches.

NOTE: The intent here is to develop a high-level understanding only. Subsequent chapters in this unit will actually teach you the underlying techniques.

> Model-Driven Analysis Approaches

Structured analysis, information engineering, and object-oriented analysis are examples of **model-driven analysis.** Model-driven analysis uses pictures to communicate

model-driven analysis a problem-solving approach that emphasizes the drawing of pictorial system models to document and validate existing and/or proposed systems. Ultimately, the system model becomes the blueprint for designing and constructing an improved system.

model a representation of either reality or vision. Since "a picture is worth a thousand words," most models use pictures to represent the reality or vision.

business problems, requirements, and solutions. Examples of **models** with which you may already be familiar include flowcharts, structure or hierarchy charts, and organization charts.

Today, model-driven approaches are almost always enhanced by the use of automated tools. Some analysts draw system models with general-purpose graphics software such as Microsoft *Visio*. Other analysts and organizations require the use of repository-based CASE or modeling tools such as *System Architect, Visible Analyst,* or *Rational ROSE*. CASE tools offer the advantage of consistency and completeness analysis as well as rule-based error checking.

Model-driven analysis approaches are featured in the model-driven methodologies and routes that were introduced in Chapter 3. Let's briefly examine today's three most popular model-driven analysis approaches.

Traditional Approaches Various traditional approaches to system analysis and design were developed beginning in the 1970s. One of the first formal approaches, which is still widely used today, is *structured analysis*. **Structured analysis** focuses on the flow of data through business and software processes. It is said to be *process-centered*. By process-centered, we mean that the emphasis is on the PROCESS building bocks in your information system framework.

structured analysis a model-driven, PROCESS-centered technique used to either analyze an existing system or define business requirements for a new system, or both. The models are pictures that illustrate the system's component pieces: processes and their associated inputs, outputs, and files.

One of the key tools used to model processes is the *data flow diagram* (Figure 5-2), which depicts the existing and/or proposed processes in a system along with their inputs, outputs, and data. The models show the flow of data between and through processes and show the places where data is stored. Ultimately these process models serve as blueprints for business processes to be implemented and software to be purchased or constructed.

FIGURE 5-2

A Simple Process Model (Also Called a Data Flow Diagram)

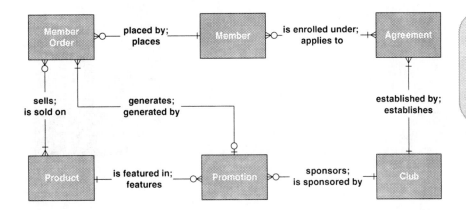

FIGURE 5-3

A Simple Data Model (Also Called an Entity Relationship Diagram)

The practice of structured analysis for software design has greatly diminished in favor of object-oriented methods. However, process modeling is enjoying something of a revival thanks to the renewed emphasis on business process redesign, which is discussed later in this chapter.

Another traditional approach, called **information engineering (IE),** focuses on the structure of stored data in a system rather than on processes. Thus, it was said to be *data-centered,* emphasizing the analysis of KNOWLEDGE (or data) requirements. The key tool to model data requirements is the entity relationship diagram (Figure 5-3). Entity relationship diagrams are still widely used in designing relational databases.

Originally, information engineering was seen as a competing approach to structured analysis. But over time many people made them as complementary: using data flow diagrams to model a system's processes and entity relationship diagrams to model a system's data.

Object-Oriented Approach   Traditional approaches deliberately separated the concerns of KNOWLEDGE (data) from those of PROCESSES. Although most systems analysis methods attempted to synchronize data and process models, the attempt did not always work well in practice. **Object** technologies have since emerged to eliminate this artificial separation of data and processes. The **object-oriented approach** views information systems not as data and processes but as a collection of objects that encapsulate data and processes. Objects can contain data attributes. However, the only way to create, read, update, or delete an object's data is through one of its embedded processes (called methods). Object-oriented programming languages, such as *Java, C++,* and the *.NET* languages, are becoming increasingly popular.

The object-oriented approach has a complete suite of modeling tools known as the Unified Modeling Language (UML). One of the UML diagrams, an object class diagram, is shown in Figure 5-4. Some of the UML tools have gained acceptance for systems projects even when the information system will not be implemented with object-oriented technologies.

> Accelerated Systems Analysis Approaches

Discovery prototyping and rapid architected development are examples of accelerated systems analysis approaches that emphasize the construction of prototypes to more rapidly identify business and user requirements for a new system. Most such approaches derive from some variation on the construction of **prototypes,** working but incomplete samples of a desired system. Prototypes cater to the "I'll know what I want when I see it" way of thinking that is characteristic of many users and managers. By "incomplete," we mean that a prototype will not include the error checking, input data validation, security, and processing completeness of a finished application. Nor will it be as polished or offer the user help as in a final system. But because it can be

information engineering (IE) a model-driven and DATA-centered, but PROCESS-sensitive, technique for planning, analyzing, and designing information systems. IE models are pictures that illustrate and synchronize the system's data and processes.

object the encapsulation of the data (called *properties*) that describes a discrete person, object, place, event, or thing, with all of the processes (called *methods*) that are allowed to use or update the data and properties. The only way to access or update the object's data is to use the object's predefined processes.

object-oriented approach a model-driven technique that integrates data and process concerns into constructs called *objects*. Object models are pictures that illustrate the system's objects from various perspectives, such as the structure, behavior, and interactions of the objects.

prototype a small-scale, incomplete, but working sample of a desired system.

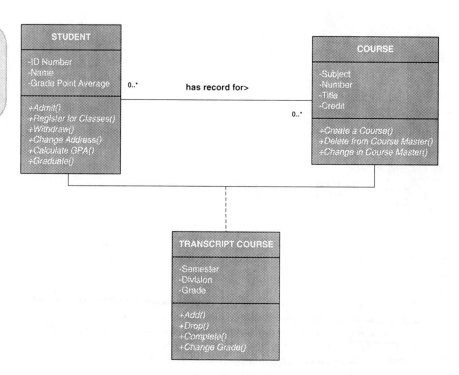

FIGURE 5-4

An Object Model (Using the Unified Modeling Language Standard)

developed quickly, it can quickly identify the most crucial of business-level requirements. Sometimes, prototypes can evolve into the actual, completed information systems and applications.

In a sense, accelerated analysis approaches place much emphasis on the COMMUNICATIONS building blocks in your information system framework by constructing sample forms and reports. At the same time, the software tools used to build prototypes also address the DATA and PROCESS building blocks.

These accelerated approaches are common in the rapid application development (RAD) methodologies and routes that were introduced in Chapter 3. RAD approaches require automated tools. While some repository-based CASE tools include very simple RAD facilities, most analysts use true RAD programming environments such as Sybase *Powerbuilder,* Microsoft *Access,* Microsoft *Visual Basic .NET,* or IBM *Websphere Studio for Application Development (Java-*based).

Let's briefly examine two popular accelerated analysis approaches.

discovery prototyping a technique used to identify the users' business requirements by having them react to a quick-and-dirty implementation of those requirements.

Discovery Prototyping   **Discovery prototyping** uses rapid development technology to help users discover their business requirements. For example, it is very common for systems analysts to use a simple development tool like Microsoft *Access* to rapidly create a simple database, user input forms, and sample reports to solicit user responses as to whether the database, forms, and reports truly represent business requirements. The intent is usually to develop the final new system in a more sophisticated application development tool and language, but the simpler tool allows the analyst to more quickly prototype the user's requirements.

In discovery prototyping, we try to discourage users from becoming preoccupied with the final "look and feel" of the system prototypes—that can be changed during system design! Therein lies the primary criticism of prototyping—software templates exist in prototyping tools to quickly generate some very elegant and visually appealing prototypes. Unfortunately, this can encourage a premature focus on, and commitment to, design represented in the prototype. Users can also be misled to believe (1) that the completed system can be built just as rapidly or (2) that tools like *Access* can be used to build the final system. While tools like *Access* can indeed accelerate systems development, their use in discovery prototyping is fast only because we omit most of the detailed database and application programming required for a complete and secure application. Also, tools like *Access* typically cannot support the database sizes, number of users, and network traffic that are required of most enterprise applications.

Regardless, discovery prototyping is a preferred and recommended approach. Unfortunately, some systems analysts and developers are using discovery prototyping to completely replace model-driven design, only to learn what true engineers have known for years: you cannot prototype without some amount of more formal design . . . enter rapid architected analysis.

Rapid Architected Analysis **Rapid architected analysis** is an accelerated analysis approach that also builds system models. Rapid architecture analysis is made possible by **reverse-engineering** technology that is included in many automated tools such as CASE and programming languages (as introduced in Chapter 3). Reverse-engineering tools generate system models from existing software applications or system prototypes. The resulting system models can then be edited and improved by systems analysts and users to provide a blueprint for a new and improved system. It should be apparent that rapid architected analysis is a blending of model-driven and accelerated analysis approaches.

There are two different techniques for applying rapid architected analysis:

- Most systems have already been automated to some degree and exist as legacy information systems. Many CASE tools can read the underlying database structures and/or application programs and reverse engineer them into various system models. Those models serve as a point of departure for defining model-driven user requirements analysis.
- If prototypes have been built into tools like Microsoft *Access* or *Visual Basic*, those prototypes can sometimes be reverse engineered into their equivalent system models. The system models usually better lend themselves to analyzing the users' requirements for consistency, completeness, stability, scalability, and flexibility to future change. Also, the system models can frequently be forward engineered by the same CASE tools and ADEs (application development environments) into databases and application templates or skeletons that will use more robust enterprise-level database and programming technology.

Both techniques address the previous issue that engineers rarely prototype in the total absence of a more formal design, and, at the same time, they preserve the advantages of accelerating the systems analysis phases.

> Requirements Discovery Methods

Both model-driven and accelerated systems analysis approaches attempt to express user requirements for a new system, either as models or as prototypes. But both approaches are, in turn, dependent on the more subtle need to actually identify and manage those requirements. Furthermore, the requirements for systems are dependent on the analysts' ability to discover the problems and opportunities that exist in the current system—thus, analysts must become skilled in identifying problems, opportunities, and requirements! Consequently, all approaches to systems analysis require some form of **requirements discovery.** Let's briefly survey a couple of common requirements discovery approaches.

Fact-Finding Techniques **Fact-finding** is an essential skill for all systems analysts. The fact-finding techniques covered in this book (in fact, in the next chapter) include:

- Sampling of existing documentation, reports, forms, files, databases, and memos.
- Research of relevant literature, benchmarking of others' solutions, and site visits.

rapid architected analysis an approach that attempts to derive system models (as described earlier in this section) from existing systems or discovery prototypes.

reverse engineering the use of technology that reads the program code for an existing database, application program, and/or user interface and automatically generates the equivalent system model.

requirements discovery the process, used by systems analysts, of identifying or extracting system problems and solution requirements from the user community.

fact-finding the process of collecting information about system problems, opportunities, solution requirements, and priorities. Also called *information gathering.*

- Observation of the current system in action and the work environment.
- Questionnaires and surveys of the management and user community.
- Interviews of appropriate managers, users, and technical staff.

Joint Requirements Planning   The fact-finding techniques listed above are invaluable; however, they can be time-consuming in their classic forms. Alternatively, requirements discovery and management can be significantly accelerated using **joint requirements planning (JRP)** techniques. A JRP-trained or -certified analyst usually plays the role of *facilitator* for a workshop that will typically run from three to five full working days. This workshop can replace weeks or months of classic fact-finding and follow-up meetings.

JRP provides a working environment in which to accelerate all systems analysis tasks and deliverables. It promotes enhanced SYSTEM OWNER and SYSTEM USER participation in systems analysis. But it also requires a facilitator with superior mediation and negotiation skills to ensure that all parties receive appropriate opportunities to contribute to the system's development.

JRP is typically used in conjunction with the model-driven analysis approaches we described earlier, and it is typically incorporated into rapid application development (RAD) methodologies and routes (which were introduced in Chapter 3).

joint requirements planning (JRP) the use of facilitated workshops to bring together all of the system owners, users, and analysts and some systems designers and builders to jointly perform systems analysis. JRP is generally considered a part of a larger method called *joint application development (JAD),* a more comprehensive application of the JRP techniques to the entire systems development process.

> Business Process Redesign Methods

One of the most interesting contemporary applications of systems analysis methods is **business process redesign (BPR).** The interest in BPR was driven by the discovery that most current information systems and applications have merely automated existing and inefficient business processes. Automated bureaucracy is still bureaucracy; automation does not necessarily contribute value to the business, and it may actually subtract value from the business. Introduced in Chapter 1, BPR is one of many types of projects triggered by the trends we call *total quality management (TQM)* and *continuous process improvement (CPI)*.

Some BPR projects focus on all business processes, regardless of their automation. Each business process is thoroughly studied and analyzed for bottlenecks, value returned, and opportunities for elimination or streamlining. Process models, such as data flow diagrams (discussed earlier), help organizations visualize their processes. Once the business processes have been redesigned, most BPR projects conclude by examining how information technology might best be applied to the improved business processes. This may create new information system and application development projects to implement or support the new business processes.

business process redesign (BPR) the application of systems analysis methods to the goal of dramatically changing and improving the fundamental business processes of an organization, independent of information technology.

BPR is also applied within the context of information system development projects. It is not uncommon for IS projects to include a study of existing business processes to identify problems, bureaucracy, and inefficiencies that can be addressed in requirements for new and improved information systems and computer applications.

BPR has also become common in IS projects that will be based on the purchase and integration of commercial off-the-shelf (COTS) software. The purchase of COTS software usually requires that a business adapt its business processes to fit the software. An analysis of existing business processes during systems analysis is usually a part of such projects.

> *FAST* Systems Analysis Strategies

agile method the integration of various approaches of systems analysis and design for application as deemed appropriate to the problem being solved and the system being developed.

Like most commercial methodologies, our hypothetical *FAST* methodology does not impose a single approach on systems analysts. Instead, it integrates all the popular approaches introduced in the preceding paragraphs into a collection of **agile methods.** The SoundStage case study will demonstrate these methods in the context of a typical first assignment for a systems analyst. The systems analysis techniques will be applied within the framework of:

- Your information system building blocks (from Chapter 2).
- The *FAST* phases (from Chapter 3).
- *FAST* tasks that implement a phase (described in this chapter).

Given this context for studying systems analysis, we can now explore the systems analysis phases and tasks.

The Scope Definition Phase

Recall from Chapter 3 that the *scope definition phase* is the first phase of the classic systems development process. In other methodologies this might be called the *preliminary investigation phase, initial study phase, survey phase,* or *planning phase.* The scope definition phase answers the question, "Is this project worth looking at?" To answer this question, we must define the scope of the project and the perceived problems, opportunities, and directives that triggered the project. Assuming the project *is* deemed worth looking at, the scope definition phase must also establish the project plan in terms of scale, development strategy, schedule, resource requirements, and budget.[1]

The context for the scope definition phase is shaded in Figure 5-5. Notice that the scope definition phase is concerned primarily with the SYSTEM OWNERS' view of the existing system and the problems or opportunities that triggered the interest. System owners tend to be concerned with the big picture, not details. Furthermore, they determine whether resources can and will be committed to the project.

Figure 5-6 is the first of five task diagrams we will introduce in this chapter to take a closer look at each systems analysis phase. A *task diagram* shows the work (= tasks) that should be performed to complete a phase. Our task diagrams do not mandate any specific methodology, but we will describe in the accompanying paragraphs the approaches, tools, and techniques you might want to consider for each task. Figure 5-6 shows the tasks required for the scope definition phase. It is important to remember that these task diagrams are only templates. The project team and project manager may expand on or alter these templates to reflect the unique needs of any given project.

As shown in Figure 5-6, the final deliverable for the preliminary investigation phase is completion of a PROJECT CHARTER. (Such major deliverables are indicated in each task diagram in all-capital letters.) A project charter defines the project scope, plan, methodology, standards, and so on. Completion of the project charter represents the first milestone in a project.

The scope definition phase is intended to be quick. The entire phase should not exceed two or three days for most projects. The phase typically includes the following tasks:

1.1 Identify baseline problems and opportunities.
1.2 Negotiate baseline scope.
1.3 Assess baseline project worthiness.
1.4 Develop baseline schedule and budget.
1.5 Communicate the project plan.

Let's now examine each of these tasks in greater detail.

---

[1]If your course or reading has already included Chapter 4, you should recognize these planning elements as part of project management. Chapter 4 surveyed and demonstrated the process used by project managers to develop a project plan.

FIGURE 5-5 The Context of the Scope Definition Phase of Systems Analysis

THE BUSINESS COMMUNITY

SYSTEM OWNERS AND USERS
(OR STEERING COMMITTEE)

PROJECT CHARTER

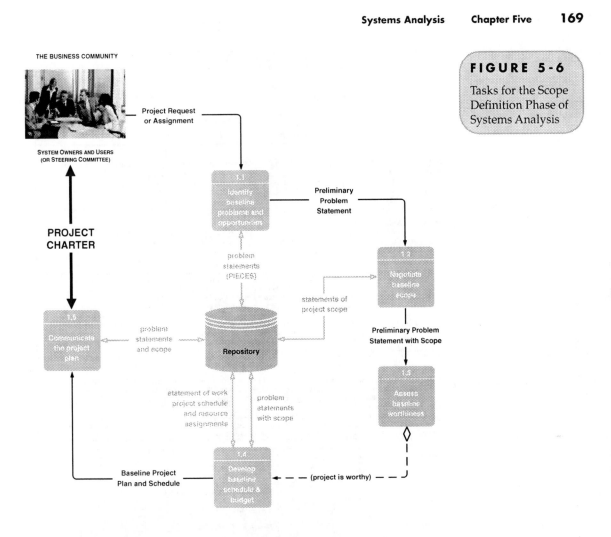

FIGURE 5-6

Tasks for the Scope Definition Phase of Systems Analysis

> Task 1.1—Identify Baseline Problems and Opportunities

One of the most important tasks of the **scope** definition phase is establishing an initial baseline of the problems, opportunities, and/or directives that triggered the project. Each problem, opportunity, and directive is assessed with respect to urgency, visibility, tangible benefits, and priority. Any additional, detailed analysis is not relevant at this stage of the project. It may, however, be useful to list any perceived constraints (limits) on the project, such as deadlines, maximum budget, or general technology.

A senior systems analyst or project manager usually leads this task. Most of the other participants are broadly classified as SYSTEM OWNERS. This includes the executive sponsor(s), the highest-level manager(s) who will pay for and support the project. It also includes managers of all organizational units that may be impacted by the system and possibly includes information systems managers. SYSTEM USERS, SYSTEM DESIGNERS, and SYSTEM BUILDERS are not typically involved in this task.

As shown in Figure 5-6, a PROJECT REQUEST OR ASSIGNMENT triggers the task. This trigger may take one of several alternative forms. It may be as simple as a memorandum of authority from an information systems steering body. Or it may be a memorandum from a business team or unit requesting systems development. Some organizations require that all project requests be submitted on some standard request-for-service form, such as Figure 5-7.

scope the boundaries of a project—the areas of a business that a project may (or may not) address.

FIGURE 5-7

A Request for
Systems Services

SoundStage Entertainment Club	REQUEST FOR
Information System Services Phone: 494-0666 Fax: 494-0999 Internet: http://www.soundstage.com Intranet: http://www.soundstage.com/iss	**INFORMATION SYSTEM SERVICES**

DATE OF REQUEST	SERVICE REQUESTED FOR DEPARTMENT(S)
January 9, 2003	Member Services, Warehouse, Shipping

SUBMITTED BY (key user contact)
- Name   Sarah Hartman
- Title   Business Analyst, Member Services
- Office   B035
- Phone   494-0867

EXECUTIVE SPONSOR (funding authority)
- Name   Galen Kirkhoff
- Title   Vice President, Member Services
- Office   G242
- Phone   494-1242

TYPE OF SERVICE REQUESTED:
- ☐ Information Strategy Planning
- ☒ Business Process Analysis and Redesign
- ☒ New Application Development
- ☐ Other (please specify) _____
- ☐ Existing Application Enhancement
- ☐ Existing Application Maintenance (problem fix)
- ☐ Not Sure

BRIEF STATEMENT OF PROBLEM, OPPORTUNITY, OR DIRECTIVE (attach additional documentation as necessary)
The information strategy planning group has targeted member services, marketing, and order fulfillment (inclusive of shipping) for business process redesign and integrated application development. Currently serviced by separate information systems, these areas are not well integrated to maximize efficient order services to our members. The current systems are not adaptable to our rapidly changing products and services. In some cases, separate systems exist for similar products and services. Some of these systems were inherited through mergers that expanded our products and services. There also exist several marketing opportunities to increase our presence to our members. One example includes Internet commerce services. Finally, the automatic identification system being developed for the warehouse must fully interoperate with member services.

BRIEF STATEMENT OF EXPECTED SOLUTION
We envision completely new and streamlined business processes that minimize the response time to member orders for products and services. An order shall not be considered fulfilled until it has been received by the member. The new system should provide for expanded club and member flexibility and adaptability of basic business products and services.
   We envision a system that extends to the desktop computers of both employees and members, with appropriate shared services provided across the network, consistent with the ISS distributed architecture. This is consistent with strategic plans to retire the AS/400 central computer and replace it with servers.

ACTION (ISS Office Use Only)

- ☐ Feasibility assessment approved
- ☒ Feasibility assessment waived

- ☐ Request delayed
- ☐ Request rejected

Assigned to <u>Sandra Shepherd</u>

Approved Budget $ <u>450,000</u>

Start Date   <u>ASAP</u>   Deadline   <u>ASAP</u>

Backlogged until date: _____

Reason: _____

Authorized Signatures:

Rebecca J. Todd
Chair, ISS Executive Steering Body

Galen Kirkhoff
Project Executive Sponsor

FORM ISS-100-RFSS (Last revised December, 1999)

The key deliverable of this task, the PRELIMINARY PROBLEM STATEMENT, consists of the problems, opportunities, and directives that were identified. The PROBLEM STATEMENTS are stored in the repository for later use in the project. Figure 5-8 is a sample document that summarizes problems, opportunities, and directives in terms of:

- *Urgency*—In what time frame must/should the problem be solved or the opportunity or directive be realized? A rating scale could be developed to consistently answer this question.
- *Visibility*—To what degree would a solution or new system be visible to customers and/or executive management? Again, a rating scale could be developed for the answers.
- *Benefits*—Approximately how much would a solution or new system increase annual revenues or reduce annual costs? This is often a guess, but if all participants are involved in that guess, it should prove sufficiently conservative.

Problem Statements

Project:	Member services information system	Project manager:	Sandra Shepherd
Created by:	Sandra Shepherd	Last updated by:	Robert Martinez
Date created:	January 9, 2003	Date last updated:	January 15, 2003

Brief Statements of Problem, Opportunity, or Directive	Urgency	Visibility	Annual Benefits	Priority or Rank	Proposed Solution
1. Order response time as measured from time of order receipt to time of customer delivery has increased to an average of 15 days.	ASAP	High	$175,000	2	New development
2. The recent acquisitions of Private Screenings Video Club and Game-Screen will further stress the through-put requirements for the current system.	6 months	Med	75,000	2	New development
3. Currently, three different order entry systems service the audio, video, and game divisions. Each system is designed to interface with a different warehousing system; therefore, the intent to merge inventory into a single warehouse has been delayed.	6 months	Med	515,000	2	New development
4. There is a general lack of access to management and decision-making information. This will become exasperated by the acquisition of two additional order processing systems (from Private Screenings and Game-Screen).	12 months	Low	15,000	3	After new system is developed, provide users with easy-to-learn and -use reporting tools.
5. There currently exist data inconsistencies in the member and order files.	3 months	High	35,000	1	Quick fix; then new development
6. The Private Screenings and GameScreen file systems are incompatible with the SoundStage equivalents. Business data problems include data inconsistencies and lack of input edit controls.	6 months	Med	Unknown	2	New development. Additional quantification of benefit might increase urgency.
7. There is an opportunity to open order systems to the Internet, but security and control are an issue.	12 months	Low	Unknown	4	Future version of newly developed system
8. The current order entry system is incompatible with the forthcoming automatic identification (bar-coding) system being developed for the warehouse.	3 months	High	65,000	1	Quick fix; then new development

FIGURE 5-8 Sample Problem Statements

- *Priority*—Based on the above answers, what are the consensus priorities for each problem, opportunity, or directive. If budget or schedule becomes a problem, these priorities will help to adjust project scope.
- *Possible solutions* (OPT)—At this early stage of the project, possible solutions are best expressed in simple terms such as (a) leave well enough alone, (b) use a quick fix, (c) make a simple to moderate enhancement of the existing system, (d) redesign the existing system, or (e) design a new system. The participants listed for this task are well suited to an appropriately high-level discussion of these options.

The PIECES framework that was introduced in Chapter 3 can be used as a framework for categorizing problems, opportunities, directives, and constraints. For example, Problem 1 in Figure 5-8 could be classified according to PIECES as P.B.—Performance, Response Times. (See Figure 3-4 in Chapter 3). Problem 4 in Figure 5-8 could be classified as I.A.2—Information, Outputs, Lack of necessary information.

The primary techniques used to complete this task include fact-finding and meetings with SYSTEM OWNERS. These techniques are taught in Chapter 6.

> Task 1.2—Negotiate Baseline Scope

Scope defines the boundary of the project—those aspects of the business that will and will not be included in the project. Scope can change during the project; however, the initial project plan must establish the preliminary or baseline scope. Then if the scope changes significantly, all parties involved will have a better appreciation for why the budget and schedule have also changed. This task can occur in parallel with the prior task.

Once again, a senior systems analyst or project manager usually leads this task. Most of the other participants are broadly classified as SYSTEM OWNERS. This includes the executive sponsor, managers of all organizational units that may be impacted by the system, and possibly information systems managers. SYSTEM USERS, SYSTEM DESIGNERS, and SYSTEM BUILDERS are not typically involved in this task.

As shown in Figure 5-6, this task uses the PRELIMINARY PROBLEM STATEMENT produced by the previous task. It should make sense that those problems, opportunities, and directives form the basis for defining scope. The STATEMENTS OF PROJECT SCOPE are added to the repository for later use. These statements are also formally documented as the task deliverable, PRELIMINARY PROBLEM STATEMENT WITH SCOPE.

Scope can be defined easily within the context of your information system building blocks. For example, a project's scope can be described in terms of:

- What types of DATA describe the system being studied? For example, a sales information system may require data about such things as CUSTOMERS, ORDERS, PRODUCTS, and SALES REPRESENTATIVES.
- What business PROCESSES are included in the system being studied? For example, a sales information system may include business processes for CATALOG MANAGEMENT, CUSTOMER MANAGEMENT, ORDER ENTRY, ORDER FULFILLMENT, ORDER MANAGEMENT, and CUSTOMER RELATIONSHIP MANAGEMENT.
- How must the system INTERFACE with users, locations, and other systems? For example, potential interfaces for a sales information system might include CUSTOMERS, SALES REPRESENTATIVES, SALES CLERKS AND MANAGERS, REGIONAL SALES OFFICES, and the ACCOUNTS RECEIVABLE and INVENTORY CONTROL INFORMATION SYSTEMS.

Notice that each statement of scope can be described as a simple list. We don't necessarily "define" the items in the list. Nor are we very concerned with precise requirements analysis. And we definitely are not concerned with any time-consuming steps such as modeling or prototyping.

Once again, the primary techniques used to complete this task are fact-finding and meetings. Many analysts prefer to combine this task with both the previous and the next tasks and accomplish them within a single meeting.

> Task 1.3—Assess Baseline Project Worthiness

This is where we answer the question, "Is this project worth looking at?" At this early stage of the project, the question may actually boil down to a "best guess": Will solving the problems, exploiting the opportunities, or fulfilling the directives return enough value to offset the costs that we will incur to develop this system? It is impossible to do a thorough feasibility analysis based on the limited facts we've collected to date.

Again, a senior systems analyst or project manager usually leads this task. But the SYSTEM OWNERS, inclusive of the executive sponsor, the business unit managers, and the information systems managers, should make the decision.

As shown in Figure 5-6, the completed PRELIMINARY PROBLEM STATEMENT WITH SCOPE triggers the task. This provides the level of information required for this preliminary assessment of worth. There is no physical deliverable other than the GO OR NO-GO DECISION. There are actually several alternative decisions. The project can be approved or canceled, and project scope can be renegotiated (increased or decreased!). Obviously, the remaining tasks in the preliminary investigation phase are necessary only if the project has been deemed worthy and approved to continue.

> Task 1.4—Develop Baseline Schedule and Budget

If the project has been deemed worthy to continue, we can now plan the project in depth. The initial project plan should consist of at least the following:

- A preliminary master plan that includes schedule and resource assignments for the entire project. This plan will be updated at the end of each phase of the project. It is sometimes called a *baseline plan*.
- A detailed plan and schedule for completing the next phase of the project (the problem analysis phase).

The task is the responsibility of the *project manager.* Most project managers find it useful to include as much of the project team, including SYSTEM OWNERS, USERS, DESIGNERS, and BUILDERS, as possible. Chapter 4 coined the term *joint project planning* to describe the team approach to building a project plan.

As shown in Figure 5-6, this task is triggered by the GO OR NO-GO DECISION to continue the project. This decision represents a consensus agreement on the project's scope, problems, opportunities, directives, and worthiness. (This "worthiness" must still be presented and approved.) The PROBLEM STATEMENTS WITH SCOPE are the key input (from the repository). The deliverable of this task is the BASELINE PROJECT PLAN AND SCHEDULE. The STATEMENT OF WORK (see Chapter 4) and PROJECT SCHEDULE AND RESOURCE ASSIGNMENTS are also added to the repository for continuous monitoring and, as appropriate, updating. The schedule and resources are typically maintained in the repository as a project management software file.

The techniques used to create a project plan were covered in depth in Chapter 4. Today, these techniques are supported by project management software such as Microsoft *Project.* Chapter 4 also discussed the detailed steps for completing the plan.

> Task 1.5—Communicate the Project Plan

In most organizations, there are more potential projects than resources to staff and fund those projects. Unless our project has been predetermined to be of the highest priority (by some sort of prior tactical or strategic planning process), then it must be presented and defended to a **steering body** for approval. Most organizations use a steering body to approve and monitor projects and progress. The majority of any steering body should consist of non–information systems professionals or managers. Many organizations designate vice presidents to serve on a steering body. Other

steering body a committee of executive business and system managers that studies and prioritizes competing project proposals to determine which projects will return the most value to the organization and thus should be approved for continued systems development. Also called a *steering committee.*

organizations assign the direct reports of vice presidents to the steering body. And some organizations utilize two steering bodies, one for vice presidents and one for their direct reports. Information systems managers serve on the steering body only to answer questions and to communicate priorities back to developers and project managers.

Regardless of whether or not a project requires steering committee approval, it is equally important to formally launch the project and communicate the project, goals, and schedule to the entire business community. Opening the lines of communication is an important capstone to the preliminary investigation. For this reason, we advocate the "best practices" of conducting a *project kickoff event* and creating an *intranet project Web site*. The project kickoff meeting is open to the entire business community, not just the business units affected and the project team. The intranet project Web site establishes a community portal to all nonsensitive news and documentation concerning the project.

Ideally, the executive sponsor should jointly facilitate the task with the chosen project manager. The visibility of the executive sponsor establishes instant credibility and priority to all who participate in the kickoff meeting. Other kickoff meeting participants should include the entire project team, including assigned SYSTEM OWNERS, USERS, ANALYSTS, DESIGNERS, and BUILDERS. Ideally, the kickoff meeting should be open to any and all interested staff from the business community. This builds community awareness and consensus while reducing both the volume and the consequences of rumor and misinformation. For the intranet component, a Webmaster or Web author should be assigned to the project team.

As shown in Figure 5-6, this task is triggered by the completion of the BASELINE PROJECT PLAN AND SCHEDULE. The PROBLEM STATEMENTS AND SCOPE are available from the repository. The deliverable is the PROJECT CHARTER. The project charter is usually a document. It includes various elements that define the project in terms of participants, problems, opportunities, and directives; scope; methodology; statement of work to be completed; deliverables; quality standards; schedule; and budget. The project charter should be added to the project Web site for all to see. Elements of the project charter may also be reformatted as slides and handouts (using software such as Microsoft *PowerPoint*) for inclusion in the project kickoff event.

Effective interpersonal and communications skills are the keys to this task. These include principles of persuasion, selling change, business writing, and public speaking.

This concludes our discussion of the scope definition phase. The participants in the scope definition phase might decide the project is not worth proposing. It is also possible the steering body may decide that other projects are *more* important. Or the executive sponsor might not endorse the project. In each of these instances, the project is terminated. Little time and effort have been expended. On the other hand, with the blessing of all the system owners and the steering committee, the project can now proceed to the problem analysis phase.

The Problem Analysis Phase

There is an old saying, "Don't try to fix it unless you understand it." That statement aptly describes the *problem analysis phase* of systems analysis. There is always a current or existing system, regardless of the degree to which it is automated with information technology. The problem analysis phase provides the analyst with a more thorough understanding of the problems, opportunities, and/or directives that triggered the project. The problem analysis phase answers the questions, "Are the problems really worth solving?" and "Is a new system really worth building?" In other methodologies, the problem analysis phase may be known as the *study phase, study of the current system, detailed investigation phase,* or *feasibility analysis phase.*

Can you ever skip the problem analysis phase? Rarely! You almost always need some level of understanding of the current system. But there may be reasons to accelerate the problem analysis phase. First, if the project was triggered by a strategic or tactical plan, the worthiness of the project is probably not in doubt—the problem analysis phase would be reduced to understanding the current system, not analyzing it. Second, a project may be initiated by a directive (such as compliance with a governmental directive and deadline). Again, in this case project worthiness is not in doubt. Finally, some methodologies and organizations deliberately consolidate the problem analysis and requirements analysis phases to accelerate systems analysis.

The goal of the problem analysis phase is to study and understand the problem domain well enough to thoroughly analyze its problems, opportunities, and constraints. Some methodologies encourage a very detailed understanding of the current system and document that system in painstaking detail using system models such as data flow diagrams. Today, except when business processes must be redesigned, the effort required and the value added by such detailed modeling is questioned and usually bypassed. Thus, the current version of our hypothetical *FAST* methodology encourages only enough system modeling to refine our understanding of project scope and problem statement, and to define a common vocabulary for the system.

The context for the problem analysis phase is shaded in Figure 5-9. Notice that the problem analysis phase is concerned primarily with both the SYSTEM OWNERS' and the SYSTEM USERS' views of the existing system. Notice that we build on the lists created in the preliminary investigation phase to analyze the KNOWLEDGE, PROCESS, and COMMUNICATIONS building blocks of the existing system. Also notice that we imply minimal system modeling. We may still use the PIECES framework to analyze each building block for problems, causes, and effects.

Figure 5-10 is the task diagram for the problem analysis phase. The final phase deliverable and milestone is producing SYSTEM IMPROVEMENT OBJECTIVES that address problems, opportunities, and directives. Depending on the size of the system, its complexity, and the degree to which project worthiness is already known, the illustrated tasks may consume one to six weeks. Most of these tasks can be accelerated by JRP-like sessions. The problem analysis phase typically includes the following tasks:

2.1 Understand the problem domain.
2.2 Analyze problems and opportunities.
2.3 Analyze business processes.
2.4 Establish system improvement objectives.
2.5 Update or refine the project plan.
2.6 Communicate findings and recommendations.

Let's now examine each of these tasks in greater detail.

> Task 2.1—Understand the Problem Domain

During the problem analysis phase, the *team* initially attempts to learn about the current system. Each SYSTEM OWNER, USER, and ANALYST brings a different level of understanding to the system—different detail, different vocabulary, different perceptions, and different opinions. A well-conducted study can prove revealing to all parties, including the system's own management and users. It is important to study and *understand the problem domain,* that domain in which the business problems, opportunities, directives, and constraints exist.

This task will be led by the project manager but facilitated by the lead systems analyst. It is not uncommon for one individual to play both roles (as Sandra does in the SoundStage case). Other SYSTEMS ANALYSTS may also be involved since they conduct interviews, scribe for meetings, and document findings. A comprehensive study should include representative SYSTEM OWNERS and USERS from all business units that will be supported or impacted by the system and project. It is extraordinarily important that enough users be included to encompass the full scope of the

FIGURE 5-9 The Context of the Problem Analysis Phase of Systems Analysis

FIGURE 5-10

Tasks for the
Problem Analysis
Phase of Systems
Analysis

FIGURE 5-10

Tasks for the
Problem Analysis
Phase of Systems
Analysis

system being studied. In some organizations, one or more experienced users are "loaned" to the project <u>full-time</u> as *business analysts;* however, it is rare that any one user can fully represent the interests of all users. Business analysts can, however, serve as facilitators to get the right people involved and sustain effective communication back to the business units and management. SYSTEM DESIGNERS and BUILDERS are rarely involved in this task unless they are interviewed to determine any technical limitations of the current system.

In Figure 5-10, this task is triggered by APPROVAL TO CONTINUE THE PROJECT—from the scope definition phase. (The dashed line indicates this approval is an event or trigger, not a data or information flow.) The approval comes from the SYSTEM OWNERS or steering committee. The key informational input is the PROJECT CHARTER and any CURRENT SYSTEM DOCUMENTATION that may exist in the repository and program libraries for the current system. Current system documentation doesn't always exist. And when it does exist, it must be carefully checked for currency—most such documentation is notoriously out of date because analysts and programmers are not always diligent about updating that documentation as changes occur throughout the lifetime of a system.

The deliverables of this task are an understanding of the PROBLEM DOMAIN AND BUSINESS VOCABULARY. Your understanding of the existing problem domain should be documented so that it can be verified that you truly understand it. There are several ways to document the problem domain. Certainly, drawing SYSTEM MODELS of the current system can help, but they can lead to a phenomenon called "analysis paralysis," in which the desire to produce perfect models becomes counterproductive to the schedule. Another approach might be to use your information system building blocks as a framework for listing and defining the system domain:

- KNOWLEDGE—List all the "things" about which the system currently stores data (in files, databases, forms, etc.). Define each thing in business terms. For example, "An ORDER is a business transaction in which a customer requests to purchase products."

    Additionally, we could list all the reports produced by the current system and describe their purpose or use. For example, "The open orders report describes all orders that have not been filled within one week of their approval to be filled. The report is used to initiate customer relationship management through personal contact."

- PROCESSES—Define each business event for which a business response (process) is currently implemented. For example, "A customer places a new order," or "A customer requests changes to a previously placed order," or "A customer cancels an order."

- COMMUNICATIONS—Define all the locations that the current system serves and all of the users at each of those locations. For example, "The system is currently used at regional sales offices in San Diego, Dallas, St. Louis, Indianapolis, Atlanta, and Manhattan. Each regional sales office has a sales manager, assistant sales manager, administrative assistant, and 5 to 10 sales clerks, all of whom use the current system. Each region is also home to 5 to 30 sales representatives who are on the road most days but who upload orders and other transactions each evening."

    Another facet of interfaces is system interfaces—that is, interfaces that exist between the current information system and other information systems and computer applications. These can be quickly listed and described by the information systems staff.

Ultimately, the organization's systems development methodology and project plan will determine what types and level of documentation are expected.

The business vocabulary deliverable is all too often shortchanged. Understanding the business vocabulary of the system is an excellent way of understanding the system itself. It bridges the communication gap that often exists or develops between business and technology experts.

If you elect to draw SYSTEM MODELS during this task, we suggest that "if you want to learn *anything*, you must not try to learn *everything*—at least not all in this task." To avoid analysis paralysis, we suggest that the following system models may be appropriate:

- KNOWLEDGE—A one-page data model is very useful for establishing business vocabulary and rules. Data modeling is taught in Chapter 8.
- PROCESSES—Today, it is widely accepted that a one- or two-page functional decomposition diagram should prove sufficient to get a feel for the current system processing. Decomposition modeling is taught in Chapter 9.
- COMMUNICATIONS—A one-page context diagram or use-case diagrams are very useful for illustrating the system's inputs and outputs with other organizations, business units, and systems. Context diagrams are discussed below. Use case diagrams are taught in Chapter 7.

Several other techniques and skills are useful for developing an understanding of an existing system. Obviously, fact-finding techniques (taught in the next chapter) are critical to learning about any existing system. Also, joint requirements planning, or JRP, techniques (also taught in the next chapter) can accelerate this task. Finally, the ability to clearly communicate back to users what you've learned about a system is equally crucial.

Context Diagram   The purpose of a context diagram is to analyze how the system interacts with the world around it and to specify in general terms the system inputs and outputs. Context diagrams can be drawn in various ways. Chapter 9 presents the traditional format, which was done as the first step in drawing data flow diagrams.

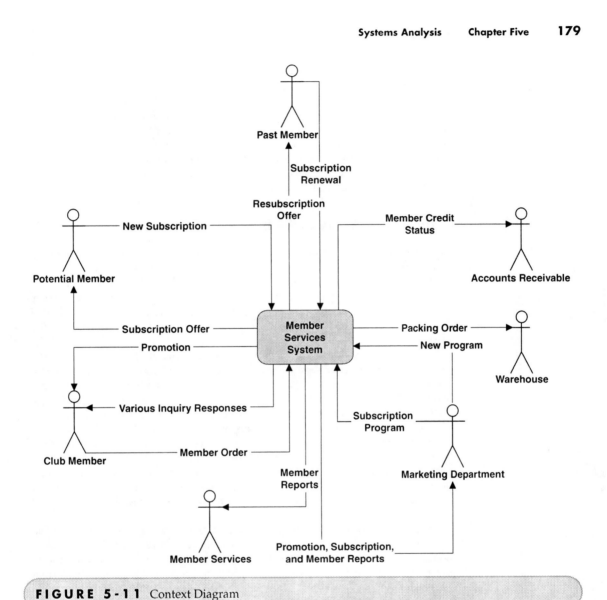

FIGURE 5-11 Context Diagram

Chapter 7 shows a different format for a context diagram. The context diagram shown in Figure 5-11 employs a hybrid approach. It employs use case symbols as use cases are becoming a generally accepted tool of the requirements analysis phase.

The system itself is shown as a "black box" in the middle of the diagram. We are not yet ready to look inside the box. For now we just want to see how everyone will use the box. The stick figures around the outside of the diagram are the persons, organizations, and other information systems that will interact with the system. In use cases, these are called actors, and we can call them that here. In traditional data flow diagrams, they are called external agents. In Chapters 7 and 9 you will learn that once you look inside the system box, other things such as time or devices like sensors can also be actors or external agents. But for a context diagram they are rarely shown.

The lines indicate the inputs (arrows pointing to the system) provided by actors to the system and the outputs (arrows pointing to the actors) created by the system. Each input and output is identified with a noun phrase that describes it.

To build a context diagram ask the users what business transactions the system must respond to; these are the inputs. Also ask the users what reports, notifications, and other outputs must be produced by the system. A system can have many reports that can quickly clutter the diagram; consolidate them as needed to keep the diagram readable. During other phases in the process they will be analyzed separately.

We certainly couldn't build an information system from a context diagram. But it is a solid first step. From this simple diagram we know what inputs the system must respond to and what outputs it must produce. In other words, it helps us understand the problem domain. We will see in Chapter 7 how to detect use cases from a context diagram. That will be the first step in cracking open the "black box." We are following the principles for systems development presented in Chapter 2: "use a problem-solving approach" and "divide and conquer."

> Task 2.2—Analyze Problems and Opportunities

In addition to learning about the current system, the project team must work with system owners and system users to *analyze problems and opportunities.* You might be asking, "Weren't problems and opportunities identified earlier, in the preliminary investigation phase?" Yes, they were. But those initial problems may be only symptoms of other problems, perhaps problems not as well known or understood by the users. Besides, we haven't yet really analyzed any of those problems in the classic sense.

True problem analysis is a difficult skill to master, especially for inexperienced systems analysts. Experience suggests that most new systems analysts (and many system owners and users) try to solve problems without truly analyzing them. They might state a problem like this: "We need to . . ." or "We want to . . ." In doing so, they are stating the problem in terms of a solution. More effective problem solvers have learned to truly analyze the problem before stating any possible solution. They analyze each perceived problem for **causes and effects.** In practice, an effect may actually be a symptom of a different, more deeply rooted or basic problem. That problem must also be analyzed for causes and effects, and so on until such a time as the causes and effects do not yield symptoms of other problems. Cause-and-effect analysis leads to true understanding of problems and can lead to not-so-obvious but more creative and valuable solutions.

cause-and-effect analysis
a technique in which problems are studied to determine their causes and effects.

SYSTEMS ANALYSTS facilitate this task; however, all SYSTEMS OWNERS and USERS should actively participate in the process of cause-and-effect analysis. They are the problem domain experts. SYSTEM DESIGNERS and BUILDERS are not usually involved in this process unless they are called on to analyze technical problems that may exist in the current system.

As shown in Figure 5-10, the team's understanding of the SYSTEM DOMAIN AND BUSINESS VOCABULARY triggers this task. This understanding of the problem domain is crucial because the team members should not attempt to analyze problems unless they understand the domain in which those problems occur. The other informational input to this task is the initial PROBLEM STATEMENTS (from the scope definition phase). The deliverables of this task are the updated PROBLEM STATEMENTS and the CAUSE-EFFECT ANALYSIS for each problem and opportunity. Figure 5-12 illustrates one way to document a cause-and-effect analysis.

Once again, fact-finding and JRP techniques are crucial to this task. These techniques, as well as cause-and-effect analysis, are taught in the next chapter.

> Task 2.3—Analyze Business Processes

This task is appropriate only to *business process redesign (BPR)* projects or system development projects that build on or require significant business process redesign. In such a project, the team is asked to examine its business processes in much greater detail to measure the value added or subtracted by each process as it relates to the total organization. Business process analysis can be politically charged. System owners and users alike can become very defensive about their existing business

PROBLEMS, OPPORTUNITIES, OBJECTIVES, AND CONSTRAINTS MATRIX

Project:	Member Services Information System	Project Manager:	Sandra Shepherd
Created by:	Robert Martinez	Last Updated by:	Robert Martinez
Date Created:	January 21, 2003	Date Last Updated:	January 31, 2003

CAUSE-AND-EFFECT ANALYSIS		SYSTEM IMPROVEMENT OBJECTIVES	
Problem or Opportunity	**Causes and Effects**	**System Objective**	**System Constraint**
1. Order response time is unacceptable.	1. Throughput has increased while number of order clerks was downsized. Time to process a single order has remained relatively constant. 2. System is too keyboard-dependent. Many of the same values are keyed for most orders. Net result is (with the current system) each order takes longer to process than is ideal. 3. Data editing is performed by the AS/400. As that computer has approached its capacity, order edit responses have slowed. Because order clerks are trying to work faster to keep up with the volume, the number of errors has increased. 4. Warehouse picking tickets for orders were never designed to maximize the efficiency of order fillers. As warehouse operations grew, order filling delays were inevitable.	1. Decrease the time required to process a single order by 30%. 2. Eliminate keyboard data entry for as much as 50% of all orders. 3. For remaining orders, reduce as many key-strokes as possible by replacing keystrokes with point-and-click objects on the computer display screen. 4. Move data editing from a shared computer to the desktop. 5. Replace existing picking tickets with a paperless communication system between member services and the warehouse.	1. There will be no increase in the order processing workforce. 2. Any system developed must be compatible with the existing Windows 95 desktop standard. 3. New system must be compatible with the already approved automatic identification system (for bar coding).

FIGURE 5-12 A Sample Cause-and-Effect Analysis

processes. The analysts involved must keep the focus on the processes, not the people who perform them, and constantly remind everyone that the goal is to identify opportunities for fundamental business change that will benefit the business and everyone in the business.

One or more systems analysts or business analysts facilitate the task. Ideally, the ANALYSTS should be experienced, trained, or certified in BPR methods. The only other participants should be appropriate SYSTEM OWNERS and USERS. Business process analysis should avoid any temptation to focus on information technology solutions until well after the business processes have been redesigned for maximum efficiency. Some analysts find it useful to assume the existence of "perfect people" and "perfect technology" that can make anything "possible." They ask, "If the world were perfect, would we need this process?"

As depicted in Figure 5-10, a business process analysis task is dependent only on some PROBLEM DOMAIN knowledge (from Task 2.1). The deliverables of this task are business "as is" PROCESS MODELS and PROCESS ANALYSES. The process models can look very much like data flow diagrams (Figure 5-2) except they are significantly annotated to show (1) the volume of data flowing through the processes, (2) the response times of each process, and (3) any delays or bottlenecks that occur in the system. The process analysis data provides additional information such as (a) the cost of each process, (b) the value added by each process, and (c) the consequences of eliminating or streamlining the process. Based on the as-is models and their analysis, the team develops "to be" models that redesign the business processes to eliminate redundancy and bureaucracy and increase efficiency and service.

Several techniques are applicable to this task. Once again, fact-finding techniques and facilitated team meetings (Chapter 6) are invaluable. Also, process modeling techniques (Chapter 9) are critical to BPR success.

> Task 2.4—Establish System Improvement Objectives

Given our understanding of the current system's scope, problems, and opportunities, we can now *establish system improvement objectives.* The purpose of this task is to establish the criteria against which any improvements to the system will be measured and to identify any constraints that may limit flexibility in achieving those improvements. The criteria for success should be measured in terms of **objectives.** Objectives represent the first attempt to establish expectations for any new system. In addition to identifying objectives, we must also identify any known constraints. **Constraints** place limitations or delimitations on achieving objectives. Deadlines, budgets, and required technologies are examples of constraints.

objective a measure of success. It is something that you expect to achieve, if given sufficient resources.

constraint something that will limit your flexibility in defining a solution to your objectives. Essentially, constraints cannot be changed.

The SYSTEMS ANALYSTS facilitate this task. Other participants include the same SYSTEM OWNERS and USERS who have participated in other tasks in this problem analysis phase. Again, we are not yet concerned with technology; therefore, SYSTEM DESIGNERS and BUILDERS are not involved in this task.

This task is triggered by the PROBLEM ANALYSES completed in Tasks 2.2 and 2.3. For each verified and significant problem, the analysts and users should define specific SYSTEM IMPROVEMENT OBJECTIVES. They should also identify any CONSTRAINTS that may limit or prevent them from achieving the system improvement objectives.

System improvement objectives should be precise, measurable statements of business performance that define the expectations for the new system. Some examples are:

Reduce the number of uncollectible customer accounts by 50 percent within the next year.

Increase by 25 percent the number of loan applications that can be processed during an eight-hour shift.

Decrease by 50 percent the time required to reschedule a production lot when a workstation malfunctions.

The following is an example of a poor objective:

Create a delinquent accounts report.

This is a poor objective because it states only a requirement, not an actual objective. Now, let's reword that objective:

Reduce credit losses by 20 percent through earlier identification of delinquent accounts.

This gives us more flexibility. Yes, the delinquent accounts report would work. But a customer delinquency inquiry might provide an even better way to achieve the same objective.

System improvement objectives may be tempered by identifiable constraints. Constraints fall into four categories, as listed below (with examples):

- *Schedule:* The new system must be operational by April 15.
- *Cost:* The new system cannot cost more than $350,000.
- *Technology:* The new system must be online, or all new systems must use the DB2 database management system.
- *Policy:* The new system must use double-declining-balance inventory techniques.

The last two columns of Figure 5-12 document typical system improvement objectives and constraints.

> Task 2.5—Update or Refine the Project Plan

Recall that project scope is a moving target. Based on our baseline schedule and budget from the scope definition phase, scope may have grown or diminished in size and complexity. (Growth is much more common!) Now that we're approaching the completion of the problem analysis phase, we should reevaluate project scope and *update or refine the project plan* accordingly.

The project manager, in conjunction with SYSTEM OWNERS and the entire project team, facilitates this task. The SYSTEMS ANALYSTS and SYSTEM OWNERS are the key individuals in this task. The analysts and owners should consider the possibility that not all objectives may be met by the new system. Why? The new system may be larger than expected, and they may have to reduce the scope to meet a deadline. In this case the system owner will rank the objectives in order of importance. Then, if the scope must be reduced, the higher-priority objectives will tell the analyst what's most important.

As shown in Figure 5-10, this task is triggered by completion of the SYSTEM IMPROVEMENT OBJECTIVES. The initial PROJECT PLAN is another key input, and the UPDATED PROJECT PLAN is the key output. The updated plan should now include a detailed plan for the requirements analysis phase that should follow. The techniques and steps for updating the project plan were taught in Chapter 4, "Project Management."

> Task 2.6—Communicate Findings and Recommendations

As with the scope definition phase, the problem analysis phase concludes with a communication task. We must *communicate findings and recommendations* to the business community. The project manager and executive sponsor should jointly facilitate this task. Other meeting participants should include the entire project team, including assigned SYSTEM OWNERS, USERS, ANALYSTS, DESIGNERS, and BUILDERS. And, as usual, the meeting should be open to any and all interested staff from the business community. Also, if an intranet Web site was established for the project, it should have been maintained throughout the problem analysis phase to ensure continuous communication of project progress.

This task is triggered by the completion of the UPDATED PROJECT PLAN. Informational inputs include the PROBLEM ANALYSES, any SYSTEM MODELS, the SYSTEM IMPROVEMENT OBJECTIVES, and any other documentation that was produced during the problem analysis phase. Appropriate elements are combined into the SYSTEM IMPROVEMENT OBJECTIVES, the major deliverable of the problem analysis phase. The format may be a report, a verbal presentation, or an inspection by an auditor or peer group (called a *walkthrough*). An outline for a written report is shown in Figure 5-13.

Interpersonal and communications skills are essential to this task. Systems analysts should be able to write a formal business report and make a business presentation without getting into technical issues or alternatives.

FIGURE 5-13   An Outline for a System Improvement Objectives and
Recommendations Report

Analysis of the Current _____ System

I. Executive summary (approximately 2 pages)
   A. Summary of recommendation
   B. Summary of problems, opportunities, and directives
   C. Brief statement of system improvement objectives
   D. Brief explanation of report contents
II. Background information (approximately 2 pages)
   A. List of interviews and facilitated group meetings conducted
   B. List of other sources of information that were exploited
   C. Description of analytical techniques used
III. Overview of the current system (approximately 5 pages)
   A. Strategic implications (if the project is part of or impacts an existing information systems strategic plan)
   B. Models of the current system
      1. Interface model (showing project scope)
      2. Data model (showing project scope)
      3. Geographic models (showing project scope)
      4. Process model (showing functional decomposition only)
IV. Analysis of the current system (approximately 5–10 pages)
   A. Performance problems, opportunities, and cause-effect analysis
   B. Information problems, opportunities, and cause-effect analysis
   C. Economic problems, opportunities, and cause-effect analysis
   D. Control problems, opportunities, and cause-effect analysis
   E. Efficiency problems, opportunities, and cause-effect analysis
   F. Service problems, opportunities, and cause-effect analysis
V. Detailed recommendations (approximately 5–10 pages)
   A. System improvement objectives and priorities
   B. Constraints
   C. Project plan
      1. Scope reassessment and refinement
      2. Revised master plan
      3. Detailed plan for the definition phase
VI. Appendixes
   A. Any detailed system models
   B. Other documents as appropriate

This concludes the problem analysis phase. One of the following decisions must be made after the conclusion of this phase:

- Authorize the project to continue, as is, to the requirements analysis phase.
- Adjust the scope, cost, and/or schedule for the project and then continue to the requirements analysis phase.
- Cancel the project due to (1) lack of resources to further develop the system, (2) realization that the problems and opportunities are simply not as important as anticipated, or (3) realization that the benefits of the new system are not likely to exceed the costs.

With some level of approval from the SYSTEM OWNERS, the project can now proceed to the requirements analysis phase.

The Requirements Analysis Phase

Many inexperienced analysts make a critical mistake after completing the problem analysis phase. The temptation at that point is to begin looking at alternative solutions, particularly technical solutions. One of the most frequently cited errors in new information systems is illustrated in the statement, "Sure the system works, and it is technically impressive, but it just doesn't do what we needed it to do." The *requirements analysis phase* defines the business requirements for a new system.

Did you catch the key word in the quoted sentence? It is "what," not "how"! Analysts are frequently so preoccupied with the *technical* solution that they inadequately define the *business* requirements for that solution. The requirements analysis phase answers the question, "What do the users need and want from a new system?" The requirements analysis phase is critical to the success of any new information system. In different methodologies the requirements analysis phase might be called the *definition phase* or *logical design phase*.

Can you ever skip the requirements analysis phase? Absolutely not! New systems will always be evaluated, first and foremost, on whether or not they fulfill business objectives and requirements, regardless of how impressive or complex the technological solution might be!

It should be acknowledged that some methodologies integrate the problem analysis and requirements analysis phases into a single phase.

Once again, your information systems building blocks (Figure 5-14) can serve as a useful framework for documenting the information systems requirements. Notice that we are still concerned with the SYSTEM USERS' perspectives. Requirements can be defined in terms of the PIECES framework or in terms of the types of data, processes, and interfaces that must be included in the system.

Figure 5-15 illustrates the typical tasks of the requirements analysis phase. The final phase deliverable and milestone is producing a BUSINESS REQUIREMENTS STATEMENT that will fulfill the system improvement objectives identified in the previous phase. One of the first things you may notice in this task diagram is that most of the tasks are not as sequential as those in previous task diagrams. Instead, many of these tasks occur in parallel as the team works toward the goal of completing the requirements statement. The requirements analysis phase typically includes the following tasks:

3.1 Identify and express system requirements.
3.2 Prioritize system requirements.
3.3 Update or refine the project plan.
3.4 Communicate the requirements statement.

Let's now examine each of these tasks in greater detail.

> Task 3.1—Identify and Express System Requirements

The initial task of the requirements analysis phase is to *identify and express requirements*. While this may seem to be an easy or trivial task, it is often the source of many errors, omissions, and conflicts. The foundation for this task was established in the problem analysis phase when we identified system improvement objectives. Minimally, this task translates those objectives into an outline of **functional** and **nonfunctional requirements** that will be needed to meet the objectives. Functional requirements are frequently identified in terms of inputs, outputs, processes, and stored data that are needed to satisfy the system improvement objectives. Examples of nonfunctional requirements include performance (throughput and response time); ease of learning and use; budgets, costs, and cost savings; timetables and deadlines; documentation and training needs; quality management; and security and internal auditing controls.

Rarely will this definition task identify *all* the functional or nonfunctional business requirements. But the outline will frame your thinking as you proceed to later

functional requirement a description of activities and services a system must provide.

nonfunctional requirement a description of other features, characteristics, and constraints that define a satisfactory system.

FIGURE 5-14   The Context of the Requirements Analysis Phase of Systems Analysis

THE BUSINESS COMMUNITY

SYSTEM OWNERS AND USERS

(approval to continue
the project—from
problem analysis phase)

**BUSINESS
REQUIREMENTS
STATEMENT**

3.1

Identify and
express
requirements

Draft
Functional
and
Nonfunctional
Requirements

system improvement objectives,
functional and nonfunctional
requirements

3.4

Communicate
requirements
statement

final
requirements
and priorities

Repository

validated
requirements
with priorities

3.2

Prioritize
system
requirements

project
plan

Completed
Requirements
and Priorities

Revised Plan Completed

3.3

Update or
refine the
project plan

FIGURE 5-15

Tasks for the
Requirements
Analysis Phase of
Systems Analysis

tasks that will add new requirements and details to the outline. Thus, neither completeness nor perfection is a goal of this task.

SYSTEMS ANALYSTS facilitate the task. They also document the results. Obviously, SYSTEM USERS are the primary source of business requirements. Some SYSTEM OWNERS may elect to participate in this task since they played a role in framing the system improvement objectives that will guide the task. SYSTEM DESIGNERS and BUILDERS should not be involved because they tend to prematurely redirect the focus to the technology and technical solutions.

As shown in Figure 5-15, this task (and phase) is triggered by the APPROVAL TO CONTINUE THE PROJECT FROM THE PROBLEM ANALYSIS PHASE. The key input is the SYSTEM IMPROVEMENT OBJECTIVES from the problem analysis phase (via the repository). Of course, any and all relevant information from the problem analysis phase is available from the repository for reference as needed.

The only deliverable of this task is the DRAFT FUNCTIONAL AND NONFUNCTIONAL REQUIREMENTS. Various formats can work. In its simplest format, the outline could be divided into four logical sections: the original list of system improvement objectives and, for each objective, a sublist of (a) inputs, (b) processes, (c) outputs, and (d) stored data needed to fulfill the objective. Increasingly, however, system analysts are

use case a business scenario or event for which the system must provide a defined response. Use cases evolved out of object-oriented analysis; however, their use has become common in many other methodologies for systems analysis and design.

expressing functional requirements using a modeling tool called **use cases.** Use cases model business scenarios and events that must be handled by a new system. They are introduced in Chapter 7 and used throughout this book.

The PIECES framework that was used earlier to identify problems, opportunities, and constraints can also be used as a framework for defining draft requirements.

Several techniques are applicable to this task. Joint requirements planning (JRP) is the preferred technique for rapidly outlining business requirements. Alternatively, the analysts could use other fact-finding methods such as surveys and interviews. Both JRP and fact-finding are taught in the next chapter.

> Task 3.2—Prioritize System Requirements

We stated earlier that the success of a systems development project can be measured in terms of the <u>degree</u> to which business requirements are met. But not all requirements are created equal. If a project gets behind schedule or over budget, it may be useful to recognize which requirements are more important than others. Thus, given the validated requirements, system owners and users should *prioritize system requirements*.

timeboxing a technique that delivers information systems functionality and requirements through versioning. The development team selects the smallest subset of the system that, if fully implemented, will return immediate value to the system owners and users. That subset is developed, ideally with a time frame of six to nine months or less. Subsequently, value-added versions of the system are developed in similar time frames.

Prioritization of requirements can be facilitated using a popular technique called **timeboxing.** Timeboxing attempts to divide requirements into "chunks" that can be implemented within a period of time that does not tax the patience of the user and management community. Timeboxing forces priorities to be clearly defined.

SYSTEMS ANALYSTS facilitate the prioritization task. SYSTEM OWNERS and USERS establish the actual priorities. SYSTEM DESIGNERS and BUILDERS are not involved in the task. The task is triggered by the VALIDATED REQUIREMENTS. It should be obvious that you cannot adequately prioritize an incomplete set of requirements. The deliverable of this task is the REQUIREMENTS WITH PRIORITIES. Priorities can be classified according to their relative importance:

- A *mandatory requirement* is one that must be fulfilled by the minimal system, version 1.0. The system is useless without it. Careful! There is a temptation to label too many requirements as mandatory. A mandatory requirement cannot be ranked because it is essential to any solution. In fact, if an alleged mandatory requirement can be ranked, it is actually a desirable requirement.
- A *desirable requirement* is one that is not absolutely essential to version 1.0. It may still be essential to the vision of some future version. Desirable requirements can and should be ranked. Using version numbers as the ranking scheme is an effective way to communicate and categorize desirable requirements.

> Task 3.3—Update or Refine the Project Plan

Here again, recall that project scope is a moving target. Now that we've identified the business system requirements, we should step back and redefine our understanding of the project scope and update our project plan accordingly. The team must consider the possibility that the new system may be larger than originally expected. If so, the team must adjust the schedule, budget, or scope accordingly. We should also secure approval to continue the project into the next phase. (Work may have already started on the design phases; however, the decisions still require review.)

The project manager, in conjunction with SYSTEM OWNERS and the entire project team, facilitates this task. As usual, the project manager and SYSTEM OWNERS are the key individuals in this task. They should consider the possibility that the requirements now exceed the original vision that was established for the project and new system. They may have to reduce the scope to meet a deadline or increase the budget to get the job done.

As shown in Figure 5-15, this task is triggered by completion of the COMPLETED REQUIREMENTS AND PRIORITIES. The up-to-date PROJECT PLAN is the other key input, and it is updated in the repository as appropriate. The tools, techniques, and steps for maintenance of the project plan were covered in Chapter 4, "Project Management."

> Task 3.4—Communicate the Requirements Statement

Communication is an ongoing task of the requirements analysis phase. We must communicate requirements and priorities to the business community throughout the phase. Users and managers will frequently lobby for requirements and priority consideration. Communication is the process through which differences of opinion must be mediated. The project manager and executive sponsor should jointly facilitate this task. Today, a project intranet or portal is frequently used to communicate requirements. Some systems allow users and managers to *subscribe* to requirements documents to ensure they are notified as changes occur. Interpersonal, communications, and negotiation skills are essential to this task.

> Ongoing Requirements Management

The requirements analysis phase is now complete. Or is it? It was once popular to freeze the business requirements before beginning the system design and construction phases. But today's economy has become increasingly fast-paced. Businesses are measured on their ability to quickly adapt to constantly changing requirements and opportunities. Information systems can be no less responsive than the business itself. Thus, requirements analysis really never ends. While we quietly transition to the remaining phases of our project, there remains an ongoing need to continuously manage requirements through the course of the project and the lifetime of the system.

Requirements management defines a process for system owners, users, analysts, designers, and builders to submit proposed changes to requirements for a system. The process specifies how changes are to be requested and documented, how they will be logged and tracked, when and how they will be assessed for priority, and how they will eventually be satisfied (if they are ever satisfied).

The Logical Design Phase

Not all projects embrace model-driven development, but most include some amount of system modeling. A logical design further documents business requirements using system models that illustrate data structures, business processes, data flows, and user interfaces (increasingly using object models, as introduced earlier in the chapter). In a sense, they validate the requirements established in the previous phase.

Once again, your information systems building blocks (Figure 5-16) can serve as a useful framework for documenting the information systems requirements. Notice that we are still concerned with the SYSTEM USERS' perspectives. In this phase, we draw various system models to document the requirements for a new and improved system. The models depict various aspects of our building blocks. Alternatively, prototypes could be built to "discover requirements." Discovery prototypes were introduced earlier in the chapter. Recall that some prototypes can be reverse engineered into system models.

Figure 5-17 illustrates the typical tasks of the logical design phase. The final phase deliverable and milestone is producing a BUSINESS REQUIREMENTS STATEMENT that will fulfill the system improvement objectives identified in the previous phase. One of the first things you may notice in this task diagram is that most of the tasks are not as sequential as in previous task diagrams. Instead, many of these tasks occur in parallel as the team works toward the goal of completing the requirements statement.

The logical design phase typically includes the following tasks:

4.1a Structure functional requirements.
4.1b Prototype functional requirements.
4.2   Validate functional requirements.
4.3   Define acceptance test cases.

Let's now examine each of these tasks in greater detail.

190   Part Two   Systems Analysis Methods

FIGURE 5-16   The Context of the Logical Design Phase of Systems Analysis

FIGURE 5-17

Tasks for the Logical Design Phase of Systems Analysis

> Task 4.1a—Structure Functional Requirements

One approach to logical design is to *structure the functional requirements*. This means that, using agile methods, you should draw or update one or more system models to illustrate the functional requirement. These may include any combination of data, process, and object models that accurately depict the business and user requirements (but not any technical solution). System models are not complete until all appropriate functional requirements have been modeled. Models are frequently supplemented with detailed logical specifications that describe data attributes, business rules and policies, and the like.

SYSTEMS ANALYSTS facilitate the task. They also document the results. Obviously, SYSTEM USERS are the primary source of factual details needed to draw the models. As shown in Figure 5-17, this task (and phase) is triggered by *each* FUNCTIONAL REQUIREMENT. The outputs are the actual SYSTEM MODELS AND DETAILED SPECIFICATIONS. The level of detail required depends on the methodology being followed. Agile methods usually require "just enough" documentation. How much is enough? That is arguable, but agile methodologists hold that every deliverable should be essential to the forthcoming design and programming phases. This textbook will teach you a variety of different system modeling tools and techniques to apply to logical design.

> Task 4.1b—Prototype Functional Requirements (alternative)

Prototyping is an alternative (and sometimes a prerequisite) to system modeling. Sometimes users have difficulty expressing the facts necessary to draw adequate system models. In such a case, an alternative or complementary approach to system modeling is to build discovery prototypes. Prototyping is typically used in the requirements analysis phase to build sample inputs and outputs. These inputs and outputs help to construct the underlying database and the programs for inputting and outputting the data to and from the database. Although discovery prototyping is optional, it is frequently applied to systems development projects, especially in cases where the users are having difficulty stating or visualizing their business requirements. The philosophy is that the users will recognize their requirements when they see them.

SYSTEMS BUILDERS facilitate this analysis task. SYSTEM ANALYSTS document and analyze the results. As usual, SYSTEM USERS are the primary source of factual input to the task. Figure 5-17 demonstrates that this task is dependent on one or more FUNCTIONAL REQUIREMENTS that have been identified by the users. The system builders and analysts respond by constructing the PROTOTYPES. As described earlier in this chapter, it may be possible to *reverse engineer* some SYSTEM MODELS directly from the prototype databases and program libraries.

> Task 4.2—Validate Functional Requirements

Both SYSTEM MODELS and PROTOTYPES are representations of the users' requirements. They must be validated for completeness and correctness. SYSTEMS ANALYSTS facilitate the prioritization task by interactively engaging system users to identify errors and omissions or make clarifications.

> Task 4.3—Define Acceptance Test Cases

While not a required task, most experts agree that it is not too early to begin planning for system testing. System models and prototypes very effectively define the processing requirements, data rules, and business rules for the new system. Accordingly, these specifications can be used to define TEST CASES that can ultimately be used to test programs for correctness. Either SYSTEM ANALYSTS or SYSTEM BUILDERS can perform this task and validate the test cases with the SYSTEM USERS.

Recall that SYSTEM IMPROVEMENT OBJECTIVES were defined earlier in the project. Test cases can be defined to test these objectives as well.

The Decision Analysis Phase

Given the business requirements for an improved information system, we can finally address how the new system—including computer-based alternatives—*might* be implemented with technology. The purpose of the *decision analysis phase* is to identify candidate solutions, analyze those candidate solutions, and recommend a target system that will be designed, constructed, and implemented. Chances are that someone has already championed a vision for a technical solution. But alternative solutions, perhaps better ones, nearly always exist. During the decision analysis phase, it is imperative that you identify options, analyze those options, and then sell the best solution based on the analysis.

Once again, your information systems building blocks (Figure 5-18) can serve as a useful framework for the decision analysis phase. One of the first things you should notice is that information technology and architecture begin to influence the decisions we must make. In some cases, we must work within standards. In other cases,

FIGURE 5-18 The Context of the Decision Analysis Phase of Systems Analysis

194   Part Two   Systems Analysis Methods

FIGURE 5-19

Tasks for the
Decision Analysis
Phase of Systems
Analysis

FIGURE 5-19

Tasks for the
Decision Analysis
Phase of Systems
Analysis

we can look to apply different or emerging technology. You should also notice that the perspectives are in transition—from those of the SYSTEM USERS to those of the SYSTEM DESIGNERS. Again, this reflects our transition from pure business concerns or technology. But we are not yet designing. The building blocks indicate our goal as developing a proposal that will fulfill requirements.

Figure 5-19 illustrates the typical tasks of the decision analysis phase. The final phase deliverable and milestone is producing a SYSTEM PROPOSAL that will fulfill the business requirements identified in the previous phase. The decision analysis phase typically includes the following tasks:

5.1 Identify candidate solutions.
5.2 Analyze candidate solutions.
5.3 Compare candidate solutions.
5.4 Update the project plan.
5.5 Recommend a system solution.

Let's now examine each of these tasks in greater detail.

> Task 5.1—Identify Candidate Solutions

Given the business requirements established in the definition phase of systems analysis, we must first identify alternative candidate solutions. Some candidate solutions will be posed by design ideas and opinions from SYSTEM OWNERS and USERS. Others may come from various sources including SYSTEMS ANALYSTS, SYSTEMS DESIGNERS, technical consultants, and other IS professionals. And some technical choices may be limited by a predefined, approved technology architecture. It is the intent of this task not to evaluate the candidates but, rather, simply to define possible candidate solutions to be considered.

The SYSTEMS ANALYSTS facilitate this task. SYSTEM OWNERS and USERS are not normally directly involved in this task, but they may contribute ideas and opinions that start the task. For example, an owner or user may have read an article about, heard about, or learned how some competitor's or acquaintance's similar system was implemented. In any case, it is politically sound to consider the ideas. SYSTEM DESIGNERS and BUILDERS such as database administrators, network administrators, technology architects, and programmers are also a source of ideas and opinions.

As shown in Figure 5-19, this task is formally triggered by the APPROVAL TO CONTINUE THE PROJECT FROM THE REQUIREMENTS ANALYSIS phase. In reality, ideas and opinions have been generated and captured since the preliminary investigation phase—it is human nature to suggest solutions throughout any problem-solving process. Notice that, in addition to coming from the project team itself, IDEAS AND OPINIONS can be generated from both internal and external sources. Each idea generated is considered to be a CANDIDATE SOLUTION to the BUSINESS REQUIREMENTS.

The amount of information describing the characteristics of any one candidate solution may become overwhelming. A candidate matrix, such as Figure 5-20, is a useful tool for effectively capturing, organizing, and comparing the characteristics of different candidate solutions.

As has been the case throughout this chapter, fact-finding and group facilitation techniques like JRP are the principle techniques used to research candidate system solutions. Fact-finding and group facilitation techniques are taught in the next chapter. Also, Chapter 10, "Feasibility Analysis and the System Proposal," will teach you how to actually generate candidate system solutions and document them in the matrix.

> Task 5.2—Analyze Candidate Solutions

Each candidate system solution must be analyzed for feasibility. This can occur as each candidate is identified or after all candidates have been identified. Feasibility analysis should not be limited to costs and benefits. Most analysts evaluate solutions against at least four sets of criteria:

- *Technical feasibility*—Is the solution technically practical? Does our staff have the technical expertise to design and build this solution?
- *Operational feasibility*—Will the solution fulfill the user's requirements? To what degree? How will the solution change the user's work environment? How do users feel about such a solution?
- *Economic feasibility*—Is the solution cost-effective?
- *Schedule feasibility*—Can the solution be designed and implemented within an acceptable time period?

When completing this task, the analysts and users must take care not to make comparisons between the candidates. The feasibility analysis is performed on each individual candidate without regard to the feasibility of other candidates. This approach discourages the analyst and users from prematurely making a decision concerning which candidate is the best.

Again, the SYSTEMS ANALYSTS facilitate the task. Usually SYSTEMS OWNERS and USERS analyze operational, economic, and schedule feasibility. SYSTEMS DESIGNERS and BUILDERS usually contribute to the analyses and play the critical role in analyzing technical feasibility.

Figure 5-19 shows that the task is triggered by the completion of each candidate solution; however, it is acceptable to delay the task until all candidate solutions have been identified. Input to the actual feasibility analyses comes from the various team

FIGURE 5-20 A Candidate Systems Matrix

Characteristics	Candidate 1	Candidate 2	Candidate 3	Candidate . . .
Portion of System Computerized Brief description of that portion of the system that would be computerized in this candidate.	COTS package Platinum Plus from Entertainment Software Solutions would be purchased and customized to satisfy Member Services required functionality.	Member Services and warehouse operations in relation to order fulfillment.	Same as candidate 2.	
Benefits Brief description of the business benefits that would be realized for this candidate.	This solution can be implemented quickly because it's a purchased solution.	Fully supports user's required business processes for SoundStage Inc. Plus more efficient interaction with member accounts.	Same as candidate 2.	
Servers and Workstations A description of the servers and workstations needed to support this candidate.	Technically, architecture dictates Pentium Pro, MS Windows NT class servers and Pentium, MS Windows NT 4.0 workstations (clients).	Same as candidate 1.	Same as candidate 1.	
Software Tools Needed Software tools needed to design and build the candidate (e.g., database management system, emulators, operating systems, languages, etc.). Not generally applicable if applications software packages are to be purchased.	MS Visual C++ and MS Access for customization of package to provide report writing and integration.	MS Visual Basic 5.0 System Architect 3.1 Internet Explorer	MS Visual Basic 5.0 System Architect 3.1 Internet Explorer	
Application Software A description of the software to be purchased, built, accessed, or some combination of these techniques.	Package solution.	Custom solution	Same as candidate 2.	
Method of Data Processing Generally some combination of online, batch, deferred batch, remote batch, and real time.	Client/server.	Same as candidate 1.	Same as candidate 1.	
Output Devices and Implications A description of output devices that would be used, special output requirements (e.g., network, preprinted forms, etc.), and output considerations (e.g., timing constraints).	(2) HP4MV department laser printers. (2) HP5SI LAN laser printers.	(2) HP4MV department laser printers. (2) HP5SI LAN laser printers. (1) PRINTRONIX bar code printer (includes software & drivers). Web pages must be designed to VGA resolution. All internal screens will be designed for SVGA resolution.	Same as candidate 2.	
Input Devices and Implications A description of input methods to be used, input devices (keyboard, mouse, etc.), special input requirements (e.g., new or revised forms from which data would be input), and input considerations (e.g., timing of actual inputs).	Keyboard & mouse.	Apple "Quick Take" digital camera and software. (15) PSC Quickscan laser bar code scanners. (1) HP Scanjet 4C flatbed scanner. Keyboard & mouse.	Same as candidate 2.	
Storage Devices and Implications Brief descriptions of what data would be stored, what data would be accessed from existing stores, what storage media would be used, how much storage capacity would be needed, and how data would be organized.	MS SQL Server DBMS with 100GB arrayed capability.	Same as candidate 1.	Same as candidate 1.	

participants; however, it is not uncommon for external experts (and influences) to also provide data. The feasibility analysis for each candidate is saved in the repository for later comparison to other candidates.

Fact-finding techniques, again, play a role in this systems analysis task. But the ability to perform a feasibility analysis on a candidate system solution is essential. That technique is taught in Chapter 10, "Feasibility Analysis and the System Proposal."

> Task 5.3—Compare Candidate Solutions

Once the feasibility analysis has been completed for each candidate solution, we can compare the candidates and select one or more solutions to recommend to the SYSTEM OWNERS and USERS. At this point, any infeasible candidates are usually eliminated from further consideration. Since we are looking for the most feasible solution of those remaining, we will identify and recommend the candidate that offers the best overall combination of technical, operational, economic, and schedule feasibilities. It should be noted that in selecting such a candidate, it is rare that a given candidate is found to be the most operational, technical, economic, and schedule feasible.

Once again, the SYSTEMS ANALYSTS facilitate the task. SYSTEM DESIGNERS and BUILDERS should be available to answer any technical feasibility questions. But ultimately, the SYSTEMS OWNERS and USERS should be empowered to drive the final analysis and recommendation.

In Figure 5-19, this task is triggered by the completion of the feasibility analysis of all candidate solutions (NO MORE CANDIDATE SOLUTIONS). The input is ALL OF THE CANDIDATES' FEASIBILITY ANALYSES. Once again, a matrix can be used to communicate the large volume of information about candidate solutions. The feasibility matrix in Figure 5-21 allows a side-by-side comparison of the different feasibility analyses for a number of candidates.

The deliverable of this task is the SOLUTION(S) TO BE RECOMMENDED. If more than one solution is recommended, priorities should be established.

Again, feasibility analysis techniques (and the matrix) will be taught in Chapter 10, "Feasibility Analysis and the System Proposal."

> Task 5.4—Update the Project Plan

Hopefully, you noticed a recurring theme throughout this chapter. We are continually updating our project plan as we learn more about a system, its problems, its requirements, and its solutions. We are adjusting scope accordingly. Thus, based on our recommended solution(s), we should once again reevaluate project scope and *update the project plan* accordingly.

The project manager, in conjunction with SYSTEM OWNERS and the entire project team, facilitates this task. The SYSTEMS ANALYSTS and SYSTEM OWNERS are the key individuals in this task. But because we are transitioning into technical system design, we need to begin involving the SYSTEM DESIGNERS and BUILDERS in the project plan updates.

As shown in Figure 5-19, this task is triggered by completion of the SOLUTION(S) TO BE RECOMMENDED. The latest PROJECT SCHEDULE AND RESOURCE ASSIGNMENTS must be reviewed and updated. The UPDATED PROJECT PLAN is the key output. The updated plan should now include a detailed plan for the system design phase that will follow. The techniques and steps for updating the project plan were taught in Chapter 4, "Project Management."

> Task 5.5—Recommend a System Solution

As with the preliminary investigation and problem analysis phases, the decision analysis phase concludes with a communication task. We must *recommend a system solution* to the business community.

FIGURE 5-21 A Feasibility Analysis Matrix

Feasibility Criteria	Weight	Candidate 1	Candidate 2	Candidate 3	Candidate ...
Operational Feasibility **Functionality.** A description of to what degree the candidate would benefit the organization and how well the system would work. **Political.** A description of how well received this solution would be from user management, user, and organization perspectives.	30%	Only supports Member Services requirements, and current business processes would have to be modified to take advantage of software functionality. **Score: 60**	Fully supports user's required functionality. **Score: 100**	Same as candidate 2. **Score: 100**	
Technical Feasibility **Technology.** An assessment of the maturity, availability (or ability to acquire), and desirability of the computer technology needed to support this candidate. **Expertise.** An assessment of the technical expertise needed to develop, operate, and maintain the candidate system.	30%	Current production release of Platinum Plus package is version 1.0 and has been on the market for only 6 weeks. Maturity of product is a risk, and company charges an additional monthly fee for technical support. Required to hire or train C++ expertise to perform modifications for integration requirements. **Score: 50**	Although current technical staff has only Powerbuilder experience, the senior analysts who saw the MS Visual Basic demonstration and presentation have agreed the transition will be simple and finding experienced VB programmers will be easier than finding Powerbuilder programmers and at a much cheaper cost. MS Visual Basic 5.0 is a mature technology based on version number. **Score: 95**	Although current technical staff is comfortable with Powerbuilder, management is concerned with recent acquisition of Powerbuilder by Sybase Inc. MS SQL Server is a current company standard and competes with SYBASE in the client/server DBMS market. Because of this we have no guarantee future versions of Power-builder will "play well" with our current version SQL Server. **Score: 60**	
Economic Feasibility **Cost to develop:** **Payback period (discounted):** **Net present value:** **Detailed calculations:**	30%	Approximately $350,000. Approximately 4.5 years. Approximately $210,000. See Attachment A. **Score: 60**	Approximately $418,040. Approximately 3.5 years. Approximately $306,748. See Attachment A. **Score: 85**	Approximately $400,000. Approximately 3.3 years. Approximately $325,500. See Attachment A. **Score: 90**	
Schedule Feasibility An assessment of how long the solution will take to design and implement.	10%	Less than 3 months. **Score: 95**	9–12 months. **Score: 80**	9 months. **Score: 85**	
Ranking	100%	**60.5**	**92**	**83.5**	

The project manager and executive sponsor should jointly facilitate this task. Other meeting participants should include the entire project team, including assigned SYSTEM OWNERS, USERS, ANALYSTS, DESIGNERS, and BUILDERS. As usual, the meeting should be open to any and all interested staff from the business community. Also, if an intranet Web site was established for the project, it should have been maintained throughout the problem analysis phases to ensure continuous communication of project progress.

This task is triggered by the completion of the UPDATED PROJECT PLAN. The TARGET SYSTEM SOLUTION (from Task 4.3) is reformatted for presentation as a SYSTEM PROPOSAL. The format may be a report, a verbal presentation, or an inspection by an auditor or peer group (called a *walkthrough*). An outline for a written report is shown in Figure 5-22.

The Next Generations: Systems Analysis

Predicting the future of systems analysis is not easy, but we'll make an attempt. CASE technology will continue to improve, making it easier to model system requirements. First, CASE tools will include object modeling to support emerging object-oriented analysis techniques. While some CASE tools will be purely object-oriented, we believe that the demand for other types of modeling support (e.g., data modeling for databases, process modeling for BPR) will place a premium on comprehensive CASE tools that can support many types of models. Second, the reverse-engineering technology in CASE tools will continue to improve our ability to more quickly generate first-draft system models from existing databases and application programs.

In the meantime, RAD technology will continue to enable accelerated analysis approaches such as prototyping. We also expect the trend for RAD and CASE tools to interoperate through reverse and forward engineering to further simplify both system modeling and discovery prototyping.

Object-oriented analysis will eventually replace structured analysis and information engineering as the best practice for systems analysis. This change may not occur as rapidly as object purists would like, but it will occur all too rapidly for a generation of systems analysts who are skilled in the older methods. There is a grand opportunity for talented young analysts to lead the transition; however, career opportunities will remain strong for analysts who know data modeling that will continue to be used for database design. Also, the process modeling renaissance will continue as BPR projects continue to proliferate.

We also predict our systems proposals will continue to get more interesting. As the Internet, e-commerce, and e-business become increasingly pervasive in our economy, systems analysts will be proposing new alternatives to old problems. There will be a fundamental change in business and information systems to use these new technologies.

One thing will *not* change! We will continue to need systems analysts who understand how to fundamentally investigate and analyze business problems and define the logical business requirements as a preface to system design. But we will all have to do that with increased speed and accuracy to meet the accelerated systems development schedules required in tomorrow's faster-paced economy.

Next Generation

Interpersonal and communications skills are essential to this task. Soft skills such as salesmanship and persuasion become important. (Many schools offer speech and communications courses on these subjects.) Systems analysts should be able to write a formal business report and make a business presentation without getting into technical issues or alternatives.

This concludes the decision analysis phase. And it also concludes our coverage of systems analysis.

FIGURE 5-22 An Outline for a Typical System Proposal

I. Introduction
   A. Purpose of the report
   B. Background of the project leading to this report
   C. Scope of the project
   D. Structure of the report
II. Tools and techniques used
   A. Solution generated
   B. Feasibility analysis (cost-benefit)
III. Information systems requirements
IV. Alternative solutions and feasibility analysis
V. Recommendations
VI. Appendixes

Learning Roadmap

This chapter provided a detailed overview of the systems analysis phases of a project. You are now ready to learn some of the systems skills introduced in this chapter. For most students, this would be the ideal time to study the fact-finding techniques that were identified as critical to almost every phase and task that was described in this chapter. Chapter 6 teaches these skills. It is recommended that you read Chapter 7, "Modeling System Requirements with Use Cases," before proceeding to any of the modeling chapters since use cases are commonly used to facilitate the activity of modeling.

The sequencing of the system modeling chapters is flexible; however, we personally prefer and recommend that Chapter 8, "Data Modeling and Analysis," be studied first. All information systems include databases, and data modeling is an essential skill for database development. Also, it is easier to synchronize early data models with later process models than vice versa. Your instructor may prefer that you first study Chapter 9, "Process Modeling." Advanced courses may elect to jump straight to Chapter 10 to learn about object-oriented analysis and modeling with UML.

If you do jump straight to a system modeling chapter from this chapter, make a commitment to return to Chapter 6 to study the fact-finding techniques. Regardless of how well you master system modeling, that modeling skill is entirely dependent on your ability to discover and collect the business facts that underlie the models.

For those of you who have already completed a systems analysis course, this chapter was probably scheduled only as a review or context for systems design. We suggest that you merely review the system modeling chapters and proceed directly to Chapter 12, "Systems Design." That chapter will pick up where this chapter left off.

Summary

1. Formally, systems analysis is the dissection of a system into its component pieces. As a problem-solving phase, it precedes systems design. With respect to information systems development, systems analysis is the preliminary investigation of a proposed project, the study and problem analysis of the existing system, the requirements analysis of business requirements for the new system, and the decision analysis for alternative solutions to fulfill the requirements.

2. The results of systems analysis are stored in a repository for use in later phases and projects.

3. There are several popular or emerging strategies for systems analysis. These techniques can be used in combination with one another.

   a. Model-driven analysis techniques emphasize the drawing of pictorial system models that represent either a current reality or a target vision of the system.

   i) Structured analysis is a technique that focuses on modeling processes.
   ii) Information engineering is a technique that focuses on modeling data.
   iii) Object-oriented analysis is a technique that focuses on modeling objects that encapsulate the concerns of data and processes that act on that data.

   b. Accelerated analysis approaches emphasize the construction of working models of a system in an effort to accelerate systems analysis.

   i) Discovery prototyping is a technique that focuses on building small-scale, functional subsystems to discover requirements.
   ii) Rapid architected analysis attempts to automatically generate system models from either prototypes or existing systems. The automatic generation of models requires reverse engineering technology.

c. Both model-driven and accelerated system analysis approaches are dependent on requirements discovery techniques to identify or extract problems and requirements from system owners and users.

  i) Fact-finding is the formal process of using research, interviews, questionnaires, sampling, and other techniques to collect information.

  ii) Joint requirements planning (JRP) techniques use facilitated workshops to bring together all interested parties and accelerate the fact-finding process.

  d. Business process redesign is a technique that focuses on simplifying and streamlining fundamental business processes before applying information technology to those processes.

4. Each phase of systems analysis (preliminary investigation, problem analysis, requirements analysis, and decision analysis) can be understood in the context of the information system building blocks: KNOWLEDGE, PROCESSES, and COMMUNICATIONS.

5. The purpose of the preliminary investigation phase is to determine the worthiness of the project and to create a plan to complete those projects deemed worthy of a detailed study and analysis. To accomplish the preliminary investigation phase, the systems analyst will work with the system owners and users to: *(a)* list problems, opportunities, and directives; *(b)* negotiate preliminary scope; *(c)* assess project worth; *(d)* plan the project, and *(e)* present the project to the business community. The deliverable for the preliminary investigation phase is a project charter that must be approved by system owners and/or a decision-making body, commonly referred to as the steering committee.

6. The purpose of the problem analysis phase is to answer the questions, Are the problems really worth solving, and is a new system really worth building? To answer these questions, the problem analysis phase thoroughly analyzes the alleged problems and opportunities first identified in the preliminary investigation phase. To complete the problem analysis phase, the analyst will continue to work with the system owner, system users, and other IS management and staff. The systems analyst and appropriate participants will *(a)* study the problem domain; *(b)* thoroughly analyze problems and opportunities; *(c)* optionally, analyze business processes; *(d)* establish system improvement objectives and constraints; *(e)* update the project plan; and *(f)* present the findings and recommendations. The deliverable for the

problem analysis phase is the system improvement objectives.

7. The purpose of the requirements analysis phase is to identify what the new system is to do without the consideration of technology—in other words, to define the business requirements for a new system. As in the preliminary investigation and problem analysis phases, the analyst actively works with system users and owners as well as other IS professionals. To complete the requirements analysis phase, the analyst and appropriate participants will *(a)* define requirements, *(b)* analyze functional requirements using system modeling and/or discovery prototyping, *(c)* trace and complete the requirements statement, *(d)* prioritize the requirements, and *(e)* update the project plan and scope. The deliverable of the requirements analysis phase is the business requirements statement. Because requirements are a moving target with no finalization, requirements analysis also includes the ongoing task of managing changes to the requirements.

8. The purpose of the logical design phase is to document business requirements using system models for the proposed system. These system models can, depending on the methodology, be any combination of process models, data models, and object models. The models depict various aspects of our building blocks. Alternatively, prototypes could be built to "discover requirements." Some discovery prototypes can be reverse engineered into system models. The systems analyst and appropriate participants will *(a)* structure or prototype functional requirements, *(b)* validate functional requirements, and *(c)* define acceptance test cases. These tasks are not necessarily sequential; they can occur in parallel. The deliverable for the logical design phase is the business requirements statement.

9. The purpose of the decision analysis phase is to transition the project from business concerns to technical solutions by identifying, analyzing, and recommending a technical system solution. To complete the decision analysis phase, the analyst and appropriate participants will *(a)* define candidate solutions; *(b)* analyze candidate solutions for feasibility (technical, operational, economic, and schedule feasibility); *(c)* compare feasible candidate solutions to select one or more recommended solutions; *(d)* update the project plan based on the recommended solution; and *(e)* present and defend the target solution. The deliverable of the decision analysis phase is the system proposal.

Review Questions

1. What are the business factors that are driving systems analysis? Based on these factors, what should systems analysis address?
2. What is model-driven analysis? Why is it used? Give several examples.
3. What is the major focus of structured analysis?
4. What is the major focus of information engineering?
5. Why has object-oriented analysis become popular? What problems does it solve?
6. What are the five phases of systems analysis?
7. What is the goal of the scope definition phase?
8. What are the five tasks that you do in the scope definition phase?
9. What is the trigger for communicating the project plan, and who is the audience? Why is communicating the project plan important?

10. Why do many new systems analysts fail to effectively analyze problems? What can they do to become more effective?
11. What is a popular tool used to identify and express the functional requirements of a system?
12. What is a commonly used technique for prioritizing system requirements?
13. When could prototyping be used instead of system modeling for determining functional requirements?
14. Why is the decision analysis phase needed?
15. What are some ways to identify candidate solutions?

Problems and Exercises

1. There are many different approaches to systems analysis. Despite these different approaches, what is the universally accepted definition of systems analysis? What is the general consensus as to when systems analysis begins and when it ends? As a project manager, what is important to know regarding the definition of systems analysis, and what is important to ensure in your organization regarding the definition?
2. As a systems analyst, you will be exposed to and use many different approaches to systems

analysis throughout your career. It is important that you understand the conceptual basis of each type of approach, and their essential differences, strengths and weaknesses. Consider the differences in structured analysis, information engineering and data modeling, and object-oriented analysis, all of which represent model-driven analysis, and fill in the matrix shown below.

	CENTRICITY (data, process, etc.)	TYPE OF MODELS USED	ESSENTIAL DIFFERENCES
STRUCTURED ANALYSIS			
INFORMATION ENGINEERING AND DATA MODELING			
OBJECT-ORIENTED ANALYSIS			

3. Accelerated systems analysis approaches are based on the premise that prototypes can help reveal the most important business requirements faster than other methods. Describe the two most commonly used approaches to accelerated analysis. What do they do and how do they do it? What is one of the criticisms of prototyping? Do the accelerated systems analysis approaches completely replace more formal approaches, such as structured analysis?

4. During the scope definition phase, what is one question that you should never lose sight of? And how do you answer this question? What five tasks should occur during the scope definition phase?

5. You are a new systems analyst and eager to prove your abilities on your first project. You are at a problem analysis meeting with the system owners and users and find yourself saying, "We need to do this to solve the problem." Into what common trap are you in danger of falling? What technique could you use to avoid this trap?

6. Your project team has completed the scope definition phase, and is now at the point in the problem analysis phase for establishing system improvement objectives. As the systems analyst on the project team, you are the facilitator of a brainstorming session to define the system improvement objectives. Since several of the project owners and users have never done this before, describe the characteristics of good system improvement objectives and provide some examples. Members of the project team suggest the following objectives:

   a. Reduce the time required to process the order.
   b. The new system must use Oracle to store data.
   c. The data input screens must be redesigned so they are more user-friendly.
   d. The customer satisfaction rate with the online ordering process must be increased by 10 percent.

   Are these examples of good system improvement objectives? Why or why not? If not, how could they be reworded? Also, objectives frequently have constraints that are tied to them; what, if any, do you think the matching constraint might be for each of these objectives?

7. You've made it through the problem analysis phase of the project, and are now beginning the requirements analysis phase. During the first meeting on the business requirements, one of the other analysts on the project team asks the system users, "How should the new system meet your needs?" What common mistake is the analyst making? What are often the consequences of making this mistake?

8. What is the difference between functional and nonfunctional requirements, and what is the purpose of categorizing them into these categories? What are two formats that an analyst can use to document the functional system requirements?

9. Is it important to prioritize system requirements, and if so, when should the requirements be prioritized? What is one technique that can be used, and what is the difference between mandatory and desirable requirements? What is one way to test whether a mandatory requirement is truly a mandatory requirement?

10. Once the system requirements are identified and prioritized, shouldn't everything be frozen to prevent scope or feature creep? Doesn't updating the project plan or allowing stakeholders to continue to request changes just delay system design and construction, and maybe even project completion itself?

11. Why should acceptance test cases be defined during the logical design phase? After all, the technical design hasn't been done yet, let alone building the system. Shouldn't testing activities at least wait until construction is actually underway?

12. How is the logical design phase different from the requirements analysis phase?

13. Let's say you are on the project team of a project that had a great deal of difficulty during the requirements analysis phase, and fell several weeks behind schedule. The project manager wants to try to catch up by either skipping or abbreviating some of the tasks in the logical design phase. After all, the project manager reasons, we really have a clear idea of the requirements now, the designers and builders are really experienced, and they don't really need the logical design in order to do the technical design. Is this a legitimate method to get back on schedule? What are the possible consequences?

14. In identifying and defining possible candidate solutions, what are the typical roles of the various stakeholders who are involved in the project?

15. You are a systems analyst and have been asked to facilitate the analysis and evaluation of several candidate system solutions for their feasibility. What sets of criteria would you typically use? Who do you involve in this task? Should you compare the candidate solutions against each other at this point? Why or why not? What is the typical deliverable coming out of this task?

Projects and Research

1. Select an information system with which you are familiar, and which you feel needs to be improved, based upon your experiences as an employee, customer, other system user, or system owner. Switch roles and perspectives as necessary to perform or answer the following:

   a. Describe the nature of the information system you have selected.
   b. Describe the organization that owns and maintains the information system.
   c. Identify the baseline problems and opportunities, per Task 1.1.
   d. Develop a preliminary problem statement, using the format shown in Figure 5-8.

2. Assume you are the now a systems analyst on the project described in the preceding question. Executive management was extremely impressed by your work on the problem statement. As a result, they have given the project the go-ahead, the baseline schedule and budget have been developed, and the project plan has been approved by the executive steering committee. As the systems analyst, you now have been tasked to do the following:

   a. Develop and document your understanding of the problem domain and business vocabulary, using the textbook's information system building blocks framework as described in Task 2.1.
   b. Analyze problems and opportunities using cause-and-effect analysis (Task 2.2).
   c. Analyze business processes and develop process models (Task 2.3).
   d. Establish system improvement objectives (Task 2.4).
   e. Prepare a Problems, Opportunities, Objectives, and Constraints Matrix, using Figure 5-12 as an example.

3. Communicating findings and recommendations is the final task in the problem analysis phase. As a systems analyst on the project, you have been tasked with preparing the System Improvement Objectives and Recommendations Report. For this exercise, prepare only the Executive Summary

portion of the report, using the format shown in Figure 5-13. The executive steering committee will use this summary to make its decisions regarding the recommendations.

4. Your strong work on the project to date has continued to impress executive management. You have received a pay increase and have been tasked with conducting the requirements analysis phase. Specifically:

   a. Identify the system requirements, and prepare an outline of functional and nonfunctional requirements, per Task 3.1. Since your organization uses structured analysis and does not employ use case modeling, list each system improvement objective, and the inputs, processes, outputs, and stored data needed to meet each objective.
   b. Assume that the requirements you identified in the preceding step have been validated. Prioritize the requirements according to their relative importance, using the method described in Task 3.2.

5. Your work has helped keep the project well ahead of schedule, so executive management gives you a couple of weeks of paid vacation. When you return, the project is moving into the decision analysis phase. Your next task is to identify candidate solutions.

   a. Describe the process for identifying candidate solutions. What should you be careful *not* to do at this point?
   b. Develop a candidate systems matrix, using the format in Figure 5-20 as an example, and include three possible solutions.

6. After identifying candidate solutions, the next step is to analyze these solutions.

   a. Describe the process for analyzing candidate solutions. What should the project team *not* do in completing this task?
   b. Develop a Feasibility Analysis Matrix, based upon the candidate solutions identified in the preceding question, and using the format shown in Figure 5-21 as an example. Determine what your weighting factors should be.

Minicases

1. You are the CIO of a major retailer. Recently, you read "Spying on the Sales Floor" in the *Wall Street Journal* on December 21, 2004. You see that your

competitors are using video mining to analyze consumer behavior. Should your company also adopt this tool (video mining)? What are the strategic

implications to your company of your competitors' move? What opportunities have been created? Threats?

2. Read "Human Reengineering," by Cooper and Markus, in the *Sloan Management Review,* Summer 1995. In this article, Okuno works on instituting a positive attitude toward change. How does he do this? Discuss the importance of change acceptance by employees to the success of a technology implementation.
3. Refer to Minicase 1. You, as the CIO, believe that the business gains for implementing video mining in your retail stores will outweigh any negative customer perceptions. Your company is Baby's R Us, a child company of Toys R Us. Do an economic feasibility study for this investment. Be sure to include a listing of intangible costs and benefits, as well as an argument for your chosen discount rate. What is the ROI of the video mining? Try to keep your analysis to under 15 pages.
4. Develop a project plan and schedule feasibility study for the video-mining investment into Baby's R Us. Be sure to include a Gantt and PERT/CPM chart, as well as a clear discussion of all tasks that need to be completed.

Team and Individual Exercises

1. How often do you think legal issues play a role in project success? Think of an example of a potentially good information system or program that was constrained or not feasible due to legal requirements.
2. As a team, brainstorm some ways to enhance employee change acceptance of new information systems or business processes.
3. Think of an example when business process improvement is more appropriate than business process reengineering. Share with the class.

Suggested Readings

Application Development Trends (monthly periodical). Natick, MA: Software Productivity Group, a ULLO International company. This is our favorite systems development periodical. It follows systems analysis and design strategies, methodologies, CASE, and other relevant trends. Visit its Web site at www.adtmag.com.

Gause, Donald C., and Gerald M. Weinberg. *Are Your Lights On? How to Figure Out What the Problem REALLY Is.* New York: Dorset House Publishing, 1990. Here's a title that should really get you thinking, and the entire book addresses one of the least published aspects of systems analysis: problem solving.

Hammer, Mike. "Reengineering Work: Don't Automate, Obliterate." *Harvard Business Review,* July–August 1990, pp. 104–11. Dr. Hammer is a noted expert on business process redesign. This seminal paper examines some classic cases where the technique dramatically added value to businesses.

Wetherbe, James. *Systems Analysis and Design: Best Practices,* 4th ed. St. Paul, MN: West Publishing, 1994. We are indebted to Dr. Wetherbe for the PIECES framework.

Wood, Jane, and Denise Silver. *Joint Application Design: How to Design Quality Systems in 40% Less Time.* New York: John Wiley & Sons, 1989. This book provides an excellent in-depth presentation of joint application development (JAD).

Yourdon, Edward. *Modern Structured Analysis.* Englewood Cliffs, NJ: Yourdon Press, 1989. This update to the classic DeMarco text on the same subject defines the current state of the practice for the structured analysis approach.

Zachman, John A. "A Framework for Information System Architecture." *IBM Systems Journal* 26, no. 3 (1987). This article presents a popular conceptual framework for information systems surveys and the development of an information architecture.

Data Modeling and Analysis

Chapter Preview and Objectives

In this chapter you will learn how to use a popular data-modeling tool, *entity relationship diagrams,* to document the data that must be captured and stored by a system, independently of showing how that data is or will be used—that is, independently of specific inputs, outputs, and processing. You will also learn about a data analysis technique called *normalization* that is used to ensure that a data model is a "good" data model. You will know data modeling and data analysis as systems analysis tools and techniques when you can:

- Define systems modeling and differentiate between logical and physical system models.

- Define data modeling and explain its benefits.

- Recognize and understand the basic concepts and constructs of a data model.

- Read and interpret an entity relationship data model.

- Explain when data models are constructed during a project and where the models are stored.

- Discover entities and relationships.

- Construct an entity relationship context diagram.

- Discover or invent keys for entities and construct a key-based diagram.

- Construct a fully attributed entity relationship diagram and describe all data structures and attributes to the repository or encyclopedia.

- Normalize a logical data model to remove impurities that can make a database unstable, inflexible, and nonscalable.

- Describe a useful tool for mapping data requirements to business operating locations.

Introduction

As the SoundStage Member Services system project moves from requirements analysis into logical design, the first task according to their methodology is to analyze the data requirements for the new system. Bob Martinez remembers a favorite professor in college who always said, "Get the data right and the system will be able to elegantly support all your present requirements and even requirements users don't yet envision; get the data wrong and it will be a pain in the neck to meet requirements today, tomorrow, and forever."

Bob enjoyed his database classes in college and always did well in them. Of course, the member services system is larger and more detailed than any data project he did in school. Fortunately, he has the database from the previous version of the system to start with, plus forms and reports from the previous system, plus notes from user interviews, plus use-case narratives created during the requirements analysis phase. Sandra has asked Bob to take the first shot at pulling it all together into a logical data model. He's determined to impress her.

What Is Data Modeling?

data modeling a technique for organizing and documenting a system's data. Sometimes called *database modeling*.

Systems models play an important role in systems development. This chapter will present **data modeling** as a technique for defining business requirements for a database. Data modeling is sometimes called *database modeling* because a data model is eventually implemented as a database.

Figure 8-1 is an example of a simple data model called an *entity relationship diagram*, or *ERD*. This diagram makes the following business assertions:

- We need to store data about CUSTOMERS, ORDERS, and INVENTORY PRODUCTS.
- The value of CUSTOMER NUMBER <u>uniquely</u> identifies one and only one CUSTOMER. The value of ORDER NUMBER <u>uniquely</u> identifies one and only one ORDER. The value of PRODUCT NUMBER <u>uniquely</u> identifies one and only one INVENTORY PRODUCT.
- For a CUSTOMER we need to know the CUSTOMER NAME, SHIPPING ADDRESS, BILLING ADDRESS, and BALANCE DUE. For an ORDER we need to know ORDER DATE and ORDER TOTAL COST. For an INVENTORY PRODUCT we need to know PRODUCT NAME, PRODUCT UNIT OF MEASURE, and PRODUCT UNIT PRICE.

FIGURE 8-1

An Entity Relationship Data Model

- A CUSTOMER has placed zero, one, or more current or recent ORDERS.
- An ORDER is placed by exactly one CUSTOMER. The value of CUSTOMER NUMBER (as recorded in ORDER) identifies that CUSTOMER.
- An ORDER sold one or more ORDERED PRODUCTS. Thus, an ORDER must contain at least one ORDERED PRODUCT.
- An INVENTORY PRODUCT may have been sold as zero, one, or more ORDERED PRODUCTS.
- An ORDERED PRODUCT identifies a single INVENTORY PRODUCT on a single ORDER. The ORDER NUMBER (for an ORDERED PRODUCT) identifies the ORDER, and the PRODUCT NUMBER (for an ORDERED PRODUCT) identifies the INVENTORY PRODUCT. Together, they identify one and only one ORDERED PRODUCT.
- For each ORDERED PRODUCT we need to know QUANTITY ORDERED and UNIT PRICE AT TIME OF ORDER.

After you study this chapter, you will be able to read data models and construct them.

System Concepts for Data Modeling

There are several notations for data modeling. The actual model is frequently called an **entity relationship diagram (ERD)** because it depicts data in terms of the entities and relationships described by the data. There are several notations for ERDs. Most are named after their inventor (e.g., Chen, Martin, Bachman, Merise) or after a published standard (e.g., IDEF1X). These data modeling "languages" generally support the same fundamental concepts and constructs. We have adopted the Martin (information engineering) notation because of its widespread use and CASE tool support.

Let's explore some basic concepts that underlie all data models.

entity relationship diagram (ERD) a data model utilizing several notations to depict data in terms of the entities and relationships described by that data.

> Entities

All systems contain data—usually lots of data! Data describes "things." Consider a school system. A school system includes data that describes things such as STUDENTS, TEACHERS, COURSES, and CLASSROOMS. For any of these things, it is not difficult to imagine some of the data that describes any given instance of the thing. For example, the data that describes a particular student might include NAME, ADDRESS, PHONE NUMBER, DATE OF BIRTH, GENDER, RACE, MAJOR, and GRADE POINT AVERAGE, to name a few.

We need a concept to abstractly represent all instances of a group of similar things. We call this concept an entity. An **entity** is something about which the business needs to store data. In system modeling, we find it useful to assign each abstract concept to a shape. In this book, an entity will be drawn as a rectangle with rounded corners (see margin). This shape represents all instances of the named entity. For example, the entity STUDENT represents all students in the system. Thus, an entity identifies specific classes of entities and is distinguishable from the other entities.

Categories of entities (and examples) include:

entity a class of persons, places, objects, events, or concepts about which we need to capture and store data.

An Entity

Persons:	AGENCY, CONTRACTOR, CUSTOMER, DEPARTMENT, DIVISION, EMPLOYEE, INSTRUCTOR, STUDENT, SUPPLIER. Notice that a person entity class can represent individuals, groups, or organizations.
Places:	SALES REGION, BUILDING, ROOM, BRANCH OFFICE, CAMPUS.
Objects:	BOOK, MACHINE, PART, PRODUCT, RAW MATERIAL, SOFTWARE LICENSE, SOFTWARE PACKAGE, TOOL, VEHICLE MODEL, VEHICLE. An object entity can represent actual objects (such as a specific software license) or specifications for a type of object (such as specifications for different software packages).
Events:	APPLICATION, AWARD, CANCELLATION, CLASS, FLIGHT, INVOICE, ORDER, REGISTRATION, RENEWAL, REQUISITION, RESERVATION, SALE, TRIP.
Concepts:	ACCOUNT, BLOCK OF TIME, BOND, COURSE, FUND, QUALIFICATION, STOCK.

entity instance a single occurrence of an entity.

It is important to distinguish between an entity and its instances. An **entity instance** is a single occurrence of an entity. For example, the entity STUDENT may have multiple instances: Mary, Joe, Mark, Susan, Cheryl, and so forth. In data modeling, we do not concern ourselves with individual students because we recognize that each student is described by similar pieces of data.

> Attributes

attribute a descriptive property or characteristic of an entity. Synonyms include *element, property,* and *field.*

If an entity is something about which we want to store data, then we need to identify what specific pieces of data we want to store about each instance of a given entity. We call these pieces of data **attributes.** As noted at the beginning of this section, each instance of the entity STUDENT might be described by the following attributes: NAME, ADDRESS, PHONE NUMBER, DATE OF BIRTH, GENDER, RACE, MAJOR, GRADE POINT AVERAGE, and others.

We can now extend our graphical abstraction of the entity to include attributes by recording those attributes inside the entity shape along with the name (see margin).

Some attributes can be logically grouped into superattributes called **compound attributes.** For example, a student's NAME is actually a compound attribute that consists of LAST NAME, FIRST NAME, and MIDDLE INITIAL. In the margin, we demonstrate one possible notation for compound attributes. Notice that a period is placed at the beginning of each primitive attribute that is included in the composite attribute.

Domains   When analyzing a system, we should define those values for an attribute that are legitimate or that make business sense. The values for each attribute are defined in terms of three properties: data type, domain, and default.

The **data type** for an attribute defines what type of data can be stored in that attribute. Data typing should be familiar to those of you who have written computer programs; declaring types for variables is common to most programming languages. For purposes of systems analysis and business requirements definition, it is useful to declare logical (nontechnical) data types for business attributes. For the sake of argument, we will use the logical data types shown in Table 8-1.

An attribute's data type constrains its domain. The **domain** of an attribute defines what values the attribute can legitimately take on. Eventually, system designers must use technology to enforce the business domains of all attributes. Table 8-2 demonstrates how logical domains might be expressed for each data type.

STUDENT

Name
.Last Name
.First Name
.Middle Initial
Address
.Street Address
.City
.State or Province
.Country
.Postal Code
Phone Number
.Area Code
.Exchange Number
.Number Within Exchange
Date of Birth
Gender
Race
Major
Grade Point Average

**Attributes and
Compound Attributes**

compound attribute an attribute that consists of other attributes. Synonyms in different data modeling languages are numerous: *concatenated attribute, composite attribute,* and *data structure.*

data type a property of an attribute that identifies what type of data can be stored in the attribute.

domain a property of an attribute that defines what values the attribute can legitimately take on.

TABLE 8-1 Representative Logical Data Types for Attributes

Logical Data Type	Logical Business Meaning
NUMBER	Any number, real or integer.
TEXT	A string of characters, inclusive of numbers. When numbers are included in a TEXT attribute, it means we do not expect to perform arithmetic or comparisons with those numbers.
MEMO	Same as TEXT but of an indeterminate size. Some business systems require the ability to attach potentially lengthy notes to a given database record.
DATE	Any date in any format.
TIME	Any time in any format.
YES/NO	An attribute that can assume only one of these two values.
VALUE SET	A finite set of values. In most cases, a coding scheme would be established (e.g., FR = freshman, SO = sophomore, JR = junior, SR = senior, etc.).
IMAGE	Any picture or image.

TABLE 8-2 Representative Logical Domains for Logical Data Types

Data Type	Domain	Examples
NUMBER	For integers, specify the range: {minimum–maximum} For real numbers, specify the range and precision: {minimum.precision–maximum.precision}	{10–99} {1.000–799.999}
TEXT	TEXT (maximum size of attribute) *Actual values are usually infinite; however, users may specify certain narrative restrictions.*	TEXT (30)
MEMO	*Not applicable. There are no logical restrictions on size or content.*	*Not applicable.*
DATE	Variation on the MMDDYYYY format. To accommodate the year 2000, do not abbreviate year to YY. Formatting characters are rarely stored; therefore, do not include hyphens or slashes.	MMDDYYYY MMYYYY YYYY
TIME	For AM/PM times: HHMMT or For military times: HHMM	HHMMT HHMM
YES/NO	{YES, NO}	{YES, NO} {ON, OFF}
VALUE SET	{value#1, value#2, . . . value#n} or {table of codes and meanings}	{FRESHMAN, SOPHO-MORE, JUNIOR, SENIOR} {FR = FRESHMAN SO = SOPHOMORE JR = JUNIOR SR = SENIOR}
IMAGE	*Not applicable; however, any known characteristics of the images will eventually prove useful to designers.*	*Not applicable.*

Finally, every attribute should have a logical **default value** that represents the value of an attribute if its value is not specified by the user. Table 8-3 shows possible default values for an attribute. Notice that NOT NULL is a way to specify that each instance of the attribute must <u>have</u> a value, while NULL is a way to specify that some instances of the attribute may be optional, or not have a value.

Identification An entity has many instances, perhaps thousands or millions. There exists a need to uniquely identify each instance based on the data value of one or more attributes. Thus, every entity must have a **key**. For example, each instance of the entity STUDENT might be uniquely identified by the key STUDENT NUMBER attribute. No two students can have the same STUDENT NUMBER.

Sometimes more than one attribute is required to uniquely identify an instance of an entity. A key consisting of a group of attributes is called a **concatenated key**. For example, each DVD entity instance in a video store might be uniquely identified by the

default value the value that will be recorded if a value is not specified by the user.

key an attribute, or a group of attributes, that assumes a unique value for each entity instance. It is sometimes called an *identifier*.

concatenated key a group of attributes that uniquely identifies an instance of an entity. Synonyms include *composite key* and *compound key*.

> **TABLE 8-3 Permissible Default Values for Attributes**

Default Value	Interpretation	Examples
A legal value from the domain (as described above)	For an instance of the attribute, if the user does not specify a value, then use this value.	0 1.00 FR
NONE or NULL	For an instance of the attribute, if the user does not specify a value, then leave it blank.	NONE NULL
REQUIRED or NOT NULL	For an instance of the attribute, requires that the user enter a legal value from the domain. (This is used when no value in the domain is common enough to be a default but some value must be entered.)	REQUIRED NOT NULL

concatenation of TITLE NUMBER plus COPY NUMBER. TITLE NUMBER by itself would be inadequate because the store may own many copies of a single title. COPY NUMBER by itself would also be inadequate since we presumably have a *copy #1* for every title we own. We need both pieces of data to identify a specific tape (e.g., *copy #7* of *Star Wars: Revenge of the Sith*). In this book, we will give a name to the group as well as the individual attributes. For example, the concatenated key for DVD would be recorded as follows:

    DVD ID
    .TITLE NUMBER
    .COPY NUMBER

Frequently, an entity may have more than one key. For example, the entity EMPLOYEE may be uniquely identified by SOCIAL SECURITY NUMBER, or company-assigned EMPLOYEE NUMBER, or E-MAIL ADDRESS. Each of these attributes is called a *candidate key*. A **candidate key** is a "candidate to become the primary key" of instances of an entity. It is sometimes called a *candidate identifier.* (A candidate key may be a single attribute or a concatenated key.) A **primary key** is that candidate key that will most commonly be used to uniquely identify a single entity instance. The default for a primary key is always NOT NULL because if the key has no value, it cannot serve its purpose to identify an instance of an entity. Any candidate key that is not selected to become the primary key is called an **alternate key.** A common synonym is *secondary key.* In the margin, we demonstrate our notation for primary and alternate keys. All candidate keys must be either primary or alternate; therefore, we do not use a separate notation for candidate keys. All attributes that are not part of the primary key are called nonkey attributes.

Sometimes, it is also necessary to identify a subset of an entity's instances as opposed to a single instance. For example, we may require a simple way to identify all male students and all female students. A **subsetting criteria** is an attribute (or concatenated attribute) whose finite values divide all entity instances into useful subsets. This is sometimes referred to as an *inversion entry.* In our STUDENT entity, the attribute GENDER divides the instances of STUDENT into two subsets: male students and female students. In general, subsetting criteria are useful only when an attribute has a finite (meaning "limited") number of legitimate values. For example, GRADE POINT AVERAGE would not be a good subsetting criteria because there are 999 possible values between 0.00 and 4.00 for that attribute. The margin art demonstrates a notation for subsetting criteria.

> Relationships

Conceptually, entities and attributes do not exist in isolation. The things they represent interact with and impact one another to support the business mission. Thus, we

candidate key one of a number of keys that may serve as the primary key of an entity. Also called *candidate identifier.*

primary key a candidate key that will most commonly be used to uniquely identify a single entity instance.

alternate key a candidate key that is not selected to become the primary key. A synonym is *secondary key.*

subsetting criteria an attribute(s) whose finite values divide entity instances into subsets. Sometimes called *inversion entry.*

introduce the concept of a relationship. A **relationship** is a natural business association that exists between one or more entities. The relationship may represent an event that links the entities or merely a logical affinity that exists between the entities. Consider, for example, the entities STUDENT and CURRICULUM. We can make the following business assertions that link students and courses:

- A current STUDENT IS ENROLLED IN one or more CURRICULA.
- A CURRICULUM IS BEING STUDIED BY zero, one, or more STUDENTS.

The underlined verb phrases define business relationships that exist between the two entities.

We can graphically illustrate this association between STUDENT and CURRICULUM as shown in Figure 8-2. The connecting line represents a relationship. Verb phrases describe the relationship. Notice that all relationships are implicitly bidirectional, meaning they can be interpreted in both directions (as suggested by the above business assertions). Data modeling methods may differ in their naming of relationships—some include both verb phrases, and others include a single verb phrase.

Cardinality   Figure 8-2 also shows the complexity or *degree* of each relationship. For example, if we know how to read it, Figure 8-2 can answer the following questions:

- Must there exist an instance of STUDENT for each instance of CURRICULUM? No!
- Must there exist an instance of CURRICULUM for each instance of STUDENT? Yes!
- How many instances of CURRICULUM can exist for each instance of STUDENT? Many!
- How many instances of STUDENT can exist for each instance of CURRICULUM? Many!

We call this concept *cardinality*. **Cardinality** defines the minimum and maximum number of occurrences of one entity that may be related to a single occurrence of the other entity. Because all relationships are bidirectional, cardinality must be defined in both directions for every relationship. A popular graphical notation for cardinality is shown in Figure 8-3. Sample cardinality symbols were demonstrated in Figure 8-2.

Conceptually, cardinality tells us the following rules about the data entities shown in Figure 8-2:

- When we insert a STUDENT instance in the database, we <u>must</u> link (associate) that STUDENT to at least one instance of CURRICULUM. In business terms, "a student cannot be admitted without declaring a major." (Most schools would include an instance of CURRICULUM called "undecided" or "undeclared.")
- A STUDENT <u>can</u> study more than one CURRICULUM, and we must be able to store data that indicates all CURRICULA for a given STUDENT.
- We must insert a CURRICULUM before we can link (associate) STUDENTS to that CURRICULUM. That is why a CURRICULUM can have zero students—no students have yet been admitted to that CURRICULUM.
- Once a CURRICULUM has been inserted into the database, we can link (associate) many STUDENTS with that CURRICULUM.

Degree   Another measure of the complexity of a data relationship is its degree. The **degree** of a relationship is the number of entities that participate in the relationship. All the relationships we've explored so far are *binary* (degree = 2). In other words, two different entities participated in the relationship.

Sidebar

STUDENT

Student Number
  (Primary Key)
Social Security Number
  (Alternate Key)
Name
  .Last Name
  .First Name
  .Middle Initial
Address
  .Street Address
  .City
  .State or Province
  .Country
  .Postal Code
Phone Number
  .Area Code
  .Exchange Number
  .Number Within Exchange
Date of Birth
Gender (Subsetting Criteria 1)
Race (Subsetting Criteria 2)
Major (Subsetting Criteria 3)
Grade Point Average

Keys and Subsetting Criteria

relationship a natural business association between one or more entities.

cardinality the minimum and maximum number of occurrences of one entity that may be related to a single occurrence of the other entity.

degree the number of entities that participate in a relationship.

FIGURE 8-2

A Relationship (Many-to-Many)

STUDENT ──>O─ is enrolled in ──────── is being studied by ─+── CURRICULUM

FIGURE 8-3

Cardinality
Notations

CARDINALITY INTERPRETATION	MINIMUM INSTANCES	MAXIMUM INSTANCES	GRAPHIC NOTATION
Exactly one (one and only one)	1	1	— or —
Zero or one	0	1	
One or more	1	many (>1)	
Zero, one, or more	0	many (>1)	
More than one	>1	>1	

recursive relationship a relationship that exists between instances of the same entity.

associative entity an entity that inherits its primary key from more than one other entity.

Relationships may also exist between different instances of the same entity. We call this a **recursive relationship** (degree = 1). For example, in your school a course may be a prerequisite for other courses. Similarly, a course may have several other courses as its prerequisite. Figure 8-4 demonstrates this many-to-many recursive relationship.

Relationships can also exist between more than two different entities. These are sometimes called *N*-ary relationships. An example of a *3-ary*, or *ternary, relationship* is shown in Figure 8-5. An *N*-ary relationship is illustrated with a new entity construct called an *associative entity*. An **associative entity** is an entity that inherits its primary key from more than one other entity (called *parents*). Each part of that concatenated key points to one and only one instance of each of the connecting entities.

In Figure 8-5 the associative entity ASSIGNMENT (notice the unique shape) matches an EMPLOYEE, a LOCATION, and a PROJECT. For each instance of ASSIGNMENT, the key

FIGURE 8-4

A Recursive
Relationship

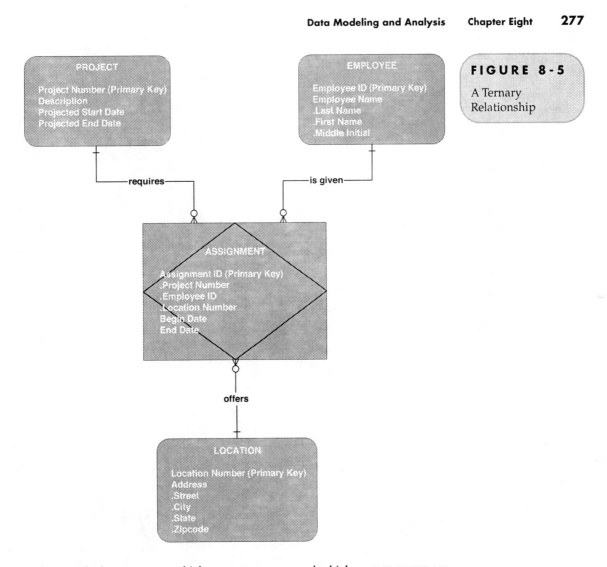

FIGURE 8-5

A Ternary
Relationship

indicates which EMPLOYEE ID, which LOCATION NUMBER, and which PROJECT NUMBER are combined to form that assignment.

Also as shown in Figure 8-5, an associative entity can be described by its own nonkey attributes. In addition to the primary key, an ASSIGNMENT is described by the attributes BEGIN DATE and END DATE. If you think about it, none of these attributes describes an EMPLOYEE, LOCATION, or PROJECT—they describe a single instance of the relationship between an instance of each of those entities.

Foreign Keys   A relationship implies that instances of one entity are related to instances of another entity. We should be able to identify those instances for any given entity. The ability to identify specific related entity instances involves establishing foreign keys. A **foreign key** is a primary key of one entity that is contributed to (duplicated in) another entity to identify instances of a relationship. A foreign key (always in a **child entity**) always matches the primary key (in a **parent entity**). In Figure 8-6(a), we demonstrate the concept of foreign keys with our simple data model. Notice that the <u>maximum</u> cardinality for DEPARTMENT is "one," whereas the maximum cardinality for CURRICULUM is "many." In this case, DEPARTMENT is called the *parent* entity and CURRICULUM is the *child* entity. The primary key is always contributed by the parent to the child as a foreign key. Thus, an instance of CURRICULUM now has a foreign key DEPARTMENT NAME whose value points to the instance of DEPARTMENT that offers that curriculum. (Foreign keys are never contributed from child to parent.)

foreign key a primary key of an entity that is used in another entity to identify instances of a relationship.

child entity a data entity that derives one or more attributes from another entity, called the parent. In a one-to-many relationship the child is the entity on the "many" side.

parent entity a data entity that contributes one or more attributes to another entity, called the child. In a one-to-many relationship the parent is the entity on the "one" side.

(a)

(b)

FIGURE 8-6   Foreign Keys

nonidentifying
relationship a relationship
in which each participating
entity has its own independent
primary key.

In our example, the relationship between CURRICULUM and DEPARTMENT is referred to as a *nonidentifying relationship*. **Nonidentifying relationships** are those in which each of the participating entities has its own independent primary key. In other words, none of the primary-key attributes is shared. The entities CURRICULUM and DEPARTMENT are also referred to as *strong* or independent entities because neither depends on any other entity for its identification. Sometimes, however, a foreign key may participate as part of the primary key of the child entity. For example, in Figure 8-6(b) the parent entity BUILDING contributes its key to the entity ROOM. Thus, BUILDING NAME serves as a foreign key to relate a ROOM and BUILDING and in conjunction with ROOM ID

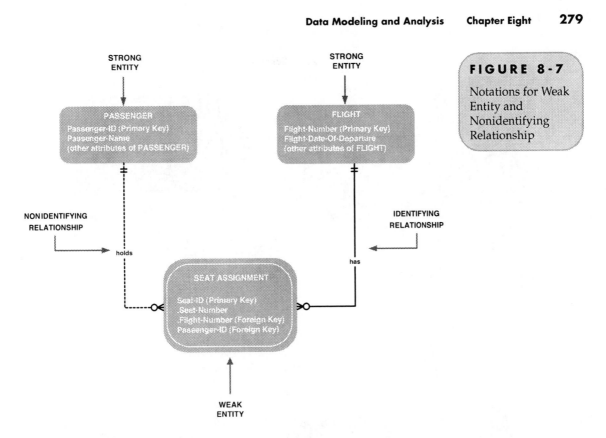

FIGURE 8-7

Notations for Weak Entity and Nonidentifying Relationship

to uniquely identify a given instance of ROOM. In those situations the relationship between the parent entity and the child entity is referred to as an *identifying relationship*. **Identifying relationships** are those in which the parent entity contributes its primary key to become part of the primary key of the child entity. The child entity of any identifying relationship is frequently referred to as a *weak entity* because its identification is dependent on the parent entity's existence.

Most popular CASE tools and data modeling methods use different notations to distinguish between identifying and nonidentifying relationships and between strong and weak entities. In Figure 8-7, we use a *dashed line* notation to represent the non-identifying relationship between PASSENGER and SEAT ASSIGNMENT. Because part of the primary key of SEAT ASSIGNMENT is the foreign key FLIGHT NUMBER from the parent entity FLIGHT, the relationship is an identifying relationship and is represented using a *solid line*. Finally, seat assignment is a weak entity because it receives the primary key of flight to compose its own primary key. A weak entity is represented using a symbol composed of a *rounded rectangle within a rounded rectangle*.

> NOTE: To reinforce the above concepts of identifying and nonidentifying relationships and strong versus weak entities and to be consistent with most popular data modeling methods and most widely used CASE tools, the authors use the above modeling notations on all subsequent data modeling examples presented in the book.

What if you cannot differentiate between parent and child? For example, in Figure 8-8(a) on page 280 we see that a CURRICULUM enrolls zero, one, or more STUDENTS. At the same time, we see that a STUDENT is enrolled in one or more CURRICULA. The maximum cardinality on both sides is "many." So, which is the parent and which is the child? You can't tell! This is called a *nonspecific relationship*. **A nonspecific relationship** (or *many-to-many relationship*) is one in which many instances of one entity are associated with many instances of another entity. Such relationships are suitable only for preliminary data models and should be resolved as quickly as possible.

identifying relationship
a relationship in which the parent entity's key is also part of the primary key of the child entity.

nonspecific relationship
a relationship where many instances of an entity are associated with many instances of another entity. Also called *many-to-many relationship*.

(a)

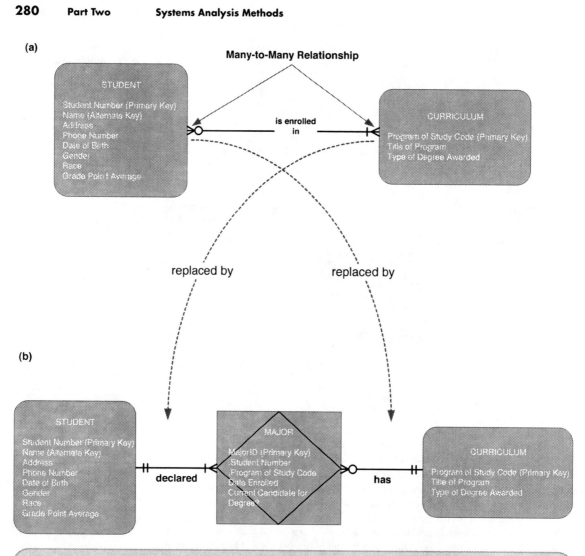

(b)

F I G U R E   8 - 8   Resolving Nonspecific Relationships with an Associative Entity

Many nonspecific relationships can be resolved into a pair of one-to-many relationships. As illustrated in Figure 8-8(b), each entity becomes a parent. A new, *associative entity* is introduced as the child of each parent. In Figure 8-8(b), each instance of MAJOR represents <u>one</u> STUDENT's enrollment in <u>one</u> CURRICULUM. If a student is pursuing two majors, that student will have two instances of the entity MAJOR.

Study Figure 8-8(b) carefully. For associative entities, the cardinality from child to parent is always <u>one and only one</u>. That makes sense because an instance of MAJOR must correspond to one and only one STUDENT and one and only one CURRICULUM. The cardinality from parent to child depends on the business rule. In our example, a STUDENT must declare <u>one or more</u> MAJORS. Conversely, a CURRICULUM is being studied by zero, one, or more MAJORS—perhaps it is new and no one has been admitted to it yet. An associative entity can also be described by its own nonkey attributes (such as DATE ENROLLED and CURRENT CANDIDATE FOR DEGREE?). Finally, associative entities inherit the primary keys of the parents; thus, all associative entities are weak entities.

Not all nonspecific relationships can and should be automatically resolved as described above. Occasionally nonspecific relationships result from the failure of the analyst to identify the existence of other entities. For example, examine the relationship between CUSTOMER and PRODUCT in Figure 8-9(a). Recognize that the relationship

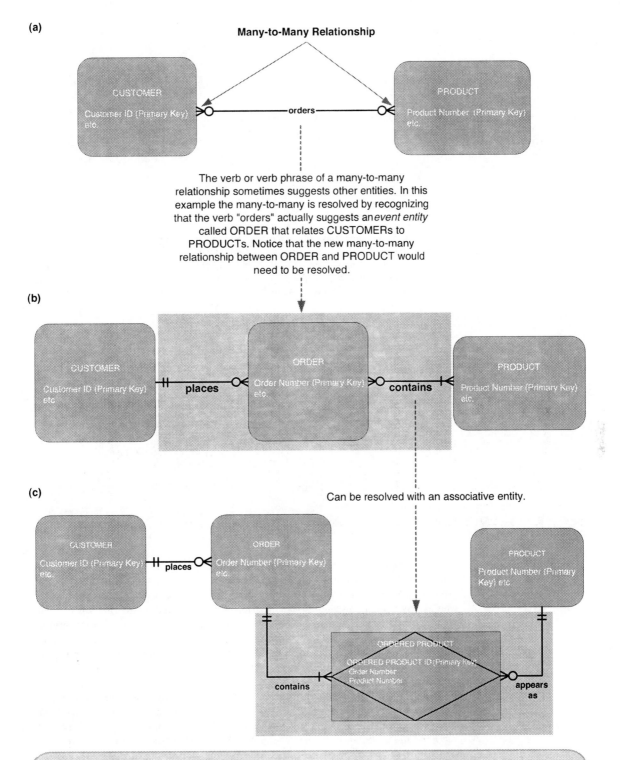

(a)

Many-to-Many Relationship

CUSTOMER

Customer ID (Primary Key)
etc.

orders

PRODUCT

Product Number (Primary Key)
etc.

The verb or verb phrase of a many-to-many relationship sometimes suggests other entities. In this example the many-to-many is resolved by recognizing that the verb "orders" actually suggests an *event entity* called ORDER that relates CUSTOMERs to PRODUCTs. Notice that the new many-to-many relationship between ORDER and PRODUCT would need to be resolved.

(b)

CUSTOMER

Customer ID (Primary Key)
etc.

places

ORDER

Order Number (Primary Key)
etc.

contains

PRODUCT

Product Number (Primary Key)
etc.

(c)

Can be resolved with an associative entity.

CUSTOMER

Customer ID (Primary Key)
etc.

places

ORDER

Order Number (Primary Key)
etc.

PRODUCT

Product Number (Primary Key) etc.

ORDERED PRODUCT

ORDERED PRODUCT ID (Primary Key)
Order Number
Product Number

contains

appears as

FIGURE 8-9 Resolving Nonspecific Relationships by Recognizing a Fundamental Business Entity

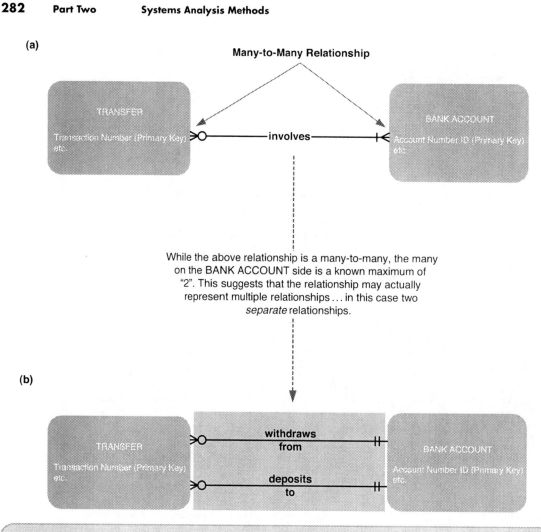

(a)

Many-to-Many Relationship

TRANSFER

Transaction Number (Primary Key)
etc.

involves

BANK ACCOUNT

Account Number ID (Primary Key)
etc.

While the above relationship is a many-to-many, the many
on the BANK ACCOUNT side is a known maximum of
"2". This suggests that the relationship may actually
represent multiple relationships... in this case two
separate relationships.

(b)

TRANSFER

Transaction Number (Primary Key)
etc.

withdraws
from

deposits
to

BANK ACCOUNT

Account Number ID (Primary Key)
etc.

FIGURE 8-10 Resolving Nonspecific Relationships by Recognizing Separate Relationships

"orders" between CUSTOMER and PRODUCT suggests an event about which a user might want to store data. That event represents an event entity called ORDER depicted in Figure 8-9(b). In reality, CUSTOMER and PRODUCT do not have a natural and direct relationship as was depicted in Figure 8-9(a). Rather, they are related indirectly, by way of an ORDER. Thus, our many-to-many relationship was replaced by separate relationships between CUSTOMER, ORDER, and PRODUCT. Notice that the relationship between ORDER and PRODUCT is a many-to-many relationship. That relationship would need to be resolved by replacing it with an associative entity and two one-to-many relationships, as is illustrated in Figure 8-9(c).

Finally, some nonspecific relationships can be resolved by introducing separate relationships. Notice the many-to-many relationship between TRANSFER and BANK ACCOUNT shown in Figure 8-10(a). While it is true that a TRANSFER transaction involves many BANK ACCOUNTS and a BANK ACCOUNT may be involved in many TRANSFER transactions, we must be careful! Data modeling notations can sometimes mislead us. Technically, a single TRANSFER transaction involves two BANK ACCOUNTS. When we know the specific maximum number of occurrences of a many-to-many relationship, it often suggests that our original relationship is weak or too general. Notice in Figure 8-10(b) that our relationship "involves" was replaced by two separate one-to-many relationships that more accurately describe the business relationships between a TRANSFER and BANK ACCOUNTS.

Generalization   Most people associate the concept of generalization with modern object-oriented techniques. In reality, the concepts have been applied by data modelers for many years. Generalization is an approach that seeks to discover and exploit the commonalities between entities. **Generalization** is a technique wherein the attributes that are common to several types of an entity are grouped into their own entity. Consider, for example, a typical school. A school enrolls STUDENTS and employs EMPLOYEES (in a university, a person could be both). There are several attributes that are common to both entities; for example, NAME, GENDER, RACE, MARITAL STATUS, and possibly even a key based on SOCIAL SECURITY NUMBER. We could consolidate these common attributes into an entity supertype called PERSON. An entity **supertype** is an entity whose instances store attributes that are common to one or more entity subtypes.

The entity supertype will have one or more *one-to-one* relationships to entity *subtypes*. These relationships are sometimes called "is a" relationships (or "was a," or "could be a") because each instance of the supertype "is also an" instance of one or more subtypes. An entity **subtype** is an entity whose instances inherit some common attributes from an entity supertype and then add other attributes that are unique to an instance of the subtype. In our example, "a PERSON is an employee, or a student, or both." The top half of Figure 8-11 illustrates this generalization ❶ as a hierarchy. Notice that the subtypes STUDENT and EMPLOYEE have inherited attributes from PERSON, as well as adding their own.

Extending the metaphor, we see that an entity can be both a supertype and a subtype. Returning to Figure 8-11, we see that a STUDENT (which was a subtype of PERSON) has its own subtypes. In the diagram, we see that a STUDENT is ❷ either a PROSPECT, or a CURRENT STUDENT, or a FORMER STUDENT (having left for any reason other than graduation), and ❸ a STUDENT could be an ALUMNUS. These additional subtypes inherit all the attributes from STUDENT as well as those from PERSON. Finally, notice that all subtypes are weak entities.

Through inheritance, the concept of generalization in data models permits us to reduce the number of attributes through the careful sharing of common attributes. The subtypes not only inherit the attributes but also the data types, domains, and defaults of those attributes. This can greatly enhance the consistency with which we treat attributes that apply to many different entities (e.g., dates, names, addresses, currency, etc.).

In addition to inheriting attributes, subtypes also inherit relationships to other entities. For instance, all EMPLOYEES and STUDENTS inherit the relationship ❹ between PERSON and ADDRESS. But only EMPLOYEES inherit the relationship ❺ with CONTRACTS. And only an ALUMNUS can be related to ❻ an AWARDED DEGREE.

generalization a concept wherein the attributes that are common to several types of an entity are grouped into their own entity.

supertype an entity whose instances store attributes that are common to one or more entity subtypes.

subtype an entity whose instances may inherit common attributes from its entity supertype.

The Process of Logical Data Modeling

Now that you understand the basic concepts of data models, we can examine the process of data modeling. When do you do it? How many data models may be drawn? What technology exists to support the process?

Data modeling may be performed during various types of projects and in multiple phases of projects. Data models are progressive; there is no such thing as the "final" data model for a business or application. Instead, a data model should be considered a living document that will change in response to a changing business. Data models should ideally be stored in a repository so that they can be retrieved, expanded, and edited over time. Let's examine how data modeling may come into play during systems planning and analysis.

> Strategic Data Modeling

Many organizations select application development projects based on strategic information systems plans. Strategic planning is a separate project. This project produces

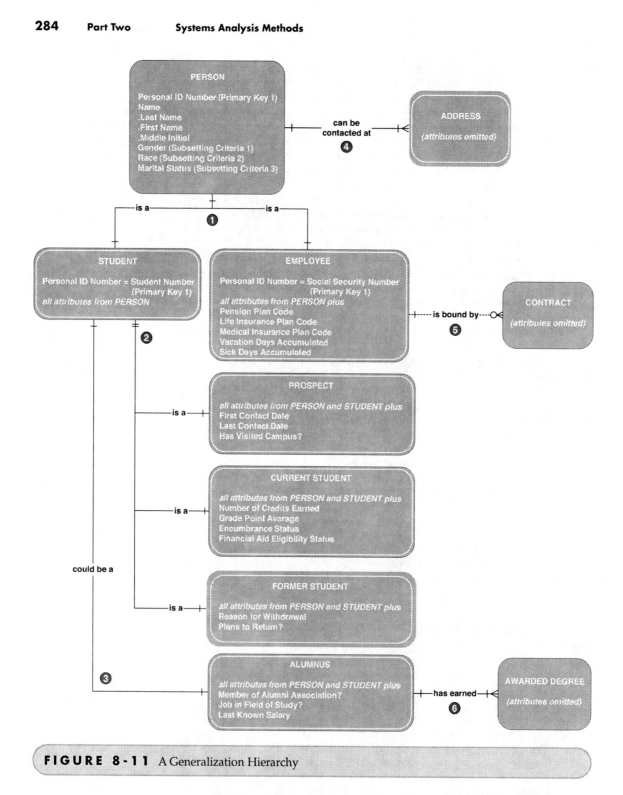

FIGURE 8-11 A Generalization Hierarchy

an information systems strategy plan that defines an overall vision and architecture for information systems. Almost always, this architecture includes an *enterprise data model.* Information engineering is a methodology that embraces this approach.

An enterprise data model typically identifies only the most fundamental of entities. The entities are typically defined (as in a dictionary), but they are not described in terms of keys or attributes. The enterprise data model may or may not include relationships (depending on the planning methodology's standards and the level of detail desired by executive management). If relationships are included, many of them will be nonspecific (a concept introduced earlier in the chapter).

How does an enterprise data model affect subsequent applications development? Part of the information strategy plan identifies application development projects and prioritizes them according to whatever criteria management deems appropriate. As those projects are started, the appropriate subsets of the information systems architecture, including a subset of the enterprise data model, are provided to the applications development team as a point of departure.

The enterprise data model is usually stored in a corporate repository. When the application development project is started, the subset of the enterprise data model (as well as the other models) is exported from the corporate repository into a project repository. Once the project team completes systems analysis and design, the expanded and refined data models are imported back into the corporate repository.

> Data Modeling during Systems Analysis

In systems analysis and in this chapter, we will focus on *logical* data modeling as a part of systems analysis. The data model for a single information system is usually called an **application data model.**

application data model
a data model for a complete, single information system.

Data models are rarely constructed during the scope definition phase of systems analysis. The short duration of that phase makes them impractical. If an enterprise data model exists, the subset of that model that is applicable to the project might be retrieved and reviewed as part of the phase requirement to establish context. Alternatively, the project team could identify a simple list of entities, the things about which team members think the system will have to capture and store data.

Unfortunately, data modeling is rarely associated with the problem analysis phase of systems analysis. Some analysts prefer to draw process models (Chapter 9) to document the current system, but many analysts report that data models are far superior for the following reasons:

- Data models help analysts to quickly identify business vocabulary more completely than process models.
- Data models are almost always built more quickly than process models.
- A complete data model can fit on a single sheet of paper. Process models often require dozens of sheets of paper.
- Process modelers frequently and too easily get hung up on unnecessary detail.
- Data models for existing and proposed systems are far more similar than process models for existing and proposed systems. Consequently, there is less work to throw away as you move into later phases.

We agree! A problem analysis phase model includes only entities and relationships, but no attributes—it is called a **context data model.** The intent is to refine our understanding of scope, not to get into details about the entities and business rules. Many relationships may be nonspecific.

context data model a
data model that includes entities and relationships but no attributes.

Many automated tools provide the ability to read existing system files and databases and translate them into "physical" data models. These physical data models can then be transformed into their equivalent "logical" data model. This translation capability benefits both the problem analysis and the requirements analysis phases.

The requirements analysis results in a logical data model that is developed in stages as follows:

1. We begin by constructing the *context data model* to establish the project scope. If a context data model was already developed during problem analysis, that model may be revised to reflect new requirements and project scope.

key-based data model a data model that includes entities and relationships with precise cardinalities resolving non-specific relationships into associative entities, and also including primary and alternate keys.

2. Next, a **key-based data model** will be drawn. This model will eliminate non-specific relationships, add associative entities, and include primary and alternate keys. The key-based model will also include precise cardinalities and any generalization hierarchies.

3. Next, a **fully attributed data model** will be constructed. The fully attributed model includes all remaining descriptive attributes and subsetting criteria. Each attribute is defined in the repository with data types, domains, and defaults (in what is sometimes called a *fully described data model*).

4. The completed data model is analyzed for adaptability and flexibility through a process called *normalization*. The final analyzed model is referred to as a *normalized data model*.

fully attributed data model a data model that includes all entities, attributes, relationships, subsetting criteria, and precise cardinalities.

This data requirements model requires a team effort that includes systems analysts, users and managers, and data analysts. A data administrator often sets standards for and approves all data models.

Ultimately, during the decision analysis phase, the data model will be used to make implementation decisions—the best way to implement the requirements with database technology. In practice, this decision may have already been standardized as part of a database architecture. For example, SoundStage has already standardized on two database management systems: Microsoft *Access* for personal and work-group databases, and Microsoft *SQL Server* for enterprise databases.

Finally, data models cannot be constructed without appropriate facts and information as supplied by the user community. These facts can be collected through a number of techniques such as sampling of existing forms and files, research of similar systems, surveys of users and management, and interviews of users and management. The fastest method of collecting facts and information and simultaneously constructing and verifying the data models is joint requirements planning. JRP uses a carefully facilitated group meeting to collect the facts, build the models, and verify the models—usually in one or two full-day sessions. Fact-finding and information-gathering techniques were fully explored in Chapter 6. Table 8-4 summarizes some questions that may be useful for fact-finding and information gathering as it pertains to data modeling.

> Looking Ahead to Systems Design

During system design, the logical data model will be transformed into a physical data model (called a *database schema*) for the chosen database management system. This model will reflect the technical capabilities and limitations of that database technology, as well as the performance tuning requirements suggested by the database administrator. Any further discussion of database design is deferred until Chapter 14.

> Automated Tools for Data Modeling

metadata data about data.

Data models are stored in a repository. In a sense, the data model is **metadata**—that is, data about the business's data. Computer-aided systems engineering (CASE) technology, introduced in Chapter 3, provides the repository for storing the data model and its detailed descriptions. Most CASE products support computer-assisted data modeling and database design. Some CASE products (such as Logic Works' *ERwin*) only support data modeling and database design. CASE takes the drudgery out of drawing and maintaining these models and their underlying details.

Using a CASE product, you can easily create professional, readable data models without the use of paper, pencil, erasers, and templates. The models can be easily modified to reflect corrections and changes suggested by end users—you don't have to start over! Also, most CASE products provide powerful analytical tools that can check your models for mechanical errors, completeness, and consistency. Some CASE

TABLE 8-4 JRP and Interview Questions for Data Modeling

Purpose	Candidate Questions
Discover the system entities	What are the subjects of the business? In other words, what types of persons, organizations, organizational units, places, things, materials, or events are used in or interact with this system about which data must be captured or maintained? How many instances of each subject exist?
Discover the entity keys	What unique characteristic (or characteristics) distinguishes an instance of each subject from other instances of the same subject? Are there any plans to change this identification scheme in the future?
Discover entity subsetting criteria	Are there any characteristics of a subject that divide all instances of the subject into useful subsets? Are there any subsets of the above subjects for which you have no convenient way to group instances?
Discover attributes and domains	What characteristics describe each subject? For each of these characteristics, (1) what type of data is stored? (2) who is responsible for defining legitimate values for the data? (3) what are the legitimate values for the data? (4) is a value required? and (5) is there any default value that should be assigned if you don't specify otherwise?
Discover security and control needs	Are there any restrictions on who can see or use the data? Who is allowed to create the data? Who is allowed to update the data? Who is allowed to delete the data?
Discover data timing needs	How often does the data change? Over what period of time is the data of value to the business? How long should we keep the data? Do you need historical data or trends? If a characteristic changes, must you know the former values?
Discover generalization hierarchies	Are all instances of each subject the same? That is, are there special types of each subject that are described or handled differently? Can any of the data be consolidated for sharing?
Discover relationships and degrees	What events occur that imply associations between subjects? What business activities or transactions involve handling or changing data about several different subjects of the same or a different type?
Discover cardinalities	Is each business activity or event handled the same way, or are there special circumstances? Can an event occur with only some of the associated subjects, or must all the subjects be involved?

products can even help you analyze the data model for consistency, completeness, and flexibility. The potential time and quality savings are substantial.

As mentioned earlier, some CASE tools support reverse engineering of existing file and database structures into data models. The resulting data models represent "physical" data models that can be revised and reengineered into a new file or database, or they may be translated into their equivalent "logical" model. The logical data model could then be edited and forward engineered into a revised physical data model, and subsequently a file or database implementation.

CASE tools do have their limitations. Not all data modeling conventions are supported by all CASE products. And different CASE tools adopt slightly different

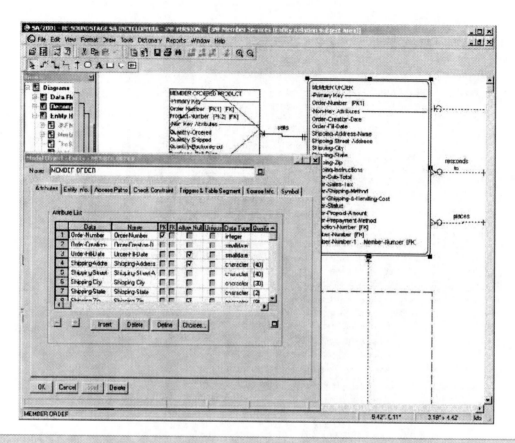

FIGURE 8-12   Screen Capture of *System Architect* CASE Tool

notations for the same data-modeling methods. Therefore, it is very likely that any given CASE product may force a company to adapt its methodology's data-modeling symbols or approach so that it is workable within the limitations of the CASE tool.

All the SoundStage data models in the next section of this chapter were created with Popkin Systems and Software's CASE tool, *System Architect 2001*. For the case study, we provide you with the printouts exactly as they came off our printers. We did not add color. The only modifications by the artist were the bullets that call your attention to specific items of interest on the printouts. All of the entities, attributes, and relationships on the SoundStage data models were automatically cataloged into *System Architect*'s project repository (which it calls an encyclopedia). Figure 8-12 illustrates some of *System Architect*'s screens as used for data modeling.

How to Construct Data Models

You now know enough about data models to read and interpret them. But as a systems analyst or knowledgeable end user, you must learn how to construct them. We will use the SoundStage Entertainment Club project to teach you how to construct data models.

NOTE: This example teaches you to draw the data model from scratch. In reality, you should always look for an existing data model. If such models exist, the data management or data administration group usually maintains them. Alternatively, you could reverse engineer a data model from an existing database.

> Entity Discovery

The first task in data modeling is relatively easy. You need to discover the fundamental entities in the system that are or might be described by data. You should not restrict your thinking to entities about which the end users know they want to store data. There are several techniques that may be used to identify entities:

- During interviews or JRP sessions with system owners and users, pay attention to key words in their discussion. For example, during an interview with an individual discussing SoundStage's business environment and activities, a user may state, "We have to keep track of all our members and their bound agreements." Notice that the key words in this statement are MEMBERS and AGREEMENTS. Both are entities!
- During interviews or JRP sessions, specifically ask system owners and users to identify things about which they would like to capture, store, and produce information. Those things often represent entities that should be depicted on the data model.
- Another technique for identifying entities is to study existing forms, files, and reports. Some forms identify event entities. Examples include ORDERS, REQUISITIONS, PAYMENTS, DEPOSITS, and so forth. But most of these same forms also contain data that describes other entities. Consider a registration form used in your school's course enrollment system. A REGISTRATION is itself an event entity. But the average registration form also contains data that describes other entities, such as STUDENT (a person), COURSES (which are concepts), INSTRUCTORS (other persons), ADVISOR (yet another person), DIVISIONS (another concept), and so forth. Studying the computerized registration system's computer files, databases, or outputs could also discover these same entities.
- If use-case narratives have been written during the requirements analysis phase, they can be a source of data attributes and entities. Scan each use-case narrative for nouns. Every noun is a potential data attribute or entity. You will have to massage the resulting list of nouns because not all of them will be attributes or entities. Some will be references to users or other information systems. Some will be references to things that are part of the user interface, not data. Some will be synonyms for other attributes or entities elsewhere on the list, and you would not want to duplicate them. Chapter 10 explains how to do this, taking an object-oriented approach to build a list of objects and their attributes. You can use a very similar approach to discover data entities and their attributes.
- Technology may also help you identify entities. Some CASE tools can reverse engineer existing files and databases into physical data models. The analyst must usually clean up the resulting model by replacing physical names, codes, and comments with their logical, business-friendly equivalents.

While these techniques may prove useful in identifying entities, they occasionally play tricks on you. A simple, quick quality check can eliminate false entities. Ask your user to specify the number of instances of each entity. A true entity has multiple instances—dozens, hundreds, thousands, or more! If not, the entity does not exist.

As entities are discovered, give them simple, meaningful, business-oriented names. Entities should be named with nouns that describe the person, event, place, object, or thing about which we want to store data. Try not to abbreviate or use acronyms. Names should be singular so as to distinguish the logical concept of the entity from the actual instances of the entity. Names may include appropriate adjectives or clauses to better describe the entity—for instance, an externally generated CUSTOMER ORDER must be distinguished from an internally generated STOCK ORDER.

For each entity, define it in business terms. Don't define the entity in technical terms, and don't define it as "data about . . . " Try this: Use an English dictionary to create a draft definition, and then customize it for the business at hand. Your entity names and definitions should establish an initial glossary of business terminology that will serve both you and future analysts and users for years.

> **TABLE 8-5 Fundamental Entities for the SoundStage Project**

Entity Name	Business Definition
AGREEMENT	A contract whereby a member agrees to purchase a certain number of products within a certain time. After fulfilling that agreement, the member becomes eligible for bonus credits that are redeemable for free or discounted products.
MEMBER	An active member of one or more clubs. Note: A target system objective is to reenroll inactive members as opposed to deleting them.
MEMBER ORDER	An order generated for a member as part of a monthly promotion, or an order initiated by a member. Note: The current system only supports orders generated from promotions; however, customer-initiated orders have been given a high priority as an added option in the proposed system.
TRANSACTION	A business event to which the Member Services System must respond.
PRODUCT	An inventoried product available for promotion and sale to members. Note: System improvement objectives include (1) compatibility with new bar code system being developed for the warehouse, and (2) adaptability to a rapidly changing mix of products.
PROMOTION	A monthly or quarterly event whereby special product offerings are made available to members.

Our SoundStage management and users initially identified the entities listed in Table 8-5. Notice how the definitions contribute to establishing the vocabulary of the system.

> The Context Data Model

The next task in data modeling is to construct the context data model. The context data model should include the fundamental business entities that were previously discovered as well as their natural relationships.

Relationships should be named with verb phrases that, when combined with the entity names, form simple business sentences or assertions. Some CASE tools, such as *System Architect,* let you name the relationships in both directions. Otherwise, always name the relationship from parent to child.

We have completed this task in Figure 8-13. This figure represents a data model created in *System Architect.* Once we begin mapping attributes, new entities and relationships may surface. The numbers below reference the same numbers in Figure 8-13. The ERD communicates the following:

❶ An AGREEMENT <u>binds</u> one or more MEMBERS. While relationships may be named in only one direction (parent to child), the other direction is implicit. For example, it is implicit that a MEMBER <u>is bound to</u> one and only one AGREEMENT.

❷ A MEMBER <u>has conducted</u> zero, one, or more TRANSACTIONS. Implicitly, a given TRANSACTION was <u>conducted by</u> one and only one MEMBER.

❸ A MEMBER ORDER <u>is a</u> TRANSACTION. In fact, a given MEMBER ORDER may correspond to many TRANSACTIONS (for example, a new member order, a canceled member order, a changed member order, etc.). But a given TRANSACTION may or may not <u>represent</u> a MEMBER ORDER.

❹ A PROMOTION <u>features</u> one or more PRODUCTS. Implicitly, a PRODUCT <u>is featured in</u> zero, one, or more PROMOTIONS. For example, a CD that appeals to both

FIGURE 8-13 The SoundStage Context Data Model

country/western and light-rock audiences might be featured in the promotion for both. Since products greatly outnumber promotions, most products are never featured in a promotion.

❺ A PROMOTION <u>generates</u> many MEMBER ORDERS. Implicitly, a MEMBER ORDER <u>is generated for</u> zero or one PROMOTION. Why zero? In the new system, a member will be able to initiate his or her own order.

❻ It is permissible for more than one relationship to exist between the same two entities if the separate relationships communicate different business events or associations. Thus, a MEMBER <u>responds to</u> zero, one, or more MEMBER ORDERS. This relationship supports the promotion-generated orders. A MEMBER <u>places</u> zero, one, or more MEMBER ORDERS. This relationship supports member-initiated orders. In both cases, a MEMBER ORDER <u>is placed by</u> (<u>is responded to by</u>) exactly one MEMBER.

Although we didn't need it for this double relationship, some CASE tools (including *System Architect*) provide a symbol for recording Boolean relationships (such as AND, OR). Thus, for any two relationships, a Boolean symbol could be used to establish that instances of the relationships must be mutually exclusive (= OR) or mutually contingent (= AND).

❼ A MEMBER ORDER <u>sells</u> one or more PRODUCTS. Implicitly, a PRODUCT is <u>sold on</u> zero, one, or more MEMBER ORDERS. Note that this is a nonspecific relationship, which will later be resolved.

If you read each of the preceding items carefully, you probably learned a great deal about the SoundStage system. Data models have become increasingly popular as a tool for describing the business context for system projects.

> The Key-Based Data Model

The next task is to identify the keys of each entity. The following guidelines are suggested for keys:[1]

1. The value of a key should not change over the lifetime of each entity instance. For example, NAME would be a poor key since a person's last name could change by marriage or divorce.
2. The value of a key cannot be null.
3. Controls must be installed to ensure that the value of a key is valid. This can be accomplished by precisely defining the domain and using the database management system's validation controls to enforce that domain.

intelligent key a business code whose structure communicates data about an entity instance.

4. Some experts (Bruce) suggest you avoid **intelligent keys.** An intelligent key is a business code whose structure communicates data about an entity instance (such as its classification, size, or other properties). A code is a group of characters and/or digits that identifies and describes something in the business system. Some experts argue that because those characteristics can change, it violates rule 1 above.

   We disagree. Business codes can return value to the organization because they can be quickly processed by humans without the assistance of a computer.

   a. There are several types of codes. They can be combined to form effective means for entity instance identification.

      (1) *Serial codes* assign sequentially generated numbers to entity instances. Many database management systems can generate and constrain serial codes to a business's requirements.

[1]Adapted from Thomas A. Bruce, *Designing Quality Databases with IDEF1X Information Models.* Copyright © 1992 by Thomas A. Bruce. Reprinted by permission of Dorset House Publishing, 353 W. 12th St., New York, NY 10014 (212-620-4053/1-800-DH-BOOKS/www.dorsethouse.com). All rights reserved.

(2) *Block codes* are similar to serial codes except that block numbers are divided into groups that have some business meaning. For instance, a satellite television provider might assign 100–199 as PAY PER VIEW channels, 200–299 as CABLE channels, 300–399 as SPORT channels, 400–499 as ADULT PROGRAMMING channels, 500–599 as MUSIC-ONLY channels, 600–699 as INTERACTIVE GAMING channels, 700–799 as INTERNET channels, 800–899 as PREMIUM CABLE channels, and 900–999 as PREMIUM MOVIE AND EVENT channels.

(3) *Alphabetic codes* use finite combinations of letters (and possibly numbers) to describe entity instances. For example, each STATE has a unique two-character alphabetic code. Alphabetic codes must usually be combined with serial or block codes to uniquely identify instances of most entities.

(4) In *significant position codes,* each digit or group of digits describes a measurable or identifiable characteristic of the entity instance. Significant digit codes are frequently used to code inventory items. The codes you see on tires and lightbulbs are examples of significant position codes. They tell us about characteristics such as tire size and wattage, respectively.

(5) *Hierarchical codes* provide a top-down interpretation for an entity instance. Every item coded is factored into groups, subgroups, and so forth. For instance, we could code employee positions as follows:
   — First digit identifies classification (clerical, faculty, etc.).
   — Second and third digits indicate level within classification.
   — Fourth and fifth digits indicate calendar of employment.

b. The following guidelines are suggested when creating a business coding scheme:
   (1) Codes should be expandable to accommodate growth.
   (2) The full code must result in a unique value for each entity instance.
   (3) Codes should be large enough to describe the distinguishing characteristics but small enough to be interpreted by people *without a computer.*
   (4) Codes should be convenient. A new instance should be easy to create.

5. Consider inventing a surrogate key instead to substitute for large concatenated keys of independent entities. This suggestion is not practical for associative entities because each part of the concatenated key is a foreign key that must precisely match its parent entity's primary key.

Figure 8-14 is the key-based data model for the SoundStage project. Notice that the primary key is specified for each entity.

❶ Many entities have a simple, single-attribute primary key.

❷ We resolved the nonspecific relationship between MEMBER ORDER and PRODUCT by introducing the associative entity MEMBER ORDERED PRODUCT. Each associative entity instance represents one product on one member order. The parent entities contributed their own primary keys to comprise the associative entity's concatenated key. *System Architect* places a "PK1" next to ORDER NUMBER to indicate that it is "part one" of the concatenated primary key and a "PK2" beside PRODUCT NUMBER to indicate that it is "part two" of the concatenated key. Also notice that each attribute in that concatenated key, by itself, is a foreign key that points back to the correct parent entity instance.

Likewise, the nonspecific relationship between PRODUCT and PROMOTION was resolved using an associative entity, TITLE PROMOTION, that also inherits the keys of the parent entities.

When developing this model, look out for a couple of things. If you cannot define keys for an entity, it may be that the entity doesn't really exist—that is, multiple occurrences of the so-called entity do not exist. Thus, assigning keys is a good quality check before fully attributing the data model. Also, if two or more entities have identical keys, they are in all likelihood the same entity.

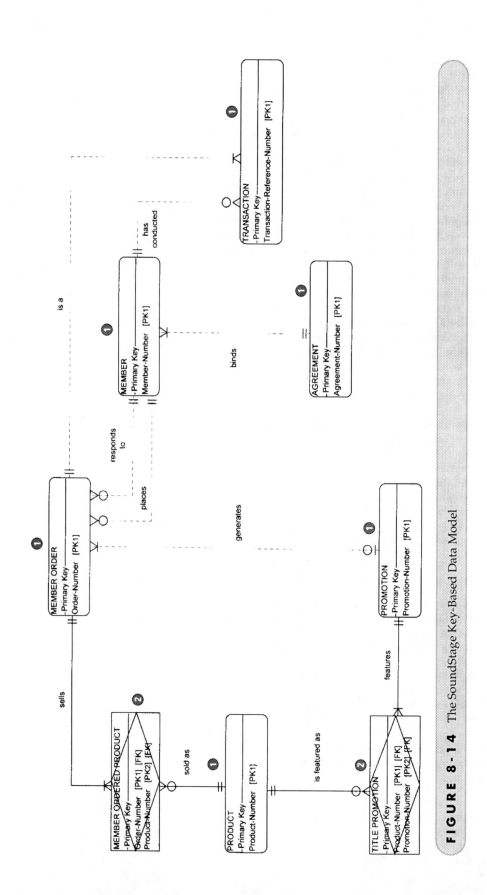

FIGURE 8-14 The SoundStage Key-Based Data Model

> Generalized Hierarchies

At this time, it would be useful to identify any generalization hierarchies in the business domain. The SoundStage project at the beginning of this chapter identified at least one supertype/subtype structure. Subsequent discussions did uncover a generalization hierarchy. Thus, our key-based model was revised as shown in Figure 8-15. We had to lay out the model somewhat differently because of the hierarchy; however, the relationships and keys that were previously defined have been retained. We call your attention to the following:

❶ The SoundStage CASE tool automatically draws a dashed box around a generalization hierarchy.
❷ The subtypes inherit the keys of the supertypes.
❸ We disconnected PROMOTION from PRODUCT as it was shown earlier and reconnected it to the subtype TITLE. This was done to accurately assert the business rule that MERCHANDISE is never featured on a PROMOTION—only TITLES.

> The Fully Attributed Data Model

It may seem like a trivial task to identify the remaining data attributes; however, analysts not familiar with data modeling frequently encounter problems. To accomplish this task, you must have a thorough understanding of the data attributes for the system. These facts can be discovered using top-down approaches (such as brainstorming) or bottom-up approaches (such as form and file sampling). If an enterprise data model exists, some (perhaps many) of the attributes may have already been identified and recorded in a repository.

The following guidelines are offered for attribution:

• Many organizations have naming standards and approved abbreviations. The data administrator usually maintains such standards.
• Choose attribute names carefully. Many attributes share common base names such as NAME, ADDRESS, DATE. Unless the attributes can be generalized into a supertype, it is best to give each variation a unique name such as:

CUSTOMER NAME	CUSTOMER ADDRESS	ORDER DATE
SUPPLIER NAME	SUPPLIER ADDRESS	INVOICE DATE
EMPLOYEE NAME	EMPLOYEE ADDRESS	FLIGHT DATE

Also, remember that a project does not live in isolation from other projects, past or future. Names must be distinguishable across projects.
Some organizations maintain reusable, global templates for these common base attributes. This promotes consistent data types, domains, and defaults across all applications.
• Physical attribute names on existing forms and reports are frequently abbreviated to save space. Logical attribute names should be clearer—for example, translate the order form's attribute COD into its logical equivalent, AMOUNT TO COLLECT ON DELIVERY; translate QTY into QUANTITY ORDERED; and so forth.
• Many attributes take on only YES or NO values. Try naming these attributes as questions. For example, the attribute name CANDIDATE FOR A DEGREE? suggests the values are YES and NO.
Each attribute should be mapped to only one entity. If an attribute truly describes different entities, it is probably several different attributes. Give each a unique name.
• Foreign keys are the exception to the nonredundancy rule—they identify associated instances of related entities.

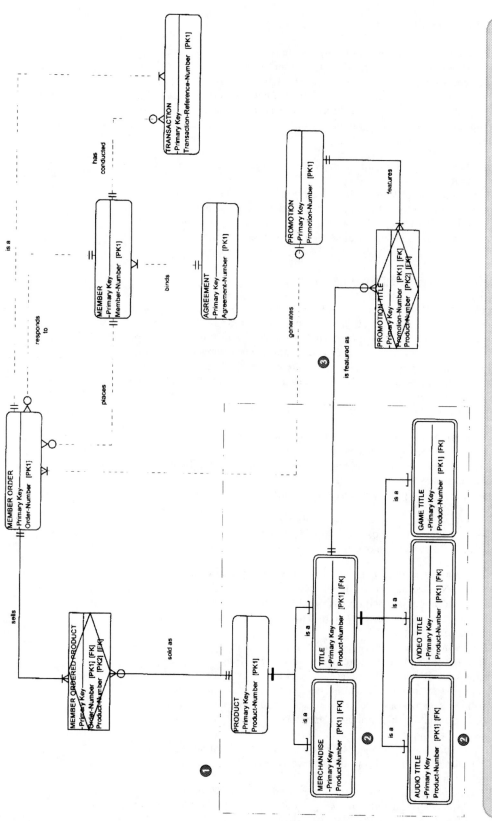

FIGURE 8-15 The SoundStage Key-Based Data Model with a Generalization Hierarchy

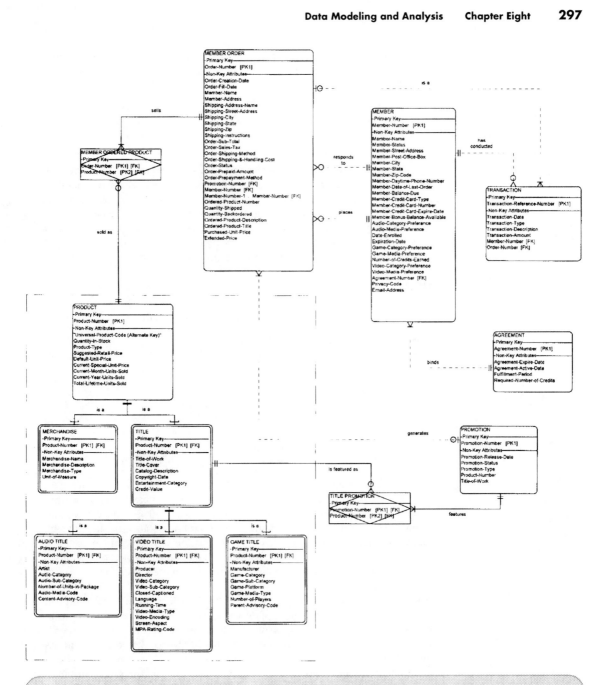

FIGURE 8-16 The SoundStage Fully Attributed Data Model

- An attribute's domain should not be based on logic. For example, in the SoundStage case we learned that the values of MEDIA were dependent on the type of product. If the product type is a video, the media could be VHS tape, 8mm tape, laserdisc, or DVD. If the product type is audio, the media could be cassette tape, CD, or MD. The best solution would be to assign separate attributes to each domain: AUDIO MEDIA and VIDEO MEDIA.

Figure 8-16 provides the mapping of data attributes to entities for the definition phase of our SoundStage systems project. While the fully attributed model identifies all the attributes to be captured and stored in our future database, the descriptions for those attributes are incomplete; they require domains. Most CASE tools provide extensive facilities for describing the data types, domains, and defaults for all attributes to the repository. Additionally, each attribute should be defined for future reference.

Analyzing the Data Model

While a data model effectively communicates database requirements, it does not necessarily represent a *good* database design. It may contain structural characteristics that reduce flexibility and expansion or create unnecessary redundancy. Therefore, we must prepare our fully attributed data model for database design and implementation.

This section will discuss the characteristics of a *quality* data model—one that will allow us to develop an ideal database structure. We'll also present the process used to analyze data model quality and make necessary modifications before database design.

> What Is a Good Data Model?

What makes a data model good? We suggest the following criteria:

- *A good data model is simple.* As a general rule, the data attributes that describe any given entity should describe only that entity. Consider, for example, the following entity definition:

COURSE REGISTRATION =   COURSE REGISTRATION NUMBER (PRIMARY KEY) +
                           COURSE REGISTRATION DATE +
                           STUDENT ID NUMBER (A FOREIGN KEY) +
                           STUDENT NAME +
                           STUDENT MAJOR +
                           One or more COURSE NUMBERS

    Do STUDENT NAME and STUDENT MAJOR really describe an instance of course registration? Or do they describe a different entity, say, STUDENT? The same argument could be applied to STUDENT ID NUMBER, but on further inspection, that attribute is needed to "point" to the corresponding instance of the STUDENT entity. Another aspect of simplicity is stated as follows: Each attribute of an entity instance can have only one value. Looking again at the previous example, we see that COURSE NUMBER can have as many values for one COURSE REGISTRATION as the student elects.

- *A good data model is essentially nonredundant.* This means that each data attribute, <u>other than foreign keys</u>, describes at most one entity. In the prior example, it is not difficult to imagine that STUDENT NAME and STUDENT MAJOR might also describe a STUDENT entity. We should choose. Based on the previous bullet, the logical choice would be the STUDENT entity. There may also exist subtle redundancies in a data model. For example, the same attribute might be recorded more than once under different names (synonyms).

- *A good data model should be flexible and adaptable to future needs.* In the absence of this criterion, we would tend to design databases to fulfill only today's business requirements. Then, when a new requirement becomes known, we can't easily change the databases without rewriting many or all of the programs that used those databases. While we can't change the reality that most projects are application-driven, we can make our data models as application-independent as possible to encourage database structures that can be extended or modified without impact to current programs.

    So how do we achieve the above goals? How can you design a database that can adapt to future requirements that you cannot predict? The answer lies in data analysis.

> Data Analysis

The technique used to improve a data model in preparation for database design is called *data analysis*. **Data analysis** is a process that prepares a data model for implementation as a simple, nonredundant, flexible, and adaptable database. The specific technique is called *normalization*. **Normalization** is a data analysis technique that organizes data attributes such that they are grouped to form nonredundant, stable, flexible, and adaptive entities. Normalization is a three-step technique that places the data model into first normal form, second normal form, and third normal form.[2] Don't get hung up on the terminology—it's easier than it sounds. For now, let's establish an initial understanding of these three formats:

- Simply stated, an entity is in **first normal form (1NF)** if there are no attributes that can have more than one value for a single instance of the entity. Any attributes that can have multiple values actually describe a separate entity, possibly an entity and relationship.
- An entity is in **second normal form (2NF)** if it is already in 1NF and if the values of all non-primary-key attributes are dependent on the full primary key—not just part of it. Any nonkey attributes that are dependent on only part of the primary key should be moved to any entity where that partial key is actually the full key. This may require creating a new entity and relationship on the model.
- An entity is in **third normal form (3NF)** if it is already in 2NF and if the values of its non-primary-key attributes are not dependent on any other non-primary-key attributes. Any nonkey attributes that are dependent on other nonkey attributes must be moved or deleted. Again, new entities and relationships may have to be added to the data model.

> Normalization Example

There are numerous approaches to normalization. We have chosen to present a nontheoretical and nonmathematical approach. We'll leave the theory, relational algebra, and detailed implications to the database courses and textbooks.

As usual, we'll use the SoundStage case study to demonstrate the steps. Let's begin by referring to the fully attributed data model that was developed earlier (see Figure 8-16). Is it a normalized data model? No. Let's identify the problems and walk through the steps of normalizing our data model.

First Normal Form   The first step in data analysis is to place each entity into 1NF. In Figure 8-16, which entities are not in 1NF?

You should find two—MEMBER ORDER and PROMOTION. Each contains a *repeating group*, that is, a group of attributes that can have multiple values for a single instance of the entity *(denoted by the brackets)*. These attributes repeat many times "as a group." Consider, for example, the entity MEMBER ORDER. A single MEMBER ORDER may contain many products; therefore, the attributes ORDERED PRODUCT NUMBER, ORDERED PRODUCT DESCRIPTION, ORDERED PRODUCT TITLE, QUANTITY ORDERED, QUANTITY SHIPPED, QUANTITY BACKORDERED, PURCHASED UNIT PRICE, and EXTENDED PRICE may (and probably do) repeat for each instance of MEMBER ORDER.

Similarly, since a PROMOTION may feature more than one PRODUCT TITLE, the PRODUCT NUMBER and TITLE OF WORK attributes may repeat. How do we fix these anomalies in our model?

Figures 8-17 and 8-18 demonstrate how to place these two entities into 1NF. The original entity is depicted on the left side of the page. The 1NF entities are on the right

---

data analysis a technique used to improve a data model for implementation as a database.

normalization a data analysis technique that organizes data into groups to form nonredundant, stable, flexible, and adaptive entities.

first normal form (1NF) an entity whose attributes have no more than one value for a single instance of that entity.

second normal form (2NF) an entity whose non-primary-key attributes are dependent on the full primary key.

third normal form (3NF) an entity whose non-primary-key attributes are not dependent on any other non-primary-key attributes.

---

[2]Database experts have identified additional normal forms. Third normal form removes most data anomalies. We leave a discussion of advanced normal forms to database textbooks and courses.

300   **Part Two**   **Systems Analysis Methods**

FIGURE 8-17 First Normal Form (1NF)

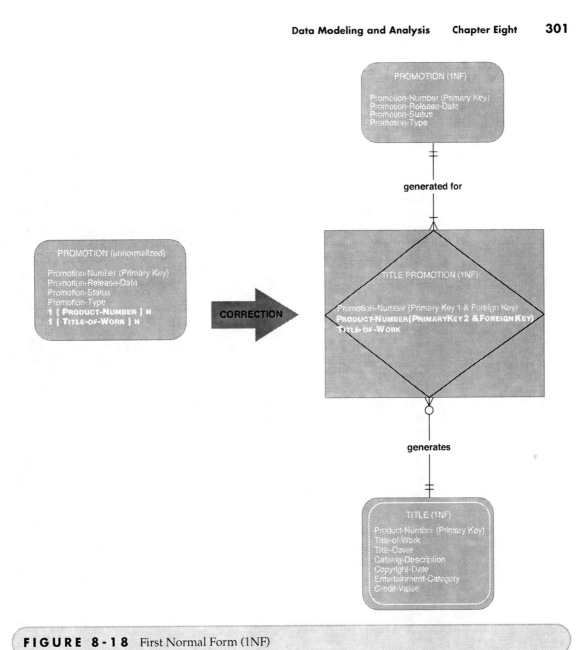

FIGURE 8-18 First Normal Form (1NF)

side of the page. Each figure shows how normalization changed the data model and attribute assignments. For your convenience, the attributes that are affected are in boldface type and in small capital letters.

In Figure 8-17, we first removed the attributes that can have more than one value for an instance of the MEMBER ORDER entity. That alone places MEMBER ORDER in 1NF. But what do we do with the removed attributes? We can't remove them entirely from the model—they are part of the business requirements! Therefore, we moved the entire group of attributes to a new entity, MEMBER ORDERED PRODUCT. Each instance of these attributes describes one PRODUCT on a single MEMBER ORDER. Thus, if a specific order contains five PRODUCTS, there will be five instances of the MEMBER ORDERED PRODUCT entity. Each entity instance has only one value for each attribute; therefore, the new entity is also in first normal form.

Another example of 1NF is shown in Figure 8-18 for the PROMOTION entity. As before, we moved the repeating attributes to a different entity, TITLE PROMOTION.

All other entities are already in 1NF because they do not contain any repeating groups.

Second Normal Form The next step of data analysis is to place the entities into 2NF. Recall that it is required that you have already placed all entities into 1NF. Also recall that 2NF looks for an attribute whose value is determined by only part of the primary key—not the entire concatenated key. Accordingly, entities that have a single-attribute primary key are already in 2NF. That takes care of PRODUCT (and its subtypes), MEMBER ORDER, MEMBER, PROMOTION, AGREEMENT, and TRANSACTION. Thus, we need to check only those entities that have a concatenated key—MEMBER ORDERED PRODUCT and TITLE PROMOTION.

First, let's check the MEMBER ORDERED PRODUCT entity. Most of the attributes are dependent on the full primary key. For example, QUANTITY ORDERED makes no sense unless you have *both* an ORDER NUMBER and a PRODUCT NUMBER. Think about it! By itself, ORDER NUMBER is inadequate since the order could have as many quantities ordered as there are products on the order. Similarly, by itself, PRODUCT NUMBER is inadequate since the same product could appear on many orders. Thus, QUANTITY ORDERED requires both parts of the key and is dependent on the full key. The same could be said of QUANTITY SHIPPED, QUANTITY BACKORDERED, PURCHASE UNIT PRICE, and EXTENDED PRICE.

But what about ORDERED PRODUCT DESCRIPTION and ORDERED PRODUCT TITLE? Do we really need ORDER NUMBER to determine a value for either? No! Instead, the values of these attributes are dependent only on the value of PRODUCT NUMBER. Thus, the attributes are *not* dependent on the full key; we have uncovered a *partial dependency* anomaly that must be fixed. How do we fix this type of normalization error?

Refer to Figure 8-19 on the next page. To fix the problem, we simply move the nonkey attributes, ORDERED PRODUCT DESCRIPTION and ORDERED PRODUCT TITLE, to an entity that has only PRODUCT NUMBER as its key. If necessary, we would have to create this entity, but the PRODUCT entity with that key already exists. But we have to be careful because PRODUCT is a supertype. Upon inspection of the subtypes, we discover that the attributes are already in the MERCHANDISE and TITLE entities, albeit under a synonym. Thus, we didn't actually have to move the attributes from the MEMBER ORDERED PRODUCT entity; we just deleted them as redundant attributes.

Next, let's examine the TITLE PROMOTION entity. The concatenated key is the combination of PROMOTION NUMBER and PRODUCT NUMBER. TITLE OF WORK is dependent on the PRODUCT NUMBER portion of the concatenated key. Thus, TITLE OF WORK is removed from TITLE PROMOTION (see Figure 8-20). Notice that TITLE OF WORK already existed in the entity TITLE, which has a product number as its primary key.

Third Normal Form We can further simplify our entities by placing them into 3NF. Entities are required to be in 2NF before beginning 3NF analysis. Third normal form analysis looks for two types of problems, *derived data* and *transitive dependencies*. In both cases, the fundamental error is that nonkey attributes are dependent on other nonkey attributes.

The first type of 3NF analysis is easy—examine each entity for derived attributes. **Derived attributes** are those whose values can be either calculated from other attributes or derived through logic from the values of other attributes. If you think about it, storing a derived attribute makes little sense. First, it wastes disk storage space. Second, it complicates what should be simple updates. Why? Every time you change the base attributes, you must remember to reperform the calculation and also change its result.

For example, look at the MEMBER ORDERED PRODUCT entity in Figure 8-21. The attribute EXTENDED PRICE is calculated by multiplying QUANTITY ORDERED by PURCHASED UNIT PRICE. Thus, EXTENDED PRICE (a nonkey attribute) is not dependent on the primary key

derived attribute an attribute whose value can be calculated from other attributes or derived from the values of other attributes.

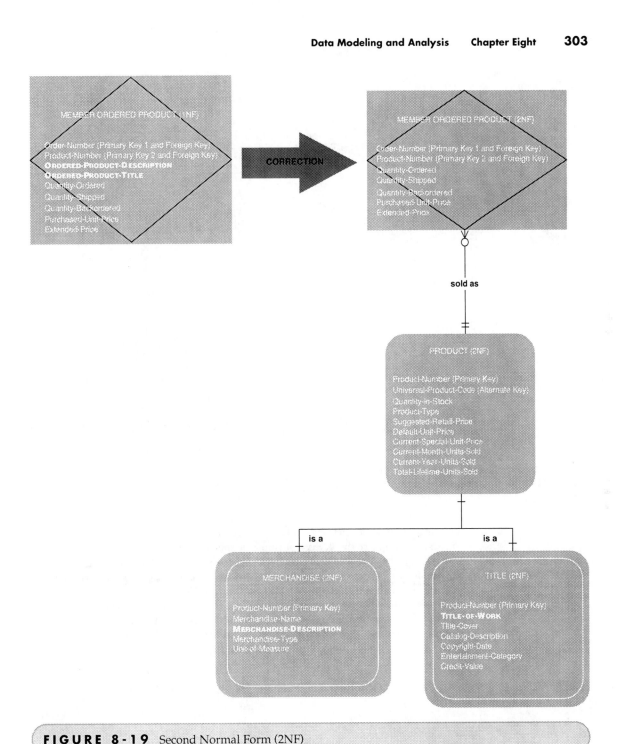

FIGURE 8-19 Second Normal Form (2NF)

as much as it is dependent on the nonkey attributes, QUANTITY ORDERED and PURCHASED
UNIT PRICE. Thus, we correct the entity by deleting EXTENDED PRICE.

 Sounds simple, right? Well, not always! There is disagreement on how far you take
this rule. Some experts argue that the rule should be applied only within a single entity. Thus, these experts would not delete a derived attribute if the attributes required
for the derivation were assigned to *different* entities. We agree based on the argument
that a derived attribute that involves multiple entities presents a greater danger for

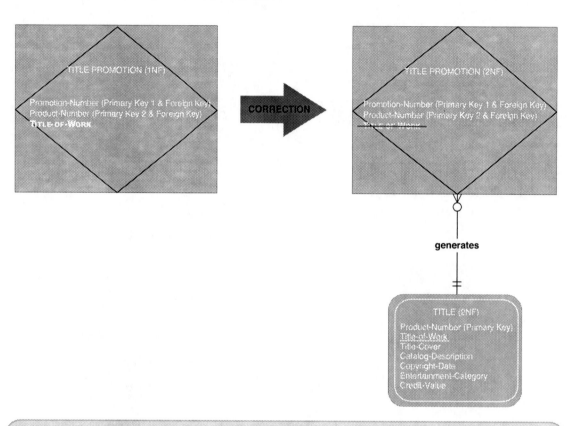

FIGURE 8-20 Second Normal Form (2NF)

data inconsistency caused by updating an attribute in one entity and forgetting to subsequently update the derived attribute in another entity.

Another form of 3NF analysis checks for *transitive dependencies*. A **transitive dependency** exists when a nonkey attribute is dependent on another nonkey attribute (other than by derivation). This error usually indicates that an undiscovered entity is still embedded within the problem entity. Such a condition, if not corrected, can cause future flexibility and adaptability problems if a new requirement eventually requires that we implement that undiscovered entity as a separate database table.

transitive dependency when the value of a nonkey attribute is dependent on the value of another nonkey attribute other than by derivation.

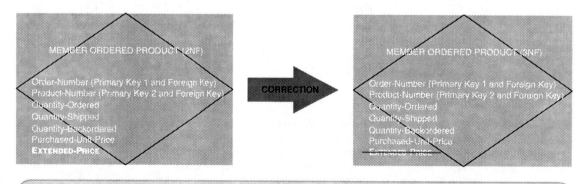

FIGURE 8-21 Third Normal Form (3NF)

FIGURE 8-22 Third Normal Form (3NF)

Transitive analysis is performed only on entities that do not have a concatenated key. In our example, this includes PRODUCT, MEMBER ORDER, PROMOTION, AGREEMENT, MEMBER, and TRANSACTION. For the entity PRODUCT, all the nonkey attributes are dependent on the primary key and only the primary key. Thus, PRODUCT is already in third normal form. A similar analysis of PROMOTION, AGREEMENT, and TRANSACTION reveals that they are also in third normal form.

But look at the entity MEMBER ORDER in Figure 8-22. In particular, examine the attributes MEMBER NAME and MEMBER ADDRESS. Are these attributes dependent on the primary key, ORDER NUMBER? No! The primary key ORDER NUMBER in no way determines the value of MEMBER NAME and MEMBER ADDRESS. On the other hand, the values of MEMBER NAME and MEMBER ADDRESS are dependent on the value of another non-*primary* key in the entity, MEMBER NUMBER.

How do we fix this problem? MEMBER NAME and MEMBER ADDRESS need to be moved from the MEMBER ORDER entity to an entity whose primary key is just MEMBER NUMBER. If necessary, we would create that entity, but in our case we already have a MEMBER entity with the required primary key. As it turns out, we don't need to really move the problem attributes because they are already assigned to the MEMBER entity. We did, however, notice that MEMBER ADDRESS was a synonym for MEMBER STREET ADDRESS. We elected to keep the latter term in MEMBER.

Several normal forms beyond 3NF exist. Each successive normal form makes the data model simpler, less redundant, and more flexible. However, systems analysts (and most database experts) rarely take data models beyond 3NF. Consequently, we will leave further discussion of normalization to database textbooks.

The first few times you normalize a data model, the process will appear slow and tedious. However, with time and practice, it becomes quick and routine. Many experienced modelers significantly reduce the modeling time and effort by doing normalization during attribution (they are able to do normalization at the time they are developing the fully attributed data model). It may help to always remember the following ditty (source unknown), which nicely summarizes first, second, and third normal forms:

> An entity is said to be in third normal form if every non-primary-key attribute is dependent on the primary key, the whole primary key, and nothing but the primary key.

Simplification by Inspection   Normalization is a fairly mechanical process. But it is dependent on naming consistencies in the original data model (before normalization). When several analysts work on a common application, it is not unusual to create problems that won't be taken care of by normalization. These problems are best solved through simplification by inspection, a process wherein a data entity in 3NF is further simplified by such efforts as addressing subtle data redundancy.

The final, normalized data model is presented in Figure 8-23 on the next page.

CASE Support for Normalization   Many CASE tools claim to support normalization concepts. They read the data model and attempt to isolate possible normalization errors. On close examination, most CASE tools can normalize only to first normal form. They accomplish this in one of two ways. They look for many-to-many relationships and resolve those relationships into associative entities. Or they look for attributes specifically described as having multiple values for a single entity instance. (One could argue that the analyst should have recognized that as a 1NF error and not described the attributes as such.)

It is exceedingly difficult for a CASE tool to identify second and third normal form errors. That would require that the CASE tool have the intelligence to recognize partial and transitive dependencies. In reality, such dependencies can be discovered only through less-than-routine examination by the systems analysts or database experts.

Mapping Data Requirements to Locations

While a logical data model is effective for describing what data is to be stored for a new system, it does not communicate the requirements on a business operating location basis. We need to identify what data and access rights are needed at which locations. Specifically, we might ask the following business questions:

- Which subsets of the entities and attributes are needed to perform the work at each location?
- What level of access is required?

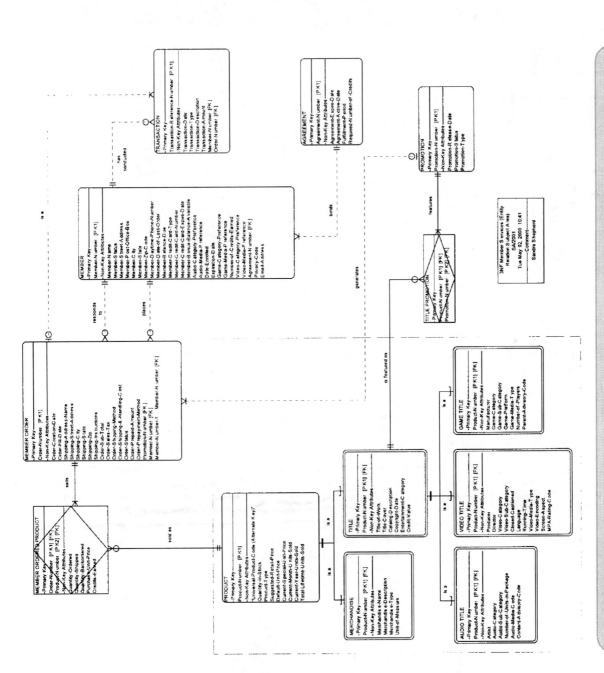

Entity . Attribute	Location / Customers	Kansas City	Marketing	Advertising	Warehouse	Sales	A/R	Boston	Sales	Warehouse	San Francisco	Sales	San Diego	Warehouse
Customer	INDV					ALL	ALL		SS	SS		SS		SS
Customer Number	R				R	CRUD	R		CRUD	R		CRUD		R
Customer Name	RU				R	CRUD	R		CRUD	R		CRUD		R
Customer Address	RU				R	CRUD	R		CRUD	R		CRUD		R
Customer Credit Rating	X					R	RU		R			R		
Customer Balance Due	R					R	RU		R			R		
Order	INDV		ALL		SS	ALL			SS	SS		SS		SS
Order Number	SRD		R	CRUD	R	CRUD	R		CRUD	R		CRUD		R
Order Date	SRD		R	CRUD	R	CRUD	R		CRUD	R		CRUD		R
Order Amount	SRD		R	CRUD		CRUD	R		CRUD	R		CRUD		R
Ordered Product	INDV		ALL		SS	ALL			SS	SS		SS		SS
Quantity Ordered	SUD		R	CRUD	R	CRUD	R		CRUD			CRUD		
Ordered Item Unit Price	SUD		R	CRUD		CRUD	R		CRUD			CRUD		
Product	ALL		ALL	ALL	ALL	ALL			ALL	ALL		ALL		ALL
Product Number	R		CRUD	R	R	R			R	R		R		R
Product Name	R		CRUD	R	R	R			R	R		R		R
Product Description	R		CRUD	RU	R	R			R	R		R		R
Product Unit of Measure	R		CRUD	R	R	R			R	R		R		R
Product Current Unit Price	R		CRUD	R		R			R	R		R		R
Product Quantity on Hand	X				RU	R			R	RU		R		RU

INDV = individual   **ALL** = ALL   **SS** = subset   **X** = no access

S = submit   **C** = create   **R** = read   **U** = update   **D** = delete

FIGURE 8-24 Data-to-Location-CRUD Matrix

- Can the location *create* instances of the entity?
- Can the location *read* instances of the entity?
- Can the location *delete* instances of the entity?
- Can the location *update* existing instances of the entity?

data-to-location-CRUD matrix a matrix that is used to map data requirements to locations.

Systems analysts have found it useful to define these logical requirements in the form of a *data-to-location-CRUD matrix*. A **data-to-location-CRUD matrix** is a table in which the rows indicate entities (and possible attributes); the columns indicate locations; and the cells (the intersection of rows and columns) document level of access where C = create, R = read, U = update or modify, and D = delete or deactivate. Figure 8-24 illustrates a typical data-to-location-CRUD matrix. The decision to include or not include attributes is based on whether locations need to be restricted as to which attributes they can access. Figure 8-24 also demonstrates the ability to document that a location requires access only to a subset (designated SS) of entity instances. For example, each sales office might need access only to those customers in its region.

In some methodologies and CASE tools, you can define *views* of the data model for each location. A view includes only the entities and attributes to be accessible for a single location. If views are defined, they must also be kept in sync with the master data model. (Most CASE tools do this automatically.)

Learning Roadmap

Most of you will proceed directly to Chapter 9, "Process Modeling." Whereas data modeling was concerned with data independently from how that data is captured and used (data at rest), process modeling shows how the data will be captured and used (data in motion). To take an object-oriented approach, you may jump to Chapter 10, "Object-Oriented Analysis and Modeling with UML." Object modeling has many parallels with data modeling. An object includes attributes, but it also includes all the processes that can act on and use those methods.

If you want to immediately learn how to implement data models as databases, you should skim or read Chapter 14, "Designing Databases." In that chapter, the logical data models are transformed into physical database schemas. With CASE tools, the code for creating the database can be generated automatically.

 Summary

1. Data modeling is a technique for organizing and documenting a system's DATA. Data modeling is sometimes called database modeling because a data model is usually implemented as a database.

2. There are several notations for data modeling. The actual model is frequently called an entity relationship diagram (ERD) because it depicts data in terms of the entities and relationships described by the data.

3. An entity is something about which the business needs to store data. Classes of entities include persons, places, objects, events, and concepts.

4. An entity instance is a single occurrence of an entity class.

5. Pieces of data we want to store about each instance of a given entity are called attributes. An attribute is a descriptive property or characteristic of the entity. Some attributes can be logically grouped into superattributes called compound attributes.

6. When analyzing a system, we should define those values for an attribute that are legitimate or that make business sense. The values for each attribute are defined in terms of three properties—data type, domain, and default:

   a. The data type defines what class of data can be stored in the attribute.

   b. The domain of an attribute defines what values an attribute can legitimately take on.

   c. The default value for an attribute is the value that will be recorded if not specified by the user.

7. Every entity must have an identifier or key. A key is an attribute, or a group of attributes, that assumes a unique value for each entity instance.

   a. A group of attributes that uniquely identifies an instance of an entity is called a concatenated key.

   b. A candidate key is a "candidate to become the primary identifier" of instances of an entity.

    c. A primary key is the candidate key that will most commonly be used to uniquely identify a single entity instance.

    d. Any candidate key that is not selected to become the primary key is called an alternate key.

    e. Sometimes, it is also necessary to identify a subset of entity instances as opposed to a single instance. A subsetting criteria is an attribute (or concatenated attribute) whose finite values divide all entity instances into useful subsets.

8. A relationship is a natural business association that exists between one or more entities. The relationship may represent an event that links the entities or merely a logical affinity that exists between the entities. All relationships are implicitly bidirectional, meaning they can be interpreted in both directions.

9. Cardinality defines the minimum and maximum number of occurrences of one entity for a single occurrence of the related entity. Because all relationships are bidirectional, cardinality must be defined in both directions for every relationship.

10. The degree of a relationship is the number of entity classes that participate in the relationship. Not all relationships are binary. Some relationships may be recursive relationships, wherein the relationship exists between different instances of the same entity. Relationships can also exist between more than two different entities, as in the case of a 3-ary, or ternary, relationship.

11. An associative entity is an entity that inherits its primary key from more than one other entity (parents). Each part of that concatenated key points to one and only one instance of each of the connecting entities.

12. A foreign key is a primary key of one entity that is contributed to (duplicated in) another entity to identify instances of a relationship. A foreign key (always in a child entity) always matches the primary key (in a parent entity).

13. Nonidentifying relationships are those in which each of the participating entities has its own independent primary key, of which none of the primary-key attributes is shared. The entities in a nonidentifying relationship are referred to as *strong* or independent entities because neither depends on any other entity for its identification. Identifying relationships are those in which the parent entity contributes its primary key to become part of the primary key of the child

entity. The child entity of any identifying relationship is referred to as a *weak* entity because its identification is dependent on the existence of the parent entity's existence.

14. A nonspecific relationship (or many-to-many relationship) is one in which many instances of one entity are associated with many instances of another entity. Such relationships are suitable only for preliminary data models and should be resolved as quickly as possible.

15. Generalization is an approach that seeks to discover and exploit the commonalities between entities. It is a technique wherein the attributes are grouped to form entity supertypes and subtypes.

    a. An entity supertype is an entity whose instances store attributes that are common to one or more entity subtypes.

    b. An entity subtype is an entity whose instances inherit some common attributes from an entity supertype and then add other attributes that are unique to an instance of the subtype.

16. A logical data model is developed in the following stages:

    a. Entities are discovered and defined.

    b. A context data model is built. A context data model contains only business entities and relationships identified by the system owners and users.

    c. A key-based data model is built. The key-based model eliminates nonspecific relationships and adds associative entities. All entities in the model are given keys.

    d. A fully attributed model is built. This model shows all the attributes to be stored in the system.

    e. A fully described model is built. Each attribute is defined in the dictionary and described in terms of properties such as domain and security.

    f. The completed data model is then analyzed for adaptability and flexibility through a process called normalization. The final analyzed model is referred to as a third normal form data model.

17. A logical data model does not communicate data requirements on a business operating location basis. Systems analysts have found it useful to define these requirements in the form of a data-to-location-CRUD matrix.

Review Questions

1. What is the difference between logical and physical models?
2. Why is it important to create an implementation-independent model of a system?
3. Why is it necessary to create an implementation-dependent model of a system?
4. What is an entity? What are entity instances?

5. A *relationship* is a natural business association between entities. What is the relationship between student and teacher? Does it depend on how many classes a student can take, or how many classes a teacher can teach?
6. What is cardinality? Give an example.

 ## Problems and Exercises

1. What is a reasonable domain for the data attribute for a student's last name?
2. What default value would you choose for a student's last name?
3. What default value would you choose for gender?
4. The student table you are working with contains the attributes: STUDENT ID, NAME, PHONE NUMBER, and MAJOR. Normalize to 3NF.
5. What attributes would you have in a table to describe a movie?
6. A many-to-many relationship (also called a nonspecific relationship) can and generally should be resolved into a pair of one-to-many relationships with an associative entity. When is this not the case?

7. Give an example of a many-to-many relationship. Resolve using an entity or an associative entity. Which did you use? Why?
8. Describe each of the first three normal forms. Give an example of each.
9. A customer goes to a shoe store and purchases several pairs of shoes. Diagram this relationship.
10. Give an example each of ternary, identifying, and nonidentifying relationships.
11. On the surface, data modeling appears not to require much creativity. Why is this incorrect?
12. Can a well-designed database give a business a strategic advantage? How?

 ## Projects and Research

1. Go to the school library. Ask the librarian at the circulation desk to print out a copy of the information they keep on you. What types of data are being stored? Is there anything that surprises you or seems irrelevant to checking out books? If so, ask why the information is collected.
2. Create a list of attributes for the student entity from the information you found in the previous problem. Normalize to third normal form.
3. Go to a grocery store and make a purchase. What type of data would a good information system maintain on a transaction? What does a good information system do for a business?
4. Compare your answer from the above question (grocery store) to that of at least one other student. How were your answers different?

5. What legal and privacy issues are related to databases used by grocery stores? Go to *http://www.findlaw.com* and research some recent court cases on the topic. Present your work in a short (five-page) paper to your class.
6. How can databases, and the information kept in databases, be used by businesses for a strategic advantage? In a small group, go to a business of your choosing. Brainstorm to create a database that offers that company either a solution to an existing problem, or exploits an existing opportunity in business. Remember to be creative.

312   **Part Two**   **Systems Analysis Methods**

Minicases

1. Consider a fictitious online grocery store called Wow Munchies. This is a national franchise, complete with marketing, accounting, shipping, and customer service departments. The CIO has decided to update the database corresponding to the Web store so that it collects pertinent transaction and shopping information for the different departments. She is undecided what software or hardware will support this database.

   Step 1.   How will you determine what data is important to collect and maintain in the new database? Be specific.

   Step 2.   Create surveys, questionnaires, and the like, and administer them to appropriate personnel in the affected departments. Review the forms that each department uses.

   Step 3.   What kind of responses did you get? Go to an online grocery store, and see what data is being collected by "rival" companies. Did you miss anything? Did any of the responses you get require a secondary meeting with department personnel? If so, revise your surveys and questions and reinterview.

   Step 4.   Utilize the methods you outlined in the above question, and ascertain the entities and attributes you will need to include in your data.

   Step 5.   Draft the relationships and cardinality between the entities. What kind of data model are you using? Implementation specific or nonspecific? Why?

   Step 6.   Revise your data model so that there are no many-to-many relationships, and the model is normalized to third normal form.

   Step 7.   Submit all questionnaires, surveys, forms, and responses to your professor, along with your final data model draft. Include a short explanation as to how you derived your entities and attributes and the relationships and any assumptions or limitations your data model may have.

2. Research a car rental agency and create a data model for its database for car rentals. What departments are affected by the rental of a car? Review any forms publicly available and create surveys and interviews as necessary to help you determine what your database should contain. Be sure to normalize to third normal form and to resolve any many-to-many relationships. Submit your data model and all supporting documents to your professor.

3. Consider the Mafia. Assuming that organized crime groups maintain databases to evade capture and to run their businesses, what information would they keep? Why?

4. What legal, ethical, and privacy issues are associated with databases used in crime fighting? Research and present a short paper (ten pages or less) to your class.

Team and Individual Exercises

1. Project management in a geographically and culturally dispersed team is difficult. For each team member, assign the member to a country with a different time zone and different languages. Assume all members share one common language, although that language will not be a first language for all members. Example countries: USA, India, Israel, China, Pakistan, Iran, France, Peru, and Japan.

2. Individual exercise: It is said that the boundaries of our own creativity are ourselves, and our experiences. That is, the very things that make us who we are also constrain us. What does it mean to be creative? How do you become creative and to think freely?

3. Individual or team exercise: Reengineer a common life process. If the "sky was the limit," how would you change this process? Identify each of the steps in the old process and then each step in the new process (e.g., putting on makeup, cleaning the house, going to the grocery store, going to class). Bring your notes to class for a roundtable discussion.

Suggested Readings

Bruce, Thomas A. *Designing Quality Databases with IDEF1X Information Models.* New York: Dorset House Publishing, 1992. We actually use this book as a textbook in our database analysis and design course. IDEF1X is a rich, standardized syntax for data modeling (which Bruce calls information modeling). The graphical language looks different, but it communicates the same system concepts presented in our book. The language is supported by at least two CASE tools: Logic Works' *ERwin* and Popkin's *System Architect.* The book includes two case studies.

Hay, David C. *Data Model Patterns: Conventions of Thought.* New York: Dorset House Publishing, 1996. What a novel book! This book starts with the premise that most business data models are derivatives of some basic, repeatable patterns. CASE vendors, how about including these patterns in CASE tools as reusable templates?

Martin, James, and Clive Finkelstein. *Information Engineering,* 3 vols. New York: Savant Institute, 1981. Information engineering is a formal, database, and fourth-generation language-oriented methodology. The graphical data modeling language of information engineering is virtually identical to ours. Data modeling is covered in Volumes I and II.

Reingruber, Michael, and William Gregory. *The Data Modeling Handbook.* New York: John Wiley & Sons, 1994. This is an excellent book on data modeling and is particularly helpful in ensuring the quality and accuracy of data models.

Schlaer, Sally, and Stephen J. Mellor. *Object-Oriented Systems Analysis: Modeling the World in Data.* Englewood Cliffs, NJ: Yourdon Press, 1988. Forget the title! "Object-oriented" means something different today than it did in 1988, but the book is still one of the easiest-to-read books on the subject of data modeling.

Teorey, Toby J. *Database Modeling & Design: The Fundamental Principles,* 2nd ed. San Francisco: Morgan Kaufman Publishers, 1994. This book is somewhat more conceptual than the others in the list, but it provides useful insights into the practice of data modeling.

Process Modeling

Chapter Preview and Objectives

In this chapter you will learn how to draw data flow diagrams, a popular process model that documents a system's processes and their data flows. You will know process modeling as a systems analysis tool when you can:

▌ Define systems modeling and differentiate between logical and physical system models.

▌ Define process modeling and explain its benefits.

▌ Recognize and understand the basic concepts and constructs of a process model.

▌ Read and interpret a data flow diagram.

▌ Explain when to construct process models and where to store them.

▌ Construct a context diagram to illustrate a system's interfaces with its environment.

▌ Identify use cases and external and temporal business events for a system.

▌ Perform event partitioning and organize events in a functional decomposition diagram.

▌ Draw event diagrams and then merge those event diagrams into system diagrams.

▌ Draw primitive data flow diagrams and describe the elementary data flows and processes in terms of data structures and procedural logic (Structured English and decision tables), respectively.

▌ Document the distribution of processes to locations.

▌ Synchronize data and process models using a CRUD matrix.

Introduction

Bob Martinez has been working on the SoundStage Member Services system for several weeks. He understands the system pretty well, but it is still easy to get confused and to forget details.

"The problem," Bob said to his boss, Sandra Shepherd, "is that the system is too big to keep it all in your head at one time."

"I'm glad you said that," Sandra answered, "because your next assignment is to break the system down into parts that you can get your head around. Each part is called a process, and you'll need to define the inputs and outputs to that process plus who or what each input and output comes from or goes to. And, by the way, you'll need to specify the logic for the process."

"I thought the use cases did all that," Bob replied.

"They aren't specific enough," Sandra stated. "Would you like to turn a project over to a programmer located across the country with no more specifics than what a use case has? Who knows what you'd end up with? Welcome to the world of process modeling, Bob. Get to work."

An Introduction to Process Modeling

model a pictorial representation of reality.

In Chapter 5 you were introduced to systems analysis activities that called for drawing system models. System models play an important role in system development. As a systems analyst or user, you will constantly deal with unstructured problems. One way to structure such problems is to draw models. A **model** is a representation of reality. Just as a picture is worth a thousand words, most system models are pictorial representations of reality. Models can be built for existing systems as a way to better understand those systems or for proposed systems as a way to document business requirements or technical designs. An important concept is the distinction between logical and physical models.

logical model a nontechnical pictorial representation that depicts what a system is or does. Synonyms are *essential model, conceptual model,* and *business model.*

Logical models show *what* a system is or does. They are implementation-*in*dependent; that is, they depict the system independent of any technical implementation. As such, logical models illustrate the *essence* of the system. Popular synonyms include *essential model, conceptual model,* and *business model.* **Physical models** show not only *what* a system is or does but also *how* the system is physically and technically implemented. They are implementation-*de*pendent because they reflect technology choices and the limitations of those technology choices. Synonyms include *implementation model* and *technical model.*

physical model a technical pictorial representation that depicts what a system is or does and how the system is implemented. Synonyms are *implementation model* and *technical model.*

Systems analysts have long recognized the value of separating business and technical concerns. That is why they use logical system models to depict business requirements and physical system models to depict technical designs. Systems analysis activities tend to focus on the logical system models for the following reasons:

- Logical models remove biases that are the result of the way the current system is implemented or the way that any one person thinks the system might be implemented. Thus, we overcome the "we've always done it that way" syndrome. Consequently, logical models encourage creativity.
- Logical models reduce the risk of missing business requirements because we are too preoccupied with technical details. Such errors can be costly to correct after the system is implemented. By separating what the system must do from how the system will do it, we can better analyze the requirements for completeness, accuracy, and consistency.
- Logical models allow us to communicate with end users in nontechnical or less technical languages. Thus, we don't lose requirements in the technical jargon of the computing discipline.

In this chapter we will focus exclusively on *logical* process modeling during systems analysis. **Process modeling** is a technique for organizing and documenting the structure and flow of data through a system's PROCESSES and/or the logic, policies, and procedures to be implemented by a system's PROCESSES. In the context of information system building blocks (see the home page at the beginning of the chapter), *logical* process models are used to document an information system's PROCESS focus from the system owners' and users' perspective (the intersection of the PROCESS column with the system owner and system user rows). Also notice that one special type of process model, called a *context diagram*, illustrates the COMMUNICATION focus from the system owners' and users' perspective.

Process modeling originated in classical software engineering methods; therefore, you may have encountered various types of process models such as program structure charts, logic flowcharts, or decision tables in an application programming course. In this chapter, we'll focus on a systems analysis process model, *data flow diagrams*.

A **data flow diagram (DFD)** is a tool that depicts the flow of data through a system and the work or processing performed by that system. Synonyms include *bubble chart, transformation graph,* and *process model.* We'll also introduce a DFD planning tool called *decomposition diagrams.* Finally, we'll also study *context diagrams,* a processlike model that actually illustrates a system's interfaces to the business and outside world, including other information systems.[1]

A simple data flow diagram is illustrated in Figure 9-1. In the design phase, some of these business processes might be implemented as computer software (either built in-house or purchased from a software vendor). If you examine this data flow diagram, you should find it easy to read, even before you complete this chapter—that has always been the advantage of DFDs. There are only three symbols and one connection:

- The rounded rectangles represent *processes* or work to be done. Notice that they are illustrated in the PROCESS color from your information system framework.
- The squares represent *external agents*—the boundary of the system. Notice that they are illustrated in the INTERFACE color from your information system framework.
- The open-ended boxes represent *data stores,* sometimes called files or databases. If you have already read Chapter 8, these data stores correspond to all instances of a single entity in a data model. Accordingly, they have been illustrated with the DATA color from your information systems framework.
- The arrows represent *data flows,* or inputs and outputs, to and from the processes.

There is sometimes a tendency to confuse data flow diagrams with flowcharts because program design frequently involves the use of flowcharts. However, data flow diagrams are very different. Let's summarize the differences.

- Processes on a data flow diagram can operate in parallel. Thus, several processes might be executing or working simultaneously. This is consistent with the way businesses work. On the other hand, processes on flowcharts can execute only one at a time.
- Data flow diagrams show the flow of data through the system. Their arrows represent paths down which data can flow. Looping and branching are not typically shown. On the other hand, flowcharts show the sequence of processes or operations in an algorithm or program. Their arrows represent pointers to the next process or operation. This may include looping and branching.

process modeling a technique used to organize and document a system's processes.

data flow diagram (DFD) a process model used to depict the flow of data through a system and the work or processing performed by the system. Synonyms are *bubble chart, transformation graph,* and *process model.*

Author's Note: there are several competing symbol sets for DFDs. Throughout this chapter, the authors have chosen to use the Gane and Sarson notation because of its wide popularity.

---

[1]In classic structured analysis, context diagrams are considered to be another type of process model. But in object-oriented analysis, they illustrate scope and interfaces. In this edition, we have chosen the latter definition.

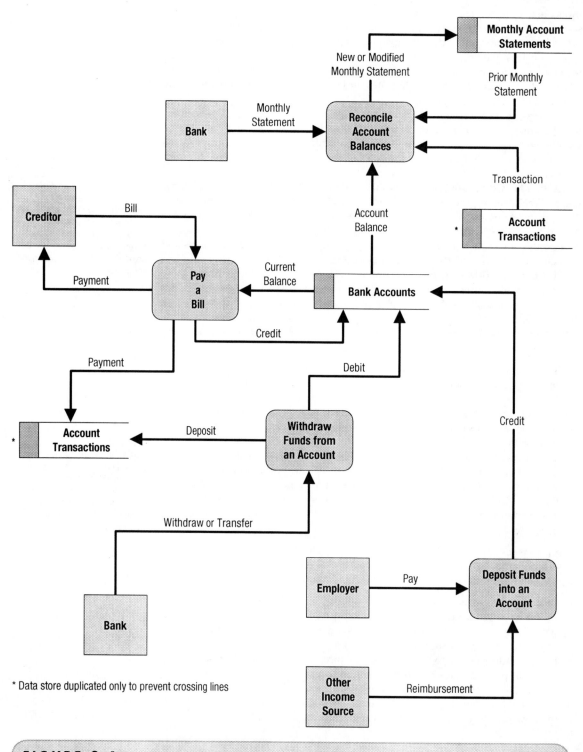

* Data store duplicated only to prevent crossing lines

FIGURE 9-1 A Simple Data Flow Diagram

- Data flow diagrams can show processes that have dramatically different timing. For example, a single DFD might include processes that happen hourly, daily, weekly, yearly, and on demand. This doesn't happen in flowcharts.

Data flow diagrams have been popular for more than 20 years, but the interest in DFDs has been recently renewed because of their applicability in *business process redesign (BPR)*. As businesses have come to realize that most data processing systems have merely automated outdated, inefficient, and bureaucratic business processes, there is renewed interest in streamlining the business processes. This is accomplished by first modeling the business processes for the purpose of analyzing, redesigning, and/or improving them. Subsequently, information technology can be applied to the improved business processes in creative ways that maximize the value returned to the business. We'll revisit this trend at the end of the chapter.

System Concepts for Process Modeling

> External Agents

All information systems respond to events and conditions in the system's environment. The environment of an information system includes *external agents* that form the boundary of the system and define places where the system interfaces with its environment. An **external agent** defines a person, an organization unit, another system, or another organization that lies outside the scope of the project but that interacts with the system being studied. External agents provide the net inputs into a system and receive net outputs from a system. A common synonym is *external entity* (not to be confused with *data entity* as introduced in Chapter 8).

The term *external* means "external to the system being analyzed or designed." In practice, an external agent may actually be outside of the business (such as government agencies, customers, suppliers, and contractors), or it may be inside the business but outside the project and system scope (such as other departments, other business functions, and other internal information systems). An external agent is represented by a square on the data flow diagram. The DeMarco/Yourdon equivalent is a rectangle (see margin).

It is important to recognize that work and activities are occurring inside the external agent, but that work and those activities are said to be "out of scope" and not subject to change. Thus, the data flows between your system and these boundaries should not cause substantive change to the work or activities performed by the external agents.

The external agents of an information system are rarely fixed. As project scope and goals change, the scope of an information system can either grow or shrink. If the system scope grows, it can consume some of the original external agents—in other words, what was once considered outside the system is now considered inside the system (*as new processes*).

Similarly, if the system scope shrinks (because of budget or schedule constraints), processes that were once considered to be inside the system may become external agents.

External agents on a logical data flow diagram may include people, business units, other internal systems with which a system must interact, and external organizations. Their inclusion on the logical DFD means that your system interacts with these agents. They are almost always one of the following:

- An office, department, division, or individual within your company that provides net inputs to that system, receives net outputs from that system, or both.
- An organization, agency, or individual that is outside your company but that provides net inputs to, or receives net outputs from, your system. Examples include CUSTOMERS, SUPPLIERS, CONTRACTORS, BANKS, and GOVERNMENT AGENCIES.

external agent an outside person, organization unit, system, or organization that interacts with a system. Also called *external entity.*

Gane and Sarson shape

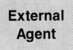

DeMarco/Yourdon shape

External Agent Symbols

- Another business or information system—possibly, though not necessarily, computer-based—that is separate from your system but with which your system must interface. It is becoming common to interface information systems with those of other businesses.
- A system's end users or managers. In this case, the user or manager is either a net source of data to be input to a system and/or a net destination of outputs to be produced by a system.

External agents should be named with descriptive, singular nouns, such as REGISTRAR, SUPPLIER, MANUFACTURING SYSTEM, or FINANCIAL INFORMATION SYSTEM. External agents represent fixed, *physical* systems; therefore, they can have physical names or acronyms—even on a <u>logical</u> DFD. For example, an external agent representing our school's financial management information system would be called FMIS. If an external agent describes an individual, we recommend job titles or role names instead of proper names (for example, use ACCOUNT CLERK, not *Mary Jacobs*).

To avoid crossing data flow lines on a DFD, it is permissible to duplicate external agents on DFDs. But as a general rule, external agents should be located on the perimeters of the page, consistent with their definition as a system boundary.

> Data Stores

Most information systems capture data for later use. The data is kept in a data store, the last symbol on a data flow diagram. It is represented by the open-end box (see margin). A **data store** is an "inventory" of data. Synonyms include *file* and *database* (although those terms are too implementation-oriented for essential process modeling). If data flows are *data in motion,* think of data stores as *data at rest.*

Ideally, essential data stores should describe "things" about which the business wants to store data. These things include:

data store stored data intended for later use. Synonyms are *file* and *database.*

Persons: AGENCY, CONTRACTOR, CUSTOMER, DEPARTMENT, DIVISION, EMPLOYEE, INSTRUCTOR, OFFICE, STUDENT, SUPPLIER. Notice that a person entity can represent either individuals, groups, or organizations.

Places: SALES REGION, BUILDING, ROOM, BRANCH OFFICE, CAMPUS.

Objects: BOOK, MACHINE, PART, PRODUCT, RAW MATERIAL, SOFTWARE LICENSE, SOFTWARE PACKAGE, TOOL, VEHICLE MODEL, VEHICLE. An object entity can represent actual objects (such as SOFTWARE LICENSE) or specifications for a type of object (such as SOFTWARE PACKAGE).

Events: APPLICATION, AWARD, CANCELLATION, CLASS, FLIGHT, INVOICE, ORDER, REGISTRATION, RENEWAL, REQUISITION, RESERVATION, SALE, TRIP.

Concepts: ACCOUNT, BLOCK OF TIME, BOND, COURSE, FUND, QUALIFICATION, STOCK.

	Data Store	

Gane and Sarson shape

Data Store

DeMarco/Yourdon shape

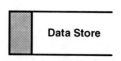

NOTE: If the above list looks familiar, it should: A data store represents *all occurrences* of a data entity—defined in Chapter 8 as something about which we want to store data. As such, the data store represents the synchronization of a system's process model with its data model.

If data modeling is done before process modeling, identification of most data stores is simplified by the following rule:

There should be one data store for each data entity on an entity relationship diagram. (We even include associative and weak entity data stores on our models.)

If, on the other hand, process modeling is done before data modeling, data store discovery tends to be more arbitrary. In that case, our best recommendation is to identify existing implementations of files or data stores (e.g., computer files and databases, file cabinets, record books, catalogs) and then rename them to reflect the logical "things" about which they store data. Consistent with information engineering strategies, we recommend that data models precede the process models.

Generally, data stores should be named as the plural of the corresponding data model entity. Thus, if the data model includes an entity named CUSTOMER, the process models will include a data store named CUSTOMERS. This makes sense because the data store, by definition, stores all instances of the entity. Avoid physical terms such as *file, database, file cabinet, file folder,* and the like.

As was the case with boundaries, it is permissible to duplicate data stores on a DFD to avoid crossing data flow lines. Duplication should be minimized.

> Process Concepts

Recall from Chapter 2 that a fundamental building block of information systems is PROCESSES. All information systems include processes—usually many of them. Information system processes respond to business events and conditions and transform DATA (another building block) into useful information. Modeling processes helps us to understand interactions with the system's environment, other systems, and other processes.

A System Is a Process   We have used the word *system* throughout this book to describe almost any orderly arrangement of ideas or constructs. People speak of educational systems, computer systems, management systems, business systems, and, of course, information systems. In the oldest and simplest of all system models, a system *is* a process.

In systems analysis, models are used to view or present a system. As shown in Figure 9-2, the simplest process model of a system is based on inputs, outputs, and the system itself—viewed as a process. The process symbol defines the boundary of the system. The system is inside the boundary; the environment is outside that boundary. The system exchanges inputs and outputs with its environment. Because the environment is always changing, well-designed systems have a feedback and control loop to allow the system to adapt itself to changing conditions.

Consider a business as a system. It operates within an environment that includes customers, suppliers, competitors, other industries, and the government. Its inputs include materials, services, new employees, new equipment, facilities, money, and orders (to name but a few). Its outputs include products and/or services, waste

Process name

Gane & Sarson shape;
used throughout
this book

FIGURE 9-2

The Classic Process
Model of a System

materials, retired equipment, former employees, and money (payments). It monitors its environment to make necessary changes to its product line, services, operating procedures, competitors, and the economy.

A rounded rectangle (the Gane and Sarson notation) is used throughout this chapter to represent a process (see margin). A **process** is work performed on, or in response to, incoming data flows or conditions. A synonym is *transform*. Different process modeling notations use a circle (the DeMarco/Yourdon notation) or a rectangle (the SSADM/IDEF0 notation). The choice is often dependent on your methodology and CASE tool features.

Although processes can be performed by people, departments, robots, machines, or computers, we once again want to focus on *what* work or action is being performed (the *logical* process), not on who or what is doing that work or activity (the *physical* process). For instance, in Figure 9-1 we included the logical process WITHDRAW FUNDS FROM AN ACCOUNT. We did not indicate how this would be done. Intuitively, we can think of several physical implementations such as using an ATM, using a bank's drive-through service, or actually going inside the bank.

Process Decomposition   A complex system is usually too difficult to fully understand when viewed as a whole (meaning *as a single process*). Therefore, in systems analysis we separate a system into its component subsystems, which are decomposed into smaller subsystems, until we have identified manageable subsets of the overall system (see Figure 9-3). We call this technique *decomposition*. **Decomposition** is the act of breaking a system into its component subsystems, processes, and subprocesses. Each level of *abstraction* reveals more or less detail (as desired) about the overall system or a subset of that system. You have already applied decomposition in various ways. Most of you have *outlined* a term paper—this is a form of decomposition. Many of you have partitioned a medium- to large-size computer program into subprograms that could be developed and tested independently before they are integrated. This is also decomposition.

In systems analysis, decomposition allows you to partition a system into logical subsystems of processes for improved communication, analysis, and design. A diagram similar to Figure 9-3 can be a little difficult to construct when dealing with all

process work performed by a system in response to incoming data flows or conditions. A synonym is *transform*.

decomposition the act of breaking a system into subcomponents.

FIGURE 9-3

A System Consists of Many Subsystems and Processes

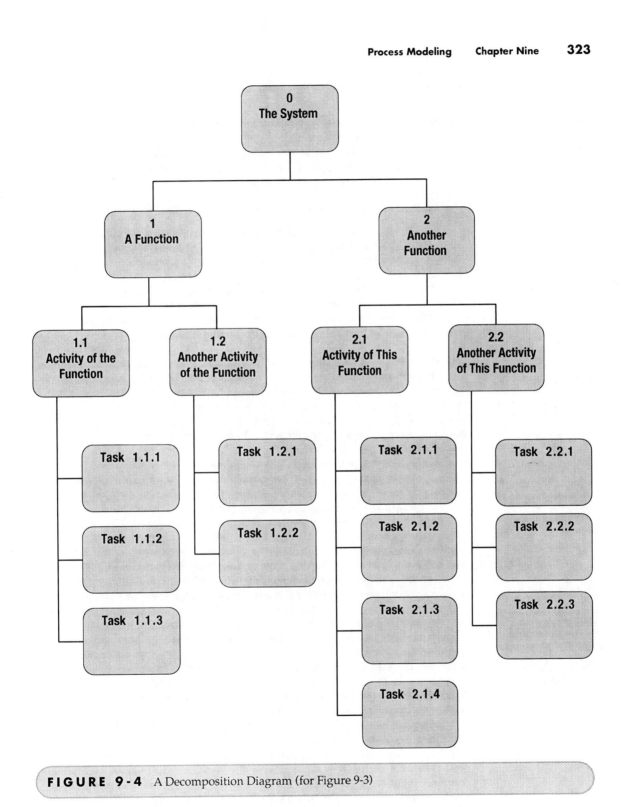

FIGURE 9-4 A Decomposition Diagram (for Figure 9-3)

but the smallest of systems. Figure 9-4 demonstrates an alternative layout that is supported by many CASE tools and development methodologies. It is called a *decomposition diagram.* We'll use it extensively in this chapter. A **decomposition diagram,** also called a *hierarchy chart,* shows the top-down functional decomposition and structure of a system. A decomposition diagram is essentially a planning

decomposition diagram
a tool used to depict the decomposition of a system. Also called *hierarchy chart.*

tool for more detailed process models, namely, data flow diagrams. The following rules apply:

- Each process in a decomposition diagram is either a *parent process*, a *child process* (of a parent), or both.
- A parent *must* have two or more children—a single child does not make sense because that would not reveal any additional detail about the system.
- In most decomposition diagramming standards, a child may have only one parent.
- Finally, a child of one parent may be the parent of its own children.

The upper and lower halves of the decomposition diagram in Figure 9-4 demonstrate two styles for laying out the processes and connections. You may use either or both as necessary to present an uncluttered model. Some models may require multiple pages for maximum clarity.

The connections on a decomposition diagram do not contain arrowheads because the diagram is meant to show *structure*, not *flow.* Also, the connections are not named. Implicitly they all have the same name—CONSISTS OF—since the sum of the child processes for a parent process *equals* the parent process.

Logical Processes and Conventions   *Logical* processes are work or actions that <u>must</u> be performed no matter <u>how</u> you implement the system. Each logical process is (or will be) implemented as one or more physical processes that may include work performed by people, work performed by robots or machines, or work performed by computer software. It doesn't matter which implementation is used, however, because logical processes should only indicate <u>that</u> there is work that must be done.

Naming conventions for logical processes depend on where the process is in the decomposition diagram/data flow diagram and the type of process depicted. There are three types of logical processes: *functions, events,* and *elementary processes.*

function a set of related and ongoing activities of a business.

A **function** is a set of related and <u>ongoing</u> activities of the business. A function has no start or end; it just continuously performs its work as needed. For example, a manufacturing system may include the following functions (subsystems): PRODUCTION PLANNING, PRODUCTION SCHEDULING, MATERIALS MANAGEMENT, PRODUCTION CONTROL, QUALITY MANAGEMENT, and INVENTORY CONTROL. Each of these functions may consist of dozens or hundreds of more discrete processes to support specific activities and tasks. Function names are nouns that describe the entire function. Additional examples are ORDER ENTRY, ORDER MANAGEMENT, SALES REPORTING, CUSTOMER RELATIONS, and RETURNS AND REFUNDS.

event a logical unit of work that must by completed as a whole. Sometimes called a *transaction.*

An **event** is a logical unit of work that must be completed as a whole. An event is triggered by a discrete input and is completed when the process has responded with appropriate outputs. Events are sometimes called *transactions.* Functions consist of processes that respond to events. For example, the MATERIALS MANAGEMENT function may respond to the following events: TEST MATERIAL QUALITY, STOCK NEW MATERIALS, DISPOSE OF DAMAGED MATERIALS, DISPOSE OF SPOILED MATERIALS, REQUISITION MATERIALS FOR PRODUCTION, RETURN UNUSED MATERIALS FROM PRODUCTION, ORDER NEW MATERIALS, and so on. Each of these events has a trigger and response that can be defined by its inputs and outputs.

Using *modern* structured analysis techniques such as those advocated by McMenamin, Palmer, Yourdon, and the Robertsons (see the Suggested Readings at the end of the chapter), analysts decompose system functions into business events. Each business event is represented by a single process that will respond to that event. Event process names tend to be very general. We will adopt the convention of naming event processes as follows: PROCESS _____, RESPOND TO _____, or GENERATE _____, where the blank would be the name of the event (or its corresponding input). Sample event process names are PROCESS CUSTOMER ORDER, PROCESS CUSTOMER ORDER CHANGE, PROCESS CUSTOMER CHANGE OF ADDRESS, RESPOND TO CUSTOMER COMPLAINT, RESPOND TO ORDER INQUIRY, RESPOND TO PRODUCT PRICE CHECK, GENERATE BACK-ORDER REPORT, GENERATE CUSTOMER ACCOUNT STATEMENT, and GENERATE INVOICE.

An event process can be further decomposed into elementary processes that illustrate in detail how the system must respond to an event. **Elementary processes** are discrete, detailed activities or tasks required to complete the response to an event. In other words, they are the lowest level of detail depicted in a process model. A common synonym is *primitive process*. Elementary processes should be named with a strong action verb followed by an object clause that describes what the work is performed on (or for). Examples of elementary process names are VALIDATE CUSTOMER IDENTIFICATION, VALIDATE ORDERED PRODUCT NUMBER, CHECK PRODUCT AVAILABILITY, CALCULATE ORDER COST, CHECK CUSTOMER CREDIT, SORT BACK ORDERS, GET CUSTOMER ADDRESS, UPDATE CUSTOMER ADDRESS, ADD NEW CUSTOMER, and DELETE CUSTOMER.

elementary process
discrete, detailed activity or task required to complete the response to an event. Also called *primitive process*.

Logical process models omit any processes that do nothing more than move or route data, thus leaving the data unchanged. Thus, you should omit any process that corresponds to a secretary or clerk receiving and simply forwarding a variety of documents to the next processing location. In the end, you should be left only with logical processes that:

- *Perform computations* (calculate grade point average).
- *Make decisions* (determine availability of ordered products).
- *Sort, filter, or otherwise summarize data* (identify overdue invoices).
- *Organize data into useful information* (generate a report or answer a question).
- *Trigger other processes* (turn on the furnace or instruct a robot).
- *Use stored data* (create, read, update, or delete a record).

Be careful to avoid three common mechanical errors with processes (illustrated in Figure 9-5):

- Process 3.1.2 has inputs but no outputs. We call this a *black hole* because data enters the process and then disappears. In most cases, the modeler simply forgot the output.
- Process 3.1.3 has outputs but no input. In this case, the input flows were likely forgotten.
- In Process 3.1.1 the inputs are insufficient to produce the output. We call this a *gray hole*. There are several possible causes, including (1) a misnamed process, (2) misnamed inputs and/or outputs, or (3) incomplete facts. Gray holes are the most common errors—and the most embarrassing. Once handed to a programmer, the input data flows to a process (to be implemented as a program) must be sufficient to produce the output data flows.

> Data Flows

Processes respond to inputs and generate outputs. Thus, at a minimum, all processes have at least one input and one output *data flow*. Data flows are the communications between processes and the system's environment. Let's examine some of the basic concepts and conventions of data flows.

Data in Motion   A data flow is *data in motion*. The flow of data between a system and its environment or between two processes inside a system is *communication*. Let's study this form of communication.

A **data flow** represents an input of data to a process or the output of data (or information) from a process. A data flow is also used to represent the creation, reading, deletion, or updating of data in a file or database (called a *data store* on the DFD). Think of a data flow as a highway down which packets of known composition travel. The name implies what type of data may travel down that highway. This highway is depicted as a solid line with arrow (see margin).

data flow data that is input or output to or from a process.

Data flow name →

Data Flow Symbol

The *packet* concept is critical. Data that should travel together should be shown as a single data flow, no matter how many *physical* documents might be included. The

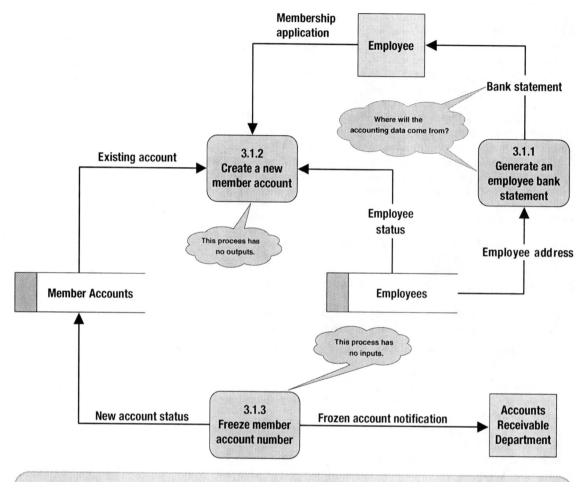

FIGURE 9-5 Common Errors on Data Flow Diagrams

packet concept is illustrated in Figure 9-6, which shows the correct and incorrect ways to show a logical data flow packet.

The *known composition* concept is equally important. A data flow is composed of either actual data attributes (also called *data structures*—more about them later) or other data flows. **A composite data flow** is a data flow that consists of other data flows. They are used to combine similar data flows on high-level data flow diagrams

composite data flow a data flow that consists of other data flows.

FIGURE 9-6

The Data Flow Packet Concept

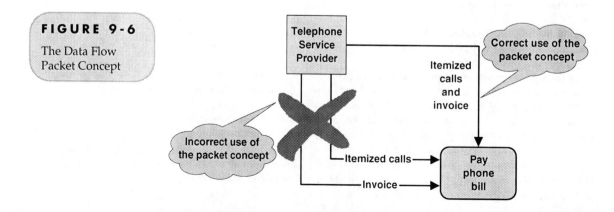

(a) High-Level DFD

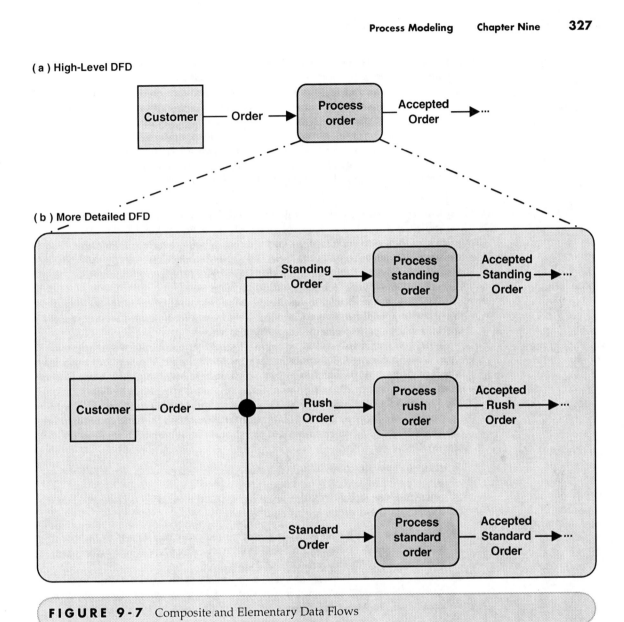

(b) More Detailed DFD

FIGURE 9-7 Composite and Elementary Data Flows

to make those diagrams easier to read. For example, in Figure 9-7(a), a high-level DFD consolidates all types of orders into a composite data flow called ORDER. In Figure 9-7(b), a more detailed data flow diagram shows specific types of orders: STANDING ORDER, RUSH ORDER, and STANDARD ORDER. These different orders require somewhat different processing. (The small, black circle is called a *junction*. It indicates that any given ORDER is an instance of only one of the order types.)

Another common use of composite data flows is to consolidate all reports and inquiry responses into one or two composite flows. There are two reasons for this. First, these outputs can be quite numerous. Second, many modern systems provide extensive user-defined reports and inquiries that cannot be predicted before the system's implementation and use.

Some data flow diagramming methods also recognize *nondata* flows called *control flows*. A **control flow** represents a condition or nondata event that triggers a process. Think of it as a condition to be monitored while the system works. When the system realizes that the condition meets some predetermined state, the process to

control flow a condition or nondata event that triggers a process.

_ _ <u>Control flow name</u> _ _ ▷

Control Flow
Symbol

which it is input is started. The classic information system example is *time*. For example, a report generation process may be triggered by the temporal event END-OF-MONTH. In real-time systems, control flows often represent real-time conditions such as TEMPERATURE and ALTITUDE. In most methodologies that distinguish between data and control flows, the control flow is depicted as a dashed line with arrow (see margin).

Typically, information systems analysts have dealt mostly with data flows; however, as information systems become more integrated with real-time systems (such as manufacturing processes and computer-integrated manufacturing), the need to distinguish the concept of control flows becomes necessary.

Logical Data Flows and Conventions   While we recognize that data flows can be implemented a number of ways (e.g., telephone calls, business forms, bar codes, memos, reports, computer screens, and computer-to-computer communications), we are interested only in *logical* data flows. Thus, we are only interested <u>that</u> the flow is needed (not <u>how</u> we will implement that flow). Data flow names should discourage premature commitment to any possible implementation.

Data flow names should be descriptive nouns and noun phrases that are singular, as opposed to plural (ORDER—not ORDERS). We do not want to imply that occurrences of the flow <u>must</u> be implemented as a *physical* batch.

Data flow names also should be unique. Use adjectives and adverbs to help to describe how processing has changed a data flow. For example, if an input to a process is named ORDER, the output should not be named ORDER. It might be named VALID ORDER, APPROVED ORDER, ORDER WITH VALID PRODUCTS, ORDER WITH APPROVED CREDIT, or any other more descriptive name that reflects what the process <u>did</u> to the original order.

Logical data flows to and from data stores require special naming considerations (see Figure 9-8). (Data store names are plural, and the numbered bullets match the note to the figure.)

- Only the *net* data flow is shown. Intuitively, you may realize that you have to get a record to update it or delete it. But unless data is needed for some other purpose (e.g., a calculation or decision), the "read" action is not shown. This keeps the diagram uncluttered.

❶ A data flow from a data store to a process indicates that data is to be "read" for some specific purpose. The data flow name should clearly indicate what data is to be read. This is shown in Figure 9-8.

❷ A data flow from a process to a data store indicates that data is to be created, deleted, or updated in/from that data store. Again, as shown in Figure 9-8, these data flows should be clearly named to reflect the specific action performed (such as NEW CUSTOMER, CUSTOMER TO BE DELETED, or UPDATED ORDER ADDRESS).

Notice that the names suggest the classic actions that can be performed on a file, namely, CREATE, READ, UPDATE, and DELETE (CRUD). In a real DFD, we would not actually record these action names on the diagram.

No data flow should never go unnamed. Unnamed data flows are frequently the result of flowchart thinking (step 1, step 2, etc.). If you can't give the data flow a reasonable name, it probably does not exist. Consistent with our goal of *logical* modeling, data flow names should describe the data flow without describing how the flow is or could be implemented. Suppose, for example, that end users explain their system as follows: *"We fill out Form 23 in triplicate and send it to . . ."* The logical name for the "Form 23" data flow might be COURSE REQUEST. This logical name eliminates physical, implementation biases—the idea that we must use a *paper form* and the notion that we must use carbon copies. Ultimately, this will free us to consider other physical alternatives such as Touch-Tone phone responses, online registration screens, or even e-business Internet pages.

Finally, all data flows must begin and/or end at a process because data flows are the inputs and outputs of a process. Consequently, all the data flows on the left side of Figure 9-9 are illegal. The corrected diagrams are shown on the right side.

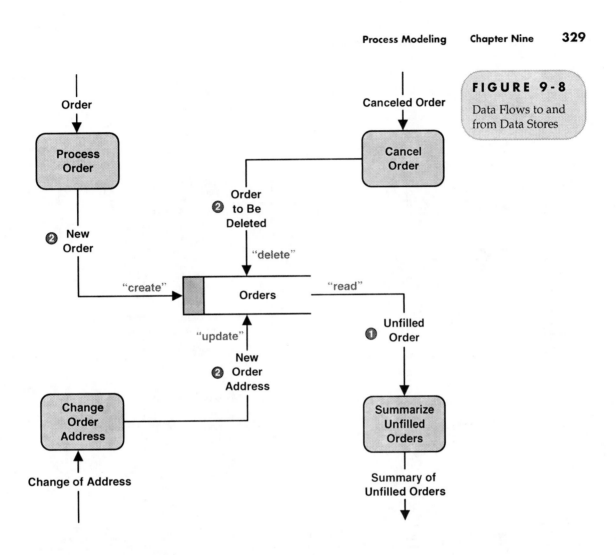

FIGURE 9-8
Data Flows to and from Data Stores

Data Flow Conservation   For many years we have tried to improve business processes by automating them. It hasn't always worked or worked well because the business processes were designed to process data flows in a precomputing era. Consider the average business form. It is common to see the form divided into sections that are designed for different audiences. The first recipient completes his part of the form, the next recipient completes her part, and so forth. At certain points in this processing sequence, a copy of the form might even be detached and sent to another recipient who initializes a new multiple-part form that requires transcribing much of the same data from the initial form. In our own university, we've seen examples where poor form design requires that the same data be typed a dozen times.

Now, if the flow of current data is computerized based on the current business forms and processes, the resulting computer programs will merely automate these inefficiencies. This is precisely what has happened in most businesses! Today, a new emphasis on *business process redesign* encourages management, users, and systems analysts to identify and eliminate these inefficiencies <u>before</u> designing any new information system. We can support this trend in *logical* data flow diagrams by practicing data conservation. **Data conservation,** sometimes called "starving the processes," requires that a data flow contain only the data that is truly needed by the receiving process. By ensuring that processes receive only as much data as they really need, we simplify the interface between those processes. To practice data conservation, we must precisely define the data composition of each (noncomposite) data flow. Data composition is expressed in the form of *data structures*.

data conservation the practice of ensuring that a data flow contains only data needed by the receiving process.

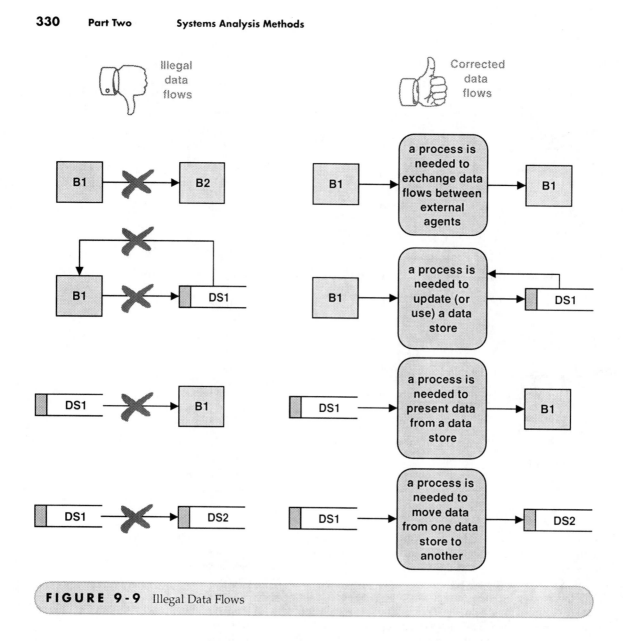

FIGURE 9-9 Illegal Data Flows

data attribute the smallest piece of data that has meaning to the users and the business.

Data Structures   Ultimately, a data flow contains data items called *attributes*. A **data attribute** is the smallest piece of data that has meaning to the end users and the business. (This definition also applies to *attributes* as they were presented in Chapter 8.) Sample attributes for the data flow ORDER might include ORDER NUMBER, ORDER DATE, CUSTOMER NUMBER, SHIPPING ADDRESS (which consists of attributes such as STREET ADDRESS, CITY, and ZIP CODE), ORDERED PRODUCT NUMBERS, QUANTITY(ies) ORDERED, and so on. Notice that some attributes occur once for each instance of ORDER, while others may occur several times for a single instance of ORDER.

data structure a specific arrangement of data attributes that define a single instance of a data flow.

The data attributes that comprise a data flow are organized into **data structures**. Data flows can be described in terms of the following types of data structures:

- A *sequence* or group of data attributes that occur one after another.
- The *selection* of one or more attributes from a set of attributes.
- The *repetition* of one or more attributes.

The most common data structure notation is a Boolean algebraic notation that is required by many CASE tools. Other CASE tools and methodologies support proprietary,

FIGURE 9-10   A Data Structure for a Data Flow

Data Structure	English Interpretation

ORDER =
   ORDER NUMBER +
   ORDER DATE +
   [PERSONAL CUSTOMER NUMBER,
     CORPORATE ACCOUNT NUMBER]
   SHIPPING ADDRESS = ADDRESS +
   (BILLING ADDRESS = ADDRESS) +
   1 {PRODUCT NUMBER +
     PRODUCT DESCRIPTION +
     QUANTITY ORDERED +
     PRODUCT PRICE +
     PRODUCT PRICE SOURCE +
     EXTENDED PRICE} N +
   SUM OF EXTENDED PRICES +
   PREPAID AMOUNT
   (CREDIT CARD NUMBER + EXPIRATION DATE)
   (QUOTE NUMBER)
 	
ADDRESS =
   (POST OFFICE BOX NUMBER) +
   STREET ADDRESS +
   CITY +
   [STATE MUNICIPALITY] +
   (COUNTRY) +
   POSTAL CODE
	An instance of ORDER consists of:
	   ORDER NUMBER and
	   ORDER DATE and
	   Either PERSONAL CUSTOMER NUMBER
	     or CORPORATE ACCOUNT NUMBER
	   and SHIPPING ADDRESS (which is equivalent
	     to ADDRESS)
	   and optionally: BILLING ADDRESS (which is
	     equivalent to ADDRESS)
	   and one or more instances of:
	     PRODUCT NUMBER and
	     PRODUCT DESCRIPTION and
	     QUANTITY ORDERED and
	     PRODUCT PRICE and
	     PRODUCT PRICE SOURCE and
	     EXTENDED PRICE
	   and SUM OF EXTENDED PRICES and
	   PREPAID AMOUNT and
	   optionally: both CREDIT CARD NUMBER and
	     EXPIRATION DATE
	   and optionally: QUOTE NUMBER
	
	An instance of ADDRESS consists of:
	   optionally: POST OFFICE BOX NUMBER and
	   STREET ADDRESS and
	   CITY and
	   Either STATE OR MUNICIPALITY
	   and optionally: COUNTRY
	     and POSTAL CODE

but essentially equivalent, notations. A sample data structure for the data flow ORDER is presented in Figure 9-10. This algebraic notation uses the following symbols:

=   Means "consists of" or "is composed of."

+   Means "and" and designates *sequence*.

[. . .]   Means "only one of the attributes within the brackets may be present"—designates *selection*. The attributes in the brackets are separated by commas.

{. . .}   Means that the attributes in the braces may occur many times for one instance of the data flow—designates *repetition*. The attributes inside the braces are separated by commas.

(. . .)   Means the attribute(s) in the parentheses are optional—no value—for some instances of the data flow.

In our experience, <u>all</u> data flows can be described in terms of these fundamental constructs. Figure 9-11 demonstrates each of the fundamental constructs using examples. Returning to Figure 9-10, notice that the constructs are combined to describe the data content of the data flow.

FIGURE 9-11 Data Structure Constructs

Data Structure	Format by Example (relevant portion is **boldfaced**)	English Interpretation (relevant portion is **boldfaced**)
Sequence of Attributes—The sequence data structure indicates one or more attributes that may (or must) be included in a data flow.	WAGE AND TAX STATEMENT = **TAXPAYER IDENTIFICATION NUMBER** + **TAXPAYER NAME** + **TAXPAYER ADDRESS** + **WAGES, TIPS, AND COMPENSATION** + **FEDERAL TAX WITHHELD** + ...	An instance of WAGE AND TAX STATEMENT consists of: **TAXPAYER IDENTIFICATION NUMBER and** **TAXPAYER NAME and** **TAXPAYER ADDRESS and** **WAGES, TIPS, AND COMPENSATION and** **FEDERAL TAX WITHHELD and** . . .
Selection of Attributes—The selection data structure allows you to show situations where different sets of attributes describe different instances of the data flow.	ORDER = [**PERSONAL CUSTOMER NUMBER,** **CORPORATE ACCOUNT NUMBER**] + ORDER DATE + ...	An instance of ORDER consists of: **Either PERSONAL CUSTOMER NUMBER or** **CORPORATE ACCOUNT NUMBER;** and ORDER DATE and . . .
Repetition of Attributes—The repetition data structure is used to set off a data attribute or group of data attributes that may (or must) repeat themselves a specified number of times for a single instance of the data flow. The minimum number of repetitions is usually zero or one. The maximum number of repetitions may be specified as "n" meaning "many" where the actual number of instances varies for each instance of the data flow.	CLAIM = POLICY NUMBER + POLICYHOLDER NAME + POLICYHOLDER ADDRESS + **0** {**DEPENDENT NAME** + **DEPENDENT'S RELATIONSHIP**} **N** + **1** {**EXPENSE DESCRIPTION** + **SERVICE PROVIDER** + **EXPENSE AMOUNT**} **N**	An instance of CLAIM consists of: POLICY NUMBER and POLICYHOLDER NAME and POLICYHOLDER ADDRESS and **zero or more instances of:** **DEPENDENT NAME and** **DEPENDENT'S RELATIONSHIP and** **one or more instances of:** **EXPENSE DESCRIPTION and** **SERVICE PROVIDER and** **EXPENSE ACCOUNT**
Optional Attributes—The optional notation indicates that an attribute, or group of attributes in a <u>sequence or selection data structure</u> may not be included in all instances of a data flow. *Note: For the repetition data structure, a minimum of "zero" is the same as making the entire repeating group "optional."*	CLAIM = POLICY NUMBER + POLICYHOLDER NAME + POLICYHOLDER ADDRESS + (**SPOUSE NAME** + **DATE OF BIRTH**) + ...	An instance of CLAIM consists of: POLICY NUMBER and POLICYHOLDER NAME and POLICYHOLDER ADDRESS and **optionally, SPOUSE NAME and** **DATE OF BIRTH and** . . .
Reusable Attributes—For groups of attributes that are contained in many data flows, it is desirable to create a separate data structure that can be reused in other data structures.	DATE = MONTH + DAY + YEAR	Then, the reusable structures can be included in other data flow structures as follows: ORDER = ORDER NUMBER . . . + DATE INVOICE = INVOICE NUMBER . . . + DATE PAYMENT = CUSTOMER NUMBER . . . + DATE

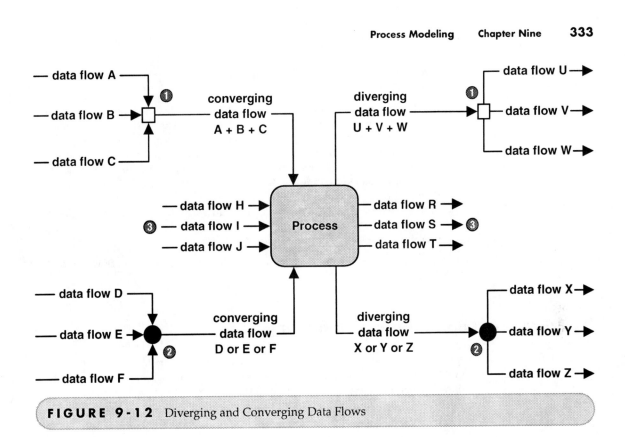

FIGURE 9-12 Diverging and Converging Data Flows

The importance of defining the data structures for every data flow should be apparent—you are defining the business data requirements for each input and output! These requirements must be determined before any process could be implemented as a computer program. This standard notation provides a simple but effective means for communicating between end users and programmers.

Domains An attribute is a piece of data. In analyzing a system, it makes sense that we should define those values for an attribute that are legitimate, or that make sense. The values for each attribute are defined in terms of two properties: data type and domain. The **data type** for an attribute defines what class of data can be stored in that attribute, whereas the **domain** of an attribute defines what values an attribute can legitimately take on. The concepts of data type and domain were introduced in Chapter 8. See that discussion and Tables 8-1 and 8-2 for a more complete description of data type and domain.

data type a class of data that can be stored in an attribute.

domain the legitimate values for an attribute.

Divergent and Convergent Flows It is sometimes useful to depict diverging or converging data flows on a data flow diagram. A **diverging data flow** is one that splits into multiple data flows. Diverging data flows indicate that all or parts of a single data flow are routed to different destinations.[2] A **converging data flow** is the merger of multiple data flows into a single data flow. Converging data flows indicate that data flows from different sources can (must) come together as a single packet for subsequent processing.

Diverging and converging data flows are depicted as shown in Figure 9-12. Notice that we do not include a process to "route" the flows. The flows simply diverge from

diverging data flow a data flow that splits into multiple data flows.

converging data flow the merger of multiple data flows into a single data flow.

---

[2]Some experts suggest that diverging data flows should be used only when all data in the flow is routed to all destinations. We prefer the classic DeMarco definition that allows all *or* parts of the flow to be routed to different processes.

or converge to a common flow. The following notations, not supported by all CASE tools, are used in this book:

❶ The small square *junction* means "and." This means that each time the process is performed, it must input (or output) all the diverging or converging data flows. *(Some DFD notations simply place a + between the data flows.)*

❷ The small black *junction* means "exclusive or." This means that each time the process is performed, it must input (or output) only one of the diverging or converging data flows. *(Some DFD notations simply place an * between the data flows.)*

❸ In the absence of one diverging or converging data flow, the reader should assume an "inclusive or." This means that each time the process is performed, it may input any <u>or</u> all of the depicted data flows.

With the above rules, the most complex of business process and data flow combinations can be depicted.

The Process of Logical Process Modeling

Now that you understand the basic concepts of process models, we can examine building a process model. When do you do it? How many process models may be drawn? What technology exists to support the development of process models?

> Strategic Systems Planning

Many organizations select application development projects based on strategic information system plans. Strategic planning is a separate project that produces an information systems strategy plan that defines an overall vision and architecture for information systems. This architecture frequently includes an *enterprise process model*. (The plan usually has other architectural components that are not important to this discussion.)

An enterprise process model typically identifies only business areas and functions. Events and detailed processes are rarely examined. Business areas and functions are identified and mapped to other enterprise models such as the enterprise data model (Chapter 8). Business areas and functions are subsequently prioritized into application development projects. Priorities are usually based on which business areas, functions, and supporting applications will return the most value to the business as a whole.

An enterprise process model is stored in a corporate repository. Subsequently, as application development projects are started, subsets of the enterprise process model are exported to the project teams to serve as a starting point for building more detailed process models (including data flow diagrams). Once the project team completes systems analysis and design, the expanded and refined process models are returned to the corporate repository.

> Process Modeling for Business Process Redesign

Business process redesign (BPR) has been discussed several times in this book and chapter. Recall that BPR projects analyze business processes and then redesign them to eliminate inefficiencies and bureaucracies before any (re)application of information technology. To redesign business processes, we must first study the existing processes. Process models play an integral role in BPR.

Each BPR methodology recommends its own process model notations and documentation. Most of the models are a cross between data flow diagrams and flowcharts. The diagrams tend to be very *physical* because the BPR team is trying to isolate the implementation idiosyncrasies that cause inefficiency and reduce value. BPR data flow diagrams/flowcharts may include new symbols and information to illustrate timing, throughput, delays, costs, and value. Given this additional data, the BPR team then attempts to simplify the processes and data flows in an effort to maximize efficiency and return the most value to the organization.

Opportunities for the efficient use of information technology may also be recorded on the physical diagrams. If so, the BPR diagram becomes an input to systems analysis (described next).

> Process Modeling during Systems Analysis

In systems analysis and in this chapter, we focus exclusively on *logical* process modeling as a part of business requirements analysis. In your information system framework, logical process models have a process focus and a SYSTEM OWNER and/or SYSTEM USER perspective. They are typically constructed as deliverables of the requirements analysis phase of a project. While logical process models are not concerned with implementation details or technology, they may be constructed (through *reverse engineering*) from existing application software, but this technology is much less mature and reliable than the corresponding reverse *data* engineering technology.

In the heyday of the original structured analysis methodologies, process modeling was also performed in the problem analysis phase of systems analysis. Analysts would build a *physical process model of the current system*, a *logical model of the current system*, and a *logical model of the target system*. Each model would be built top-down—from very general models to very detailed models. While conceptually sound, this approach led to modeling overkill and significant project delays, so much so that even structured techniques guru Ed Yourdon called it "analysis paralysis."

Today, most modern structured analysis strategies focus exclusively on the *logical model of the target system* being developed. Instead of being built either top-down or bottom-up, they are organized according to a commonsense strategy called *event partitioning*. **Event partitioning** factors a system into subsystems based on business events and responses to those events. This strategy for event-driven process modeling is illustrated in Figure 9-13 and described as follows:

❶ A system **context data flow diagram** is constructed to establish *initial* project scope. This simple, one-page data flow diagram shows only the system's main interfaces with its environment.

❷ A **functional decomposition diagram** is drawn to partition the system into logical subsystems and/or functions. (This step is omitted for very small systems.)

❸ An **event-response** or **use-case list** is compiled to identify and confirm the business events to which the system must provide a response. The list will also describe the required or possible responses to each event.

❹ One process, called an **event handler**, is added to the decomposition diagram for each event. The decomposition diagram now serves as the outline for the system.

❺ Optionally, an **event diagram** is constructed and validated for each event. This simple data flow diagram shows only the event handler and the inputs and outputs for each event.

❻ One or more **system diagrams** are constructed by merging the event diagrams. These data flow diagrams show the "big picture" of the system.

❼ **Primitive diagrams** are constructed for event processes that require additional processing details. These data flow diagrams show all the elementary processes, data stores, and data flows for single events. ❽ The logic of each elementary process and ❾ the data structure of each elementary data flow are described using the tools described earlier in the chapter.

event partitioning a structured analysis strategy in which a system is factored into subsystems based on business events and responses to those events.

context data flow diagram a diagram that shows the system as a "black box" and its main interfaces with its environment.

functional decomposition diagram a diagram that partitions the system into logical subsystems and/or functions.

event-response list a list of the business events to which the system must provide a response similar to a use-case list.

event handler a process that handles a given event in the event-response list.

event diagram a data flow diagram for a single event handler and the agents and data stores that provide inputs or receive outputs.

system diagram a data flow diagram that merges event diagrams for the entire system or part of the system.

primitive diagram a data flow diagram that depicts the elementary processes, data stores, and data flows for a single event.

FIGURE 9-13 Event-Driven Process Modeling Strategy

The above process models collectively document all the business processing requirements for a system. We'll demonstrate the technique in our SoundStage case study.

The logical process model from systems analysis describes business processing requirements of the system, not technical solutions. Recall from Chapter 5 that the purpose of the decision analysis phase is to determine the best way to implement those requirements with technology. In practice, this decision may have already been standardized as part of an application architecture. For example, the SoundStage application architecture requires that the development team first determine if an acceptable system can be purchased. If not, the current application architecture specifies that software built in-house be written in either Microsoft's *Visual Basic .NET* or *C#*.

> Looking Ahead to Systems Design

During system design, the logical process model will be transformed into a physical process model (called an *application schema*) for the chosen technical architecture. This model will reflect the technical capabilities and limitations of the chosen technology. Any further discussion of physical process/application design is deferred until Chapter 13.

> Fact-Finding and Information Gathering for Process Modeling

Process models cannot be constructed without appropriate facts and information as supplied by the user community. These facts can be collected through a number of techniques such as sampling of existing forms and files, research of similar systems, surveys of users and management, and interviews of users and management. The fastest method of collecting facts and information and simultaneously constructing and verifying the process models is *joint requirements planning (JRP)*. JRP uses a carefully facilitated group meeting to collect the facts, build the models, and verify the models—usually in one or two full-day sessions.

Fact-finding, information gathering, and JRP techniques were explored in Chapter 6.

> Computer-Aided Systems Engineering (CASE) for Process Modeling

Like all system models, process models are stored in the repository. Computer-aided systems engineering (CASE) technology, introduced in Chapter 3, provides the repository for storing the process model and its detailed descriptions. Most CASE products support computer-assisted process modeling. Most support decomposition diagrams and data flow diagrams. Some support extensions for business process analysis and redesign.

Using a CASE product, you can easily create professional, readable process models without using paper, pencil, eraser, and templates. The models can be easily modified to reflect corrections and changes suggested by end users. Also, most CASE products provide powerful analytical tools that can check your models for mechanical errors, completeness, and consistency. Some CASE products can even help you analyze the data model for consistency, completeness, and flexibility. The potential time savings and quality are substantial.

CASE tools do have their limitations. Not all process model conventions are supported by all CASE products. Therefore, any given CASE product may force the company to adapt its methodology's process modeling symbols or approach so that it is workable within the limitations of its CASE tool.

All the SoundStage process models in the next section of this chapter were created with Popkin's CASE tool, *System Architect 2001*. For the case study, we provide you with the printouts exactly as they came off our printers. We did not add color. The only modifications by the artist were the occasional bullets that call your attention to specific items of interest on the printouts. All the processes, data flows, data stores, and boundaries on the SoundStage process models were automatically cataloged into *System Architect*'s project repository (which it calls an encyclopedia). Figure 9-14 illustrates some of *System Architect*'s screens as used for data modeling.

How to Construct Process Models

As a systems analyst or knowledgeable end user, you must learn how to draw decomposition and data flow diagrams to model business process requirements. We will use the SoundStage Entertainment Club project to teach you how to draw these process models.

Let's assume the preliminary investigation and problem analysis phases of the project have been completed and the project team understands the current system's strengths, weaknesses, limitations, problems, opportunities, and constraints. The team has also already built the data model (in Chapter 8) to document business data requirements for the new system. Team members will now build the corresponding process models.

> The Context Data Flow Diagram

First, we need to document the initial project scope. All projects have scope. A project's scope defines what aspect of the business a system or application is supposed to support and how the system being modeled must interact with other systems and the business as a whole. In your information system framework, scope is defined as the COMMUNICATION focus from the SYSTEM OWNERS' perspective. It is documented with a **context data flow diagram.** Because the scope of any project is always subject to change, the context diagram is also subject to constant change. A synonym is *environmental model* [Yourdon, 1990].

We suggest the following strategy for documenting the system's boundary and scope:

context data flow diagram a process model used to document the scope for a system. Also called *environmental model*.

1. Think of the system as a container in order to distinguish the inside from the outside. Ignore the inner workings of the container. This is sometimes called "black box" thinking.
2. Ask your end users what business transactions a system must respond to. These are the *net inputs* to the system. For each net input, determine its source. Sources will become *external agents* on the context data flow diagram.
3. Ask your end users what responses must be produced by the system. These are the net outputs to the system. For each net output, determine its destination. Destinations will also become *external agents.* Requirements for reports and queries can quickly clutter the diagram. Consider consolidating them into composite data flows.
4. Identify any *external* data stores. Many systems require access to the files or databases of other systems. They may use the data in those files or databases. Sometimes they may update certain data in those files and databases. But generally, they are not permitted to change the structure of those files and databases—therefore, they are outside the project scope.
5. Draw a context diagram from all of the preceding information.

If you try to include all the inputs and outputs between a system and the rest of the business and outside world, a typical context data flow diagram might show as many as 50 or more data flows. Such a diagram would have little, if any, communication value. Therefore, we suggest you show only those data flows that represent the main objective or most important inputs and outputs of the system. Defer less common data flows to more detailed DFDs to be drawn later.

The context data flow diagram contains one and only one process (see Figure 9-15). Sometimes, this process is identified by the number "0"; however, our CASE tool did not allow this. External agents are drawn around the perimeter. Data flows define the interactions of your system with the boundaries and with the external data stores.

As shown in the context data flow diagram, the main purpose of the system is to process NEW SUBSCRIPTIONS in response to SUBSCRIPTION OFFERS, create NEW PROMOTIONS for products, and respond to MEMBER ORDERS by sending PACKING ORDERS to the warehouse to be filled. (Notice that we made all data flow names singular.) Management has also emphasized the need for VARIOUS REPORTS. Finally, the Web extensions to this system require that the system provide members with VARIOUS INQUIRY RESPONSES regarding orders and accounts.

> The Functional Decomposition Diagram

Recall that a decomposition diagram shows the top-down functional decomposition or structure of a system. It also provides us with the beginnings of an outline for drawing our data flow diagrams.

Figure 9-16 on page 341 is the functional decomposition diagram for the SoundStage project. Let's study this diagram. First, notice that the processes are depicted as rectangles, not rounded rectangles. This is merely a limitation of our CASE tool's implementation of decomposition diagrams—you also may have to adapt to your CASE tool.

FIGURE 9-15   The Context Data Flow Diagram (created with *System Architect 2001*)

The following is an item-by-item discussion of the decomposition diagram. The circled numbers correspond to specific points of interest on the diagram.

❶ The root process corresponds to the entire system.

❷ The system is initially factored into subsystems and/or functions. These subsystems and functions do not necessarily correspond to organization units on an organization chart. Increasingly, analysts and users are being asked to ignore organizational boundaries and to build cross-functional systems that streamline processing and data sharing.

❸ We like to separate the operational and reporting aspects of a system. Thus, we factored each subsystem accordingly. Later, if this structure doesn't make sense, we can change it.

Larger systems might have first been factored into subsystems *and* functions. There is no limit to the number of child processes for a parent process. Many authors used to recommend a maximum of five to nine processes per parent, but any such limit is too artificial. Instead, structure the system such that it makes sense for the business!

Factoring a parent process into a single child process doesn't make sense. It would provide no additional detail. Therefore, if a process is to be factored, it should be factored into at least two child processes.

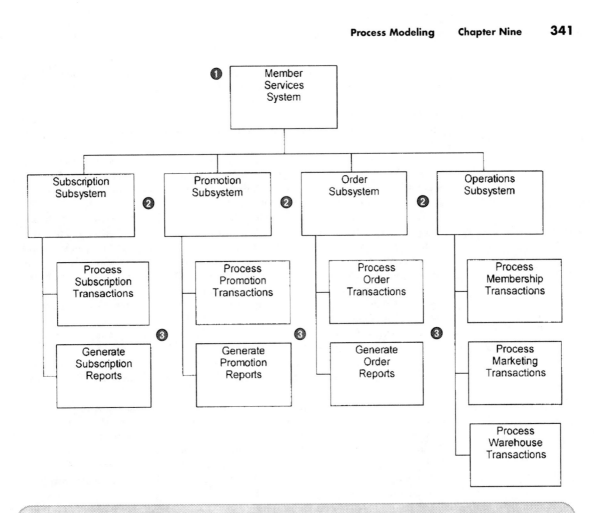

FIGURE 9-16 A Functional Decomposition Diagram (created with *System Architect 2001*)

> The Event-Response or Use-Case List

After constructing the decomposition diagram, we next determine what business events the system must respond to and what responses are appropriate. Events are not hard to find. Some of the inputs on the context diagram are associated with events, but the context diagram rarely shows all the events. Essentially, there are three types of events:

- *External events* are so named because they are initiated by external agents. When these events happen, an input data flow occurs for the system. For example, the event CUSTOMER PLACES A NEW ORDER is recognized in the form of the input data flow ORDER from the external agent CUSTOMER.
- *Temporal events* trigger processes on the basis of time, or something that merely happens. When these events happen, an input *control flow* occurs. Examples of temporal events include TIME TO REMIND CUSTOMERS TO PAY PAST INVOICES or END OF MONTH.
- *State events* trigger processes based on a system's change from one state or condition to another. Like temporal events, state events will be illustrated as an input *control flow*.

Information systems usually respond mostly to external and temporal events. State events are usually associated with real-time systems such as elevator or robot control.

One of the more popular and successful approaches for finding and identifying events and responses is a technique called *use cases* (Chapter 7) developed by Dr. Ivar Jacobson. This technique is rooted in object-oriented analysis but is easily adapted to structured analysis and data flow diagramming. **Use-case** analysis is the process of identifying and modeling business events, who initiated them, and how the system responds to them.

use case an analysis tool for finding and identifying business events and responses.

Use cases identify and describe necessary system processes from the perspective of users. Each use case is initiated by users or external systems called *actors*. An actor is anything that needs to interact with the system to exchange information and so is analogous to external agents in DFDs.

The context data flow diagram identifies the key actors as *external agents*. It also identifies *some* of the use cases. The key word is "some." Recall that the context diagram shows only the main inputs and outputs of a system. There are almost always more inputs and outputs than are depicted—usually many more. Some of the inputs and outputs depicted are really composites of many types of and variations on those inputs and outputs (e.g., the "various reports" on our context diagram). Also, the context diagram may not illustrate the many exception inputs and outputs such as errors, inquiries, and follow-ups.

One way to expand the use cases is to interview the external agents (actors) depicted on the diagram. The agents can (1) identify the events (use cases) for which they believe the system may have to provide a response and (2) identify other actors (new external agents) that were not originally shown on the context diagram.

Another way to identify use cases (events) is to study the data model, assuming a data model was developed before drawing data flow diagrams, and study the life history of each entity on that data model. Instances of these entities must be created, updated, and eventually deleted. Events or use cases trigger these actions on the entity. It is not difficult to get users talking about the events that could create, update, and delete entity instances. After all, they live these events daily. This approach was used to build the use-case list for the SoundStage project.

A partial table of use cases is illustrated in Figure 9-17 (pages 343–344). For each use case, you will find:

- The actor that initiates the event (which will become an external agent on our DFDs).
- The event (which will be handled by a process on our DFDs).
- The input or trigger (which will become a data or control flow on our DFDs).
- All outputs and responses (which will also become data flows on our DFDs). Notice that we used parentheses to denote temporal events.
- Outputs (but be careful not to imply implementation). When we used the term *report* we were not necessarily implying a paper-based document. Notice that our responses include changes to stored data about entities from the data model. These include create new instances of the entity, update existing instances of the entity, and delete instances of the entity.

The number of use cases for a system is usually quite large. This is necessary to ensure that the system designers build a complete system that will respond to all the business events. As a final step, consider assigning each event to one of the subsystems and functions identified in the decomposition diagram (drawn in the previous step).

> Event Decomposition Diagrams

To further partition our functions in the decomposition diagram, we simply add event handling processes (one per use case) to the decomposition (see Figure 9-18 on page 345). If the entire decomposition diagram will not fit on a single page, add separate pages for subsystems or functions. The root process on a subsequent page

FIGURE 9-17 A Partial Use-Case Table

Actor/External Agent	Event (or Use Case)	Trigger	Responses
Marketing	Establishes a new membership subscription plan to entice new members.	NEW MEMBER SUBSCRIPTION PROGRAM	Generate SUBSCRIPTION PLAN CONFIRMATION. Create AGREEMENT in the database.
Marketing	Establishes a new membership resubscription plan to lure back former members.	PAST MEMBER RESUBSCRIPTION PROGRAM	Generate SUBSCRIPTION PLAN CONFIRMATION. Create AGREEMENT in the database.
Marketing	Changes a subscription plan for current members (e.g., extending the fulfillment period).	SUBSCRIPTION PLAN CHANGE	Generate AGREEMENT CHANGE CONFIRMATION. Update AGREEMENT in the database.
(time)	A subscription plan expires.	(current date)	Generate AGREEMENT CHANGE CONFIRMATION. Logically Delete (void) AGREEMENT in the database.
Marketing	Cancels a subscription plan before its planned expiration date.	SUBSCRIPTION PLAN CANCELLATION	Generate AGREEMENT CHANGE CONFIRMATION. Logically Delete (void) AGREEMENT in the database.
Member	Joins the club by subscribing. ("Take any 12 CDs for one penny and agree to buy 4 more at regular prices within two years.")	NEW SUBSCRIPTION	Generate MEMBER DIRECTORY UPDATE CONFIRMATION. Create MEMBER in the database. Create first MEMBER ORDER and MEMBER ORDERED PRODUCTS in the database.
Member	Changes address (including e-mail and privacy code).	CHANGE OF ADDRESS	Generate MEMBER DIRECTORY UPDATE CONFIRMATION. Update MEMBER in the database.
Accounts Receivable	Changes member's credit status.	CHANGE OF CREDIT STATUS	Generate CREDIT DIRECTORY UPDATE CONFIRMATION. Update MEMBER in the database.

F I G U R E 9 - 1 7 (Concluded)

Actor/External Agent	Event (or Use Case)	Trigger	Responses
(time)	90 days after Marketing decides to no longer sell a product.	(current date)	Generate CATALOG CHANGE CONFIRMATION. Logically Delete (deactivate) PRODUCT in the database.
Member	Wants to pick products for possible purchase. (Logical requirement is driven by vision of Web-based access to information.)	PRODUCT INQUIRY	Generate CATALOG DESCRIPTION.
Member	Places order.	NEW MEMBER ORDER	Generate MEMBER ORDER CONFIRMATION. Create MEMBER ORDER and MEMBER ORDERED PRODUCT in the database.
Member	Revises order.	MEMBER ORDER CHANGE REQUEST	Generate MEMBER ORDER CONFIRMATION. Update MEMBER ORDER and/or MEMBER ORDERED PRODUCTS in the database.
Member	Cancels order.	MEMBER ORDER CANCELLATION	Generate MEMBER ORDER CONFIRMATION. Logically Delete MEMBER ORDER and MEMBER ORDERED PRODUCTS in the database.
(time)	90 days after the order.	(current date)	Physically Delete MEMBER ORDER and MEMBER ORDERED PRODUCTS in the database.
Member	Inquires about his or her purchase history (three-year time limit).	MEMBER PURCHASE INQUIRY	Generate MEMBER PURCHASE HISTORY.
(each) Club	(end of month).	(current date)	Generate MONTHLY SALES ANALYSIS. Generate MONTHLY MEMBER AGREEMENT EXCEPTION ANALYSIS. Generate MEMBERSHIP ANALYSIS REPORT.

FIGURE 9-18 A Partial Event Decomposition Diagram (created with *System Architect 2001*)

should be duplicated from an earlier page to provide a cross-reference. Figure 9-18 shows only the event processes for the MEMBERSHIPS subsystem. Events for the PROMOTIONS and ORDERS functions would be on separate pages.

There is no need to factor the decomposition diagram beyond the events and reports. That would be like outlining down to the final paragraphs or sentences in a paper. The decomposition diagram, as constructed, will serve as a good outline for the later data flow diagrams.

> Event Diagrams

Using our decomposition diagram as an outline, we can draw one event diagram for each event process. This is an optional, but useful, step. An **event diagram** is a context diagram for a single event. It shows the inputs, outputs, and data store interactions for the event. By drawing an event diagram for each process, users do not become overwhelmed by the overall size of the system. They can examine each use case as its own context diagram.

Before drawing any event diagrams, you may find it helpful to have a list of all the data stores available. Because SoundStage already completed the data model for this project, team members simply created a list of each entity name on that data model

event diagram a data flow diagram that depicts the context for a single event.

(see margin). It is useful to review the definition and attributes for each entity/data store on the list.

Most event diagrams contain a single process—the same process that was named to handle the event on the decomposition diagram. For each event, illustrate the following:

- The inputs and their sources. Sources are depicted as external agents. The data structure for each input should be recorded in the repository.
- The outputs and their destinations. Destinations are depicted as external agents. The data structure for each output should be recorded in the repository.
- Any data stores from which records must be "read" should be added to the event diagram. Data flows should be added and named to reflect what data is read by the process.
- Any data stores in which records must be created, deleted, or updated should be included in the event diagram. Data flows to the data stores should be named to reflect the nature of the update.

The simplicity of event diagramming makes the technique a powerful communication tool between users and technical professionals.

A complete set of event diagrams for the SoundStage case study would double the length of this chapter without adding substantive educational value. Thus, we will demonstrate the model with three simple examples.

Figure 9-19 illustrates a simple event diagram for an external event. Most systems have many such simple event diagrams because all systems must provide for routine maintenance of data stores.

Figure 9-20 depicts a somewhat more complex external event, one for the business transaction MEMBER ORDER. Notice that business transactions tend to use and update more data stores and have more interactions with external agents.

Can an event diagram have more than one process on it? The answer is maybe. Some event processes may trigger other event processes. In this case, the combination of events should be shown on a single event diagram. In our experience, most event diagrams have one process. An occasional event diagram may have two or perhaps three processes. If the number of processes exceeds three, you are probably drawing what is called an *activity diagram* (prematurely), not an event diagram—in other words, you're getting too involved with details. Most event processes do not directly communicate with one another. Instead, they communicate across shared data stores. This allows each event process to do its job without worrying about other processes keeping up.

Figure 9-21 on page 348 shows an event diagram for a temporal event. We added an external entity CALENDAR OR TIME to serve as a source for this control flow.

FIGURE 9-19 A Simple External Event Diagram (created with *System Architect 2001*)

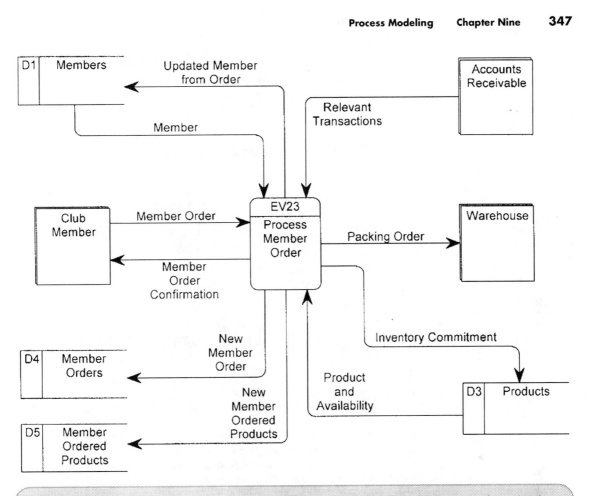

Each event process should be described to the CASE repository with the following properties:

- Event sentence—for business perspective.
- Throughput requirements—the volume of inputs per some time period.
- Response time requirements—how fast the typical event must be handled.
- Security, audit, and control requirements.
- Archival requirements (from a business perspective).

For example, consider the event diagram in Figure 9-19: "A member submits a change of address."

- Occurs 25 times per month.
- Should be processed within 15 days.
- Must protect privacy of addresses unless the member authorizes release.
- Should retain a semipermanent record of some type.

All the above properties can be added to the descriptions associated with the appropriate processes, data flows, and data stores on the model.

> The System Diagram(s)

The event diagrams serve as a meaningful context to help users validate the accuracy of each event to which the system must provide a response. But these events do not

FIGURE 9-21 A Temporal Event Diagram (created with *System Architect 2001*)

exist in isolation. They collectively define systems and subsystems. It is, therefore, useful to construct one or more system diagrams that show all the events in the system or a subsystem.

The system diagram is said to be "exploded" from the single process that we created on the original context diagram (Figure 9-15). The system diagram shows either (1) all the events for the system on a single diagram or (2) all the events for a single subsystem on a single diagram. Depending on the size of the system, a single diagram may be too large.

While the SoundStage project is moderate in size, it still responds to too many events to squeeze all those processes onto a single diagram. Instead, Bob Martinez elected to draw a subsystem diagram for each of the major subsystems. Figure 9-22 (pages 350–351) shows the subsystem diagram for the ORDERS SUBSYSTEM. It consolidates all the transaction and report-writing events for that subsystem onto a single diagram. (The reporting events may be omitted or consolidated into composites if the diagram is too cluttered.) Notice that the system diagram demonstrates how event processes communicate using shared data stores.

If necessary, and after drawing the four subsystem diagrams for this project, Bob could have drawn a system diagram that illustrates only the interactions between those four subsystems. This is a relic of the original top-down data flow diagramming strategy of the original structured analysis methodology. In practice, this higher-level diagram requires so much consolidation of data flows and data stores that its communication value is questionable. To Bob, this was busywork, and his time was better spent on the next set of data flow diagrams.

We now have a set of event diagrams (one per business event) and one or more system/subsystem diagrams. The event diagram processes are merged into the system diagrams. It is very important that each of the data flows, data stores, and external agents that were illustrated on the event diagrams be represented on the system diagrams. Notice that we duplicate data stores and external agents to minimize crossing of lines. Most CASE tools include facilities to check for balancing errors.

Before we leave this topic, we should introduce the concept of balancing. **Balancing** is the synchronizing of data flow diagrams at different levels of detail to preserve consistency and completeness of the models. Balancing is a quality assurance technique. Balancing requires that, if you explode a process to another DFD to reveal

balancing a concept that requires that data flow diagrams at different levels of detail reflect consistency and completeness.

more detail, you must include the same data flows and data stores on the child diagram that you included in the parent diagram's original process (or their logical equivalents).

> Primitive Diagrams

Some event processes on the system diagram may be exploded into a primitive data flow diagram to reveal more detail. This is especially true of the more complex business transaction processes (e.g., order processing). Other events, such as generation of reports, are simple enough that they do not require further explosion.

Event processes with more complex event diagrams should be exploded into a more detailed, primitive data flow diagram such as that illustrated in Figure 9-23 on page 352. This primitive DFD shows detailed processing requirements for the event. This DFD shows several elementary processes *for* the event process. Each elementary process is cohesive—that is, it does only one thing. On a primitive diagramming it is permissable to have flows connecting the elementary processes.

When Bob drew this primitive data flow diagram, he had to add new data flows between the processes. In doing so, he tried to practice good data conservation, making sure each process has only the data it truly needs. The data structure for each data flow had to be described in his CASE tool's repository. Also notice that he used data flow junctions to split and merge appropriate data flows on the diagram.

Note that the primitive DFD contains some new exception data flows that were *not* introduced in Figure 9-22. It should not be hard to imagine a computer program structure when examining this DFD.

The combination of the context diagram, system diagram, event diagrams, and primitive diagrams completes our process models. Collectively, this *is* the process model. A well-crafted and complete process model can effectively communicate business requirements between end users and computer programmers, eliminating much of the confusion that often occurs in system design, programming, and implementation.

> Completing the Specification

The data flow diagrams are complete. Where do you go from here? That depends on your choice of methodology. If you are practicing the pure structured analysis methodology (from which data flow diagramming was derived), you must complete the specification. To do so, each data flow, data store, and *elementary* process (meaning one that is not further exploded into a more detailed DFD) must be described to the encyclopedia or data dictionary. CASE tools provide facilities for such descriptions.

Data flows are described by data structures, as explained earlier in this chapter. Figure 9-24 (page 353) demonstrates how *System Architect 2001*, the SoundStage CASE tool, can be used to describe a data flow. Notice that this CASE tool uses an algebraic notation for data structures, as described in this chapter. Ultimately, each data element or attribute should also be described in the data dictionary to specify data type, domain, and default value (as was described in Chapter 8). Data stores correspond to all instances of a data entity from our data model. Thus, they are best described in the data dictionary that corresponds to each entity and its attributes, as was taught in Chapter 8. Some analysts like to translate each data store's content into a relational data structure similar to that used in Figure 9-24 to describe data flows. We consider this to be busywork—let the entity descriptions from the data model describe the contents of a data store. Besides, defining data structures for data stores could lead to synchronization errors between the data and process models—if you would make any changes to an entity in the data model, you would be forced to remember to make those same changes in the corresponding data store's data structure. This requires too much effort (unless you have a CASE tool capable of doing it automatically for you).

Process Logic   Decomposition diagrams and data flow diagrams will prove very effective tools for identifying processes, but they are not good at showing the logic inside

350   Part Two   Systems Analysis Methods

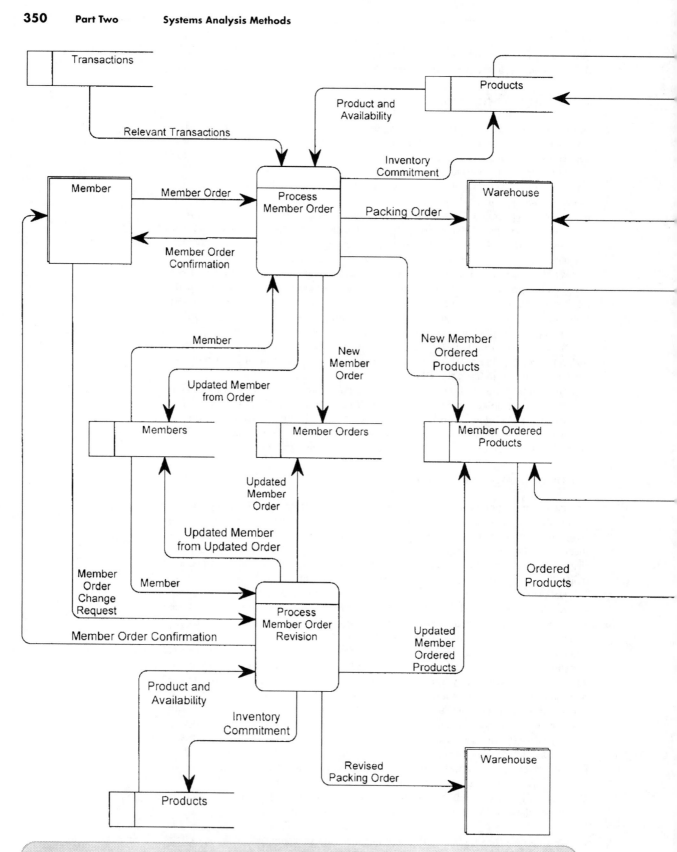

FIGURE 9-22 A System Diagram (created with *System Architect 2001*)

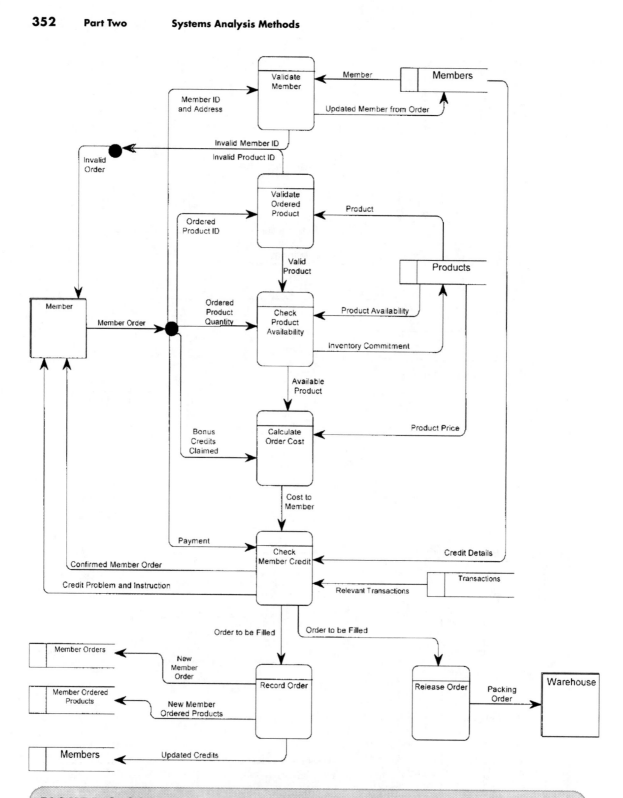

FIGURE 9-23 A Primitive Diagram (created with *System Architect 2001*)

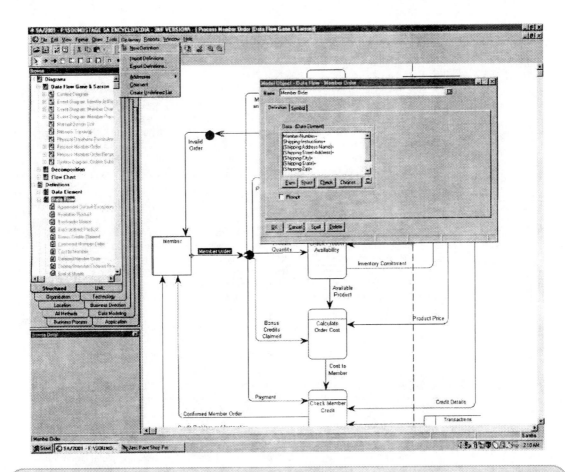

FIGURE 9-24 A Data Flow (created with *System Architect 2001*)

those processes. Eventually, we will need to specify detailed *instructions* for the elementary processes on a data flow diagram. Consider, for example, an elementary process named CHECK CUSTOMER CREDIT. By itself, the named process is insufficient to explain the logic needed to CHECK CUSTOMER CREDIT. We need an effective way to model the logic of an elementary process. Ideally, our logic model should be equally effective for communicating with users (who must verify the business accuracy of the logic) and programmers (who may have to implement the business logic in a programming language).

We can rule out flowcharts. While they do model process logic, most end users tend to be extremely intimidated by them. The same would be true of pseudocode and other popular programming logic tools. We can also rule out natural English. It is too often imprecise and frequently subject to interpretation (and misinterpretation). Figure 9-25 summarizes some common problems encountered by those who attempt to use natural English as a procedural language.

To address this problem, we require a tool that marries some of the advantages of natural English with some of the rigor of programming logic tools. **Structured English** is a language and syntax, based on the relative strengths of structured programming and natural English, for specifying the underlying logic of elementary processes on process models (such as *data flow diagrams*). An example of Structured English is shown in Figure 9-26. (The numbers and letters at the beginning of each statement are optional. Some end users like them because they further remove the programming "look and feel" from the specification.)

Structured English a language syntax for specifying the logic of a process.

> **FIGURE 9-25** Problems with Natural English as a Procedure Specification Language
>
> - Many of us do not write well, and we also tend not to question our writing abilities.
> - Many of us are too educated! It's often difficult for a highly educated person to communicate with an audience that may not have had the same educational opportunities. For example, the average college graduate (including most analysts) has a working vocabulary of 10,000 to 20,000 words; on the other hand, the average noncollege graduate has a working vocabulary of around 5,000 words.
> - Some of us write everything like it was a program. If business procedures required such precision, we'd write everything in a programming language.
> - Too often, we allow the jargon and acronyms of computing to dominate our language.
> - English statements frequently have an excessive or confusing scope. How would you carry out this procedure: "If customers walk in the door and they do not want to withdraw money from their account or deposit money to their account or make a loan payment, send them to the trust department." Does this mean that the only time you should not send the customer to the trust department is when he or she wishes to do all three of the transactions? Or does it mean that if a customer does not wish to perform at least one of the three transactions, that customer should not be sent to the trust department?
> - We overuse compound sentences. Consider the following procedure: "Remove the screws that hold the outlet cover to the wall. Remove the outlet cover. Disconnect each wire from the plug, but first make sure the power to the outlet has been turned off." An unwary person might try to disconnect the wires before turning off the power!
> - Too many words have multiple definitions.
> - Too many statements use imprecise adjectives. For example, a loan officer asks a teacher to certify that a student is in good academic standing. What is "good"?
> - Conditional instructions can be imprecise. For example, if we state that "all applicants under the age of 19 must secure parental permission," do we mean less than 19, or less than or equal to 19?
> - Compound conditions tend to show up in natural English. For example, if credit approval is a function of several conditions—credit rating, credit ceiling, annual dollar sales for the customer in question—then different combinations of these factors can result in different decisions. As the number of conditions and possible combinations increases, the procedure becomes more and more tedious and difficult to write.

Source: Adapted from Leslie Matthies, *The New Playscript Procedure* (Stamford, CT: Office Publications, Inc., 1977)

Structured English is *not* pseudocode. It does not concern itself with declarations, initialization, linking, and such technical issues. It does, however, borrow some of the logical constructs of *structured programming* to overcome the lack of structure and precision in the English language. Think of it as the marriage of natural English language with the syntax of structured programming.

FIGURE 9-26

Using Structured English to Document an Elementary Process

> 1. For each CUSTOMER NUMBER in the data store CUSTOMERS:
>   a. For each LOAN in the data store LOANS that matches the above CUSTOMER NUMBER:
>   1) Keep a running total of NUMBER OF LOANS for the CUSTOMER NUMBER.
>   2) Keep a running total of ORIGINAL LOAN PRINCIPAL for the CUSTOMER NUMBER.
>   3) Keep a running total of CURRENT LOAN BALANCE for the CUSTOMER NUMBER.
>   4) Keep a running total of AMOUNTS PAST DUE for the CUSTOMER NUMBER.
>   b. If the TOTAL AMOUNTS PAST DUE for the CUSTOMER NUMBER is greater than 100.00 then
>   1) Write the CUSTOMER NUMBER and data in the data flow LOANS AT RISK.
>   Else
>   1) Exclude the CUSTOMER NUMBER and data from the data flow LOANS AT RISK.

The overall structure of a Structured English specification is built using the fundamental constructs that have governed structured programming for nearly three decades. These constructs (summarized in Figure 9-27) are:

- A *sequence* of simple, declarative sentences—one after another. Compound sentences are discouraged because they frequently create ambiguity. Each sentence uses strong, action verbs such as GET, FIND, RECORD, CREATE, READ, UPDATE, DELETE, CALCULATE, WRITE, SORT, MERGE, or anything else recognizable or understandable to users. A formula may be included as part of a sentence (e.g., CALCULATE GROSS PAY = HOURS WORKED × HOURLY WAGE).
- A *conditional* or *decision structure* indicates that a process must perform different steps under well-specified conditions. There are two variations (and a departure) on this construct.
  — The IF-THEN-ELSE construct specifies that one set of steps should be taken if a specified condition is true but that a different set of steps should be specified if the specified condition is false. The steps to be taken are typically a *sequence* of one or more sentences as described above.
  — The CASE construct is used when there are more than two sets of steps to choose from. Once again, these steps usually consist of the aforementioned *sequential* statements. The case construct is an elegant substitute for an IF-THEN-ELSE IF-THEN-ELSE IF-THEN . . . construct (which is very convoluted to the average user).
  — For logic based on multiple conditions and combinations of conditions (which programmers call a *nested IF*), *decision tables* are a far more elegant logic modeling tool. Decision tables will be introduced shortly.
- An *iteration,* or *repetition,* structure specifies that a set of steps should be repeated based on some stated condition. There are two variations on this construct:
  — The DO-WHILE construct indicates that certain steps are repeated zero, one, or more times based on the value of the stated condition. Note that these steps may not execute at all if the condition is not true when the condition is first tested.
  — The REPEAT-UNTIL construct indicates that certain steps are repeated one or more times based on the value of the stated condition. Note that a REPEAT-UNTIL set of steps must execute at least once, unlike the DO-WHILE set of actions.

Additionally, Structured English places the following restrictions on process logic:

- Only strong, imperative verbs may be used.
- Only names that have been defined in the project dictionary may be used. These names may include those of data flows, data stores, entities (from data models; see Chapter 8), attributes (the specified data fields or properties contained in a data flow, data store, or entity), and domains (the specified legal values for attributes).
- Formulas should be stated clearly using appropriate mathematical notations. In short, you can use whatever notation is recognizable to the users. Make sure each operand in a formula is either input to the process in a data flow or a defined constant.
- Undefined adjectives and adverbs (the word *good,* for instance) are not permitted unless clearly defined in the project dictionary as legal values for data attributes.
- Blocking and indentation are used to set off the beginning and ending of constructs and to enhance readability. (Some authors and models encourage the use of special verbs such as ENDIF, ENDCASE, ENDDO, and ENDREPEAT to terminate constructs. We dislike this practice because it gives the Structured English too much of a pseudocode or programming look and feel.)
- When in doubt, user readability should always take priority over programmer preferences.

Structured English Procedural Structures

Construct	Sample Template
Sequence of steps – Unconditionally perform a sequence of steps.	[Step 1] [Step 2] … [Step n]

Simple condition steps – If the specified condition is true, then perform the first set of steps. Otherwise, perform the second set of steps.
 	
Use this construct if the condition has only two possible values.
 	
(Note: The second set of conditions is optional.)
	If [truth condition]
	  then
	    [sequence of steps or other conditional steps]
	  else
	    [sequence of steps or other conditional steps]
	  ~~End If~~

Complex condition steps – Test the value of the condition and perform the appropriate set of steps.
 	
Use this construct if the condition has more than two values.
	Do the following based on [condition]:
	  Case 1: If [condition] = [value] then
	    [sequence of steps or other conditional steps]
	  Case 2: If [condition] = [value] then
	    [sequence of steps or other conditional steps]
	  …
	  Case n: If [condition] = [value] then
	    [sequence of steps or other conditional steps]
	  ~~End Case~~

Multiple conditions – Test the value of multiple conditions to determine the correct set of steps. Use a decision table instead of nested if-then-else Structured English constructs to simplify the presentation of complex logic that involves combinations of conditions. *A decision table is a tabular presentation of complex logic in which rows represent conditions and possible actions and columns indicate which combinations of conditions result in specific actions.*	<table><tr><td>DECISION TABLE</td><td>Rule</td><td>Rule</td><td>Rule</td><td>Rule</td></tr><tr><td>[Condition]</td><td>value</td><td>value</td><td>value</td><td>value</td></tr><tr><td>[Condition]</td><td>value</td><td>value</td><td>value</td><td>value</td></tr><tr><td>[Condition]</td><td>value</td><td>value</td><td>value</td><td>value</td></tr><tr><td>[Sequence of steps or conditional steps]</td><td>X</td><td></td><td></td><td></td></tr><tr><td>[Sequence of steps or conditional steps]</td><td></td><td>X</td><td>X</td><td></td></tr><tr><td>[Sequence of steps or conditional steps]</td><td></td><td></td><td></td><td>X</td></tr></table> Although it isn't a Structured English construct, a decision table can be named, and referenced within a Structured English procedure.

One-to-many iteration – Repeat the set of steps until the condition is false.
 	
Use this construct if the set of steps must be performed <u>at least</u> once, regardless of the condition's initial value.
	Repeat the following until [truth condition]:
	  [sequence of steps or conditional steps]
	  ~~End Repeat~~

Zero-to-many iteration – Repeat the set of steps until the condition is false.
 	
Use this construct if the set of steps is conditional based on the condition's initial value.
	Do while [truth condition]:
	  [sequence of steps or conditional steps]
	  ~~End Do~~
	        - OR -
	For [truth condition]:
	  [sequence of steps or conditional steps]
	  ~~End For~~

FIGURE 9-27 Structured English Constructs

Structured English should be precise enough to clearly specify the required business procedure to a programmer or user. Yet it should not be so inflexible that a programmer or user spends hours arguing over syntax.

Many processes are governed by complex combinations of conditions that are not easily expressed with Structured English. This is most commonly encountered in business policies. A **policy** is a set of rules that governs some process in the business.

In most firms, policies are the basis for decision making. For instance, a credit card company must bill cardholders according to various policies that adhere to restrictions imposed by state and federal governments (maximum interest rates and minimum payments, for instance). Policies consist of *rules* that can often be translated into computer programs if the users and systems analysts can accurately convey those rules to the computer programmer.

There are ways to formalize the specification of policies and other complex combinations of conditions. One such logic modeling tool is a **decision table**. While people who are unfamiliar with them tend to avoid them, decision tables are very useful for specifying complex policies and decision-making rules. Figure 9-28 illustrates the three components of a simple decision table:

- *Condition stubs* (the upper rows) describe the conditions or factors that will affect the decision or policy.

> **policy** a set of rules that governs how a process is to be completed.

> **decision table** a tabular form of presentation that specifies a set of conditions and their corresponding actions.

A SIMPLE POLICY STATEMENT

CHECK CASHING IDENTIFICATION CARD

A customer with check cashing privileges is entitled to cash personal checks of up to $75.00 and payroll checks from companies pre-approved by *LMART*. This card is issued in accordance with the terms and conditions of the application and is subject to change without notice. This card is the property of *LMART* and shall be forfeited upon request of *LMART*.

SIGNATURE   *Charles C. Parker, Jr.*

EXPIRES   May 31, 2003

THE EQUIVALENT POLICY DECISION TABLE

Conditions and Actions	Rule 1	Rule 2	Rule 3	Rule 4
C1: Type of check	personal	payroll	personal	payroll
C2: Check amount less than or equal to $75.00	yes	doesn't matter	no	doesn't matter
C3: Company accredited by *LMART*	doesn't matter	yes	doesn't matter	no
A1: Cash the check	X	X		
A2: Don't cash the check			X	X

Condition Stubs (C1–C3)   Action Stubs (A1–A2)   Rules

FIGURE 9-28   A Sample Decision Table

- *Action stubs* (the lower rows) describe, in the form of statements, the possible policy actions or decisions.
- *Rules* (the columns) describe which actions are to be taken under a specific combination of conditions.

The figure depicts a check-cashing policy that appears on the back of a check-cashing card for a grocery store. This same policy has been documented with a decision table. Three conditions affect the check-cashing decision: the type of check, whether the amount of the check exceeds the maximum limit, and whether the company that issued the check is accredited by the store. The actions (decisions) are either to cash the check or to refuse to cash the check. Notice that each combination of conditions defines a rule that results in an action, denoted by an X.

Both decision tables and Structured English can describe a single elementary process. For example, a legitimate statement in a Structured English specification might read DETERMINE WHETHER OR NOT TO CASH THE CHECK USING THE DECISION TABLE, LMART CHECK CASHING POLICY.

Elementary processes can be described by Structured English and/or decision tables. Because they are "elementary," they should be described in one page or less of either tool. Figure 9-29, demonstrates how *System Architect 2001* can be used to describe an elementary process. Like many CASE tools, *System Architect* does not support decision table construction. Fortunately, decision tables are easily constructed using the table features in most word processors and spreadsheets.

FIGURE 9-29 An Elementary Process (created with *System Architect 2001*)

Synchronizing of System Models

Data and process models represent different views of the same system, but these views are interrelated. Modelers need to synchronize the different views to ensure consistency and completeness of the total system specification. In this section, we'll review the basic synchronization concepts for data and process models.

> Data and Process Model Synchronization

The linkage between data and process models is almost universally accepted by all major methodologies. In short, there should be one data store in the process models for each entity in the data model. Some methodologies exempt associative entities from this requirement, but we believe it is simpler (and more consistent) to apply the rule to all entities on the data model.

Figure 9-30 illustrates a typical *data-to-process-CRUD matrix*. The decision to include or not include attributes is based on whether processes need to be restricted as to which attributes they can access.

Data-to-Process-CRUD Matrix

Entity . Attribute	Process Customer Application	Process Customer Credit Application	Process Customer Change of Address	Process Internal Customer Credit Change	Process New Customer Order	Process Customer Order Cancellation	Process Customer Change to Outstanding Order	Process Internal Change to Customer Order	Process New Product Addition	Process Product Withdrawal from Market	Process Product Price Change	Process Change to Product Specification	Process Product Inventory Adjustment
Customer	C	C			R	R	R	R					
.Customer Number	C	C			R	R	R	R					
.Customer Name	C	C	U		R		R	R					
.Customer Address	C	C	U		RU		RU	RU					
.Customer Credit Rating		C		U	R		R	R					
.Customer Balance Due					RU	U	R	R					
Order					C	D	RU	RU					
.Order Number					C		R	R					
.Order Date					C		U	U					
.Order Amount					C		U	U					
Ordered Product					C	D	CRUD	CRUD		RU			
.Quantity Ordered					C		CRUD	CRUD					
.Ordered Item Unit Price					C		CRUD	CRUD					
Product					R	R	R	R	C	D	RU	RU	RU
.Product Number					R	R	R	R	C			R	
.Product Name					R		R	R	C			RU	
.Product Description					R		R	R	C			RU	
.Product Unit of Measure					R		R	R	C		RU	RU	
.Product Current Unit Price					R		R	R			U		
.Product Quantity on Hand					RU	U	RU	RU					RU

C = create   R = read   U = update   D = delete

FIGURE 9-30 Sample Data-to-Process-CRUD Matrix

The synchronization quality check is stated as follows:

Every entity should have *at least* one C, one R, one U, and one D entry for system completeness. If not, one or more event processes were probably omitted from the process models. More importantly, users and management should validate that all possible creates, reads, updates, and deletes have been included.

The matrix provides a simple quality check that is simpler to read than either the data or process models. Of course, any errors and omissions should be recorded both on the matrix and in the corresponding data and process models to ensure proper synchronization.

> Process Distribution

Process models illustrate the essential work to be performed by the system as a whole. However, processes must be distributed to locations where work is to be performed. Some work may be unique to one location. Other work may be performed at multiple locations. Before we design the information system, we should identify and document what processes must be performed at which locations. This can be accomplished through a *process-to-location-association matrix*. A **process-to-location-association matrix** is a table in which the rows indicate processes (event or elementary processes), the columns indicate locations, and the cells (the intersection of rows and columns) document which processes must be performed at which locations. Figure 9-31 illustrates a typical process-to-location-association matrix. Once it is validated for accuracy, the system designer will use this matrix to determine which processes should be implemented centrally or locally.

Some methodologies and CASE tools may support views of the process model that are appropriate to a location. If so, these views (subsets of the process models) must be kept in sync with the master process models of the system as a whole.

process-to-location-association matrix a table used to document processes and the locations at which they must be performed.

Process-to-Location-Association Matrix

Process	Customers	Kansas City	.Marketing	.Advertising	.Warehouse	.Sales	.Accounts Receivable	Boston	.Sales	.Warehouse	San Francisco	.Sales	San Diego	.Warehouse
Process Customer Application	X					X			X			X		
Process Customer Credit Application	X						X							
Process Customer Change of Address	X					X			X			X		
Process Internal Customer Credit Change							X							
Process New Customer Order	X					X			X			X		
Process Customer Order Cancellation	X					X			X			X		
Process Customer Change to Outstanding Order	X					X			X			X		
Process Internal Change to Customer Order						X			X			X		
Process New Product Addition			X											
Process Product Withdrawal from Market			X											
Process Product Price Change			X											
Process Change to Product Specification			X	X										
Process Product Inventory Adjustment					X					X				X

FIGURE 9-31 Sample Process-to-Location-Association Matrix

Learning Roadmap

If you are taking a traditional approach you will proceed directly to Chapter 11, "Feasibility Analysis and the System Proposal." Given data and process models that describe *logical* system requirements, Chapter 11 will examine the methods and techniques for identifying candidate *physical* solutions that will fulfill the logical requirements, techniques for analyzing the feasibility of each of those solutions, and approaches for presenting the solution that you deem most feasible. This system proposal culminates systems analysis in our *FAST* methodology.

At your instructor's discretion, some of you may jump to Chapter 10, "Object-Oriented Modeling and Analysis with UML." This alternative to data and process modeling is rapidly gaining acceptance in industry and may eventually make both data and process modeling obsolete. Of course, object modeling presents many parallels with data and process modeling. You'll see some similar constructs because an object is defined as the encapsulation of related data and the processes that will be allowed to create, read, update, and use that data.

If you are interested in how we will use the logical DFDs in this chapter during systems design, you might want to preview Chapter 13, "Process Design and Modeling." In that chapter, we will teach you how to transform the logical data flow diagrams into physical data flow diagrams that model the technology architecture of a system to be designed and implemented.

Chapter Review

1. We construct logical models to better understand business problem domains and business requirements.

2. Process modeling is a technique for organizing and documenting the process requirements and design for a system. This chapter focused on a process model called a data flow diagram, which depicts the flow of data through a system's processes.

3. External agents are entities that are outside the scope of a system and project but that provide net inputs to or net outputs from a system. As such, they form the boundary of the system.

4. Data stores present files of data to be used and maintained by the system. A data store on a process model corresponds to all instances of an entity on a data model.

5. A system *is* a process. A process is work performed on, or in response to, inputs and conditions.

6. Just as systems can be recursively decomposed into subsystems, processes can be recursively decomposed into subprocesses. A decomposition diagram shows the functional decomposition of a system into processes and subprocesses. It is a planning tool for subsequent data flow diagrams.

7. Logical processes show essential work to be performed by a system without showing how the processes will be implemented. There are three types of logical processes: functions (very high level), events (middle level of detail), and elementary processes (very detailed).

8. Elementary processes are further described by procedural logic. Structured English is a tool for expressing this procedural logic. Structured English is a derivative of structured programming logic constructs married to natural English.

9. Complex elementary processes may be described by policies that are expressed in decision tables, which show complex combinations of conditions that result in specific actions.

10. Data flows are the inputs to and the outputs from processes. They also illustrate data store accesses and updates.

11. All data flows consist of either other data flows or discrete data structures that include descriptive attributes. A data flow should contain only the amount of data needed by a process; this is called data conservation.

12. Process modeling may be used in different types of projects, including business process redesign and application development. For application

development projects, this chapter taught an event-driven data flow diagramming strategy as follows:

a. Draw a context data flow diagram that shows how the system interfaces to other systems, the business, and external organizations.

b. Draw a functional decomposition diagram that shows the key subsystems and/or functions that comprise the system.

c. Create an event list that identifies the external and temporal events to which the system must provide a response. External events are triggered by the external agents of a system. Temporal events are triggered by the passing of time.

d. Update the decomposition diagram to include processes to handle the events (one process per event).

e. For each event, draw an event diagram that shows its interactions with external entities,

data stores, and, on occasion, other triggers to other events.

f. Combine the event diagrams into one or more system diagrams.

g. For each event on the system diagram, either describe it as an elementary process using Structured English or explode it into a primitive data flow diagram that includes elementary processes that must be subsequently described by either Structured English or decision tables, or by both. When processes are exploded on data flow diagrams to reveal greater detail, it is important to maintain consistency between the different types of diagrams; this is called synchronization.

13. Most computer-aided software engineering tools support both decomposition diagramming and data flow diagramming.

Review Questions

1. What is a logical model, and what are its common synonyms?

2. Why are logical models valuable tools for systems analysts?

3. What is a data flow diagram, and what are its common synonyms?

4. How is a data flow diagram different from a flowchart?

5. Why is a system considered to a process?

6. What is decomposition, and why is it needed? What is the tool used to depict the decomposition of a system?

7. What are the three types of logical processes?

8. What are the common mechanical errors when depicting processes on a data flow diagram and other process models?

9. What is Structured English, and why is it used when constructing process logic?

10. What are the naming conventions of logical data flows?

11. What is data conservation and why is it needed?

12. What are external agents and why can the external agents of an information system change?

13. What are some examples of the event-driven modeling used in systems analysis?

14. What process model is used to document the scope for an information system, and what is depicted in this process model?

15. Why is it important to synchronize data and process models?

Problems and Exercises

1. You are working as a student assistant for an engineering firm and are paid by the hour. Every two weeks, you turn in a time sheet to your supervisor, and three workdays later, your paycheck is direct deposited into your checking account. List the different entities or objects, logical processes, data flows, and data stores that are involved, starting from the time you submit your time sheet.

2. Match the terms in the first column with the definitions or examples in the second column:

1. Structured English	A. Disassembling a system into its components
2. Process	B. Logical unit of work that must be completed as a whole
3. Logical model	C. Tool for logic modeling
4. Primitive process	D. Set of business activities that are related and ongoing

5. Policy

6. DFD

7. Decision table

8. Decomposition

9. Event

10. Physical model

11. Function

12. Hierarchy chart

13. Process modeling

E. Technique for organizing and documenting a system's processes

F. Procedure specification language

G. Depiction of what a system is or does

H. Depiction of system data flow

I. Depiction of system decomposition

J. Work performed by system in response to incoming data flows

K. Detailed, separate activity/task needed to complete event response

L. Process completion rules

M. Depiction of what a system is or does, and how it is implemented

3. In a decomposition diagram, how do you show one child for a parent, and how do you show more than one parent for a child? Why don't the connections on a decomposition diagram show arrowheads, like most other diagrams? Why aren't the connections named?

4. Consider carpool lanes in Sacramento, California. Between the hours of 6:00 a.m. and 10:00 a.m. and 3:00 p.m. and 7:00 p.m., Monday through Friday, they are restricted to passenger vehicles with two or more people of any age, motorcycles, and hybrid (gas/electric) vehicles with one or more persons. For all other vehicles or conditions, the driver is subject to a traffic citation. Outside those time periods, there are no restrictions as to their usage. Based upon this information, write a policy decision table for use by highway patrol officers.

5. You work in the headquarters office of the investigation division of a law enforcement agency and are developing an automated case-tracking system for your headquarters office to replace the current manual system. Cases are opened when a request-for-investigation form is received from other divisions in your agency; no cases are initiated internally. A new case folder is created, containing any criminal record information based upon checking various criminal justice databases, then sent to the appropriate field investigation office. When the case is completed, headquarters receives an investigation report from the field office, the case is closed, and

a copy of the completed investigation report is sent to the originating office. Every week, a listing showing cases opened, completed, and in progress is sent to each field office. What are some of the strategies you might use for setting the scope and boundaries of the system?

6. Based upon the preceding question, what did you determine are the system's:

    a. Net inputs
    b. Net outputs
    c. External agents
    d. External stores

7. Now that you have your net inputs, net outputs, external agents, and external stores, draw a context data flow diagram.

8. You are now modeling the logic of each elementary process for the case-tracking system and have decided to write it in Structured English in order to communicate effectively with both users and programmers. For the Open/Closed/In Progress Case Listing Report to Field Office, write a Structured English statement to document the process of keeping a running total of cases opened, closed, and in progress. Additionally, you want to add another column to the report showing the number of cases still in progress that are over six months old.

9. You are now ready to create the functional decomposition diagram for the case-tracking system. What is the root process for the function decomposition diagram? What subsystems would you typically include? What processes would you show, and to what subsystem would they belong? Use this information to create a functional decomposition diagram.

10. Your next step, after drawing the decomposition diagram, is creating the event-response or use-case list. There should be a use case for each event initiated by an external agent. Temporal events should also be shown. For each external agent, there should be at least one use case. Start a partial use-case table that includes the events OTHER DIVISION SENDS REQUEST FOR INVESTIGATION and FIELD OFFICE SENDS COMPLETED INVESTIGATION REPORT. Also include the event GENERATE OPEN/CLOSED/IN PROGRESS CASE LISTING REPORT.

11. An event diagram is equivalent to a context diagram for one event. The event diagram includes the inputs, outputs, and data store interactions related to that specific event. Its purpose is to help users focus on a single event without becoming overwhelmed or confused by a picture of the entire system. Select one of the events from the case-tracking system, and draw an event diagram.

12. Match the definitions or examples in the first column with the terms in the second column:

A. Smallest meaningful data segment

1. Domain

B. Combination of data flows that are similar

2. Junction

C. Expressed in the form of data structures

3. External agent

D. Condition to be monitored

4. Event partitioning

E. An attribute's legitimate values

5. Composite data flow

F. "Starving the processes"

6. Control flow

G. Output of data from a process or input to the process

7. Data composition

H. Data class that can be stored in an attribute

8. Data attribute

I. Arrangement of data attributes that comprise a data flow

9. Data conservation

J. Outside entity that interacts with a system

10. Data flow

K. Symbol that given data flow is instance of only one type

11. Data structure

L. Data at rest

12. Data type

M. System broken into subsystems based on business events

13. Data store

13. Although data and process models depict the same system with different views, system designers must synchronize these different views to make sure that their models are consistent and complete. One way to ensure this is through a data-to-process-CRUD matrix. Select a system with which you are familiar. Identify at least three of the entities used in that system and their attributes. Next, identify the processes associated with those entities. Then build a data-to-process-CRUD matrix, using Figure 9-30 as your template. As a quality check, show your matrix to someone else who is familiar with the system, and have her or him review it for completeness and correctness.

Projects and Research

1. Suppose you are starting work on a project for an organization that has never used any modeling techniques or tools in designing a system. (Yes, it is hard to imagine, but it does exist.) Your manager is reluctant to change from the way they have always done things. Write a one- to two-page issue paper (or a PowerPoint presentation as an alternative) on why systems modeling is worth the time and resources involved.

2. The textbook uses the Gane and Sarson process modeling notations and compares them to the notations used by the DeMarco/Yourdon and SSADM/IDEF0 process modeling methodologies. Research at least two of these or other process modeling methodologies, then compare and contrast them.

   a. What other process modeling methodologies did you find?

   b. What, if any, are the significant differences in their process modeling methodologies, other than in their notation methods?

   c. What are their similarities?

   d. Which notation method does your organization use?

   e. If you were asked to recommend one of these methodologies for your organization, which one would you choose? Why?

3. Until fairly recently, magazines and periodicals were available in printed versions only. Publishers are now offering an increasing number of periodicals in either the traditional printed version or in a digital format that can be downloaded over the Internet. Consider the processes involved in these two methods and:

   a. Create a high-level data flow diagram describing the typical traditional methods of renewing a subscription via mail to the print version of a magazine.

   b. Create another high-level data flow diagram describing the processes for renewing a subscription via the Internet to the digital format version of a magazine.

c. What, if any, are the essential differences between the two diagrams?

d. Based upon the data flow diagrams, which format is more efficient in renewing a magazine subscription? Do you think the same holds true from the perspective of the subscriber? What about from the perspective of the publisher?

e. What about receiving and reading the magazine? From your own perspective, what are the advantages and disadvantages of a magazine published in digital format versus the traditional print version?

4. In 1978, Tom DeMarco wrote what is considered to be the classic text on structured systems analysis methodology—*Structured Analysis and System Specification.* James Wetherbe is considered by the authors of the textbook to be "one of the strongest advocates of system concepts and system thinking as part of the discipline of systems analysis and design," and has written numerous articles and books on "systems think." Edward Yourdon is another widely acknowledged leader in systems design and is noted for formalizing the event-driven approach methodology in his 1989 book, *Modern Structured Analysis.* Search the Internet for their Web sites, if any, and for recent articles and/or books by these three leaders in systems analysis and design.

a. What articles and/or Web sites did you find?

b. Describe some of their more recent work.

c. Compare and contrast each of these authors in terms of their perspective on systems analysis

and design; specifically, do you see their approaches as complementary or opposed?

d. What emerging changes or trends in systems analysis and design do they foresee?

e. Do you feel that they still represent the leading thinkers in systems analysis and design? Why or why not?

5. Look at the different information systems used in your school or organization. Find a system with incomplete and/or outdated documentation (this should not be hard to do in most organizations!). Update and complete the documentation for this system using data flow diagrams, data structures, and other process models described in this chapter. Use the Gane and Sarson notation method, unless your organization supports a different notation method.

6. At the conclusion of this chapter, the textbook mentions that data and process modeling may eventually become obsolete due to the increasing popularity and usage of object-oriented modeling and analysis with UML. Research articles discussing this topic in your school library and/or the Internet.

a. What articles did you find?

b. What were the authors' positions on this topic?

c. Compare and contrast the articles you found; which one made the more convincing case?

As you gaze into your crystal ball, what modeling methodology do you think will be the most widely used one 10 years from now? Do you predict it will be either of these two methodologies or a different one entirely? Why?

Minicases

1. Go to a small company of your choice. What does the business do? Write a one- to two-page paper describing the business and its existing system. Then draw a context-level diagram and a system-level diagram for the existing system. Do you see any inefficiencies or weaknesses in the current system? Describe.

2. In the previous case, you documented (at a high level) an existing information system at a business of your choice. Now describe the system *you* think is appropriate for this business. Consider efficiency, flow of information from one department to another, and so forth. Is there pertinent information that the previous system did not utilize? How can your new system offer a business advantage? Document this advantage in a two-page paper, as well as in a context- and system-level diagram.

3. In Chapter 2 you addressed the following problem: Government service departments are deeply burdened by the amount of data that they hold and process. Interview someone from a service department and draft a short essay. Example service departments that must sift through vast amounts of data are those that deal with, for example, missing persons, child protective services, DMV, and tracking of persons on probation following a crime. You should include, but are not limited to topics such as:

- What is the department (or person's) job?
- What kind of data do they collect and analyze?
- What kind of analyses do they do on the data?
- How much information do they collect and from whom, and what programs do they use?

366   **Part Two**   **Systems Analysis Methods**

In this exercise, utilize the information you gathered from your interview and draft a complete DFD of the *existing* information system for that department. You may need to go back and reinterview your contact or get forms, reports, and soon, so that you have a complete picture of the flow of data.

4. In the previous case, you documented the existing information system of a government department.

Now think about what the flow of information *should* be like. Discuss in a short paper the existing flow of information, and what type of information you think should be in the system. Is there a big difference between what you think they should have and what they do have?

Team and Individual Exercises

1. Individual/class roundtable discussion: It has been said that information is power and that the separation between the economically well-off nations, individuals, companies, and the like, and those that are not (economically well-off) is the use and control of information. What is the value of information? How does it affect the viability and competitiveness of nations or companies? How does your access to and use of information affect your ability to be successful in a work-related setting?

2. Individual/class roundtable discussion: Suppose a software company is hired to create a very complex and groundbreaking software package for a company. The company would like to own the

rights (including modification and sale) of that software, but the software company also wants the rights to the software. Find an example of this situation in real life. Who do you think *should* own the software? Why? Whose side does the law take? Why?

3. Roundtable discussion: Tech start-ups were known in the late 1990s for having a culture of extended workdays. That is, many times programmers would be expected to work 60–80 hours a week without overtime pay. Find out about the labor laws in your state and then discuss in a class roundtable format the impact of labor laws and corporate culture on tech employees.

Suggested Readings

Copi, I. R. *Introduction to Logic.* New York: Macmillan, 1972. Copi provides a number of problem-solving illustrations and exercises that aid in the study of logic. The poker chip problem in our exercises was adapted from one of Copi's reasoning exercises.

DeMarco, Tom. *Structured Analysis and System Specification.* Englewood Cliffs, NJ: Prentice Hall, 1978. This is the classic book on the structured systems analysis methodology, which is built heavily around the use of data flow diagrams. The progression through (1) *current physical system DFDs,* (2) *current logical system DFDs,* (3) *target logical system DFDs,* and (4) *target physical system DFDs* is rarely practiced anymore, but the essence of DeMarco's pioneering work lives on in event-driven structured analysis. DeMarco created the data structure and logic notations used in this book.

Gildersleeve, T. R. *Successful Data Processing Systems Analysis.* Englewood Cliffs, NJ: Prentice Hall, 1978. The first edition of this book includes an entire chapter on the construction of decision tables. Gildersleeve does an excellent job of demonstrating how narrative process

descriptions can be translated into condition and action entries in decision tables. Unfortunately, the chapter was deleted from the second edition.

Harmon, Paul, and Mark Watson. *Understanding UML: The Developers Guide.* San Francisco: Morgan Kaufman Publishers, 1998. This book does an excellent job of introducing use cases.

Martin, James, and Carma McClure. *Action Diagrams: Towards Clearly Specified Programs.* Englewood Cliffs, NJ: Prentice Hall, 1986. This book describes a formal grammar of Structured English that encourages the natural progression of a process (program) from Structured English to code. Action diagrams are supported directly in some CASE tools.

Matthies, Leslie H. *The New Playscript Procedure.* Stamford, CT: Office Publications, 1977. This book provides a thorough explanation and examples of the weaknesses of the English language as a tool for specifying business procedures.

McMenamin, Stephen M., and John F. Palmer. *Essential Systems Analysis.* New York: Yourdon Press, 1984. This was the first book to suggest event partitioning as a formal strategy to improve structured analysis. The book also strengthened the distinction between logical and physical process models and the increased importance of the logical models (which they called *essential* models).

Robertson, James, and Suzanne Robertson. *Complete Systems Analysis* (Vols. 1 and 2). New York: Dorset House Publishing, 1994. This is the most up-to-date and comprehensive book on the event-driven approach to structured analysis, even though we feel it still overemphasizes the current system and physical models more than the Yourdon book described below.

Seminar notes for *Process Modeling Techniques.* Atlanta: Structured Solutions, Inc., 1991. You probably can't get a copy of these notes, but we wanted to acknowledge the instructors of the *AD/Method* methodology course that stimulated our thinking and motivated our departure from classical structured analysis techniques to the event-driven structured analysis techniques taught in this chapter. Structured Solutions was acquired by Protelicess, Inc.

Wetherbe, James, and Nicholas P. Vatarli. *Systems Analysis and Design: Best Practices,* 4th ed. St. Paul, MN: West Publishing, 1994. Jim Wetherbe has always been one of the strongest advocates of system concepts and system thinking as part of the discipline of systems analysis and design. Jim has shaped many minds, including our own. The authors provide a nice chapter on system concepts in this book—and the rest of the book is must reading for those of you who truly want to learn to "systems think."

Yourdon, Edward. *Modern Structured Analysis.* Englewood Cliffs, NJ: Yourdon Press, 1989. This was the first mainstream book to abandon classic structured analysis's overemphasis on the current physical system models and to formalize McMenamin and Palmer's event-driven approach.